Co-Compounds and Natural Coordination

OXFORD STUDIES IN TYPOLOGY AND LINGUISTIC THEORY

SERIES EDITORS: Ronnie Cann, *University of Edinburgh*, William Croft, *University of Manchester*, Scott DeLancey, *University of Oregon*, Martin Haspelmath, *Max Planck Institute Leipzig*, Nicholas Evans, *University of Melbourne*, Anna Siewierska, *University of Lancaster*

PUBLISHED

Classifiers: A Typology of Noun Categorization Devices
by Alexandra Y. Aikhenvald

Pronouns
by D. N. S. Bhat

Subordination
by Sonia Cristofaro

The Paradigmatic Structure of Person Marking
by Michael Cysouw

Indefinite Pronouns
by Martin Haspelmath

Anaphora
by Yan Huang

Copulas
by Regina Pustet

The Noun Phrase
by Jan Rijkhoff

Intransitive Predication
by Leon Stassen

Co-Compounds and Natural Coordination
Bernhard Wälchli

PUBLISHED IN ASSOCIATION WITH THE SERIES

The World Atlas of Language Structures
edited by Matthew Dryer, Bernard Comrie, David Gil, and Martin Haspelmath

IN PREPARATION
Reciprocals
by Nicholas Evans

Applicative Constructions
by David Peterson

Double Object Constructions
by Maria Polinsky

Sign Languages
by Ulrike Zesham

Co-Compounds and Natural Coordination

BERNHARD WÄLCHLI

OXFORD
UNIVERSITY PRESS

OXFORD
UNIVERSITY PRESS

Great Clarendon Street, Oxford OX2 6DP
Oxford University Press is a department of the University of Oxford.
If furthers the University's objective of excellence in research, scholarship,
and education by publishing worldwide in

Oxford New York

Auckland Cape Town Dar es Salaam Hong Kong Karachi
Kuala Lumpur Madrid Melbourne Mexico City Nairobi
New Delhi Shanghai Taipei Toronto

With offices in

Argentina Austria Brazil Chile Czech Republic France Greece
Guatemala Hungary Italy Japan Poland Portugal Singapore
South Korea Switzerland Thailand Turkey Ukraine Vietnam

Oxford is a registered trade mark of Oxford University Press in the UK and in certain
other countries

Published in the United States
by Oxford University Press Inc., New York

© Bernhard Wälchli 2005

The moral rights of the author have been asserted
Database right Oxford University Press (maker)

First published 2005
First published in paperback 2009

All rights reserved. No part of this publication may be reproduced,
stored in a retrieval system, or transmitted, in any form or by any means,
without the prior permission in writing of Oxford University Press,
or as expressly permitted by law, or under terms agreed with the appropriate
reprographics rights organization. Enquiries concerning reproduction
outside the scope of the above should be sent to the Rights Department,
Oxford University Press, at the address above

You must not circulate this book in any other binding or cover
and you must impose this same condition on any acquirer

British Library Cataloguing in Publication Data
Data available

Library of Congress Cataloging-in-Publication Data
Wälchli, Bernhard.
  Co-compounds and natural coordination/Bernhard Wälchli
    p. cm.
  Includes bibliographical references and indexes.
  ISBN 0–19–927621–8 (alk. paper)
    1. Grammar, Comparitive and general–Coordinate constructions. 2. Grammar, Comparitive
  and general–Compound words. 3. Markedness (Linguistics) 4. Semantics. 1. Title.
  P293.W35 2005
  415–dc22
2004030581
Library of Congress Cataloging in Publication Data
Typeset by SPI Publisher Services, Pondicherry, India.
Printed in Great Britain on acid-free paper by MPG Books Group, Bodmin and King's Lynn

ISBN 978–0–19–927621–9 (Hbk.)   978–0–19–956332–6 (Pbk.)

1 3 5 7 9 10 8 6 4 2

Contents

Preface and Acknowledgements x
List of Figures xii
List of Maps xiii
List of Tables xiv
Conventions xv

1 Introduction 1
  1.1 Basics of co-compounds 1
    1.1.1 The form of co-compounds 2
    1.1.2 The meaning of co-compounds 5
    1.1.3 The use of co-compounds 8
    1.1.4 Differences and similarities with phrase-like tight coordination 10
    1.1.5 Are co-compounds a form of parallelism? 15
  1.2 Co-compounds in the linguistic literature 17
  1.3 Theoretical background, method, and material 22
    1.3.1 Why this is not a classical typological study? 22
      (i) Universal 'semantic' domains and 'language-specific' classes 23
      (ii) Discrete and continuous typological variables 24
      (iii) The problem of sampling for features that are highly biased areally 25
      (iv) Explanations in typology 25
      (v) Summary 26
    1.3.2 Meaning in language 26
      (i) Meaning in natural languages is not systematically taxonomic 27
      (ii) Partial cover meanings 28
      (iii) The form-related-ergo-meaning-related approach and its limits 29
      (iv) Semantic relativity and the level of cross-linguistic semantic comparison (morpheme vs. utterance) 30
      (v) Contextual semantic sharpening 32

vi Contents

    1.3.3 The linguistic material considered in this study   33
    1.3.4 Summary   34
  1.4 Organization of the following chapters   35

2 The Marking Patterns of Natural Coordination   38
  2.1 Different kinds of markedness   38
  2.2 Relational marking in natural coordination   45
  2.3 Non-relational marking in natural coordination   48
    2.3.1 Distinctive non-relational single marking   49
    2.3.2 Distinctive non-relational double marking   51
    2.3.3 Distinctive non-relational zero marking   54
    2.3.4 Iconicity of the distinctive non-relational marking strategies   55
  2.4 The syntax of single non-relational marking in coordination   57
    2.4.1 Group inflection   58
    2.4.2 Is coordination with single non-relational marking syntactically asymmetric?   60
    2.4.3 Phonological-syntactic non-isomorphism   60
  2.5 Conclusions   64

3 Tight Coordination   67
  3.1 The first dimension: the length of the coordination   67
  3.2 The second dimension: the marking patterns of coordination   69
  3.3 The third dimension: the semantic correlates of tight coordination   74
    3.3.1 Group vs. separate coordination   74
    3.3.2 Intersective vs. non-intersective coordination   76
    3.3.3 Overlapping vs. non-overlapping coordination   77
    3.3.4 Contrast   78
    3.3.5 Non-exhaustive vs. exhaustive listing coordination   81
    3.3.6 Disjunction   81
    3.3.7 Explicative disjunction   83
    3.3.8 Repair and pseudo-repair   84
    3.3.9 Enumeration   85
    3.3.10 Pseudo-coordination   85
    3.3.11 Conclusions   86
  3.4 Conclusions   87

4 Co-compounds as a Lexical Class Type   90
  4.1 The traditional morphological (and indirectly syntactic) approach to compounding   90

4.2	Are (co-)compounds really words?	92
	4.2.1 What is word? Laying out the problem	92
	4.2.2 Deconstructing the notion of word	93
	4.2.3 Criteria for the 'wordhood' of compounds (with special reference to co-compounds)	97
	(i) Semantic criteria for compounds	97
	(ii) Conventionalized prosodic patterns	98
	(iii) Compounding forms and clippings	99
	(iv) Bound stems	100
	(v) Word slots	101
	(vi) Continuity	101
	(vii) Fixed order	103
	(viii) Conclusion	104
4.3	An alternative approach to co-compounds: lexical classes	105
	4.3.1 The middle as a typical example for a lexical class type	107
	4.3.2 More examples of lexical class types	110
	4.3.3 Co-compounds as a lexical class type	113
	4.3.4 Reconsidering lexicalization and the lexicon	114
	4.3.5 Differences and similarities of lexical and grammatical classes	117
4.4	The form of co-compounds and the problem of formal non-distinctiveness	121
	4.4.1 Distinguishing co-compounds and sub-compounds	122
	4.4.2 Distinguishing co-compounds and serial verbs	124
	4.4.3 Distinguishing co-compounds and coordination	126
4.5	Meronomic structure	130
4.6	Conclusions	131
5	**A Semantic Classification of Co-compounds**	**135**
5.1	The basis of the semantic classification	136
5.2	The various semantic types of co-compounds	137
	5.2.1 Additive co-compounds	137
	5.2.2 Generalizing co-compounds	139
	5.2.3 Collective co-compounds	141
	5.2.4 Synonymic co-compounds	143
	5.2.5 Ornamental co-compounds	146
	5.2.6 Imitative co-compounds	147
	5.2.7 Figurative co-compounds	149
	5.2.8 Alternative and approximate co-compounds	151

	5.2.9 Scalar co-compounds	152
	5.2.10 Basic and non-basic co-compounds	154
5.3	Contextual semantic sharpening in co-compounds	158
5.4	Compounds that are closely related to co-compounds	161
	5.4.1 Appositional compounds	161
	5.4.2 Intermediate-denoting compounds	162
	5.4.3 Comparative (or figurative-appositional) compounds	163
	5.4.4 Ideophones and ideophone compounds	164
	5.4.5 Reduplication	166
	5.4.6 Echo-words	167
	5.4.7 Affirmative–negative compounds	170
	5.4.8 Conclusions	170
5.5	Contextual motivation of co-compounds	171
	5.5.1 Additive contextual co-compounds	173
	5.5.2 Emphasis	174
	5.5.3 Generalizing context	175
	5.5.4 Contrast (in adversative sequences)	175
	5.5.5 Non-referential contexts and restricted evidence	176
	(i) Negation	176
	(ii) Question	178
	(iii) Irrealis, potentialis, conditional, and future	178
	5.5.6 Distributivity	180
	5.5.7 Pictorial contexts	181
	5.5.8 Conclusions	182
5.6	Conclusions	183
6 The Areal Distribution of Co-compounds in the Languages of Eurasia		186
6.1	Patterns of areal coherence	186
6.2	Consideration of parallel texts	187
6.3	More evidence for a continuous diminishment of co-compounds from east to west throughout Eurasia	198
	6.3.1 Turkic, Mongolian, and Tungus	198
	6.3.2 The languages of the Caucasus	201
	6.3.3 Indo-European	203
	6.3.4 Uralic	206
	6.3.5 Dravidian	207
	6.3.6 Sino-Tibetan	208
	6.3.7 Austroasiatic	210
	6.3.8 Austronesian	211

6.3.9 Language isolates	212
6.3.10 Synthesis	214
6.4 Language internal diversity: the example of Mordvin	218
6.5 Diversity in co-compounding in Eurasia	225
6.6 The independence of co-compounds from other typological features	229
6.6.1 Head and dependent marking	229
6.6.2 Isolating morphological type and monosyllabic words	230
6.6.3 Sub-compounds	231
6.6.4 The type of ordinary coordination	231
6.6.5 Dyad constructions and family group classifiers	232
6.6.6 Loanwords	235
6.6.7 Conclusions	235
6.7 Conclusions	236
6.A Appendix: Beyond Eurasia	237
7 Some Considerations about the Diachronic Evolution of Co-compounds	243
7.1 The evolution of markers, patterns, and constructions vs. the evolution of classes	243
7.2 The diachronic relationship between co-compounds and coordination	245
7.2.1 The condensation hypothesis	245
7.2.2 The introduction of new 'heavy forms'	250
7.2.3 Conclusions	251
7.3 Co-compounds as a lexical class evolve gradually	252
7.4 The role of textual markedness for the acceptability of co-compounds	257
7.5 Co-compounds in folk poetry and desemantization	264
7.6 Conclusions	270
8 Conclusions	274
Appendix A: Languages and their Linguistic Affiliation	281
Appendix B: Map of Languages	286
References	288
Index of Persons	311
Index of Languages	317
Index of Subjects	323

Preface and Acknowledgements

The aim of this study is both descriptive and theoretical. Descriptively, it is a contribution to the cross-linguistic investigation of co-compounds and related phenomena within the functional domain of natural coordination. But its scope goes beyond that of cross-linguistic description. This was unavoidable because some time-honored traditional concepts in linguistics—notably the strict division between word and phrase, the listeme model of the lexicon, the view of coordination as a syntactic phrase, lexical semantics as a static rather than a context-dependent dynamic field—are not descriptively adequate for the phenomena under consideration. Thus, as concerns linguistic theory, the study does not present a coherent model of language structure or competence, nor does it follow any given theoretical framework. Rather, it challenges widely accepted approaches and attempts to provide some solutions that are descriptively more adequate.

This book is a revised version of my doctoral dissertation, defended at the University of Stockholm in May 2003. I consider it a distinct privilege that this dissertation was supervised by Maria Koptjevskaja-Tamm and Östen Dahl, both of whom spent countless hours with me, working through and discussing long and difficult drafts. Without their innumerable suggestions and challenges, this work would never have become a book. I would like to thank also the opponent for the defense, Andrew Spencer, for his thoughtful and valuable comments. The origin of my research, long before I started thinking about co-compounds, lies in a study trip to the Republic of Mordovia in Autumn 1996 and I remain grateful to Rajsa N. Buzakova who devoted so much of her time to teaching me Erźa Mordvin.

My dissertation project was supported by the Swiss National Science Foundation during 1999. Between March 2000 and September 2004 I have been working at the Linguistics Department of the University of Bern, and I would like to thank Iwar Werlen for always encouraging me to carry on with my research. Some of the subjects discussed in this book were presented in public on several occasions in Stockholm and Bern, at the ALT III Conference in Amsterdam in September 1999, at a workshop organized by W. Bisang and M. Haspelmath at the Fachtagung der Deutschen Gesellschaft für Sprachwissenschaft in Leipzig in February/March 2001, at the Department of Linguistics of the Max Planck Institute for Evolutionary Anthropology in Leipzig in

October 2003, and at the Departments of Linguistics in Kiel in November 2000 and Bremen in November 2003.

I would like to thank the following persons for having served as informants or for providing important material from their languages of expertise: Brita Bergman (Swedish Sign Language), Barbara Buri (Mandarin), Östen Dahl (Swedish), Enkhtuvshin Dorjgotov (Khalkha Mongolian), Volker Gast (Tzotzil), Natalja Gluxova and Z. Učaev (Mari), Pétur Helgason (Icelandic), Alan R. King (Basque), Maria Koptjevskaja-Tamm (Russian), Birgit Schlyter Nilsson (Uzbek), Yaron Matras (Romani), Nawzad Shokri (Bahdinani Kurdish), Jennifer Spenader (English), and Ljuba Veselinova (Bulgarian).

I am grateful to the following persons for their helpful suggestions: Jan Anward, Roland Bielmeier, Vladan Bošković, Barbara Buri, Michael Cysouw, Karen Ebert, Martin Gaenszle, John Haiman, Kristine Hildebrandt, Päivi Juvonen, Jussi Karlgren, René Lanszweert, Eva Lindström, Jan Peter Locher, Wiltrud Mihatsch, Ulrike Mosel, Nicole Nau, Anatolij P. Nepokupnyj, Lukas Neukom, Mikael Parkvall, Frans Plank, Birgit Schlyter Nilsson, Eva Schultze-Berndt, Leon Stassen, Pirkko Suihkonen, Robert Wälchli, Ursula Wegmüller, Björn Wiemer, and Fernando Zúñiga.

Special thanks go to Nicholas Evans, Martin Haspelmath, Irina Nikolaeva, Thomas Stolz, and an anonymous reviewer who provided me with valuable comments while I was revising the dissertation for publication. Furthermore, I would like to thank John Davey, Stuart Fowkes, and Kim Allen at Oxford University Press for their assistance. I am extremely grateful to Donald Fillinger for having made a tremendous effort to improve the draft text.

It remains for me to thank my parents and my sister, who always encouraged me to go my way, and especially my wife, Inga, for their support. I don't know how I would have done it without you!

Bernhard Wälchli
Bern, August 24, 2004

Figures

1.1	Different semantic maps to represent the meanings of the same linguistic class in an idealized way by partial cover meanings	29
3.1	Some nominal coordination patterns in Turkish	70
3.2	Different semantic kinds of coordination	77
5.1	Basic and non-basic types of co-compounds	156
5.2	Different types of reduplication	166
6.1	Frequency of co-compounds in the UDHR	189
6.2	Frequency of co-compounds in the UDHR (continued)	190
6.3	Token frequency of co-compounds in different translations of Mark	192
6.4	Semantic profiles of co-compounds in different translations of Mark	195
6.5	Frequency of co-compounds in Turkic languages	199
6.6	Co-compounds in three Mordvin texts	220
6.7	The semantic types of co-compounds in three Mordvin texts	221
6.8	The semantic profiles of co-compounds in three Mordvin texts	222
6.9	The word class profiles of co-compounds in three Mordvin texts	223
6.10	The profile of additive co-compounds in three Mordvin texts	223

Maps

6.1 Frequency of co-compounds in the languages of Eurasia 216
6.2 Co-compounds in the most lexicalized expression for 'parents' 217
Appendix B: Map of languages 286

Tables

1.1.	The iconic relationship between different kinds of coordination	13
1.2.	Examples for superordinate, basic, and subordinate concepts in Mari	27
2.1.	Different kinds of markedness	42
2.2.	Double marking in natural coordination and elsewhere in coordination	53
2.3.	Iconicity in non-relational marking strategies for natural coordination	57
2.4.	Group inflection in coordination (for case) in some languages with group inflection in subordination in the group Adj N (for case)	59
4.1.	The functions of noun incorporation	112
4.2.	Some concepts above the basic level of conceptualization in the text of the UDHR in several co-compounding languages	113
4.3.	Local (un)markedness of the plural of 'foot' in some unrelated languages	119
4.4.	Some body parts in English, Mari, Czech, and Bahasa Indonesia	127
5.1.	The various semantic types of co-compounds	138
6.1.	Languages considered in the two parallel texts ranked according to their frequency of co-compounds	197
6.2.	'Head' in several Tibeto-Burman languages	209
6.3.	The levels of co-compounding represented on Map 6.1	215
6.4.	Sub-compounds and co-compounds	232
6.5.	'Also'/'with'-coordinators and co-compounds	233
6.6.	Relational marking type in ordinary nominal coordination and co-compounds	233
6.7.	Deranked vs. non-deranked verbal coordination and co-compounds	233
7.1.	The evolution of dvandva compounds from Vedic to Sanskrit	248
7.2.	Syllable structure in Old and Middle Chinese	253

Conventions

Although it is common to use hyphens to delimitate morphemes, here dots are used instead since hyphens in many orthographies are characteristic for co-compounds. Hyphens are used only where they are present in orthography or in unanalyzed sources. The following notation is used for translations of co-compounds: 'A-B > C' (also 'A-B', '> C') where A and B are the meaning of the parts and C the meaning of the whole.

The orthography of examples from individual languages from different sources has not been standardized everywhere. If nothing else is indicated I have retained the orthography of the source (as far as the diacritic marks could be reproduced). Examples which are not written in Latin script have been transcribed according to common standards. Whenever possible, the same letters for the transcription of examples in Cyrillic script have been used as for the transcription of Russian. The orthography of Erźa Mordvin examples has been standardized; palatalization (*d'*, *l'*, *ń*, *ŕ*, *ś*, *t'*, *ź*) is indicated only at the end of a sequence of consonants (which has palatalization harmony anyway) and after *l* (as in the Cyrillic script). Avar is transcribed according to Charachidzé (1981). Georgian is transcribed according to Tschenkéli (1965–74). For the transcription of Khmer in Section 6.5.3, the orthography of Gaudes (1985) has been used.

List of abbreviations used in interlinear glosses

-	hyphen in orthography or source
*	ungrammatical example, or reconstructed form
.	morpheme segmentation
?	acceptability problematic, or element with unclear meaning
=	marks off a clitic
>	[person subject]>[person object]
1	1st person
2	2nd person
3	3rd person
ABL	ablative
ABS	absolutive
ABST	abstract
ACC	accusative

ADESS	adessive
ADJ	adjective, adjectivizer
ADV	adverbial (case), adverb
AMAN	morpheme for natural coordination (Malagasy)
ANIM	animate
AOR	aorist
APPL	applicative
ASRT	assertive (Meithei)
AUX	auxiliary
CAUS	causative
CL	classifier
CMPR	comparative
COM	comitative
COMP	comparative
COMPL	completive
COND	conditional
CONJ	conjunctive
CONT	contingent mood (Kannada)
CONV	converb
DAT	dative
DEF	definite, (definite) article
DIM	diminutive
DISTAL	distal (action initiated at some other place; Meithei)
DLMT	delimitative (Meithei)
DU	dual
ECHO	echo-word
ERG	ergative
EVID	evidential
EX	existential
F	feminine
FOC	focus
FREQ	frequentative
FUT	future
GEN	genitive
HON	honorific
ILL	illative
IMI	imitative
IMP	imperative
IMPF	imperfect
IMPV	imperfective

INAN	inanimate
INCH	inchoative
IND	indicative
INDEF	indefinite (pronoun)
INESS	inessive
INF	infinitive
INFL	inflection marker
INST	instrumental
INT	interrogative particle
INTRNS	intransitive
IO	indirect object
IZAF	izafe
LAT	lative
LINK	linker
LOC	locative
M	masculine
N	neuter
NA	agent nominal
NATCOM	natural comitative
NEG	negative
NEK	marker in Mordvin generalizing co-compounds
NOM	nominative
NOML	nominalizer
NPST	nonpast
∅	zero marking
OBJ	object
OBL	oblique
PART	partitive
PASS	passive
PER	periphrasis form
PF	perfect
PFV	perfective
PL	plural
POSS	possessive, possessive affix
PP	adposition
PREV	preverb
PROL	prolative
PROP	proprietive
PRS	present
PRT	particle

PST	past
PTC	participle
RFL	reflexive
SFP	semifinal particle
SRESS	superessive
SS	same subject
SUBR	subordinator
SV	subjective version (Georgian)
TPE	truncated personal ending
TRNS	transitive
TRNSF	transformative
TRNSL	translative
VN	verbal noun
VOC	vocative
VOL	voluntative

1

Introduction

1.1 Basics of Co-compounds

Co-compounds are also known under the names of dvandva compounds, pair words (Russian *parnye slova*), and copulative compounds (German *Kopulativkomposita*). These are word-like units consisting of two or more parts which express NATURAL COORDINATION.[1] Natural coordination (for a more detailed description see Section 1.1.2 below) implies, among other things, that the parts express semantically closely associated concepts, such as 'brother and sister', 'hands and feet', 'eat and drink', 'knife and fork', etc., which are on the same hierarchical level, and that the whole meaning ('siblings', 'limbs', etc.) is more general than the meaning of the parts. Co-compounds are especially found in many languages of Asia, easternmost Europe, and New Guinea. Consider the following examples from Indian English and Erźa Mordvin,[2] where co-compounds are given in boldface:

(1) Indian English: reported speech in an English novel (Rushdie 1981/1995: 403, 228)
    a 'Are you maybe married already, captain? Got **wife-children** waiting somewhere?'
    b 'However we can help our **father-mother** that is what it is for us to do.'

(2) Erźa Mordvin: examples from fairytales (Kemajkina 1993: 42, 86, 37, 70)
    a T'et'a.t-ćora.t   tu.s.t'   kudo.v.
        father.PL-son.PL depart.PST.3PL house.LAT
        'Father and son went home.'
    b Vard.ińe   saj.sinźe   ruća.t-panar.ot.
        slave.DIM   take.PRS3SG>3PL skirt.your-shirt.your
        '[(The mother:) Don't go swimming on the way!] The slave girl will take your clothes.'
    c At'a.ś   kil'd.ś-povod.ś   alaša.
        old:man.DEF harness.PST3SG-bridle.PST3SG horse.
        'The old man harnessed and bridled the horse.'

2 Introduction

   d S'e.t'   śim.d.s.t'-and.s.t'   ejsenze, son
      that.PL drink.CAUS.PST.3PL-feed.PST.3PL them   she
      pid'e.ś-pan.ś   t'enst.
      cook.PST3SG-bake.PST3SG   DAT3PL
      'They provided food and drink for her, she prepared food for them.'

Note that the meanings of the parts of co-compounds in the examples are closely related and that the compounds tend to form CONCEPTUAL UNITS, such as 'family', 'parents', 'male members of a family', 'clothes', 'make ready a horse for drawing a carriage', 'feed', 'prepare food', which are in a SUPER-ORDINATE relationship to the meaning of the parts. In this respect, the meaning of co-compounds is diametrically opposed to that of subordinating compounds (henceforth: SUB-COMPOUNDS), such as *fingertip, apple tree, workhorse*, in which there is a hierarchical relationship between determinant (first part in English) and determinee (second part in English), such that the determinant makes the determinee more specific, the result being that the whole sub-compound is more specific in meaning than the determinee. Sub-compounds are also known under the names of determinative compounds or tatpurusha compounds and are often called compounds *tout court*, because they are the most salient type of compound in Germanic and in classical Indo-European languages.

This section introduces some basic issues for a cross-linguistic description of co-compounds as addressed in this study: what are the formal, semantic, and use-specific properties of co-compounds in particular languages and in general? How do word-like co-compounds behave in relation to phrase-like tight coordination, such as 'bare binomials' in Germanic languages? What is the relevant cross-linguistic variation, how do languages differ with regard to co-compounds?

1.1.1 *The form of co-compounds*

As can be seen from the examples in (2), co-compounds in Erźa Mordvin are tight units whose parts consist of single word forms, so co-compounds do not look like typical syntactic phrases. On the other hand, they are not just simply words (as might be expected from the name 'compounds'). According to Koljadenkov (1959: 56), co-compounds in Mordvin hold an intermediate position between compounds and phrases. Their intermediate character between words and phrases in Mordvin can be seen already from their hyphenation in orthography. In Erźa Mordvin co-compounds, each part has a word stress[3] and in most cases each part is inflected. Inflection is not, however, as free as in phrases because—with some few exceptions—both parts will have exactly the same inflection. Since each inflection class always has the same or almost the same form for all words, the parts of Mordvin co-compounds typically have the same phonological ending (a kind of rhyme). The tendency toward 'inflection harmony' in Mordvin co-compounds is so strong that the parts of co-compounds which would be in the formally unmarked nominative singular indefinite will usually take the plural suffix *-t/-t'*, as in *t'et'a.t-ava.t* 'father.PL-mother.PL > father and mother, parents' (literally 'fathers-mothers'). Co-compounds in Mordvin thus have a number of formal properties that characterize them as a class of forms, notably parallel word stress and parallel inflection.

These formal properties cannot, however, be generalized cross-linguistically. In each language where they occur, co-compounds have specific formal properties that characterize them as a class of forms and these characteristics need not necessarily differentiate co-compounds from all other classes of forms of that language. There are very few languages where co-compounds are undoubtedly words. A language in point is Modern Greek (see Mirambel 1959: 382f). In Greek co-compounds there is only one word stress. As in sub-compounds, the first part typically has a stem form and is typically (but not always) followed by a linking vowel *-o-*. A difference between co-compounds and sub-compounds is that the former as a whole need not have the same gender and/or the same ending as the second part would have as an independent word. Thus the parts which appear in the co-compound *tó anðr.ɔ́.jin.ɔ* 'the:N man.LINK.woman.N > the (married) couple' differ considerably from the independent words *ɔ ándras* 'the:M man:M' and *i jinéka* 'the:F woman:F'. Neither the form of the parts of co-compounds, nor the gender of whole co-compounds, are predictable by a simple rule, even if most examples are neuter:[4] *tá jinɛk.ɔ́.peð.a* 'the:PL:N woman.LINK.child.N:PL > women and children' (*tá peðiá* 'the:N:PL child:PL:N > the children'), *i aγɔra.pulis.í.a* 'the:F purchase.sale.VOWEL.F > the deal' (*i aγɔrá* 'the:F market, purchase', *i púlisi* 'the:F sale'). Verbal co-compounds are formed in a similar way: *klið.ɔ.mandalɔ́n.ɔ* 'lock.LINK.bolt.1SG > I lock and bolt'.

In Modern Georgian—a Kartvelian language spoken in the Caucasus—nominal co-compounds have single final inflection, which lets them appear rather word-like. In orthography they are hyphenated (except derivations from co-compounds). Regarding stress, they do not behave uniformly (single stress on the first stem in *dá-dzma* 'sister-brother > siblings', or on the second stem in *ded-máma* 'mother-father > parents', or double stress in *t'ól-amxánagi* 'age_mate-comrade > comrades of the same age' (Harris 2002: 233)). Verbal co-compounds have single suffixes but double prefixes (Section 2.4.3).

In many languages, co-compounds are characterized by the absence of any marking (juxtaposition) and they are often not the only class of forms with this purely negative characterization. In Vietnamese, both co-compounds and sub-compounds are simply juxtapositional. Juxtaposition is also a dominant strategy for attributive possession and serial verb constructions (Section 4.4.2). According to Thompson (1987: 128), compounds frequently occur with weak stress on their first syllable. But: 'The formal characteristics of compounds are not entirely clear, and in many individual cases it is difficult to determine whether a morpheme sequence constitutes a compound or a phrase' (ibid.: 120). In Vietnamese orthography, co-compounds are sometimes hyphenated, sometimes not; it is not clear whether co-compounds in Vietnamese represent a morphological or a syntactic pattern.

In Sentani (Cowan 1965: 12), a language of Irian Jaya, co-compounds are formed by juxtaposition and, except for some few examples with stress reduction, such as *kaji-i'fa* 'big_women's_canoe-small_men's_canoe > canoe (in general)', *isam-fə'la* 'anger-bow_and_arrow > war' (only the second part has a word stress), it is again not clear whether co-compounds represent a morphological or a syntactic pattern, as in *do-mijɛ* 'man-woman > human being', *kədə-nalə* '?-nest > (family) goods, possessions', *moni maj* 'hunger disaster > famine', *kəlu omi* 'son(s) (and) daughter(s)', *aka-bɛkə* 'elder brother-? > kith and kin, relatives'. (Neither is the hyphenation consistent.)

In some South East Asian and South Asian languages such as Hmong, co-compounds can be discontinuous. Discontinuity is highly restricted, however, mostly to the patterns ACBC and CACB, where A and B are the parts of the compound and C a single word repeated either after or before each part of the compound as in *muaj txiab muaj nkeeg* 'have illness have moaning > be ill' (*txiab nkeeg* 'illness moaning > illness'; see Section 4.2.3.vi for further discussion and evidence that these co-compounds are really discontinuous and do not simply consist of four parts).

We may summarize that even if co-compounds are characterized by a number of formal properties in each language where they occur (which do not, however, necessarily differentiate co-compounds from all other classes of forms and which need not necessarily be present in all co-compounds of that language), there is only little that can be generalized for a cross-linguistic description of the form of co-compounds. It holds for co-compounds in all languages that they are WORD-LIKE patterns with two (or sometimes three or four) lexical word slots (that is, slots which cannot be filled by phrases) which usually lack overt markers for coordination (except sometimes fossilized coordination markers). In this characterization 'word-like' there is an emphasis on 'like'. In most languages, co-compounds are not simply words. Only in a few languages are co-compounds prosodic words (Modern Greek; see Nespor and Vogel 1986: 110–15), but in many languages it is questionable whether they are grammatical words, since many co-compounds also have some properties of phrases (see Chapter 4). Generally, co-compounds are TIGHT COORDINATION patterns, there being little distance between the coordinands (often simple juxtaposition), but formally this does not always strictly distinguish co-compounds from phrase-like tight coordination patterns (Section 1.1.5).

1.1.2 *The meaning of co-compounds*

The meaning of co-compounds is more consistent cross-linguistically than their form, which is why the semantic properties of co-compounds are treated much more prominently in this study than form. As pointed out above, co-compounds express NATURAL COORDINATION, coordination of items which are expected to co-occur, which are closely related in meaning, and which form conceptual units, such as 'father and mother', 'husband and wife', 'hands and feet', 'eat and drink', 'read and write', rather than 'the man and the snake', 'toe and belly', 'knife and hammer', 'eat and read', 'read and swim', which are instances of ACCIDENTAL COORDINATION, coordination of items which are not expected to co-occur, and which do not have a close semantic relationship.

Important for the understanding of natural and accidental coordination is the difference between INHERENCE and ESTABLISHMENT, as introduced by Seiler (1972) for the description of inalienable and alienable possession. In many languages, possessive relationships with inalienable entities, such as one's body parts and blood relations, are encoded differently from accidental alienable possession, such as of food, instruments, and buildings (Nichols 1992: 116–23). For kinship terms and body parts, the possessive relationship is inherent and need not be established before it is mentioned. Possessive relationships with items that are not necessarily possessed by an individual, however, need to be established. In the same way coordination is inherent in natural coordination but has to be established in accidental coordination, so it is assumed that mother and father, hands and feet belong together, whereas it cannot be taken for granted that a man and a snake belong together.

Natural coordination has characteristic semantic properties on different meronomic (part–whole) levels:

- PART–PART: There is a coordinating relationship between the parts and the parts are very closely related in meaning. Both parts are on the same taxonomic level. There is inherent coordination between the parts.

- PARTS–WHOLE: There is a close semantic relationship between the meanings of the parts and the whole. The whole expresses a superordinate concept in relation to the parts.
- WHOLE: The whole expresses a conceptual unit, which is a superordinate rather than a basic level concept.

Superordinate concepts (such as furniture, relative(s), fruit(s), cloth(es), cutlery) are more general in meaning than basic level concepts (such as table, brother, apple, shirt, fork). There are several kinds of superordinate expressions ranging from those referring to concrete individual accumulations of things (COLLECTION COMPLEXES, such as 'knife and fork', 'brothers and sisters (those present in a concrete situation)' (Vygotskij 1962: 63); or 'groups of concept members' (Wisniewski and Murphy 1989)) over conventional expressions for certain groups (GROUP COLLECTIVES, such as 'family', 'clan', 'flock' (Leisi 1971: 31)) to abstract expressions without gestalt (GENERIC COLLECTIVES, such as 'cattle', 'fowl', 'cutlery' (Leisi 1971: 32)) and HYPERONYMS denoting single items with a general meaning (such as 'sibling', 'relative', 'a piece of cutlery'). Mihatsch (2000, 2003) shows that expressions for group collectives may develop to generic collectives and further to hyperonyms.

The semantic factor of superordination is, however, more difficult to apply to SYNONYMIC CO-COMPOUNDS (both parts and the whole have the same contextual meaning; synonymic co-compounds are also known under the name of hendiadys, literally 'one by two'), such as 'lived-be_located > lived' in (3a), and to ORNAMENTAL CO-COMPOUNDS (co-compounds in which the meaning of one part does not contribute anything to the meaning of the whole), such as 'forest-maple > forest' and 'to belly-back > have a belly, be pregnant' in (3b):

(3) Erźa Mordvin: examples from fairytales (Kemajkina 1993: 12, 24)
    a Eŕa.s.t'-ašt'e.s.t'   at'a.t-baba.t.
       live.PST.3PL-be_located.PST.3PL   old_man.PL-old_woman.PL
       'Once upon a time there were an old man and an old woman.'

    b Pek.ija.ś-lang.ija.ś   śej.ińe.ś,
       belly.DENOM.PST3SG-back.DENOM.PST3SG goat.DIM.DEF
       tu.ś   vir̆.ev-ukštor.ov   l'evksija.mo.
       depart.PST3SG   forest.LAT-maple.LAT have_young.INF
       'A goat was pregnant, (it) went into the forest to have young.'

In Chapter 5, I will argue that these represent less basic semantic types of co-compounds which deviate from the semantic prototype of co-compounds. Interestingly, language-specific classes of collectives, such as the collectives on

Ge- in German (*Geschwister* 'brother or sister', *Gedärm* 'intestines', *Gewand* 'garment') also comprise representatives with a synonymic relationship between part and whole, *Gehirn* 'brain' (*Hirn* id.) and *Gebrauch* 'use' (*Brauch* id.). We may say that even if it is not the case in all co-compounds that the meaning of the whole is superordinate in relation to the meaning of the parts, it is at least not subordinate.

Most of what are traditionally considered to be copulative compounds in West European languages (see, for example, Olsen 2001) severely violate some of the semantic criteria for co-compounds listed above, and therefore I do not consider them to be co-compounds.

- In INTERMEDIATE-DENOTING COMPOUNDS, such as *southwest, blue-green*, there is a close lexico-semantic relationship between the parts, and both parts are on the same taxonomic level, but there is no coordinate relationship between the parts, and the whole is no more general in meaning than the parts themselves.
- In APPOSITIONAL COMPOUNDS, such as *poet-doctor*, French *wagon-restaurant*, there is a kind of coordinate relationship, but there is no close lexico-semantic relationship between the parts, and the meaning of the whole is more specific in meaning than the parts. In this respect, appositional compounds have a function similar to sub-compounds.
- RELATIONAL COMPOUNDS, such as *mother–child relationship*, look at first glance like sub-compounds with a co-compound in the first slot. These are, however, appositional compounds rather than sub-compounds (note that the reverse order is possible, too: *the relationship mother–child*); thus, *mother–child* in the example is not a mother and a child, but means rather 'between mother and child'. In spoken language at least, relational compounds can also occur without the noun that denotes the relationship, as in the following Swiss German example where the relational compound is added as a kind of afterthought to a question: *Und das git nie Diskussione, Vater Suun?* 'And there are never discussions, father–son?' (example from broadcasting). A relational compound, rather than a co-compound, is also Swedish *mamma pappa barn* in *leka mamma pappa barn* 'play mummy daddy child > play house (a children's game)'. But there is no sharp borderline between co-compounds and relational co-compounds. The first parts of such compounds like *husband-wife pair, fall-winter collection* come very close to co-compounds (see also Olsen 2001: 299).
- FUSIONAL COMPOUNDS, such as *Baden-Württemberg, Austria-Hungary*. Such compounds of proper names can be formed only of entities which underwent fusion. (Thus it is possible to speak of *Austria-Switzerland* in

the context of the European football championship that the two countries will organize together in 2008, but not politically.) The whole is not really a superordinate concept but is rather on the same level as the parts, even if a country or a company after fusion is bigger than the fused countries or companies. Double-barreled names belong also to this type of compound, for example *Koptjevskaja-Tamm* (fusion of names rather than persons) and certain names for drinks and meals, such as *whiskey-soda*.

- In COMPLEX NUMERALS, such as *twenty-three*, there is undoubtedly a coordinate relationship between the parts, but the parts are not on the same hierarchical level and the whole is rather more specific, not more general than the bigger unit.

It remains to add that natural coordination is not only a matter of the lexico-semantic relationship between the parts. Often it is highly context-dependent. Thus, hands and face can form a tighter unit than hands and feet in the context of washing (washing hands and face is a tighter conceptual unit than washing hands and feet), as in (4) from Georgian where there is a co-compound 'hand-face'. The example also contains a co-compound of kinship terms:

(4) Georgian (Hewitt 1996: 143)
 ...mamamt'il-dedamt'il.is   p'ex.isa   da   xel-p'ir.is
 father_in_law-mother_in_law.GEN   feet.GEN   and   hand-face.GEN
 da.ban.a
 PREV.wash.INF
 '[It was she (the bride) who was charged] with bathing the feet, hands, and face of her parents-in-law.'

Natural coordination is also highly dependent on culture. In Sentani (Cowan 1965) the co-compound with the meaning 'animal' consists of the parts *obo-joku* 'pig-dog' (not to be confounded with the metaphorical sub-compound in German, *Schweinehund*, consisting of the same elements), because these are the prominent domestic animals in the area where the language is spoken, while another co-compound *kaji-i'fa* 'big women's canoe-small men's canoe > canoe (in general)', testifies to the importance of different kinds of canoes in the region around Lake Sentani.

1.1.3 *The use of co-compounds*

The linguistic sign has three sides, not just the two—form and meaning. The third is use. The form and meaning of a linguistic expression do not fully determine its use and, if not used, a linguistic expression does not exist. The reason why meaning and use are often not distinguished is, of course, that the two are related much more intimately than meaning and form. Nevertheless, there are at least some aspects of use that can be studied independently from meaning, notably frequency, and this makes it necessary to consider use as a separate factor on a par with meaning and form. There are specific relations between form and meaning (such as iconicity) and there are also specific relations between form and use (such as economy of encoding; see Haspelmath 2003*b*). Even if form–meaning relations are sometimes difficult to distinguish from form–use relations, they can be different and sometimes it is important to distinguish strictly between the two.[5]

Use matters at least as much as meaning and form for the understanding of co-compounds. As we will see in Chapter 6, the crucial typological question to ask about co-compounds is not, 'Do they exist in language X?' but, 'How frequent are they in language X?' In the vast majority of languages there are extremely few co-compounds or none, and the question whether they exist at all is very difficult to answer for many languages. This question may also be irrelevant, since there is little reason to assume that there would be any syntactic or morphological rule to block the production of co-compounds; rather, co-compounds are in use in a particular language or they are not in use, or more precisely, they have a certain characteristic level of text frequency in various languages, registers, and styles. A typology of co-compounds must distinguish first of all languages with high, moderate, and low levels of co-compounds (and within languages, various registers and styles with different levels of co-compounding). A distinction between languages with extremely few and languages with no co-compounds is not viable in practice, since the fewer co-compounds there are, the larger the corpus required to identify them (as an infinitely large corpus if there are none).

Use matters not only quantitatively, but also qualitatively. Irrespective of their general cover meaning of natural coordination, co-compounds appear recurrently in certain lexical domains, such as 'parents', 'siblings', 'family', 'people', 'belongings/things', 'face', and 'clothes'. For exactly which concepts there will be co-compounds in a particular language cannot be predicted; there is always a considerable amount of lexical idiosyncrasy. But it can be predicted that co-compounds in moderately and highly co-compounding languages occur in many of the characteristic LEXICAL CO-COMPOUND DOMAINS and it is essentially this that makes co-compounds a relevant object for cross-linguistic study.

Use is also the most relevant factor in distinguishing co-compounds from phrase-like tight coordination (see below). In contrast to phrase-like tight coordination, co-compounds are word-like not only in form but especially in use. In parallel texts, co-compounds typically occur where non-co-compounding languages have simple words rather than coordination. This is a remarkably reliable indicator, since languages do not vary in their degree of isolation vs. synthesis and polysynthesis in coordination to the same extent as in other domains. Thus, a co-compound 'father-mother' is typically a functional equivalent for *parents* and not *father and mother*. This can be further illustrated with the following Komi (Uralic) proverbs containing co-compounds (Komi co-compounds and English equivalents in boldface):

(5) Komi: proverbs (Timušev 1971: 37, 75, 265)
   a Myj   **lun-voj**   vaj.e,   ńinem   on   ted.
      what   **day-night**   bring.PRS3SG   nothing   NEG:2SG   know
      'Nobody knows what the **future** will bring.'

   b Myj   ger.an-ked'ź.an,   sija-j   pet.al.as.
      what   plow.PRS2SG-SOW.PRS2SG,   that-also   result.FUT.3SG
      'You reap what you **sow**.'

   c **Aj-mam**.ys   si   bur   i
      'father-mother.POSS3SG   that   good   and
      nyl.a-pi.a.ys   bur.
      daughter.PROP-son.PROP.POSS3SG   good
      'If the **parents** are good, the **children** are too.'

Proverbs are a good register for illustration because of their conciseness. But generally, word-like use is a cumulative tendency of a class of forms rather than a strict rule for every individual occurrence.

Finally, what makes it very difficult to define co-compounds is their emergent character. Co-compounds exist by virtue of their recurrence in texts and their formal and functional saliency. They are not a single coherent phenomenon in language production (some co-compounds are lexicalized and thus prefabs (prefabricated items) retrieved as whole chunks, others are derived from their components in analogy to co-compounds already in use). The more frequent co-compounds are in a language, a register, a style, or a text, the more relevant they are as a linguistic class of expressions in their own right. That is another reason why co-compounds are difficult to identify in a language with a low level of co-compounding. When co-compounds lack saliency in a language, it can be difficult to decide whether a given expression is a co-compound or not.

1.1.4 *Differences and similarities with phrase-like tight coordination*

Natural coordination is not restricted to co-compounds. Some languages have specific tight patterns of coordination which can express natural coordination and which are not equally word-like as co-compounds. Here I call those PHRASE-LIKE TIGHT COORDINATION patterns, which does not mean that they are syntactic in contrast to co-compounds, but rather that they are more syntactic than co-compounds as they typically contain overt coordinators. Consider (6) from Bulgarian:

(6) Bulgarian (Ljuba Veselinova, p.c.)
    a Na trigodišna   vǎzrast   Ivan veče   može̊e
        On three_year:ADJ:F age   Ivan already can:IMPF3SG
        da čete   i   piše.
        SUBR read:PRS3SG and write:PRS3SG
        'Ivan could already read and write when he was three years old.'
    b ... Ivan veče   može̊e   da   čete   i
        Ivan   already can:IMPF3SG SUBR read:PRS3SG and
        da   pluva.
        SUBR swim:PRS3SG
        'Ivan could already read and swim [when he was three years old].'

'Read and write' in (6a) is natural, 'read and swim' in (6b) is accidental. In the example with natural coordination, the subordinator *da* occurs only once, in the accidental example it must occur with every coordinand. We may say that *da V i V* in Bulgarian expresses natural and *da V i da V* accidental coordination. Interestingly, the difference does not reside directly in coordination. It is located in the single or double occurrence of the subordinator *da*. The difference disappears in contexts where there is no such subordinator. In a similar way, there is a difference in English between *was able to read and write* and *was able to read and to swim*, but not between *could read and write* and *could read and swim*. It should not come as a surprise that 'read and write' can be expressed as a co-compound in some languages (for instance, Mordvin) while 'read and swim' cannot.

A well-known phrase-like tight coordination pattern can be seen in the so-called 'BARE BINOMIALS' (not associated with binomial distribution in mathematics) in Germanic languages (Lambrecht 1984), such as *law and order*,[6] whose essential formal property is a lack of articles (thus 'bare'). Consider the following examples in German and English with the corresponding co-compounds in Georgian:

(7)   Georgian co-compounds   German binomials   English binomials

    da-dzma 'sister-brother:NOM'   *Bruder und Schwester*   *brother and sister*

    ts'ol-k'mar.i 'wife-   *Mann und Frau*   *husband and wife*

husband.NOM'		
mšvild-isar.i 'bow-arrow.NOM'	*Pfeil und Bogen*	*bow and arrows*
mtʻa-bar.i 'mountain-valley.NOM'	*Berg und Tal*	*hill and valley*
dγe-γame 'day-night:NOM'	*Tag und Nacht*	*night and day*
sasmel-satsʼmel.i 'eating-drinking.NOM'	*Speis und Trank*	*food and drink*

There is, however, no formal distinction between natural and accidental coordination in German and English in contexts where articles do not usually occur, as with mass nouns and plurals, for example German *Gold und Silber* 'gold and silver' vs. *Gold und Wasser* 'gold and water'; *Brüder und Schwestern* 'brothers and sisters' vs. *Brüder und Hunde* 'brothers and dogs'.

A very specific case of bare binomials can be observed in languages which have articles with proper names, such as Bernese German where the coordination of names without articles expresses a close natural relationship (husband and wife, intimate friends, siblings):

(8) Bernese German (constructed example)
    Hüt   si   Simon   u   Valeri   z   Bsuech
    Today   be:PRS3PL   Simon   and Valerie at visit
    choo.
    come:PTC:PST
    'Today Simon and Valerie came for a visit.' (Simon and Valerie are partners.)

If they were not partners, an article would be used (*dr Simon u d Valerie*). This use of bare binomials corresponds to the use of co-compounds in some co-compounding languages, such as Mordvin, where co-compounds of proper names express couples, siblings, or other pairs of two closely related persons:

(9) Erźa Mordvin (Doronin 1993: 344)
    ...Igor.tʼ-Nataša.t   tʼeje.v.s.tʼ
    Igor.PL-Natasha.PL   make.RFL/PASS.PST.3PL
    mirdʼe.ks-ńi.ks.
    husband.TRNSL-wife.TRNSL
    'Igor and Natasha were made husband and wife.'

If Igor and Natasha did not belong together, one would have to say *Igor di Nataša*. It can be said that phrase-like tight coordination patterns are a less systematic, or are an occasional device to express the difference between natural and accidental coordination, whereas co-compounds express natural coordination more systematically in all syntactic contexts.[7]

According to Lambrecht (1984), an important property of bare binomials is formulaicity: 'the step from *des Rechtes und der Ordnung* to *von Recht und Ordnung* is like the step from ordinary to FORMULAIC language use' (ibid.: 755). Of course, not all instances of phrase-like tight coordination are equally formulaic, but many make excellent slogans that evoke a certain frame. Consider the Latin *panem et circenses* 'bread and games' (a strategy of Roman politicians to appease the people), *ora et labora!* 'pray and work!' (the rule of the Benedictines), the English *checks and balances* (basic principles of government), *trial and error* (a way of solving problems), and the Italian *libertà e giustizia* (a contemporary political movement). Many instances of phrase-like tight coordination are also idioms or are essential parts of idioms, such as German *(Das hat) Hand und Fuss* '(This) makes sense, holds water' (Krohn 1994). Co-compounds may also sometimes be part of idioms or evoke certain frames, especially those co-compounds which are restricted to a certain register. Thus Erźa Mordvin *eŕast'-ast'est'* and Russian *žili-byli* 'lived-were' can almost only be the beginning of a fairytale (like *Once upon a time there were...*).

Two approaches can be taken to the study of co-compounds and natural coordination. We can look at what co-compounds and phrase-like tight coordination have in common, and at the exclusive properties of co-compounds.

In the first approach, which will be pursued in Chapters 2 and 3, the difference between morphology and syntax is completely disregarded, since co-compounds and phrase-like tight coordination patterns in many languages are intermediate between syntax and morphology anyway. What both co-compounds and phrase-like tight coordination have in common is that they express natural coordination and that they are tight forms of coordination. There is a general iconic relationship between their form and meaning in terms of Haiman's (1985) 'Natural Syntax' (Table 1.1; see also Section 2.3.4).

TABLE 1.1. The iconic relationship between different kinds of coordination

	Semantic dimension	Formal dimension
Close relationship between the coordinands	Natural coordination	Tight coordination
Distant relationship between the coordinands	Accidental coordination	Loose coordination

14   *Introduction*

Note that the iconic form–meaning relationship is not always paralleled by an economic form–use relationship; co-compounds are not always more frequent than coordination in particular domains. This is not the case, for instance, for the coordination of proper names in Mordvin (see example (9) above).

For the second approach, in which only co-compounds are considered, it is important to determine the essential difference between co-compounds and phrase-like tight coordination, which is not simply a formal difference, even if co-compounds tend to be more word-like and phrase-like tight coordination tends to be more phrase-like. Neither is it simply a difference in meaning, even if phrase-like tight coordination patterns sometimes differ in this respect from co-compounds. For instance, bare binomials in German can express contextually established coordination (in Lambrecht's (1984) terms, contextual bare binomials), as in (10):

(10)   German (constructed example)
       Arabella ging in den Supermarkt, um eine Melone für den Fruchtsalat zu kaufen. Bei den Kleidern sah sie einen Zylinder, den sie unbedingt für Franz kaufen musste. An der Kasse bezahlte sie **Melone und Zylinder.**

       'Arabella went to the supermarket to buy a melon to make fruit salad. Passing through the clothes department she saw a top hat she just had to buy for Franz. She paid for the melon and the top hat at the checkout.'

This artificial example plays with the fact that *Melone* both means 'melon' and 'bowler hat' in German. Out of context one would be inclined to assign the meaning 'bowler' to *Melone* in the binomial *Melone und Zylinder* as bowler and top hat are a more natural pair than melon and top hat. Most expressions are polysemous, but have a single meaning in a specific situation. In coordination, there is a general tendency to assign to a word in a particular context that meaning which is most closely associated with the meaning of the other coordinand or coordinands. We may call this process of disambiguation of expressions in their context CONTEXTUAL SHARPENING (Sections 1.3.2.v, 5.3). It is this process that is responsible for the fact that in the Mordvin co-compound *t'et'a.t-ava.t* 'father.PL-mother/woman.PL' = father and mother', *ava*, which means both 'woman' and 'mother', can only mean 'mother' because only as 'mother', rather than 'woman', does it form a natural pair with *t'et'a* 'father'. In our German example, however, the process of semantic sharpening from *Melone* '1. melon, 2. bowler hat' to *Melone* 'bowler hat' cannot apply, as the meaning of *Melone* has been already sharpened by the earlier context (fruit salad) to 'melon'. What we have here is an utterly accidental coordination of melon and top hat that has been established in the context (the set of products selected in the supermarket). And as German allows for contextually established coordination in bare binomials, *Melone und Zylinder* 'melon and top hat' is correct in this example. Contextually established coordination is extremely rare in co-compounds (Section 5.5.1). The reason for this is that contextually established coordination, even if not maximally accidental, is not 'natural enough' to be expressed by co-compounds.

The main differences between co-compounds and phrase-like tight coordination patterns lies in their different use. Co-compounds occur predominantly in lexical word-domains and can vary considerably in text frequency cross-linguistically (Chapter 6). An essential element for co-compounds is their class-character (Chapter 4) which is largely independent of the presence or absence of specific morpho-syntactic markers (such as the definite article in German bare binomials), which are crucial in tight coordination patterns. Distinguishing co-compounds and less specific forms of coordination is not distinguishing words and phrases; it is rather like distinguishing definite articles and demonstrative pronouns or reflexives and the middle where a strict distinction is not always possible due to ongoing grammaticalization (Chapter 7).

1.1.5 *Are co-compounds a form of parallelism?*

Pairs of words with a close lexico-semantic relationship play an important role not only in co-compounds, but also in some forms of PARALLELISM (see Fox (1988) for a survey) and in WORD ASSOCIATION (Clark 1970). In my view, a strict distinction should been made between co-compounds, parallelism, and word pairs. A WORD PAIR consists of two lexico-semantically closely associated words irrespective of their context of use. Word pairs may occur as the parts of co-compounds, as the variegated elements in parallelism, and as stimulus and response in word associations (Clark 1970). Thus the Mordvin word pair *pekıjams : langijams* 'to belly : to "back"' may occur in a co-compound, as in (3b) and in parallelism, as in (11):

(11) Parallelism in Erźa Mordvin folk poetry (Paasonen 1938: 209)
Sirě.d'.me.ń pel't' baškir ava.ś pek.ija.ś.
'In old age the Bashkir woman got a belly.'
Taštu.ma.ń pel't' nogaj ava.ś lang.ija.ś.
'In old age the Nogay woman got a back.'

Example (11) is an instance of parallelism characteristic of folk poetry in many languages of central Eurasia. The form of parallelism exemplified here may be defined as the repetition of a sequence of words with one or several slots into which the members of a word pair are inserted. In (11) there are three word pairs: *sire : tasto* 'old(person) : old(thing)' (or with derivational affixes *sired'ems : tastoms* 'become older'), *baskir : nogaj* two ethnonyms, and *peke : lango* 'belly : back' (or with derivational affixes *pekijams : langijams*). The second line, as it is often the case in parallelism, does not add any new information; it even contains misleading information since *tasto* 'old' is usually applied to inanimate objects and to become pregnant is 'to belly' and not 'to back'. As for Bashkirs and Nogays, they are not kept distinct in Mordvin folklore; they are both traditional enemies of Mordvins anyway.

In spite of a considerable degree of overlap, we do not always find the same word pairs in parallelism and in co-compounds. I don't know of a Mordvin co-compound *sire-tasto 'old-old'. There are various excellent studies of the structure of folk poetry and other kinds of formal language in different languages where parallelism and co-compounds, because of their similarities in form and function, are treated together.[8] In the present study, co-compounds are considered a phenomenon fundamentally different from parallelism, even if it is certainly true that co-compounds and parallelism are closely associated in formal registers in many languages of central, East, and South Asia. There are several reasons to consider co-compounds as a distinct and separate phenomenon. First, parallelism is a property of certain formal registers, not of languages per se. Co-compounds, on the other hand, even if their frequency may vary considerably across registers, are much more a property of individual languages than is parallelism. They also occur in texts without any parallel structuring. Secondly, many languages that are well-known for their use of parallelism in formal registers lack co-compounds (for instance, Kuna and Aranda; see Section 7.5). Even if there may be a close relationship between parallelism and co-compounds in languages where co-compounds are used frequently, there is no evidence that the frequent use of parallelism in a given language will cause co-compounds to emerge in that language. Thirdly, in spite of many language-specific (and register-specific) studies of parallelism, little is known about the cross-linguistic diversity of parallelism, or to what extent different kinds of parallelism are caused either by different structures in these languages or by different properties of the relevant registers. In this study, I chose, therefore, to consider co-compounds as distinct and separate phenomena and do not address the question of the typology of parallelism.

1.2 Co-compounds in the linguistic literature

This section does not provide an exhaustive historical survey of the treatment of co-compounds and related phenomena in the literature. It concentrates on a few important contributions.

Co-compounds, under the name of dvandva, are one of the three major types of compounds identified by Old Indian grammarians in their descriptions of Vedic and Sanskrit[9] (see also 4.1). In Sanskrit grammatical terminology, most names of types of compounds are examples of the types. Unfortunately, the term *dvaṃ.dva* 'two.two > pair' is a word reduplication (5.4.5), not a co-compound (the Sanskrit expression for word reduplication being *āmreḍita*, literally 'repetition, repeated word', considered to be a subtype of dvandva (Wackernagel 1905: 142–8)), which is the major reason for me not to use this traditional name for co-compounds. Word reduplication has a cross-linguistic typological distribution that is different from that of co-compounds and should therefore not be treated together with co-compounds. The term co-compound has not been in common use in linguistics until now, even if it is attested in the literature, as in Bhatia (1993: 319) for Punjabi.

Dvandva compounds in Vedic and Sanskrit have been studied by comparative linguists from a diachronic point of view. Wackernagel (1905) (see also Justi 1861) shows that co-compounds in Vedic and Sanskrit developed from coordination and are not inherited from Indo-European sources. Co-compounds have also been a topic of investigation in Finno-Ugric linguistics, the most important contribution being the monograph by Lewy (1911) on Hungarian, Udmurt, and Khanty, where, however, no sharp distinction is made between asyndetic coordination in general, co-compounds, and parallelism. That co-compounds are an areal phenomenon in Eurasia has been noticed by Aalto (1964) in a paper that focuses on explaining the presence of co-compounds in Tokharian (an extinct Indo-European language in East Asia) through language contact with neighboring East Asian languages. Areality is also a topic in a paper by Boeder (1991), which considers synonymic co-compounds, phrase-like tight coordination patterns, and other kinds of constructions with 'synonym pairs', mainly in Kartvelian, but also in other Eurasian languages and Tok Pisin, without clearly distinguishing between the different patterns. He observes that 'synonym pairs' in different constructions often contain loanwords and from this derives the hypothesis that 'synonym pairs' originally had a metalinguistic explicative function. It is certainly true that translations and texts in early literatures sometimes accumulate synonyms, but there is no evidence that the number of loanwords would influence the frequency of co-compounds. As far as I can see, explicativity is a marginal function of co-compounds. An important investigation of the areality of co-compounds can be found in Tkačenko (1979), who investigates the frequency of co-compounds in various dialects of East Slavic languages and comes to the conclusion that the frequency of co-compounds in some Russian dialects is very similar to that of corresponding Finno-Ugric substrate languages. In East and South East Asian languages, co-compounds have been discussed in Chinese in particular, where the major focus of interest has been the increase of synonymic compounds from Old Chinese sources to Modern Mandarin. Different explanations for this development have been proposed, the traditional one being avoidance of homonymy (Karlgren 1962). Contrastive studies of co-compounds in South East Asian languages are rare, an important contribution being Nacaskul (1976) on Thai, Khmer, Burmese, and Malay. Ourn and Haiman (2000) investigate the predilection for alliteration in co-compounds in Khmer (and related languages) in contrast to other languages of the region. Co-compounds have also been treated in countless descriptions of individual languages; it is not possible to list all of these here.

In the general linguistic literature and in morphology, very little progress has been made in the understanding of co-compounds after the contributions of Sanskrit grammarians. This is because there are rarely more than a few lines devoted to co-compounds, if they are treated at all. There is a long tradition of combining both co-compounds and appositional compounds under the notion of copulative compounds (Bloomfield 1933: 235). The distinction is maintained, however, by Jespersen (1942: 142) and Bauer (1978: 67 f), although they mean fusional compounds by copulative co-compounds rather than co-compounds. There are only a few examples in the literature where co-compounds are considered together with phrase-like tight coordination patterns, such as bare binomials. This is the case in Paul (1904: 331–3), a work which consists mainly of a list of German examples. According to Paul, the reason why 'kopulative Verbindungen' very rarely become compounds is the impeding effect of coordinators. He claims that co-compounds can develop more easily if there are no coordinators, or if coordinators are not obligatory. However, this hypothesis is not supported by the typological evidence. There are many languages without co-compounds which lack coordinators and many languages with co-compounds which have coordinators.

An interesting approach to co-compounds is found in Bühler (1934: 320), who adduces compounds as an example of how the meaning of elements can be combined in coordination in highly different ways without there being any formal indication of how the semantic combination has to take place. He bases his statements on co-compounds in Modern Greek in particular.

In typology, little attention has been paid to co-compounds. An exception is Bauer (2001a) who investigates whether different types of compounds are mentioned in reference grammars in an unbiased sample of thirty-six languages. He finds that co-compounds ('dvandvas'; as such are counted also fusional and some appositional compounds excluded from co-compounds in the present study) particularly occur in his three areas: (a) Eurasia, (b) South East Asia and Oceania, and (c) Australia-New Guinea.

In the formalist literature and in generative semantics, if co-compounds are treated at all, the lack of co-compounds in West European languages is explained by claiming that their generation must be blocked for some reason. McCawley (1974: 33) observes that Japanese has co-compounds in examples like *Yoku nite iru oya.ku desu* 'It is a **parent and child** that resemble each other a lot' where reference is made to two different participants: 'parent' and 'child'. McCawley concludes from this that Japanese, unlike English, must have a parameter setting in its prelexical transformation component which allows parts of compounds to be referential. According to Fanselow (1985: 303), it is the morphological system of Sanskrit that makes dvandvas possible, whereas the use of compounds like *Schmidt-Genscher* in German and English is blocked outside the modifier position of determinative compounds (such as *Schmidt-Genscher-Konflikt*) because plural marking is not possible. Such parametric ad hoc explanations, which are based on the comparison of two languages or two types of languages, fail to account for the complex cross-linguistic situation where co-compounds have varying degrees of frequency and are not simply either present or lacking in a certain language.

Co-compounds have not been described in spoken and written languages only, but also in signed languages, notably by Klima and Bellugi (1979) in American Sign Language (ASL). A very important contribution of these authors is that they realize that co-compounds typically express superordinate level concepts, as also holds for spoken and written languages. In ASL there is a type of co-compound of three to four parts: three or four basic level signs are strung together and followed optionally by a sign glossed as ETC. Thus, APPLE-ORANGE-BANANA-ETC. can mean 'fruit', BEANS-CARROTS-CORN-ETC. 'vegetables' (the words in small capitals stand for ASL signs). There is no fixed order for the elements, though not all possible sequences may occur. The preferred sequences are those in which the signs more easily join to each other. Thus, the order RING-BRACELET-NECKLACE-EARRINGS-ETC., or the reverse order, is used for 'jewelry' where the location of the signs is ordered up the body from hand to ear or the other way round. Unordered combinations such as *RING-NECKLACE-BRACELET-EARRINGS-ETC. are not acceptable.

The stock of basic level concepts that can be used in co-compounds to denote superordinate concepts is highly limited. Thus, only PIANO, FLUTE, GUITAR, VIOLIN, and DRUM may be used in the co-compound for 'musical instrument', but not HARP, ACCORDION, or HARMONICA. According to Klima and Bellugi (1979), co-compounds of this type are a syntactic process. There are some other lexicalized co-compounds, such as KNIFE-FORK 'silverware' that consist of only two elements with fixed order and that show the typical reduction of compounds in sign language (implying that the first part is shorter than the second and the whole compound is roughly of equal length to a non-compound sign).[10] Co-compounds consisting of three or four members are, however, not specific to signed languages. There are some languages where co-compounds of three members, especially for collective concepts, are quite frequent, for example in Ālu-Kuṟumba (Dravidian, Kapp 1982) *mara-cëḍi-koḍi* 'trees, plants, and climbers > plants' (Section 6.3.5). In many East and South East Asian languages (such as Thai), co-compounds of four members are quite common.

Closely associated to co-compounds is word reduplication (as in the name dvandva) and echo-words (word reduplication with replacement of one segment; Section 5.4.6). In this connection the typological study on reduplication by Pott (1862) must be mentioned; this also lists examples of co-compounds from many languages. Among the studies of echo-words, the investigation of the use of echo-words in Toda and other South Asian languages by Emeneau (1938*a*, 1938*b*) is especially relevant for co-compounds.

In the literature on coordination, with few exceptions, little attention has been paid to co-compounds and the phenomena of natural and tight coordination. One of the most important contributions to the understanding of the syntax of coordination is Brettschneider (1978), who also briefly mentions co-compounds. His model of the syntax of coordination (with the distinction of adjunction, expansion, and fusion) is one of few that are compatible with the concepts of natural and tight coordination. An important contributor to the understanding of the semantics of coordination is Lang (1977), who investigates the mechanisms that determine the semantic interpretation of coordination. Lang also briefly discusses co-compounds in Chinese and finds that co-compounds consisting of the same lexical parts can have different meanings and partly, also, different formal properties (ibid.: 260).

In the typological literature on coordination, it has been noticed that tight forms of coordination often express tight conceptual units of coordinands. Important contributions have come from Mithun (1988) and Stassen (2003) (see Section 2.2.1 for a discussion). Anderson (1985: 50) comes close to the idea of natural coordination in his discussion of co-compounds in Mandarin: 'the meanings of all these sorts follow from the same basic principle: the interpretation of a coordinate compound is found (more or less) as the sum of what the elements of the compound have in common.'

The expression 'natural coordination', like co-compound, has been in the linguistic literature for some time without having been a technical term. It occurs, for instance, in Chomsky (1970b/1972: 94).

Some important work on bare binomials in West European languages includes Malkiel (1959), the Swedish monograph by Bendz (1965), Cooper and Ross (1975), and Lambrecht (1984). The central topic of interest of most work on binomials is the irreversibility of the order of coordinands in many binomials. An important issue in the study of phrase-like tight coordination is formulaicity, notably Lambrecht (1984). (For a current survey of various approaches to formulaic language see Wray (2002), who does not, however, mention bare binomials). A pioneering study in this field, unfortunately little known outside Sweden, is Anward and Linell (1975/76) on lexicalized phrases, who also treat bare binomials among other subjects.

The major sources of inspiration for the present study came not from the literature on compounds, but from various other areas of linguistic research. Studies of phenomena which are intermediate between syntax and morphology are very important, notably clitics (Klavans 1985, Anderson 1992, Spencer 1991, Nübling 1992) and approaches that make it possible to treat syntactic and morphological phenomena with similar semantic and formal properties together, such as in Haiman's 'Natural Syntax' (1985). In Haiman's monograph, coordination is a central issue. He concentrates particularly on clausal coordination and finds, among other things, that formally asymmetric coordination of verbs (S1 x (and) S2 y) often corresponds to a conceptual asymmetry (protasis + apodosis, cause + result, etc.), while formally symmetric coordination of verbs (S1 x (and) S2 x) often corresponds to conceptual symmetry (reciprocity, simultaneity; ibid.: 72 ff). Haiman exemplifies this point in languages from New Guinea, such as Kâte, in which there is a distinction between final (independent) and medial (dependent) verbal inflection markers. In Kâte, verbal co-compounds, like expressions for reciprocity with two verbs, are always dependent on an auxiliary (*e* 'do'), which has the consequence that there is never asymmetric marking on the two verbs of a co-compound.

Co-compounds partly overlap in function with other phenomena, some of which have been investigated cross-linguistically. DYAD CONSTRUCTIONS (Evans 2003, forthcoming) denote relationally-linked groups of the type 'pair/group of brothers' or 'mother and child(ren)' and have a wide variety of different formal expressions. Co-compounds can cover the domain of dyads (see example (2a) above) and specific dyad constructions can develop from co-compounds (see Section 6.3.6). Verbal co-compounds have been treated in connection with SERIAL VERB CONSTRUCTIONS in East and South East Asian languages by Bisang (1992, 1995) and Durie (1997), and by Steever (1988, 1993) in Dravidian languages.

Haiman (forthcoming) investigates co-compounds in Khmer and other languages with repetitive function ('symmetrical compounds', essentially what I call synonymic and ornamental co-compounds) in the context of repetition and redundancy in general, for which he coins the term DECORATIVE IMAGERY. He presents a detailed subclassification of 'symmetrical compounds' in Khmer. Co-compounds serve Haiman as one among many examples to illustrate that language has a playful aspect, which is often underestimated in linguistics, and that style matters for grammar. The approach taken in the present book is less comprehensive. I consider co-compounds to be a phenomenon *sui generis* following their own tendencies and principles. However, Haiman is certainly right in that the instinct for play may have a role in the production of co-compounds and for other grammatical structures, and that style is notoriously underestimated in linguistics.

Recently, in the study of compounds in morphological theory, there have been tendencies towards considering at least some compounds to be syntactic rather than morphological. This is the case in Olsen (2001) for what she calls copulative compounds, which are, however, mainly appositional compounds.[11] In a very interesting study on English sub-compounds, Spencer (2003) claims that most N N compounds in English are syntactic. All of this suggests that it is time to use more than just morphology to describe compounds.

1.3 Theoretical background, method, and material

In the rest of this chapter I will focus on some theoretical and methodological aspects of crucial interest for the present investigation. Section 1.3.1 is a discussion of why a cross-linguistic investigation of co-compounds and natural coordination cannot be done in the same way as a classical typological study. In Section 1.3.2, some general aspects of meaning in natural languages are discussed that are especially important for the study of co-compounds and natural coordination. In Section 1.3.3, finally, the kinds of language material considered in this study are discussed.

1.3.1 *Why this is not a classical typological study*
When first starting to work on co-compounds, I intended to write a classical typological study with its essential attributes: a well-defined universal seman-

tic domain, a small number of types, an unbiased sample of languages, and a convincing explanation for the typology. Now, years later, I find myself with quite a different kind of study. In this section I will try to explain why this is.

(i) *Universal 'semantic' domains and 'language-specific' classes* In what may be called classical typological studies, the starting point is a SEMANTIC DOMAIN—such as negation (Dahl 1979, Payne 1985a), comparison (Stassen 1985), predicative possession (Heine 1997)—which is universal in the sense that it is expressed in all languages, and languages are classified according to the different kinds of markers or CONSTRUCTION TYPES used to express that domain in that language. In another kind of typological study, classes of forms that occur in only some languages are chosen as the starting point—for example, various tenses and aspects (Dahl 1985, Bybee et al. 1994), the middle (Kemmer 1993), noun incorporation (Mithun 1984)—and it is investigated in which languages they occur and to what extent these classes form a cross-linguistically uniform CLASS TYPE. At first glance it would seem that the object of the two kinds of studies is fundamentally different. But there is no such fundamental difference, since the object in both studies is actually semantic and formal at the same time, even if the formal component is a very general one in the case of 'semantic' domains. This can already be seen from the fact that there are typological studies whose object is intermediate between 'semantic' domain and formal class types, notably Koptjevskaja-Tamm (1993) on nominalization.

'Semantic' domains cannot be fully abstracted from form as they are always represented in language as COMMUNICATIVE DOMAINS, that is, not just meaning, but meaning as it is expressed in language. Typologists do not study all kinds of communicative domains; they are not interested, for example, in advice, gossip, and declarations of love (at least not professionally), but only in such domains that are highly restricted in form and typically expressed in highly recurrent CONSTRUCTIONS, that is, types of clauses, sentences, or noun phrases with characteristic formal and semantic properties. Typically, constructions have the structure of sentences, clauses, and noun phrases. Thus, possession is investigated in typology not as a communicative domain, but as a CONSTRUCTION DOMAIN, that is, either in noun phrases (attributive possession) or in clauses (predicative possession). Construction domains always have a formal component (for a similar point see Haspelmath 1997: 9). Language-specific classes, on the other hand, always have a semantic component. As we saw in Section 1.1.1, the investigation of a cross-linguistic class type requires a great deal of abstraction from language-specific formal properties of classes. The main difference between the two typological approaches is thus not at the level of form vs. meaning, but at the level of construction vs. class. Constructions happen to be more universal cross-linguistically than classes. Classes of forms typically occur at a sub-constructional level. A form that belongs to a certain functional class—such as *Mary's*, which is an instance of a dependent-marked possessor class (better known as genitive)—usually does not form a construction, but only a fragment of a construction, or a morpho-syntactic PATTERN.

The present study investigates a functional–formal class type, co-compounds, which do not occur in all languages and which, even if they have recurrent characteristic lexical domains, are not simply a functional domain, but are used differently in different languages (especially with regard to frequency). This study is thus class- rather than domain-oriented.

(ii) *Discrete and continuous typological variables* The very designation 'typology' suggests that the items investigated (constructions, classes or categories, languages) can be classified in a small number of neatly distinct clear-cut types, and for many features this works quite well. Thus, for instance, either a language has an inclusive–exclusive distinction in pronouns and/or agreement markers of the first person plural or it has not (see Nichols 1992: 123 f). Such typological properties are DISCRETE VARIABLES.

Other typological properties can be considered as either discrete or CONTINUOUS VARIABLES; for example, word order. Interestingly, such properties are usually considered discrete variables in typological studies. One speaks of dominant SVO (subject–object–verb), SOV, and VSO word order. On the other hand, Dryer (1995: 119) argues that the basic word order is also the most frequent one; frequency thus plays a crucial role in word order, even if it is considered a discrete variable. Now, as Dryer points out, we have the problem that frequency is basically a property of texts[12] and discourse types and not of languages.

This means that frequency is problematic in typology to the extent that it varies language-internally, and typology has to face this problem, whether properties are viewed as discrete or continuous.[13] Unfortunately, there have been few studies of continuous variables in typology. Quantitative typology played a role in the work of Joseph H. Greenberg (1960, and 1974 with O'Sullivan), the father of modern typology, but it has not been a central issue in typology in recent times, even if it is well-known that frequency plays an important role in many typological questions (consider Givón 1995: 81 and Cooreman 1982, 1987 on the role of frequency for the typology of voice). Most cross-linguistic studies which take text frequency into account are based on only a few languages, mainly due to practical difficulties. This does not mean, however, that it would be impossible to compare frequencies cross-linguistically.

As pointed out in Section 1.1.3, what is most relevant about co-compounds is not whether they exist or not in a language, but to what extent they occur. Co-compounds are therefore viewed as a continuous typological variable in this study.

(iii) *The problem of sampling for features that are highly biased areally* Recent research in typology (especially Dryer 1989a and Nichols 1992) has shown that many typological features have specific macro-areal patterns of distribution. For some features there are even large continuous areas of almost continental size.

Co-compounds happen to be a feature distributed in a very specific way cross-linguistically. Although they demonstrate little sensitivity to the grammatical structure of a language and can vary considerably in frequency in closely related languages and even dialects (Indian English vs. British and American English, see example (1) above; Turkic languages, see 6.3.1), co-compounds have highly regular macro-areal distribution patterns (see Chapter 6). Traditional typological sampling that strives to exclude bias toward certain linguistic stocks and areas does not make sense for a feature with such a highly areally determined distribution. Therefore, I will concentrate on Eurasian languages where there are both many languages in which co-compounds are a characteristic phenomenon and many languages for which sufficient material is available. It turns out that for some purposes it is very useful to consider a number of languages from the same language family, as there may be considerable differences in co-compounding even in very closely related languages. Therefore I will not use a simple general method of sampling for the whole study. For many purposes, there is no need for a large and unbiased typological sample. To show that a certain phenomenon exists, it is enough to describe it in a single language and, to make a universal correspondence between two features look implausible, it often suffices to look at a small number of areally related languages.

(iv) *Explanations in typology* Explanations why certain languages have a certain property, and others do not, can be roughly classified into four types: hidden-structure explanations, functional explanations, emergent-structure explanations, and historical explanations.

HIDDEN-STRUCTURE EXPLANATIONS postulate certain non-observable factors which cause, block, or allow certain observable phenomena to appear. These factors, not directly observable, are often presented in a coherent theory, such as parameters in generative syntax, schemas or metaphors in cognitive linguistics, and conceptual space in 'Radical Construction Grammar'.

In FUNCTIONAL EXPLANATIONS it is claimed that a phenomenon emerges because there is a need for it. If a language lacks an expression for a certain domain or if that domain is not expressed in an optimal way, a certain phenomenon will arise because it can fulfill this function. The problem with theories which focus on functional explanations is that they have to claim explicitly or implicitly that natural languages—because they change constantly—are highly deficient and that everything in language has a function (otherwise it would not have developed).

The basic assumption of EMERGENT-STRUCTURE EXPLANATIONS is that language use shapes the language structure, and that languages are similar in many respects because language is used in very much the same way in all linguistic communities. Important pioneering studies in emergent structure in linguistics include Hopper (1987), Keller (1994), Lüdtke (1980), and Lindblom (1992).

The kinds of explanations mentioned so far can best be applied to recursive phenomena, but are not very good at explaining unique events. HISTORICAL EXPLANATIONS account for unique situations by explaining unique constellations as the consequences of other unique constellations. This is the only type of explanation possible if a typological feature occurs in only a single area.

All four kinds of explanations are doubtless needed in linguistics. In my study of co-compounds, it transpired that emergent-structure explanations and historical explanations were the essential ones, and these are not as neat as hidden-structure and functional explanations, since they account for general tendencies and unique constellations rather than for exceptionless rules.

(v) *Summary* This study is not a classical typological study because the phenomenon to be considered calls for a different treatment. It has a functional–formal class type as its object, rather than a universal construction domain. This class of co-compounds is best viewed as a continuous, not a discrete, variable. This continuous variable, in spite of showing little sensitivity to the grammatical structure of a language, is distributed cross-linguistically in areally highly characteristic patterns which makes traditional sampling useless, and it cannot be accounted for by neat explanations.

1.3.2 *Meaning in language*

In this section, I will discuss some aspects of meaning in natural languages which are highly relevant for the topics discussed in this monograph.

(i) *Meaning in natural languages is not systematically taxonomic* Compounds are sensitive to taxonomic levels of abstraction in conceptualization to a certain extent. Rosch (1975, Rosch et al. 1976) distinguishes three levels of abstraction in conceptualization: superordinate, middle, and subordinate. She holds that the concepts belonging to her middle level are the most basic in terms of psychological salience (measured by text frequency, ease of recall, etc.). Put differently, the concepts of Rosch's middle level of abstraction, such as *apple, dog,* and *table,* are more prototypical concepts[14] than *kitchen table* and *ankle socks* or *fruit, furniture,* and *clothing,* which is one reason why the former tend to be expressed by simple words while the latter are often expressed by derived words, compounds, or even phrases. It has been observed that sub-compounds often denote subordinate concepts (see Taylor 1989: 49 for English) and co-compounds often denote superordinate concepts (see Klima and Bellugi 1979 for American Sign Language). Consider Table 1.2 which has examples from Mari.

There is, however, no simple correlation between form and the level of abstraction in conceptualization. Simple forms need not necessarily belong to a middle level; simple and shorter forms merely tend to be more frequent than complex and longer forms (see Zipf 1935/1965, Haspelmath 2003b), as can be especially seen in cases where the cultural importance of a concept has changed drastically (see Witkowski and Brown (1983) for 'marking-reversals' between 'deer' and 'sheep' and 'tapir' and 'horse' in Meso-American languages due to cultural changes). Put differently, meaning in language is not systematically taxonomic. After all, *chicken* and *bird,* which are in a subordinate–superordinate relationship, are equally basic concepts. There is nothing like Linné's biological taxonomy built into the semantic component of lexemes denoting plants and animals in natural languages, and it is certainly unhelpful to search for folk taxonomies that would be as rigid as scientific taxonomies. Basic concepts are therefore best considered as taxonomically neutral, being concepts that are most salient and familiar to humans, irrespective of their hierarchical status in a taxonomy. It happens to be the case that non-basic concepts can (but need not necessarily) be related to basic

TABLE 1.2. Examples for superordinate, basic, and subordinate concepts in Mari

Concept above basic level	*kid-jol* 'hand/arm-foot/leg > limbs, arms and legs'	Co-compound
Basic level concept	*kid* 'hand, arm'	Simple word
Concept below basic level	*kid.tup* 'hand/arm.back > back of the hand'	Sub-compound

concepts in terms of taxonomic relationships; sub- and superordinate levels can therefore be considered as relative in respect to the basic level. The superordinate level may then also be considered as the domain of those concepts (including collection complexes, collectives, hyperonyms, and abstracts; see 1.1.2 above) that are typically related to basic level concepts by superordination and which lack 'shape' (considered to be an essential property of the basic level in cognitive linguistics). Thus, superordination can be conceived of on two different meronomic levels: as a semantic relationship between parts and whole and as the meaning of wholes.

Compounds, which are sensitive to taxonomic levels, are the best example for the lack of systematic taxonomies in language. This can be seen from the fact that sub-compounds sometimes express a subordinate taxonomic level (basic level term plus modifier), and sometimes not; thus *blackbird* and *lyrebird* are birds, but a *ladybird* is not (and there is no reason to believe that speakers of British and Australian English conceive of ladybirds as birds).

We may conclude that natural languages do not classify systematically and that this is what makes them extraordinarily plastic and flexible, and compatible with many different taxonomic systems (including different systems of cultural beliefs) at the same time. A lack of systematic taxonomic classification is also the reason why classes of co- and sub-compounds are idiosyncratic, that is, it cannot be predicted with certainty which concepts will be expressed by co-compounds and which by sub-compounds in languages where these classes occur.

(ii) *Partial cover meanings* The European structuralists claimed that the meaning of linguistic categories is to be considered in terms of *Gesamtbedeutung*, where a grammatical class has one meaning that holds equally for all of its occurrences and distinguishes it from all occurrences of all other grammatical classes (see notably Jakobson 1936/1971). However, most modern linguists agree that linguistic categories are polysemous (that is, have several directly or indirectly related meanings). This position can be traced back to pre-structuralist times and is taken in particular by linguists working in the framework of grammaticalization. It has now become common to represent semantic networks by means of SEMANTIC MAPS (see Haspelmath 2003*a* for a survey). However, it has to be kept in mind that semantic maps are always strong simplifications with specific foci. They are a powerful tool for representing very general synchronic semantic relationships that happen to coincide largely with diachronic grammaticalization paths. However, semantic maps have great difficulties with multidimensional semantic relationships. They fail whenever several ways of slicing the same cake semantically should be accounted for. For a powerful semantic map of coordination, see Haspelmath (2004). Its strength lies in the fact that it abstracts from almost all the subtle semantic differentiations made in Chapter 3.

Some linguists who reject *Gesamtbedeutung* or RADICAL COVER MEANING, as we might call it, tend to reject all forms of cover meanings (for instance, Croft 2001: 116ff). While there may be no radical cover meanings, there are still PARTIAL COVER MEANINGS.[15] Let us illustrate this with the perfect tense. According to Dahl (1985: 132f), the perfect tense has the following types of uses: (i) perfect of result, (ii) experiential perfect, (iii) perfect of persistent situation, and (iv) perfect of recent past. These uses are types of situations which may partly overlap each other, that is, each is a partial cover meaning which can already be seen from the fact that languages with a perfect expressing all these four functions do not completely agree in their use of the perfect tense. Dahl (1985: 133) further points out that uses (i) and (iv) have a common semantic factor which comes close to a 'Gesamtbedeutung', 'that both involve a point of reference ... which is different from the "point of event"'. This is also a partial cover meaning, just a more general one. There are thus several alternative ways to represent the meaning of the perfect tense, each of which is legitimate and none of which is the only correct solution, because each is a strong idealization based on partial cover meanings (Figure 1.1).

It is characteristic of functional–formal class types to have several uses which are often very closely associated semantically. Fully developed functional–formal classes must be so general that they can account for a number of different (though preferably related) situation types. Partial cover meanings are highly important for the semantic coherence of classes even if they do not apply to all members of the class equally well and do not exclude all items which are not members of that class.

(iii) *The form-related-ergo-meaning-related approach and its limits* It is a common approach in grammaticalization and typology to consider meanings

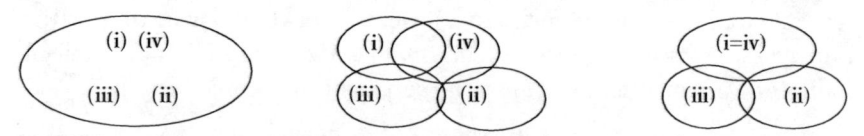

FIG. 1.1. Different semantic maps to represent the meanings of the same linguistic class in an idealized way by partial cover meanings

as being related if they are recurrently expressed by the same means in various languages. Kemmer (1993: 4), for instance, holds that 'recurring instances of different meanings being expressed by the same formal or structural means is an indication that the meanings in question are related' (see also Haiman 1985: 26ff).

One idea behind the form-related-ergo-meaning-related approach is that cross-linguistically recurrent formal identity is an argument in favor of recurrent diachronic identity. If reflexives and middles often have the same form, this supports the argument that the middle generally often develops from the reflexive and that this happens because reflexive and middle are closely related conceptually. One problem with this approach is that it presupposes a strong parallelism between diachronic and synchronic semantic relationships, which cannot be taken for granted at all. In the context of natural coordination, however, we have to face a much more intractable problem, namely that the most characteristic form of natural coordination is zero marking, which it shares with a number of other meanings, such as inalienable possession and temporal sequence (in serial verb constructions, see Section 4.4.2). Can we deduce from this that coordination, possession, and temporal sequence are semantically related? Hardly.

The form-related-ergo-meaning-related approach reaches its limits in the case of iconically motivated zero marking. While the phonological form of words expressing concepts and explicit markers expressing grammatical classes is largely arbitrary, the form of constructions for natural coordination and inalienable possession tends to be iconic and is usually not at all arbitrary. In such cases, identity or similarity of form is unreliable for synchronic semantic similarity and diachronic identity. From a common lack of a marker in possession and coordination we cannot deduce that possession and coordination would have common diachronic sources and would be semantically related. The recurrent absence of any marker is thus a much weaker common formal characteristic than the recurrent presence of a specific marker.

To summarize: recurring instances of different meanings being expressed by the same formal means may be an indicator that these meanings are related, but primarily for diachronic semantic relatedness and only indirectly for synchronic semantic relatedness. However, for two zero marked construction types, cross-linguistically recurrent identity in form is not a reliable indicator for semantic relatedness and recurrent diachronic identity.

(iv) *Semantic relativity and the level of cross-linguistic semantic comparison (morpheme vs. utterance)* It is widely believed that because of their differences in form, different languages necessarily represent different cultures and different mentalities. This common belief that meaning is language-specific is known in linguistics under various names, notably semantic relativity, or the Sapir/Whorf hypothesis (see Werlen (2002) for the history of semantic relativity in linguistics). In its strongest form, semantic relativity means that the native language inevitably determines the thinking and perception of its speakers in a specific way.

Croft (2001: ch. 3) has shown that it is characteristic for relativistic positions that they are extremely absolute in some respects. He identifies the following four hidden assumptions in relativistic argumentation (given here in a compressed formulation).

Hidden assumptions in semantic relativity approaches according to Croft (2001):

- #1: Seemingly equivalent expressions in two different languages differ in meaning if they differ in their formal construction (DIFFERENCE IN FORM IMPLIES DIFFERENCE IN MEANING).
- #2: There is a 1:1 correspondence between meaning and form (NO POLYSEMY).
- #3: There is NO REDUNDANCY in a construction.
- #4: Determining the semantic relativity of one constructional element necessarily builds on the absoluteness of another constructional element (HIDDEN ABSOLUTENESS).

Semantic relativity concerns us here because co-compounds have not been spared untenable semantic relativity interpretations. For instance, according to Lewy (1911: 99–102), co-compounds are a manifestation of a specific worldview in Finno-Ugric languages (my translation):[16]

The Finno-Ugrian has a strong tendency to perceive and to express two points of perception agglomerates or impression groupings, where we can hardly or not at all find any pairhood. (ibid.: 100) {#1, #3}

It was impossible for me to distinguish a parallelism of form from a parallelism of meaning; the Finno-Ugric form is also completely real content. (ibid.: 101) {#2}

In the tradition of Humboldt (1836), Lewy implicitly takes for granted that languages should be compared at the level of morphemes or, put differently, that the meaning of an expression in another language is more like a morpheme-to-morpheme analysis than a free translation. So he rejects the following description by Wiedemann of Komi and Udmurt verbal co-compounds (my translation):

> The grouping of two verbs for the expression of one concept for which we have a simple specific verb in German is very common. (Wiedemann 1884: 105, quoted from Lewy 1911: 99f)

I agree that the use of concept (*Begriff*) is not unproblematic since co-compounds do not typically express basic concepts. But on the whole, I am much more comfortable with Wiedemann's description than with Lewy's. If Lewy were right, we would have to make morpheme-to-morpheme translations from other languages in order to understand what people are talking about. Obviously, we don't do this. If we want to understand by translating, we have to translate at the level of the utterance. Meaning is thus most equivalent across languages at the level of the utterance and least at the level of the morpheme. This has to do with the fact that most morphemes and words are highly polysemous in isolation, but not usually (except in poetry) in situations of concrete speech. But this is the topic of the next section. Let me just add that this section does not argue against modern approaches to semantic relativity, like Levinson (2003), which do not presuppose a cross-linguistic semantic equivalence at the morpheme level.

(v) *Contextual semantic sharpening* Most lexemes and grammatical forms are highly polysemous and it is well-known that their semantic extensions are not congruent cross-linguistically. If meaning in language were static and rigid, Whorf would be right. Fortunately, meaning in language is highly flexible. In a specific context, words and morphemes are very rarely ambiguous. Different processes of CONTEXTUAL SEMANTIC SHARPENING are responsible for selecting a single contextual meaning for words and morphemes from the variety of their possible conventionalized and non-conventionalized meanings (see also Section 1.1.4 above). The sharpening processes can also be viewed as a kind of dynamic cover meaning of constructions. For example, the construction *X is a Y* has the cover meaning of member-class sharpening consisting of the directive: select and adapt the meanings of X and Y in a way that X is a member of class Y. This same process of class sharpening is responsible for the fact that Venus in the following three sentences—*Venus is a planet, Venus is a Roman goddess,* and *Venus is a tennis star*—is sharpened to three different meanings. In some cases of member-class sharpening, the subordinate–superordinate taxonomic relationship between concepts is activated. This is the case notably if X and Y are generic (as in *The lion is an animal*). Even in such cases, the superordinate concept may be sharpened to different meanings depending on the choice of the subordinate concept, as in *The piano is an instrument, The hammer is an instrument*.

In many cases, the meaning of linguistic entities is precise only in context. This has important methodological consequences. The meanings of linguistic entities can be studied properly only in the contexts where they naturally occur. The role of contextual semantic sharpening in co-compounds will be discussed in Section 5.3.

1.3.3 *The linguistic material considered in this study*

For the investigation of co-compounds it is essential to consider texts. It does not suffice to look at word lists or sentences that are detached from their contexts because:

- the text frequency of co-compounds is the feature that gives the clearest and largest areal patterns, even if there is also considerable variation in frequency within languages, across styles and registers (Chapter 6);
- many co-compounds are highly context-dependent (5.5);
- context of use is crucial for understanding diachronic semantic developments (notably inference; see Bybee et al. 1994: 25f);
- co-compounds, in languages where they occur, are one of several devices to create lexemes for the temporary lexica of individual texts or conversations (4.3.4).

I have mainly used two classes of texts: parallel texts and original texts. To a much lesser extent, I was able to profit from material from questionnaires.

PARALLEL TEXTS are translations of the same text into other languages. Their advantage is that they express approximately the same content in about the same register and have more or less the same length; they make it possible to compare language use directly across languages. Their disadvantage is that the translations may be imprecise and even faulty, and that the texts may represent registers that are highly peripheral in a typology of texts, or that a register is even created for a translation. Another problem of parallel texts is their bias towards written language. Parallel texts are always written language (not by definition, but in practice).

It is no surprise that because of all these disadvantages, translations are avoided as material for the description of single languages. For cross-linguistic studies, the advantage of direct comparability of language use may overrule the disadvantages (see also Dahl 1985: 50), especially where parallel texts are available in many genetically and areally unrelated languages. Parallel texts also have the practical advantage that they are much easier to analyze than original texts for somebody who does not know the language. Parallel texts are used in Chapter 6 in particular for the investigation of the degree of co-compounding across different languages of Eurasia.

The semantic classification of co-compounds in Chapter 5 is based mainly on material from ORIGINAL TEXTS in central Eurasian languages. I selected a small number of languages and focused on one: Erźa Mordvin. Original texts are much more reliable than translations to determine the appropriate use of co-compounds. Original texts are essential for the study of contextual motivation (Section 5.5) and language-internal diversity across styles and registers. To a minor extent, examples from original texts reproduced and analyzed in reference grammars could be used.

QUESTIONNAIRES, at least those I could obtain, did not turn out to be ideal for the collection of material on co-compounds because co-compounds are highly idiosyncratic in lexical distribution. Moreover, in many cases speakers and writers have the choice of whether or not to use co-compounds, which would make it necessary to consult more than one informant per language and, furthermore, co-compounds are highly context-dependent. It is best to study them in real language (that is, in non-experimental language with a concrete, not only a purely scientific purpose). The most characteristic feature of cross-linguistic variation in co-compounds, viz. their text frequency, cannot be considered in questionnaires, which are necessarily restricted in length. However, questionnaires turned out to be a useful heuristic tool to discover phrase-like tight coordination patterns. Specific examples are Bulgarian (6) in this chapter, Mari (11) in Chapter 2, and Bahdinani Kurdish (12) in Chapter 2.

For the cross-linguistic investigation of co-compounds and natural coordination, it is not feasible to make excessively puristic demands on the data sources. So I followed the principle that any material that serves the purpose can be used. The diversity of material used may also compensate for the unavoidable deficits implicit in individual sources of material.

1.3.4 *Summary*

What made it interesting, and at the same time difficult, to write this book was that there was no ready-made track to follow. Even if—speaking in Anderson's (1992: viii) terms—there are many shoulders to stand on, it was not possible to adhere to a single linguistic framework. Co-compounds are not a grammatical category and cannot be described simply in terms of grammaticalization. Co-compounds are not independent isolated lexemes and cannot be described simply in terms of lexicography. Co-compounds are not simply complex words and cannot be described adequately only in terms of traditional morphology. Co-compounds do not represent a discrete typological feature without language-internal variation and cannot be described simply in terms of classical typology. Co-compounds cannot be identified mechanically in texts and cannot be investigated by automatic corpus linguistic analysis. Different patterns of coordination differ in tightness and are not simply grammatical or ungrammatical in certain contexts, but rather appropriate or inappropriate, and they cannot be described by purely formal syntactic theory. Diachronic and synchronic relationships between different types of co-compounds do not coincide, so the semantic map approach is of only limited importance for them, which makes it impossible to follow the framework of 'Radical Construction Grammar'.

To put it simply, the approach taken in this study is problem-oriented and, as there is no single existing framework that fits, various frameworks had to be combined. In the same vein, the languages considered also had to be chosen in a way that was appropriate for the purpose of the investigation. Certainly, it would have been inappropriate to consider co-compounds exclusively in West European languages, where they are almost absent. Finally, needless to say, the study in hand is not a complete description of co-compounds and natural coordination. More and more, I get the impression that I have just scratched a bit off the surface and that there is much more worth accounting for.

1.4 Organization of the following chapters

In Chapters 2 and 3, co-compounds are considered along with phrase-like tight coordination. Chapter 2 focuses on the marking patterns of natural coordination and Chapter 3, in an opposite perspective, on tight coordination and its semantic correlates.

In Chapters 4–7, co-compounds are examined as a phenomenon on their own. In Chapter 4, I develop the lexical class approach to co-compounds. In Chapter 5, co-compounds are classified into different semantic types, and their uses in original texts are studied, especially in central Eurasian languages. Chapter 6 explores the areal typology of co-compounds in Eurasia, while Chapter 7 is devoted to the way co-compounds evolve diachronically.

Notes

[1] For coordination the following terminology will be used (inspired by Haspelmath forthcoming, 2004). A COORDINATING CONSTRUCTION consists of two or more COORDINANDS (also called conjuncts). Markers of coordination (English *and*, *or*) are called COORDINATORS (the traditional term 'conjunction' is avoided in this sense; subordin-

ate conjunctions are called subordinators). Coordination consisting of a simple JUXTAPOSITION of the coordinands is ASYNDETIC in contrast to SYNDETIC coordination with one or several coordinators. CONJUNCTION is 'and'-coordination, DISJUNCTION 'or'-coordination, and ADVERSATIVE COORDINATION 'but'-coordination.

The term coordinated phrase is not used, since there is much evidence that coordinands and coordinating constructions are often not syntactic phrases (Brettschneider 1978: 150). Instead, since coordinating constructions are mostly continuous, the term COORDINATE SEQUENCE is used for continuous coordinating constructions, that is, those consisting of an immediate sequence of morphemes belonging to coordinands and coordinator(s) exclusively. As understood here, co-ordination is not restricted to syntax; co-compounds (being sometimes purely morphological and mostly intermediate between morphology and syntax) are also considered instances of coordination.

[2] Mordvin is a Finno-Ugric (Uralic) language, spoken in the European part of Russia. It has two major varieties, Erźa and Mokša. Where nothing else is indicated, Mordvin below refers to Erźa Mordvin.

[3] Word stress in Erźa Mordvin is a problem by itself as it is free but not phonological or lexically specific; almost any syllable of a word can bear the word stress without any difference in meaning.

[4] This is well in line with Zubin and Köpcke's (1986) observation that words expressing concepts of the superordinate level in German often are neuter.

[5] I do not agree with Haspelmath (2003c) that cohesive expression types can always be explained by higher frequency. Co-compounds (tighter, more cohesive) are less frequent than phrasal coordination (looser) in most languages, except for very advanced stages of co-compounding. Of course, one can claim that in this case one has to consider the frequency of individual types, that, for instance, 'father-mother' is a co-compound because it is more frequent than 'father and mother', but even this does not hold for all languages, where a co-compound 'father-mother' exists. Moreover, there are clear cases of groups of co-compounds being less frequent than corresponding ordinary coordination, as is the case for the conjunction of proper names; see example (9).

[6] For the predilection of legal English for binomials, see Hiltunen (1990: 54f, 25).

[7] This difference comes close to Whorf's distinction between overt and covert marking: 'A covert category is marked ... only in certain types of sentence and not in every sentence in which a word or element belonging to the category occurs' (Whorf 1945/1956: 89). Co-compounds, insofar as they are formally distinct from coordination, are an overt marking strategy for coordination, whereas phrase-like tight coordination patterns can express the difference only in certain morpho-syntactic environments.

[8] Nguyễn (1965: 125) holds that co-compounds in Vietnamese (his term is 'additive constructions') are at the lowest level of parallelism, while according to Nguyễn (1933: 55), co-compounds (his term is 'binôms') and the structure of Vietnamese folk poetry both result from repetition.

⁹ The earliest preserved (but not the first) Sanskrit grammar is that of Pāṇini (sixth cent. BC; Katre 1987).

¹⁰ There is little information available about other sign languages. In Swedish Sign Language (Brita Bergman, p.c.) there are only a few co-compounds, such as KNIFE-FORK-SPOON 'knife, fork and spoon', RADIO-TV-JOURNAL 'massmedia'. MUM-DAD-CHILD is a variant for 'family' for which there is, however, also a single sign. Other subordinate terms are derived from, or related to, basic level terms; FRUIT is manually identical to APPLE and differs only in mouthing, the sign for FURNITURE is similar to the sign for CHAIR. A co-compound consisting of two parts is DAD-MUM 'parents'. An older variant for 'hearing person' was formed by the signs for SPEAK-HEAR. This suggests that co-compounds are more lexicalized in Swedish Sign Language than in ASL.

¹¹ Unfortunately, Olsen (2001: 310) claims that co-compounds in Sanskrit are syntactic. Sanskrit is one of the few languages, together with Modern Greek, where co-compounds are undoubtedly morphological (compound stem, single word stress; Section 7.2.1). It may be that Vedic co-compounds are syntactic, but this does not mean that it also holds true for Classical Sanskrit as well.

¹² Here, and elsewhere in this study, the notion of text is not restricted to written languages and also comprises speech.

¹³ Typology usually neglects the possibility of language-internal diversity across registers and styles and has been criticized for this by Miller and Weinert (1998: ch. 7). They emphasize the opposition of elaborate written vs. spontaneous spoken language (but this seems to be too simple in the light of Biber's (1985) typology of texts). However, it is certainly true that most large-scale cross-linguistic investigations, including the investigation in hand, suffer from a heavy written-language bias. As traditional typology does not offer any way of dealing with variations across registers and styles, other frameworks, such as typology of texts (Biber 1985, 1988, 1995) and ethnography of speaking (Sherzer 1983), may serve as a source of inspiration, even if these approaches cannot be applied one-to-one to a large-scale cross-linguistic study. The need to consider language-internal variation is well-known from sociolinguistics (see, for instance, Labov 1972).

¹⁴ See Ungerer and Schmid (1996: ch. 2) for the relationship between basic level concepts and prototypes. Consider also Wierzbicka's (1985: ch. 3) critical remarks to Rosch's approach.

¹⁵ For linguists who are fond of German terminology, I propose the term *Sammelbedeutung* instead of *Gesamtbedeutung*.

¹⁶ For a similar position see Kaplinski (2002).

2

The Marking Patterns of Natural Coordination

In natural coordination (as introduced in Section 1.1.2) the coordinands express semantically closely associated concepts, such as *brother and sister, hands and feet, eat and drink, here and there, two or three*, etc. In this chapter I will describe how natural coordination is expressed, without distinguishing between co-compounds and phrase-like tight coordination (Sections 2.2 and 2.3). The marking patterns of natural coordination are highly relevant for markedness in general (2.1) and for the syntax of coordination (2.4). Crucial for the understanding of the marking patterns of coordination are two iconic relationships of Haiman's (1985) 'Natural Syntax': minimal distance and symmetry.

2.1 Different kinds of markedness

The notions 'marked' and 'markedness' are used in a number of different senses in linguistics. For our purposes, the following kinds of markedness must be distinguished: formal, distinctive, structural, local, typological, and textual, and as far as constructions are concerned, relational vs. non-relational markedness.[1] Let us consider them in turn.

The form *hand.s* is FORMALLY MARKED for plural. A formal marker *.s [z]* marks the plural. In the same way *the hands* is formally marked for definiteness. The definite article marks definiteness. (Formal markers can be both affixes and functional words.) In formal markedness, a clearly segmentable element, be it a morpheme or a word, is added to a word or construction.

If we consider, however, the Dinka (Nilo-Saharan) forms *ciin* 'hand' and *cin* 'hands' (Nebel 1948), the plural does not add anything, but the forms are still distinct. If the notion of formal marking is rather difficult to apply in this and other cases where word forms are not easily segmentable, *ciin* 'hand' and *cin* 'hands' are nevertheless clearly DISTINCTIVELY MARKED. Similar English examples are present *sing* vs. past *sang*, and singular *woman* vs. plural *women*.

Distinctive marking is present wherever a paradigmatic difference in meaning (such as singular vs. plural) is realized in pairs of different forms. Note that the terms distinctively marked and unmarked apply to pairs of forms, not to individual forms. Distinctively marked applies also to all pairs of formally unmarked vs. marked forms.

Distinctive markedness is also relevant for Whorf's overt vs. covert marking distinction (Whorf 1945/1956; see also Section 1.1.4 above). In an overt opposition, pairs of forms are usually distinctively marked whereas they are only rarely distinctively marked in the case of a covert opposition.

In contrast to formal and distinctive marking, which apply to single pairs of forms, STRUCTURAL MARKEDNESS applies to the sum of all pairs of forms that represent a certain semantic opposition. In English, singular and plural nouns are generally opposed to each other, even with the word *sheep*, where there is no formal or distinctive marking. An ideal domain for structural markedness are paradigms where there is a category (such as number or tense) having different values of a category (see Croft 2003: ch. 4; singular and plural, or singular, plural, and dual; present and past). Structural markedness is the main concern of the traditional markedness discussion which investigates, among other things, which members of structural oppositions are marked or unmarked. Accordingly, it is claimed that the plural is generally marked with respect to the singular (even if plural forms may occasionally be formally unmarked) because: (a) it is usually the plural that is formally marked; (b) the singular is compatible with more contexts than the plural (the singular is more indifferent in respect to meaning than the plural); and (c) other oppositions (for example, gender in languages such as French, Russian, and Avar) tend to be neutralized in the plural rather than in the singular (see Greenberg 1966, Moravcsik and Wirth 1986, Andersen 1989). As a rule, the unmarked member of the opposition is also more frequent.

For many linguists, structural markedness is markedness par excellence and other types of markedness are just symptoms of structural markedness. We may call this the monistic view of markedness. For a pluralistic view about markedness, as advocated here, different kinds of markedness are basically independent of each other, even if they often coincide, and no kind of markedness is considered to be primordial over others.[2]

If structurally unmarked values of a category are generally more frequent, this is not necessarily true for all individual oppositions of forms. Thus, there are many plural forms in English that are more frequent than corresponding singular forms, such as *teeth* and *tears*. Tiersma (1982) shows that a higher frequency of the plural forms may have consequences for diachronic behavior. If the plural is more frequent, it may prevail in analogical leveling against the singular, as in some varieties of Frisian where singular *kies*, plural *kjizzen* 'tooth, teeth' is leveled to *kjizze:kjizzen*, and *trien:trjinnen* 'tear:tears' to *trjin:trjinnen*, in contrast to the expected leveling according to the singular form as in *hoer:hworren* 'whore:whores' > *hoer:hoeren*. Other diachronic reflections of locally unmarked singulars are loanwords borrowed as plural forms (such as Chamorro *sapatos* 'shoe' < Spanish *zapatos* 'shoes'), etymologically double plurals (such as English *child.r.en*, Dutch *kind.er.en* id.), irregular plural forms (English *teeth*), and distinctively unmarked plural forms (English *sheep*, *fish*). In order to capture such phenomena, Tiersma (1982) introduces the notion of LOCAL MARKEDNESS. In my understanding of the term, the more (or most) frequent form is generally locally unmarked. It appears to me to be useful to speak of local markedness not only in the 'spectacular' cases where frequency goes against structural markedness, but also in the unspectacular cases (which are the majority) where the structurally unmarked form (in our example, the singular) is more frequent. For most English nouns, it is the singular form which is locally unmarked. In cases where the structurally marked form is locally unmarked, such as in English *feet* and *teeth*, there is a MARKEDNESS CLASH between structural and local markedness, rather than a markedness reversal, as it is usually called (see Croft 2003: 165). The term markedness reversal implies that there is only one markedness which may be locally inverted. A markedness clash implies that there are several dimensions of markedness which need not agree.

Properties that occur only in a minor part of the world's languages are TYPOLOGICALLY MARKED.[3] There is no general convention in typology as to how small the percentage of languages can be in an unbiased sample for a specific feature to be considered typologically marked (less than 50 per cent, less than 25 per cent?). Therefore, typological markedness is applied mostly in the comparison of two features; for example, duals are more marked typologically than plurals. In contrast to all other kinds of markedness, typological markedness is necessarily a cross-linguistic and not a language-specific entity. Of course, it is also possible to compare structural markedness and/or formal markedness across languages and to find specific correlations between structural and formal and typological markedness, as is often done in typology.

Typological markedness is not necessarily related to structural markedness. Any two features, which need not be related to each other structurally or semantically, can be compared concerning typological markedness. Thus, for example, click phonemes are more marked typologically than an inclusive–exclusive distinction in second person plural pronouns.

TEXTUAL MARKEDNESS is different from other kinds of markedness in that it applies to individual places in texts (and in discourse), or, in an extended sense, to certain kinds of contexts. Textual marked expressions or constructions are means of expression that are unusual in a given context (deviations from the norm). They have the function of attracting the attention of the audience and are crucial for structuring a text into more important (foregrounded) and less important (backgrounded) passages.[4] The following examples from Carroll's (1865) *Alice in Wonderland* may serve as an illustration. Example (1a), since it is a crucial passage in the story, contains several textually marked means of expression, notably the unusual word order adverb–verb–subject in *down went Alice*, a complex negative expression *never once*, and a complex interrogative expression *how in the world*. Example (1b) is a much less important passage of the same story and contains rather backgrounding expressions, such as the disjunctions *once or twice* and *no pictures or conversation*.[5]

(1) English (Carroll 1865/1994: 12, 11)
    a ...In another moment down went Alice after it, never once considering how in the world she was to get out again.
    b Alice was beginning to get very tired of sitting by her sister on the bank, and of having nothing to do: once or twice she had peeped into the book her sister was reading, but it had no pictures or conversation in it...

The different kinds of markedness discussed above are summarized in Table 2.1. All of these have in common that they apply to paradigmatic rather than syntagmatic relationships between forms. Put differently, they apply to ONE-SLOT PATTERNS but do not fully account for TWO-SLOT PATTERNS like coordination. Values of a category, such as plural, genitive, definiteness, passive, etc., are one-slot patterns. Constructions, such as coordination and attributive possession, however, have at least two lexical slots and are two-slot patterns since they express relations between at least two items. A (lexical) slot contains at least one word from an open word class (and can eventually contain more complex elements, such as a phrase or a clause).

From the point of view of a construction with two (or several) lexical slots there are two kinds of formal marking: RELATIONAL and NON-RELATIONAL MARKING. Relational markers are those that indicate the relationship between the words (or phrases) in a construction, such as genitive and possessive affixes in attributive possession, pronominal agreement, accusative and ergative in transitive verb construction, and coordinators in coordination.[6] Non-relational markers are all other morpho-syntactic markers that occur in a construction without marking the relationship between the parts of the given construction, such as coordinators in possession and articles in coordination.

TABLE 2.1. Different kinds of markedness[a]

	Applies to…	Marked means…	Unmarked means…
Formal markedness	The presence or absence of a morpho-syntactic marker	Having a morpho-syntactic marker	Not having a morpho-syntactic marker
Distinctive markedness	Formal distinction of forms or constructions with different meaning	Being formally distinct	Not being formally distinct
Structural markedness	Structural opposition between values of a category (within a language system)	Feature-bearing in an asymmetric structural opposition	Lacking the relevant feature in an asymmetric structural opposition
Local markedness	Relative frequency of an expression in a specific domain	Less frequent member	More frequent member
Typological markedness	The cross-linguistic frequency of a feature in an unbiased sample	Cross-linguistically rare or rarer	Cross-linguistically frequent or more frequent
Textual markedness	Choice of the appropriate means of expression in a concrete speech/text situation or context type	Deviation from the norm, deviation from the expected	Use of the most normal, the most neutral, the most expected expression in a given context

[a] Regarding the difference between privative and equipollent oppositions (Trubetzkoy 1939: 67), only formal and structural marking are (or at least can be) privative; all the others are equipollent. Any privative opposition can be conceived of as an equipollent one, whereas the reverse is not true, and in distinctive markedness, even if it comprises formal markedness, the perspective is such that it focuses only on difference, not on hierarchy.

Let us now consider how natural coordination behaves according to the different kinds of markedness. Natural coordination, where it is formally distinct from accidental coordination, is usually characterized by the absence of formal markers, whether relational (coordinators; Section 2.2) or, very frequently, non-relational (Section 1.1.3 above: the lack of the subordinator *da* with the second coordinand in Bulgarian, the lack of articles in German bare binomials; Section 2.3). This means that natural coordination tends to be unmarked formally where it is marked distinctively.

Special constructions for natural coordination—in languages where they occur—tend, however, to be highly restricted in use. Usually, pairs of lexemes that occur in special constructions for natural coordination can also be found in ordinary coordinate constructions, but the reverse is not true. Languages that have a special construction for natural coordination usually also have a construction for accidental coordination, but the reverse is not true. Generally, the construction expressing accidental coordination, and not the construction expressing natural coordination, tends to be the ordinary construction for coordination. It follows from this that special patterns for natural coordination are generally structurally marked with respect to the ordinary coordinate construction. There is thus a general markedness clash:

Constructions for natural coordination, if they are marked distinctively, are STRUCTURALLY MARKED, but tend to be FORMALLY UNMARKED in respect to ordinary (accidental) coordinate constructions.

This markedness clash goes against the general tendency for formal markedness and structural markedness to coincide. This 'general' tendency is, however, characteristic only for one-slot patterns and not for two-slot patterns like coordination. One- and two-slot patterns behave differently in respect to zero marking. In one-slot patterns, the absence of marking can express grammatical meaning only if there is a formally marked member of the opposition that has an opposite meaning. Thus, zero marking can mean singular only if there is a non-zero marker that means plural. This is not true for two-slot patterns. Zero marked two-slot patterns can have a specific meaning even if there is no corresponding opposed pattern that is formally marked, simply by the lexico-semantic relationship that is established between the lexical items. There can even be several formally identical unmarked two-slot patterns in the same language. Thus, Vietnamese has coordinate, possessive, and appositive N N constructions. It follows from the lexico-semantic relationship between the items, not from the form, which of these different constructions is expressed. Thus *anh em* 'elder_brother younger sibling' is coordinating ('> brothers and sisters', *anh cha* 'elder_brother father' is possessive ('> father's elder brother', and *anh Lan* 'elder_brother Lan' is appositive ('> my elder/honored friend/colleague Lan'.

It is precisely these two-slot patterns expressing natural relationships that tend to be formally unmarked. As Comrie (1986) puts it, formally unmarked expressions tend to be context-dependent to a much higher degree than formally marked expressions. He shows this by discussing local expressions in Eastern Armenian. Unmarked nouns can function as local expressions only in very specific contexts (as an argument of a verb *to live*, as in the sentence *Aprum em Yerevan* 'live I-am Erevan = I live in Erevan', ibid.: 86). The locative case may express an inessive relationship ('in something') or an adessive relationship ('on something'), depending on which relationship is more natural for the context (as in *Hodvac.n ays gərk^h.um e* 'article.DEF this book.LOC is = The article is in this book'). Only the use of an inessive postposition (GEN + *meǰ* 'in') clearly marks an inessive relationship unmistakably in all contexts. It must be used in an unnatural (unexpected) location as *Caγik.n ays gərk^h.i meǰ e* 'flower.DEF this book.GEN in is = The flower is in this book' (ibid.: 88). Generally it holds that the more explicit the marking is, the less dependent is the meaning of the whole on the lexico-semantic relationship between the lexical items in the lexical slots.

Local markedness is very important for the lexicalization of co-compounds. Usually it is such concepts as 'parents' or 'property' for which co-compounds are lexicalized first; and where lexicalization takes place, a co-compound initially has to become the most frequent (locally unmarked) expression, or at least one among several frequent expressions, in a specific lexical domain. More will be said in Section 4.3.5 about lexicalization and local markedness.

With typological markedness, there is the problem that it is more difficult to apply to continuous than to discrete variables. It is probably the majority of languages which have at least some very marginal and rare co-compounds, at least in some registers, but it is definitely a small minority of languages which have a high frequency of co-compounds (Chapter 6).

In languages with a low to moderate level of co-compounding, co-compounds often have the effect of textual marking. Example (2) from Santali exemplifies a high density of co-compounds. In the example, a girl (a single child) is to be married in the house of her parents to a stranger. When asked whether she agrees, she gives her reservation special weight by using parallelism and co-compounds in her wording (co-compounds are in boldface):

(2) Santali (Bodding 1925–29, 1: 322 f)
Ado koto nahĩ **kam kaj** (work work) menaktabona, **rua haso** (fever pain) menaktabona, **neao jhogor** (discord quarrel) menaktabona. Ado kam kaj karonte, se daka utu (cooked_grain curry) karonte...
'Now all of us have our **work** to do, we suffer all from **fever and pain**, we have **quarrels and disputes**. Now perhaps on account of the **work**, or on account of the **food**, [or for some cause or other, whatever it may be, perhaps we two may some day have words together, and perhaps he may become sulky and dissatisfied and then walk away.]

In Section 7.4 we shall see that textual markedness is crucial for understanding the evolution of co-compounds.

To summarize, the different behavior of natural coordination (and co-compounds) in different kinds of markedness (notably the systematical markedness clash between formal marking and structural marking) is strong evidence that a pluralistic view about markedness should be adopted.

Let us now consider the different distinctive relational and non-relational marking strategies in natural coordination in turn.

2.2 Relational marking in natural coordination

It has been repeatedly noted in the literature that the absence of coordinators may be used to express conceptual units or pairs in coordination. According to Mithun (1988: 332):

Noun phrases joined with no intonation break typically designate a single conceptual unit. Conjoined noun phrases of this type often refer to the sorts of concepts designated by single lexical items or compounds in many languages, such as 'parents' for 'mother and father'. By contrast, noun phrases separated by comma intonation typically designate conceptually distinct members of some set. Each new coordinand introduces a separate piece of information. This distinction is characteristic of all types of languages.

Similarly, Stassen (2003: 768) notes that: 'pairs like "husband and wife", "boys and girls", "horses and cattle", "bow and arrows", or "gold and silver" are more likely to be encoded by zero marking than other, less predictable NP-coordinations.'

The lack of an overt coordinator, however, is not always distinctively marking for natural coordination, as many languages do not have obligatory coordinators in the ordinary coordinating construction. According to Mithun (1988), this is the rule rather than the exception. However, a typology of languages with zero coordinators and languages with overt coordinators is too simple. Some languages which often lack coordinators in coordination may have coordinators in especially loose coordination. An example is Khanty. According to Lewy (1911: 12), Khanty has the coordinators *i* 'and' (borrowed from Russian) and *pa* 'and; the other (one)' that are used in traditional texts mainly in cases of sentence coordination (ibid. for examples). Another language in point is Khalkha with predominantly zero coordinator in conjunction, which occasionally has little grammaticalized overt coordinators. In (3) from the UDHR (Universal Declaration of Human Rights) there is a coordinator *bolon* (a converb of *bolox* 'to be') in a complex coordinate sequence whose coordinands differ considerably in their length, which calls for an explicit relational marking of the coordination:

(3) Khalkha (UDHR 25; 2)
...ger   bül.ees[7]   gar.san   bolon
house/family family_(members).ABL go_out.CONV:PST be.CONV
butač...
out_of_wedlock
'[All children,] whether born in or out of wedlock...'

The omission of a coordinator in natural coordination is distinctive only inasmuch as ordinary coordination usually has an overt coordinator, as is the case, for example, in Georgian where co-compounds, such as *da-dzma* 'sister-brother:NOM > brother and sister', lack coordinators in contrast to accidental coordination, such as *gvel.i da k'ac'.i* 'snake.NOM and man.NOM = the snake and the man'.

Distinctive marking of natural coordination by the reduction of the coordinator is found in Tagalog. In Tagalog natural coordination, the form of the coordinator *at* 'and' may be reduced to *'t* if the preceding coordinand ends on a vowel or *-n*, as in (4) from the UDHR:

(4) Tagalog (UDHR 16; 1)
Ang mga lalaki't babae.ng   may sapat   na
FOC PL   man'n'   woman.LINK EX   sufficiently LINK
gulang...
age
'Men and women of full age...'

Reduction of *at* 'and' is actually quite rare, at least in the written language.[8] The only other case where it is found in the UDHR is the lexicalized *isa't isa* 'everyone, one another' (< 'one'n' one'). A similar reduction is the English *'n'* in *rock 'n' roll, fish 'n' chips*.

Languages with completely different coordinators in natural and ordinary coordination are rare. A case in point is Malagasy, where there is a construction for nominal natural coordination of the form DEF A *aman*-B (Dez 1980: 2, 275); here A and B are the coordinands, DEF the definite article, and *aman-* a coordinator that occurs only in this construction (*aman-* is probably related to the preposition *amin* 'with'). Nominal coordination is usually expressed by the construction DEF A *sy* DEF B in Malagasy (*sy* is the ordinary coordinator with nominal coordinands):

(5) Malagasy (UDHR 25; 3 and 16; 3)
 a Ny ray aman-dreny...
  DEF father AMAN-mother
  'father and mother'

 b ...ny lehilahy sy ny vehivavy...
  DEF man and DEF woman
  'men and women'

But note that the difference does not only consist of the form of the coordinator, but also in the number of articles (single non-relational marking vs. double non-relational marking; see below). The use of the *aman*-construction in Malagasy is quite limited. In the text of the UDHR there is just one example.

Since 'and'-coordinators often derive from comitatives, it is important to note here that there are also natural comitative constructions (which will be treated in Section 3.3.1). Because of the formal affinity of Malagasy *aman-* with the comitative, it seems possible that the Malagasy construction for natural coordination originally had a natural comitative meaning.

In Southeastern Tepehuan (Uto-Aztecan; Willett 1988) there is a specific coordinator *gam* used to append one entity to another of a similar nature or function. *Gam* is restricted to nouns, whereas the coordinator *guio* conjoins units whose referents are not similar in nature. Consider (6) with both coordinators exemplified:

(6) Southeastern Tepehuan (Willett 1988: 324)
 cortis gam risbus guio sap valas up
 cortes and rebozos and EVID balas too
 '[Lots of things are being sold here,] (including) fabric, shawls, and bullets'

Gam may be used to conjoin more than two coordinands, in which case it is repeated, and it may occur in discontinuous coordination (in boldface), as in:

(7) Southeastern Tepehuan (Willett 1988: 323)
Jixjaná **gu pippihl** gu tobav gam **gu u'ji'**.
like DEF chicks DEF hawk and DEF birds
'The chicken hawk likes (to eat) chicks and (other) small birds.'

In discontinuous coordination articles are repeated with each coordinand. The *gam*-coordination differs from typical natural coordination in that it does not cover examples such as 'day and night' (according to Willett, because these are settings and not entities).

In some languages, coordinators of SUMMARY CONJUNCTION (Haspelmath forthcoming) may be used in natural coordination. Summary coordinators are quantifiers, such as 'two', 'three', 'both', or 'all'. In practice, it is often difficult to decide whether morphemes denoting quantifiers that occur in coordination are coordinators or non-relational markers. It seems that they start as non-relational markers that can subsequently be grammaticalized to coordinators or parts of complex coordinators, as in the case of English *both... and*.

Summary coordinators can be associated with natural coordination, which is the case in many of the languages of Asia (Yakut, Khalkha, Tibetan, Mandarin, Vietnamese, Konda). Their prototypical domain are pairs of persons, such as Yakut *aɣa.m ijä.m ikki* 'father.my mother.my **two** > my mother and father' (Böhtlingk 1851/1964: 7). However, Yakut *ikki* 'two' may also be found with abstract coordinands as in (8):

(8) Yakut (Böhtlingk 1851/1964: 5)
jol sor **ikki** kisi.ni gytta särgä syljal.lar.
luck bad_luck two man.ACC simultaneously row go:PRS.3PL
'Luck and bad luck go in a row with man.'

Summary coordinators are not necessarily associated with natural coordination. In the English and Swedish complex coordinators *both... and*, *både... och*, the summary component *both*, *både* rather adds to the meaning of separateness (Payne 1985*b*: 17–22) or of coordination counter-to-expectation (Section 3.3.1). As a rule, summary coordinators in natural coordination may occur only if there is no other coordinator present.

2.3 Non-relational marking in natural coordination

Often the difference between natural and ordinary coordination is not expressed by a difference in the form of the coordinator, but rather in a difference of other markers (expressing case, number, definiteness, possession, etc.) which are associated with one or both coordinands. In a coordination with two coordinands, affixes and functional words can be attached to both coordinands (double non-relational marking), to one coordinand (single non-relational marking), or to none of the coordinands (zero non-relational marking). Interestingly, all three non-relational marking patterns can be used to mark natural coordination distinctively.

2.3.1 *Distinctive non-relational single marking*

The most widespread distinctive marking strategy for natural coordination is single non-relational marking. This type is represented in English by articles (*the house and garden, the rights and freedoms*), by possessive pronouns (*He took his hat and coat*), and by number in some compounds, such as *hunter-gatherers*.[9] We may see from the English examples that the markers closer to the head (plural) are less inclined to single non-relational marking than more peripheral markers (articles, possessive pronouns). This does not hold only for English, but seems a very widespread tendency in which it does not seem to matter which category is expressed by the more or less peripheral affixes. In Ewe (Niger-Congo), which has a sequence of affixes different from English, the plural suffix follows after the possessive suffix. While the more central possessive suffix—where it occurs—is always double marking in coordination, the plural may show single non-relational marking in natural coordination as in (9):

(9) Ewe (Westermann 1930: 47)
    a   xɔ̃.nyè   kplé   nɔví.nyè.wó
       friend.my   with/and brother.my.PL
       'my friends and my brothers'

    b   ŋútsù   kplé   nyɔ́nù.wó
       men   with/and woman.PL
       'men and women'

A further example is Eastern Armenian, where possession and case can be distinctively single marked in natural coordination:

(10) Eastern Armenian (Minassian 1980: 164)
    a   Č'.em   moṙan.a   ał   u   hac'.d.
       not.be.1SG forget.PTC:NEG:COND salt and bread.your
       'I will not forget your hospitality (=salt and bread).'

    b   nver   dproc'.i.s   ev   usuc'ič'.ner.i.s.
       present   school.DAT.my and teacher.PL.DAT.my
       'present for my school and my teachers.'

In ordinary coordination, possession and case are marked on both coordinands (10b), whereas in natural coordination (10a), possession occurs only on the second coordinand.

Interestingly, it does not seem to matter whether the non-relational markers that show single marking are affixes or functional words. Of course, affixes tend to be more grammaticalized, and therefore closer to the stem than functional words, and that is why they show single marking less often than functional words. But the mere fact that affixes may be attached just a single time to a syntactic coordinate sequence is remarkable and highly relevant for syntactic theory (see Section 2.4 below).

The study of formal marking patterns in Mari is especially interesting, as in this language the sequence of the dative suffix (this does not hold for all other cases), the possessive suffix, and the plural suffix are 'free' (except that number always precedes case). All the following combinations are possible DAT.POSS, POSS.DAT and POSS.PL.DAT, PL.POSS.DAT, PL.DAT.POSS (Luutonen 1997).[10] In (11a) both noun phrases have a case marker and a possessive suffix. In (11b, natural coordination) only the possessive suffix appears on both coordinands. The sequence of the two categories, case and possession, is different, however; in (11a) it is DAT.POSS and in the tight phrase-like coordination in (11b) it is POSS.DAT:

(11) Mari (N. Gluxova, p.c.)
 a Tide škol.lan.em   den   tunyktyšo-vlak.lan.em pölek.
    this school.DAT.my   and/with   teacher-PL.DAT.my   present
    'This is a present for my school and my teachers.'
 b Tide ača.m   den   ava.m.lan   pölek.
    this father.my   and/with   mother.my.DAT   present
    'This is a present for my father and mother.'

Possessive suffixes are less inclined to show single marking in natural coordination (co-compounds can, however, have single possessive affixes). That is probably the reason why the sequence POSS.DAT is preferred in (11b) in natural coordination. Single and double marking in natural coordination in Mari is a subject that needs further study.

Another very intricate example of single non-relational marking in natural coordination is (12a) from Bahdinani Kurdish. Here, number is marked on the izafe, the element that links different parts of a noun phrase (in the examples, the noun and the possessive pronoun). In (12a) there is a single possessive pronoun for the whole coordination (single marking for possession) and in (12b) each coordinand has its own possessive pronoun. Accordingly, the number marking on the izafe is that of the whole coordination (plural) in (12a), and that of the coordinands (singular) in (12b). The verb agrees in number with the izafe of the absolutive noun phrase. That is why the verb is plural only in (12a). The pattern represented by (12a) (single marking for possession) seems to be restricted to natural coordination, where it is optional, as can be seen from (12a) and (12b) which express the same meaning:

(12) Bahdinani Kurdish (Nawzad Shokri, p.c.)
    a Wî   kulav û   çakît.êt   xwe bir.in   û
       he:ERG hat   and coat.IZAF:PL RFL take.PST3PL and
      der.ket.
      out.enter:PST3SG

    b Wî   kulav.ê   xwe û   çakît.ê   xwe bir
      he:ERG hat.IZAF:M RFL and coat.IZAF:M RFL take:PST3SG
      û   der.ket.
      and out.enter:PST3SG
      'He took his hat and coat and went out.'

The examples from Mari and Bahdinani Kurdish show that the alternation between single and double non-relational marking can have very complicated language-specific consequences. More examples of this kind will be considered in Section 2.4, where general questions about the syntactic representation of single non-relational marking in coordination will be discussed.

2.3.2 Distinctive non-relational double marking

Usually number in coordination is marked either once as the number of the whole coordination, or as the number of the individual coordinands with every coordinand separately. However, there is also a third possibility: the number of the whole conjunction can be marked on both coordinands. This phenomenon occurs in several Uralic languages as a distinctive marking strategy for natural coordination.

In Nenets and some other Samoyedic languages (see Tereščenko 1973) and in the Ugric languages Khanty and Mansi, double dual marking (when the coordinands refer to single items) is used in natural coordination:

(13) Mansi (Balandin 1960: 32)
    Man Marks.yg Engel's.yg xans.um   kńiga.t
    we   Marx.DU   Engels.DU   write.PTC:PASS book.PL
    lovińt.ev.
    read.PRS1PL
    'We read books written by Marx and Engels.'

Literally, the coordinate sequence in (13) means 'two Marxes and two Engelses', as each coordinand is a dual. In Mansi and Khanty, distinctive double dual marking occurs both in co-compounds and in phrase-like tight coordination, and because of formal non-distinctness (see also Section 4.4.3) it is not easy to distinguish between the two. A clear example for the latter—parts of co-compounds do not usually consist of two words—is Mansi *kati ojka.g sis'kurek ojka.g* 'cat old_man.DU chicken old_man.DU > father cat and father rooster' (Balandin 1960: 32).

Occasionally, double dual as a marker of natural coordination is extended to cases where, very obviously, the dual cannot be interpreted in its primary dual function, as in (14) from Khanty:

(14) Khanty (Bouda 1933: 28)
    Togoś.ŋən t̪iś.ŋən u̯and̪ii̯d.ən.na mola ɐndɑ̀s?
    there.DU   here.DU look.your.LOC   what profit
    'What does it help if you look here and there?'

This seems to be a co-compound, since 'there-here' is a typical domain for co-compounds. In some Uralic languages that have lost the dual, distinctive double plural marking occurs instead of double dual marking. This is the case in Mordvin (see Section 1.1.1 and passim) and sporadically in Finnic languages, as in (15) from a Finnish dialect below:

(15) Finnish (Northern Savo, Pulkkinen 1966: 114)
    Vielä.kö   isä.t   äiti.t   ellä.ä?
    still.INT father.PL mother.PL   live.PRS3SG
    'Are father and mother still alive?'

It is clear that double marking by dual or plural can serve as a distinctive marking strategy for natural coordination only for those coordinands that refer to single objects. In Mordvin, co-compounds are generally distinct from accidental/ordinary coordination (such as *t'ikše di sivel'* 'grass and meat') due to the lack of an overt coordinator.

Distinctive double marking is not restricted to number. It is also found with comitatives, proprietives,[11] focus particles, and possessive affixes. Most of these markers, when added to both coordinands, can also serve as coordinators for ordinary coordination, or other specific kinds of coordination, in at least some languages, as can be seen from Table 2.2. Note that additive focus particles and comitative markers are the two most important diachronic sources for coordinators in conjunction (Mithun 1988, Stassen 2003, Haspelmath forthcoming). Table 2.2 lists the different kinds of double

TABLE 2.2. Double marking in natural coordination and elsewhere in coordination

	Marks (at least partly) natural coordination in:	Is used in ordinary coordination or any other type of coordination:
Double dual	Khanty [2.3.2], Mansi [2.3.2], Nenets, Vedic [7.2.1], Avesta	Ngiyambaa (Donaldson 1980: 113)
Double plural	Mordvin [1.1.1], Finnish dialects [2.3.2]	Kanuri (non-exhaustive listing coordination) [3.3.5]
Double comitative	Udmurt, Mordvin (generalizing co-compounds) [5.2.2]	Tauya, Hausa, etc.
Double proprietive	Komi [1.1.3, ex. (5)c], some Turkic languages [7.2.1]	Kanuri [3.3.5]
Double focus particles	Mari [7.2.1]	Tamil, Kannada [3.2]; Latin (see below, separate/contrastive coordination)
Double possessive affixes	Mari (generalizing co-compounds) [5.2.2]	?

marking used to express natural coordination, or other kinds of coordination, and the languages in which they are found. The numbers in square brackets refer to sections where further examples are discussed. If a marking pattern applies only to a specific kind of coordination or only to a specific type of co-compound, this is also indicated in parentheses.

Distinctive double marking for natural coordination happens to occur in particular in Uralic[12] and Turkic (and to a lesser extent in early Indo-Iranian languages). However, in many languages of the world, double marking for comitative, additive focus particles, dual, and plural has grammaticalized to coordinators in ordinary or any other specific kind of coordination.

Interestingly, the double markers in both natural and other kinds of coordination have an affinity with associative plurals.[13] In many languages the same marker that is used with both coordinands in coordination occurs as a marker of associative plural or dual with a single noun (Khanty, Vedic, Ngiyambaa, Kanuri); see also Corbett (2000: 228–31). The functions of the associative or elliptic plurals/duals may, however, vary considerably (Honti 1997 and Ravila 1941 for Uralic and Indo-Iranian).

We may conclude that double marking is not a unique marking strategy for natural coordination, but rather for coordination in general. In terms of Haiman's (1985) 'Natural Syntax', it is iconic for the expression of symmetric syntactic relationships. Haiman (1988) discusses a case of double marking in parallel comparative constructions with double comparative markers in Latin and Classical Greek, such as Latin *longior quam latior acies* 'long.COMP than broad.COMP battleline = the battleline was longer than it was broad'. According to Haiman this case of symmetric parallel articulation is due to the principle that 'incorporated' (affixed) elements can be focused or contrasted only if they occur in a parallel structure. Double marking in coordination and disjunction is used often for contrastive coordination (Latin *et...et, aut...aut*), which is well in line with Haiman's claim that parallel structures have contrasting potential. Contrast does not, however, play any role in double marking in natural coordination, as natural coordination is characterized, among other things, by a lack or low degree of contrast between the coordinands (see Section 3.3.4).

2.3.3 *Distinctive non-relational zero marking*

Zero non-relational marking as a distinctive marking strategy for natural coordination is found in cases such as the bare binomials in Germanic languages previously discussed, where a marker is lacking that must be present in a corresponding non-coordinate equivalent. Consider the following almost synonymic German sentences, where (16a) has bare binomials and (16b) has single nouns with articles (both happen to be collectives, *Gezeiten* 'tide' is also a plurale tantum):

(16) German (constructed examples)
    a Ebbe und Flut werden durch Sonne und Mond verursacht.
    b Die Gezeiten werden durch die Gestirne verursacht.
       'The tide is caused by sun and moon.'

Bare binomials also occur in the Northern Germanic languages with postposed articles (as in Icelandic *Hús og garður voru í niðurníðslu* (Pétur Helgason, p.c.) 'The house and garden were in a state of decay' vs. *Hús.ið* (house.DEF) *var í niðurníðslu* 'The house was in a state of decay') and also in Romance languages, notably Italian (see also Longobardi 1994), as can be seen from (17):

(17) Italian (Croce 1922: 165)
    Se Linguistica ed Estetica paiono due scienze diverse, ciò deriva dal fatto che con la prima si pensa una grammatica...
    'If linguistics and esthetics seem to be two different sciences, this derives from the fact that a grammar is associated with the former...'

They seem, however, to be lacking in some other European languages with articles, notably Bulgarian. Interestingly, Mordvin, which has postposed definite articles, has a certain tendency to lack definiteness markers in co-compounds, even in definite contexts.

2.3.4 *Iconicity of the distinctive non-relational marking strategies*

The grammatical category of the distinctive non-relational markers is not irrelevant for the choice between zero, single, and double marking. Double marking is attested in my material only for number (dual and plural), comitative, proprietive, additive focus particles, and possessive affixes, and zero marking, as a systematic phenomenon, is confined to definiteness, although it may occasionally occur with other markers (with number in German *Pfeil und Bogen* 'bow and arrows' and not **Pfeile*[PL] *und Bogen*, and with prepositions in English *night and day* vs. *during the day, in the night*). Single marking, being the most frequent type, seems not to be restricted in any way. In nominal coordination, all major categories (number, case, definiteness, possession) are attested.

The three different non-relational marking strategies are all iconic in terms of Haiman (1985). There are two conflicting iconic relationships at work: MINIMAL DISTANCE and SYMMETRY. Minimal distance between the coordinands, as it occurs in single non-relational marking, and in zero non-relational marking where there is no intervening non-relational marker between the coordinands, is iconic for naturalness (that is, for the minimal semantic distance between the concepts denoted by the coordinands), but is counter-iconic for coordination (single marking, being asymmetric, is iconic for hierarchical rather than for coordinating constructions). Formal symmetry is iconic for coordination (coordination being a symmetric syntactic construction), but counter-iconic for naturalness, one of the diacritic symmetric markers in double non-relational marking, necessarily having to be located between the coordinands. This iconic inconvenience of the double marking type can, however, be mitigated by the lack of an overt coordinator between the coordinands. Indeed, in no case in my material is the double marking type for natural coordination compatible with an overt coordinator. On the other hand, an overt coordinator in the single marking type mitigates the counter-iconic effect of asymmetric marking for coordination. There are, however, many cases of single marking without overt coordinator (co-compounds in many languages), which might be explained by the fact that the coordinands in a co-compound may by themselves, purely through the lexico-semantic relationship between their parts, establish a semantically symmetric coordinate relationship. However, naturalness is not equally independent of the marking strategy. Any pair of words in coordination can be viewed in an accidental perspective, even if there is a close lexico-semantic relationship between the words. Consider (18) from German, where father and mother are not a pair, which is rendered formally by double non-relational marking for definiteness:

(18) German (constructed example)
Anna und Hans sind alleinerziehende Eltern. Die Mutter und der Vater trafen sich an einem Elternabend
'Anna and John are single parents. The (single) mother and the (single) father met at a parent's evening.'

This might explain why minimal distance is much more important than symmetry for the marking of natural coordination.

The zero non-relational marking type turns out to be the most complex in terms of iconicity. It combines the iconic relationships of minimal distance and symmetry. If not explicitly marked for symmetry by parallel diacritic markers, it is at least consistent with symmetry. This might suggest that zero marking is iconically the best of the three types for the expression of natural coordination. However, this advantage in iconicity is negatively overcompensated by general inherent shortcomings of the zero marking type. If a category is expressed, it should also be marked somewhere and this is not possible in the zero marking, type. If there were systematic zero marking for case, number, possession, and/or definiteness in natural coordination, the meaning of such zero marked sequences would be absolutely unclear. (Moreover, if a specific grammatical meaning is expressed, the lack of a marker is not iconic at all.)

The iconic relationships at work in the different non-relational marking strategies for natural coordination are summarized in Table 2.3.

Minimal distance, of course, is also the relevant iconic relationship if more than just affixes or functional words are repeated in coordination, as is the case in (19) from Parengi-Gorum:

(19) Parengi-Gorum (Aze and Aze 1973: 291)
bileng ona' amon le.aga'n.tu le.la'.tu, t'engia
we bow arrow we.sharpen.FUT we.AUX.FUT axe
le.aga'n.tu le.la'.tu.
we.sharpen.FUT we.AUX.FUT
'We will sharpen our bows and arrows and our axes.'

Here *ona' amon* 'bow arrow' is a co-compound whereas the coordination between *ona' amon* and *t'engia* 'axe' is very loose since almost the whole sentence is repeated (except for the subject). Note that there is also double marking for person in the main verb and auxiliary characterizing serial verbs (4.4.2) in Parengi-Gorum. From this we may see that 'unexpected' double marking is not an exclusive property of coordination.

2.4 The syntax of single non-relational marking in coordination

Coordination is traditionally believed to be a symmetric syntactic construction. In Section 2.3 we found that in coordination with single non-relational marking there is no symmetry in formal marking. Does this mean that

TABLE 2.3. Iconicity in non-relational marking strategies for natural coordination

	Symmetry	Minimal distance
Zero non-relational marking strategy	(+)	+
Single non-relational marking strategy	−	+
Double non-relational marking strategy	+	−

coordination with single non-relational marking is not symmetric syntactically? Before this question can be addressed we have to have a look at single non-relational marking with affixes (that is, with the exclusion of functional words), irrespective of whether coordination is involved or not; this marking is known as GROUP INFLECTION (or *Gruppenflexion*).

2.4.1 *Group inflection*

Group inflection is a cover term for different kinds of single inflection marking in noun phrases. Consider (20a–c) from Basque, which represent group inflection in a hierarchic syntactic structure (henceforth: group inflection in subordination):

(20)   Basque (Saltarelli 1988: 76)
    a ne.re auto berri.a
       I.GEN car   new.DEF:ABS:SG
       'my new car'

    b ne.re auto.a
       I.GEN car.DEF:ABS:SG
       'my car'

    c ne.re.a
       I.GEN.DEF:ABS:SG
       'mine'

As can be seen from (20), the portmanteau-suffix for absolutive, singular, and definiteness -*a* occurs only once at the end of noun phrases, irrespective of whether the word at the end of the noun phrase is the head (20b) or not (20a). This is why Basque noun phrase affixes are sometimes considered to be clitics, since they are affixed at a given syntactic position but to different word classes.

However, there is not only group inflection in subordination, but also in coordination. In Basque, group inflection (single marking, 21a) occurs side by side with double marking (21b). The same is the case in Azerbaijani (22):

(21)   Basque (UDHR 16;1, 14;2)
    a [gizon.ek   eta emakume.ek]
       man.ERG:PL:DEF and woman.ERG:PL:DEF
       'men and women'

    b [helburu eta erizpide].en
       purpose and criterion.GEN:PL:DEF
       'to the purposes and principles'

(22) Azerbaijani (UDHR 16;1, 14;2)
a [kiši.lər və qadın.lar]
man.PL and woman.PL
'men and women'
b [məqsəd və prinsip].lər.i.nə
purpose and principle.PL.POSS3.DAT
'to the purposes and principles'

The b-examples are instances of natural coordination with semantically overlapping coordinands (Section 3.3.3; note also the single non-relational marking in English *the purposes and principles*). The a-examples are natural, too, but the looser double non-relational marking pattern is used because of the high contrast between the coordinands (Section 3.3.4). Interestingly, Basque and Azerbaijani behave similarly with respect to group inflection in coordination in spite of the fact that the grammatical categories expressed by the markers are partly different.

There is reason to believe that group inflection in subordination (20) and group inflection in coordination as in (21b, 22b) are typologically quite distinct phenomena. Table 2.4 lists some languages that have group inflection for case in adjective-noun groups and classifies them according to whether they also have group inflection in phrase-like coordination (co-compounds are not considered).

In spite of such typological differences, in group inflection both in subordination and in coordination, affixes have scope over several words, not only the word to which they are attached. Affixes that are involved in group inflection thus typically exhibit an intermediate degree of grammaticalization. They are grammaticalized to such an extent that they have already become affixes, but may still have scope over several words, which testifies to a limited degree of grammaticalization. This also explains the frequent case of alternation between group inflection and lack of group inflection, as in Basque and Azerbaijani in (21) and (22). Affixes can more easily have scope over a

TABLE 2.4. Group inflection in coordination (for case) in some languages with group inflection in subordination in the group Adj N (for case)

No or almost no group inflection in coordination	Two options: group inflection especially in natural coordination	Always or almost always group inflection in coordination
Tatar, Mordvin	Basque, Azerbaijani	Hindi, Tibetan

coordinate sequence consisting of several words if it is tight (see also Section 3.2).

2.4.2 Is coordination with single non-relational marking syntactically asymmetric?

In Section 2.3.4 we found that the iconic relationship at work in the single non-relational marking strategy is minimal distance, the consequence being that the syntactic symmetry of coordination is not mapped iconically by this strategy. But is the syntax in coordination with single non-relational marking *A & Bx* really asymmetric? It has been claimed in the minimalist framework (especially Johannessen 1998) that coordination in general is asymmetric (see Wälchli 2001a for discussion). One of Johannessen's major arguments is group inflection in coordination, which she calls 'unbalanced coordination', such as in (23):

(23) Mari (Johannessen 1998: 12)
Myj   [Joškar Ola   den Kazan'.yšte]   paša.m   yšt.em.
I   Joškar Ola   and Kazan.INESS   work.ACC do.PRS1SG
'I am working in Yoshkar Ola and Kazan.'

Much depends on whether the delimitation of the coordinate sequence *[Joškar Ola den Kazan'.yšte]* is correct, or whether it should rather be *[Joškar Ola den Kazan'.]yšte*. This second option, which was not considered by Johannessen at all, would locate the case marker outside the coordinate sequence syntactically, even if it is suffixed to a word that is part of the coordination. Based on this second analysis, the case marker would be outside the syntactically symmetric coordinate sequence and, being outside the coordination, would have scope over both coordinands. This analysis implies, however, that there is a phonological-syntactic non-isomorphism in coordination, which is only plausible if there are other cases in need of phonological-syntactic non-isomorphism interpretations.

2.4.3 Phonological-syntactic non-isomorphism

Phonological-syntactic non-isomorphism is required not only in coordination, but also for clitics, as has been shown by Klavans (1985 and elsewhere, nota bene in a generative framework). Clitics (see Spencer 1991: ch. 9, and Nübling 1992) are elements that behave phonologically like affixes;[14] they need a host word against which to 'lean' either forwards (proclitics) or backwards (enclitics). Syntactically, clitics behave like words; their syntactic position is determined by syntactic, rather than morphological criteria. In developing a generative theory of clitics, Klavans (1985) coins the notion of a

'DOUBLE CITIZENSHIP' of clitics, meaning that clitics may lean phonologically on a host that does not belong syntactically to the constituent of the clitic. Consider (24) from Bernese German (the sign = delimitates the clitic from its phonological host):

(24) Bernese German (constructed example)
I ha=r Damaris ires Buech
I have:PRS1SG=DEF:F:SG:OBL Damaris her:SG:N book
gläse.
read:PTC:PST
'I have read Damaris' book.'

In this example =r is a reduced (asyllabic) variant of the oblique case form of the definite article (feminine singular) dər, ər, which may occur only after monosyllabic words ending in a vowel (such as u 'and', o 'auch', ga 'I go', bi 'I am', de 'then'). Syntactically, it belongs to the noun phrase *(d)ər Damaris ires Buech* 'the book of Damaris' (for clitics in Bernese German see Nübling 1992). In this and other cases exemplifying the double citizenship of clitics, syntactic entities (constituents) and phonological entities (phonological words) do not correspond to each other. Clitics with double citizenship are thus a clear case of phonological-syntactic non-isomorphism.[15]

Clitics, being phonologically dependent elements and syntactically words, are intermediate between syntax and morphology. According to Anderson (1992: ch. 8), clitics are PHRASAL AFFIXES. He compares second-position clitics to infixes that follow the first phonological segment of a word (consonant or consonant cluster, such as Tagalog *bili* 'buy' > *bumili* 'buy (actor focus)'; Chamorro *tristi* 'sad' > *trumisti* 'become sad'). If Anderson is right, this means that some morphemes can be affixed to syntactic constituents. Of course, the Basque and Azerbaijani affixes discussed above are then also to be considered phrasal affixes. An issue that remains, however, is whether all inflectional markers can be unquestionably classified as either word affixes or phrasal affixes (such that group inflection would be a sufficient and necessary criterion for phrasal affixes). What about the -s plural in English that only very rarely has single non-relational marking (as in *[hunter-gatherer].s*)? Its alternation with other plural marking strategies (*oxen, children, mice*) makes it quite clear that -s is not a phrasal affix. Consider also (25) from Georgian. Georgian has a type of verbal co-compound where the stems of the two verbs are identical (underlined) and differ only in their preverbs (in boldface).[16] In co-compounds of this kind, all prefixes (preverbs, version, person–number) are double marking, while all suffixes (tense–mood–aspect, person–number) exhibit group inflection (single marking):

(25) Georgian (K'Z 1975: 31)
[ga.i.xed-gamo.i.xed.]a
out:thither.sv.look-out:hither.sv.look.AOR3SG
'(she) looked around'

However, there is no reason to believe that the suffix (expressing tense–mood–aspect and person–number) is a looser phrasal affix than the prefixes, which would then all be word-prefixes. On the contrary, in Kartvelian languages the directional prefixes are rather loose affixes.

While fully agreeing with Anderson that morphological affixes may have scope over syntactic phrases, I doubt whether a two-way distinction between word affixes and phrasal affixes is sufficient. Such a two-way distinction would also be problematic from the point of view of grammaticalization, as markers diminish their scope step-by-step in the grammaticalization process.[17]

In any case, clitics and other phrasal affixes are strong evidence for phonological-syntactic non-isomorphism.[18] It follows from this that in the syntactic analysis of group inflection in coordination, a delimitation *[A & B]x* is possible. In my view, the analysis *[A & B]x* has many advantages over *[Aø & Bx]* because it is compatible with the concept of the general syntactic symmetry of coordination, with the concept of different degrees of tightness in coordination (*[A & B]x* is tighter than *[Ax & Bx]*), and with the notion of the wide and narrow scope of non-relational markers in coordination. A further advantage of the analysis *[A & B]x* is that no unmotivated zero morphemes or traces are required in the syntactic analysis.

Available data suggest that the position of clitics or affixes with wide scope over coordination is always determined by the structure of the coordinate sequence and not by that of the coordinands. If the clitic or affix is a prefix, it will be prefixed to the coordinate sequence as a whole; if it is a suffix, it will be suffixed to the coordinate sequence as a whole; and if it is a second-position clitic, it occurs at the second position of the whole; coordinate sequence as in (26) from Bulgarian.

In Bulgarian (26), both the definite articles and the possessive pronoun are second-position clitics. While the former have narrow scope (multiple non-relational marking; in boldface), the latter occurs only once (single non-relational marking; underlined):

(26) Bulgarian (UDHR 12)
    v   [lični.ja   mu   život, semejstvo.to, žilište.to
    in personal.DEF:OBL:M   his life   family.DEF:N   flat.DEF:N
    i   korespondencija.ta]
    and correspondence.DEF:F
    '... [to arbitrary interference] with his privacy, family, home or correspondence'

Another case of clitics with scope over two coordinands are number markers in Gooniyandi (McGregor 1990). Case and number markers (so called 'postpositions') in Gooniyandi are phrase-level clitics, which can be attached to any word of an NP, one of several options being second position (such as in *ngoorroo.ngga garndiwiddi yoowooloo* 'that.ERG two man = by these two men', ibid.: 277). The 'postpositions' for dual and plural sometimes occur only once in coordination, notably if the coordinands consist only of one word (in tight coordination), such as in (27) with a coordination of two proper names (together two people):

(27) Gooniyandi (McGregor 1990: 280; new orthography, B. McGregor p.c.)
    [wambi.yoorroo   birridbiya]
    Wampi.DU   Amee
    'Wampi and Amee' (together two people)

These examples are further evidence that single affixes and functional words are attached to coordinate sequences, while double affixes and functional words are attached to coordinands. Note that coordinate sequences need not be isomorphic with phrases in hierarchical syntax; there are many cases where this is not the case.

Let us conclude this section with some examples from Mari phrase-like coordination. As was pointed out above, the sequence of suffixes for case, possession, and number is rather free in Mari. In the following examples there are both noun–number–possession–case (28a) and noun–possession–number–case (28b, c) sequences. Possession has double marking in all examples. Case has double marking in (28b) and single marking in (28a) and (28c). The plural occurs only on the second coordinand in all examples. However, the plural can be interpreted as pluralizing the whole coordinate sequence only if it has no double non-relational marker to its right, which is the case only in (28c), and is why only (28c) is ambiguous in meaning:

(28) Mari (N. Gluxova, Z. Uchaev, p.c.)
   a Tide [ergy.m   den   üdyr-vlak.em].lan   pölek.
      this [son.my   with   daughter-PL.my].DAT   present
      'This is a present for my son and my daughters.'
   b Tide [ergy.m.lan   den   üdyr.em-vlak.lan]   pölek.
      this [son.my.DAT   with   daughter.my-PL.DAT]   present
      'This is a present for my son and my daughters.'
   c Tide [ergy.m   den   üdyr.em([])-vlak([]).lan   pölek.
      this [son.my   with   daughter.my([])-PL([]).DAT present
      'This is a present for my son (one) and my daughters.'
      'This is a present for my sons and my daughters (together more than two).'

Only (28c) is syntactically and semantically ambiguous. In one analysis, the plural attaches to the second coordinand, which gives the meaning 'for my son and my daughters', and in the other it attaches to the whole coordinate sequence, which gives the meaning that sons and daughters together are at least two.

2.5 Conclusions

There is a general markedness clash between formal and structural marking in natural coordination, due to the fact that coordination is a two-slot pattern rather than a one-slot pattern. This general markedness clash led us, in Section 2.1, to postulate a more pluralistic view about markedness.

Two kinds of formal marking in two-slot patterns, relational and non-relational, have been distinguished. It was found that natural coordination, if distinct from ordinary coordination, is usually characterized either by the lack or reduction of relational markers (Section 2.2), or by one of three specific patterns of non-relational marking (Section 2.3), whereas the use of different coordinators in natural and accidental/ordinary coordination is not frequent. In 2.3 the iconic relationships at work in the different marking strategies for natural coordination—minimal distance and symmetry—were discussed. Finally, in Section 2.4, it was found that the lack of symmetry in the single marking strategy does not mean that coordination with single marking is asymmetric syntactically. Rather, group inflection in coordination provides evidence for the non-isomorphism between phonology and syntax which has to be postulated for clitics in any case.

Notes

[1] Dryer (1995)—a very important contribution to markedness theory—also discusses distributional and pragmatical markedness, which are highly relevant in the context of word order, but which can, however, be neglected for our purposes.

[2] Recently, Haspelmath (2003c) has raised a doubt about whether it is reasonable to speak of markedness at all. While I agree with some of his arguments, I still find it useful to speak of markedness in the different senses exposed here.

[3] As it is understood here, typological markedness is not the same thing as what Croft (2001: 89, 2003: 87) calls typological markedness, which is a hypothesis about a universal relationship between structural and formal markedness.

[4] The terms background(ing) and foreground(ing) are used in different senses in the functional literature and deviate from how these terms are used here, even if foregrounding always derives from the idea of 'drawing our attention to' (Keenan 1985: 243). In the context of voice operations, foregrounding means putting an element that is not usually a topic or pivot into topical or pivotal position. Thus, topicalizations, such as *Beans I like*, and left dislocations, such as *As for the President, congressmen don't respect him anymore*, are both prominent foregrounding constructions (Keenan 1985: 243f; see also Pustet 1992). However, in the context of narrative discourse, the foreground is 'the language of the actual story line', and background 'the language of supportive material which does not itself narrate the main events' (Hopper 1979: 213). In this sense, foregrounding is associated with (although not identical to) perfectivity, and backgrounding with imperfectivity. Interestingly, in the narrative discourse sense, topics are considered to be background, whereas in the voice operation sense they are considered to be foreground.

[5] Textual marking is closely related to the psycholinguistic notion of effort as described in Clark (1992: 375 f). Note, however, that a textually unmarked expression, such as *once or twice* in (1b), may sometimes demand more effort to utter than a textually more marked expression, such as *once*.

Markedness in text has been explored by the Czech scholar Mukařovský (1940/1982: 122, 1976: 44) who distinguishes between the automated application of words (the use of usual, textually unmarked expressions) and de-automated designation.

[6] In hierarchical constructions, relational markers may be divided into head and dependent marking (Nichols 1992: 46–64). This distinction does not apply to coordination.

[7] *Ger bül* is a co-compound.

[8] If we disregard non-coordinate uses of *at* where it is attached to subordinators such as in *sapagká't* 'because' and > because'.

[9] Exists besides *hunters and gatherers*, an appositional compound rather than a co-compound (5.4.1).

[10] Unlike other affixes, the plural marker *-vlak* does not belong to the same prosodic word as the stem. The prosodic word is the domain of word stress (final non-reduced vowel), which occurs before the plural marker and the affixes

following it, and the plural marker has its own vowel harmony sequence. Prosodically, the plural marker is thus a kind of clitic.

[11] The term proprietive is common in Australian linguistics in particular to characterize classes of forms that express properties or predicative possession which are derived from nouns.

[12] For the dual in Uralic see Honti (1997), and for the general tendency for parallelism in coordination in Uralic languages, Lewy (1911: 86).

[13] Associative plurals (see Moravcsik 1994 and Corbett 2000: 101–11) consist of a single nominal plus a marker and denote a set comprised of the referent of the nominal (the main member) plus one or more associated members, such as Tagalog *sina Luis* 'Luis and his company' (*si* is a phrase marker for proper names; the associative plural with *sina* is restricted to proper names in Tagalog). Associative plurals are typically formed from proper names, kinship terms, and other animate nouns, that is, nouns that are high on the animacy hierarchy.

[14] More precisely, clitics sometimes have prosodic properties of their own which lead Nespor and Vogel (1986) to postulate the clitic group as a separate level of prosodic phonology.

[15] Note also that prosodic phonology (Nespor and Vogel 1986: 142) has identified many cases of non-isomorphism between the prosodic and morpho-syntactic hierarchies.

[16] This Georgian pattern of co-compounds resembles the coordination of inseparable preverbs in German (and Dutch), such as *be- und entladen* 'on- and unload > load and unload', which is also restricted to verbs with opposite directional prefixes (Brettschneider 1978: 91).

[17] For more recent treatments of clitics as phrasal affixes see Anderson (1996), Legendre (2000), and Spencer (2000). For a discussion of more recent approaches to clitics in different formal theories see Börjars (1998).

[18] Further evidence comes from affixes to relative clauses; see Comrie (1981: 138f).

3

Tight Coordination

Tight coordination, introduced in Section 1.1.1, is not a single uniform neat and clear-cut class, but rather a highly complex multidimensional phenomenon. Three major dimensions—each having various subdimensions—can be distinguished. Two are formal, one being the length of individual instances of coordinate sequences (Section 3.1) and the other the marking patterns of coordination (Section 3.2); the third is semantic: the semantic correlates of tight and loose coordination (Section 3.3).

While the two formal dimensions are treated only very briefly here, special attention is given to the semantic correlates of tight and loose coordination. In Chapter 2 we took a predominantly semantic phenomenon, natural coordination, as our starting point and looked at how it is represented formally across different languages. In Section 3.3 we will take the opposite approach and consider with what kinds of meanings tight coordination correlates.

3.1 The first dimension: the length of the coordination

A high degree of tightness in coordination implies minimal distance between the coordinands, and that the coordinate sequence is as short as possible so as to form a compact intonation unit with as little syntactic structure as possible. A coordinate sequence is looser the longer it is, the greater the distance between the coordinands, and the more phrase-, clause-, and sentence-like the syntactic structures are within the coordination. This can best be illustrated by examples which differ only in tightness. Consider the following German sentences:

(1) German (adapted from Heine 1826/1997: 5; see also Brettschneider 1978: 34):
    a Die Stadt Göttingen ist berühmt durch ihre [Würste und Universität].
    b Die Stadt Göttingen ist berühmt durch [ihre Würste und ihre Universität].
    c Die Stadt Göttingen ist berühmt [durch ihre Würste und durch ihre Universität].
    d Die Stadt Göttingen [ist berühmt durch ihre Würste und ist berühmt durch ihre Universität].

e [Die Stadt Göttingen ist berühmt durch ihre Würste, und die Stadt Göttingen ist berühmt durch ihre Universität]
  f [Die Stadt Göttingen ist berühmt durch ihre Würste. Und die Stadt Göttingen ist auch berühmt durch ihre Universität.]
  a. 'The city of Göttingen is famous for its sausages and university.' etc. f. 'The city of Göttingen is famous for its sausages. And the city of Göttingen is also famous for its university.'

The coordination in (a) is tighter than in (b) and so on until (f), the example with the loosest coordination. The examples in (1) show that tightness clearly has a semantic dimension. The amusing effect of the clash of the 'noble' concept 'university' with the 'profane' concept 'sausages' is most apparent in the tightest variant (a) whereas this effect is only weakly present in the much more neutral example (f). Not accidentally, Heinrich Heine uses the tightest possible variant in order to make fun of Göttingen. This shows that the choice of an inappropriate degree of tightness is not ungrammatical, but is pragmatically odd.

In early generative grammar (for a more recent variant and survey see van Oirsouw 1987), it was claimed that coordination is always sentence coordination in deep structure and that other forms of coordination may be derived from sentence coordination by deletion of identical material. This would mean that (1a–e) all have the same deep structure (1e) and that (1a–d) are derived from (1e) by coordination reduction. It is clear that coordination reduction is highly problematic given the semantic relevance of different degrees of tightness (see Chomsky 1970a: 186 for different semantic interpretations as evidence of different syntactic representations). Add to this the idea that coordination reduction is incompatible with the notion of scope in coordination (Section 2.4.3). For a critique of deletion operations in analyzing coordination, see also Mallinson and Blake (1981: ch. 4).

Even if it is clear that different instances of coordination can be described in terms of tightness and that tightness is semantically relevant, there is no single measure by which the tightness of a coordinate sequence can be measured unequivocally. This is because there are different conflicting ways of measuring the length of a coordinate sequence depending on whether the length of the whole coordinate sequence or the length of the coordinands is measured, and what is counted (number of phonemes, morphemes, words, or phrases; add to this the fact that none of these elements is easily definable). Tightness remains, therefore, a vague concept which does not, however, invalidate in any way its relevance for understanding the nature of coordination. The consequence is simply that not all instances of coordination can be ranked unequivocally according to tightness. Nor does this mean that there will be no clear cases. Examples (1a–f) can clearly be ranked according to tightness since all possible measures for tightness would rank them in the same order. The ranking is also clear when one coordination is contained within another one: the inner coordination is always tighter (coordinations in [ ] are tighter than that in { } in... *their faith {in fundamental human rights, in the [dignity and worth] of the human person and in the equal rights of [men and women]}* UDHR Preamble).[1]

3.2 The second dimension: the marking patterns of coordination

Not only individual examples of coordination, but also different marking patterns can be ranked according to tightness. If patterns are considered, we abstract from how the slots are filled: *the big blue house and the small garden* and *the house and the garden* are instances of the same *the A and the B* pattern. This pattern is generally looser than *the A and B* as represented by *the house and garden*. Any pattern with a smaller distance between the slots is tighter. The more words and affixes, coordinators, intonation breaks, or word and morpheme boundaries occur in a pattern, the looser it is. Thus, in English, PREP *the A and* PREP *the B* (PREP = preposition) is looser than PREP *the A and the B*, and the latter is looser than PREP *the A and B*. The matter is, however, complicated by the fact that markers are not always obligatory. In English, for instance, not all instances of nominal coordination require prepositions and articles; whether a preposition is needed depends on the syntactic environment, and whether a definite article is needed depends largely on the lexical properties of the noun or noun phrase. Thus, in *the state and society*, the opposition between the two patterns *the A and the B* and *the A and B* is neutralized as the second noun would not take an article anyway.

Things become even more complicated when patterns cannot be ranked unequivocally according to tightness. Let us have a look at nominal coordination in Turkish, a language in which there are many different patterns for coordination. In Turkish nominal coordination there is mostly an overt coordinator, but coordination may also be juxtapositional. Turkish nouns may take many suffixes (notably for case, number, and possession) and these may appear on both coordinands or only on one. There are different degrees of tightness of the intonation unit indicated in the written form by commas and spaces or by a lack of commas and spaces. Finally, coordination may also be expressed by the comitative construction *A ile B* 'A with B'. In (2) the following patterns are exemplified: ABx (*çerçöp* in 2a, a co-compound consisting of the two synonymic components *çer* and *çöp* 'brushwood'; x is any inflectional marker); A Bx (*çarşı pazar.da* in 2b); Ax Bx (*hava.dan su.dan* in

2c); A *ve* Bx (*mal ve mülk.ün.den* in 2d, *ve* means 'and'); Ax, Bx (*hava.dan su.dan, iş.ten* in 2c); Ax *ve* Bx (*yaprak.lar.la ve çerçöp.le* in 2a); and A *ile* Bx (*ev sahib.i ile karı.sı.nı* and *Mustafa ile Hanife'yi* in 2e):

(2) Turkish (MTK 34, 98, 96, UDHR 17; 2, MTK 100):
    a Rüzgâr kayığ.ı   kuru [yaprak.lar.la ve
       wind   little_boat.his dry   leaf.PL.with   and
       [çerçöp].le]   doldur.ur.du.
       brushwood.with fill.AOR.PST3SG
       'The wind filled the boat with dry leaves and brushwood.'

    b [Çarşı   pazar].da hep bu
       permanent_market market.LOC all   this
       konuş.ul.du.
       speak.PASS.PST3SG
       'On the market and in the shops everybody talked only about this.'

    c [[Hava.dan su.dan,]   iş.ten]   konuş.tu.k.
       air.ABL   water.ABL work/affair.ABL speak.PST.1PL
       'We talked about everything in the world and about work.'

    d ... [mal ve   mülk].ün.den   mahrum...
       property and property.POSS3SG.ABL robbed...
       '[No one shall be arbitrarily] deprived of his property...'

    e Ev   sahib.i   ile   karı.sı].nı   bağlay.ıp,
       house lord.POSS3SG with   wife.POSS3SG.ACC bind.CONV
       [Mustafa ile   Hanife]'yi de   öldür.ür.ler.
       M.   with H.'ACC   also kill.AOR.PL
       'After they had tied up the head of the house and his wife, they killed Mustafa and Hanife.'

	tight ◄--► loose
ABx	—
A Bx	———
Ax Bx	———- - - - -
A *ve* Bx	- - - ———
Ax, Bx	————
Ax *ve* Bx	————
Ax, *ve* Bx	————————
A *ile* Bx	————————- - - - - - - - - -

FIG. 3.1. Some nominal coordination patterns in Turkish

The Turkish patterns in nominal coordination can be represented on a tight–loose coordination scale as illustrated in Figure 3.1.

ABx is clearly tighter than all other patterns. A Bx comes next. Ax Bx and A *ve* Bx, however, are more difficult to rank according to tightness. The former has more non-relational, but less relational marking, while for the latter it is the other way round. It is clear, however, from the cross-linguistic study of language use that overt coordinators usually tend to occur in phrase-domains (there are very few languages with co-compounds with overt coordinators) while double non-relational marking, especially if it is harmonic (see 1.1.1), can occur in co-compounds in many languages.[2] Thus, there is some reason to believe that Ax Bx might be tighter than A *ve* Bx, but the evidence is not conclusive. The same holds for the two patterns Ax, Bx and Ax *ve* Bx, which cannot be ranked unequivocally with respect to each other, but the former is looser than Ax Bx and the latter is looser than A *ve* Bx. Finally, Ax, *ve* Bx is clearly the loosest pattern. Most problematic is the status of the comitative construction. Its lack of double non-relational marking for case suggests that it is rather tight. On the other hand, the first coordinand is marked with the comitative and cannot, therefore, take a case marker. It is thus indifferent to single vs. double non-relational marking. Clearly, the comitative construction is looser than A Bx, but otherwise it cannot be ranked in comparison with the other patterns and therefore seems to be rather indifferent to tightness.

The two dominant patterns in verbal coordination in Turkish Ax, Bx (x is a finite inflection marker) and A*Ip* Bx (-*Ip* is a converb marker) are both compatible with both tight and loose coordination. In (3a) the converb pattern is used for tight (natural) coordination ('eat and drink'), while the asyndetic, double marking pattern is used for looser coordination. In (2e) we find, however, the converb pattern in a very loose construction (where, in fact, it expresses temporal sequence rather than coordination). In (3b) we have very tight combinations of the Ax, Bx pattern (where x is zero, however, in the second person imperative):

(3) Turkish (MTK 66, 72):
    a   ... [giyin.iyor.lar.di,   [yi.yip   içi].yor.lar.dı].
         dress.PRS.PL.PST   eat.CONV   drink.PRS.PL.PST
         '(the former inhabitants) had been dressing, been eating and drinking.'
    b [[Bağır,   çağır],   [söv,   say]] ...
       cry[IMP2SG], cry[IMP2SG] curse[IMP2SG] curse[IMP2SG] ...
       de.di ...
       say.PST3SG
       'Cry, roam and curse ... she said.'

The Turkish examples discussed here show that there is a great variety of different patterns in coordination that differ in their degree of tightness, but which cannot always be clearly ranked with respect to each other according to tightness. This does not mean that for a concrete pair of slots all the patterns are always possible (there is not always opposition between all patterns at the same time).

An interesting case is Kannada, where there are two different conjunctions, whose markers both derive from additive focus particles. The diachronically older coordinator is complex, -ū...-ū (A-ū B-ū), the younger simple, *mattu* (A *mattu* B) 'and; again, further, moreover'. Now, in Kannada it is not the case, as could be expected, that the younger coordinator is always used in looser coordination than the older one. *Mattu* can actually be used in both looser and tighter coordination than -ū...-ū. On the one hand, -ū...-ū cannot be used in maximally loose coordination: 'Note that sentences cannot be coordinated by -*u:*, only subsentential constituents can' (Sridhar 1990: 104). On the other hand, -ū...-ū always requires double marking for case, whereas there can be single marking for case with *mattu*, which explains why *mattu* can be used in rather tight coordination, as in *uddēśa mattu sūtra.-gaḷ.ige* 'intention and rule.PL.DAT = to the principles and purposes' (UDHR 14; 2). (Maximally tight coordination in Kannada is expressed by the co-compound patterns ABx and A Bx).

This is not the place to analyze in detail the relative tightness of patterns of coordination in English, Turkish, Kannada, or any other language. What is important for our purpose is to show that different patterns of coordination in a language can be represented on a tight–loose coordination scale, and that there are some patterns which occupy only small parts of the scale, while others occupy large parts. We might say that the former are highly sensitive to tightness, the latter not.

Another question is how the patterns to be represented on the scale should be chosen. For Turkish, above, I decided not to distinguish between different nominal inflection markers (case, possession, number). However, it is highly possible that each category of markers behaves individually, or even that every marker behaves individually. There is even some evidence that the same marker can behave differently in different functions. The difference between single and double marking with the same marker in different functions is actually a well-known test in grammaticalization, to show that the marker is more grammaticalized in one function than in another. Consider (4) from French discussed by Haspelmath (1999: 1058):

(4) French (Haspelmath 1999: 1058):
   a Tu penses à [Paul et Marie].
      you think:PRS2SG to Paul and Mary
      'You are thinking of Paul and Mary.'
   b Ils ont emprunté ce livre [à Jean et à Marie].
      they.M have:PRS3PL borrowed this book to John and to Mary
      'They borrowed this book from John and Mary.'

In (4a) the preposition *à* has a locative function (it is pronominalized by *y* 'there'); in (4b) it has a dative function (it is pronominalized by *leur* 'they:DAT'). In dative function *à* is more grammaticalized and has narrower scope. Therefore it must occur twice in coordination. It has to be noted that this test only works if we can be confident that coordination is equally tight in both cases, as the possibility of single marking does not depend only on the degree of grammaticalization of the non-relational marker, but also on the degree of tightness of the coordination. Double marking has to be expected if the marker is highly grammaticalized, but it also has to be expected in loose coordination. Single marking has to be expected if the marker has a low degree of grammaticalization, and also in cases of tight coordination.

A central question in the study of tightness in coordination concerns the number of patterns that behave differently according to tightness. It seems probable that most languages have very many patterns with different behavior, many more than those I have listed for English and Turkish above. This follows from the fact that each marker can have its individual degree of grammaticalization or even several individual degrees of grammaticalization in several functions. We may conclude from this that grammaticalization leads to a great many coordination patterns with different behavior according to tightness, and that patterns hardly ever arise in such a way that there are just two patterns that form a clearly unequivocal tightness opposition. If there is a clear-cut pattern, as is the case for co-compounds (as far as they are formally distinct from coordination), this must have arisen by a different regularizing process. The process which leads to the emergence of coordination patterns which differ in tightness is a deregularizing process leading to a large number of only vaguely distinct patterns.

3.3 The third dimension: the semantic correlates of tight coordination

There are different semantic criteria along which coordination can be subdivided, natural vs. accidental coordination being just one of them. This section examines how different semantic dimensions in coordination interact with tightness and how they relate to natural coordination. In each subsection we will discuss different ways of slicing up the cake of coordination. Most of the different kinds of coordination to be discussed are not mutually exclusive and have therefore to be considered as partial cover meanings (Section 1.3.2.ii).

3.3.1 Group vs. separate coordination

In *John and Mary went to the market*, John and Mary can go together or separately. In the first case there is GROUP, in the second SEPARATE COORDINATION.[3] Some languages, such as Babungo (Niger-Congo), have a specific means of expression for group coordination:

(5)   Babungo (Schaub 1985: 84):
    a Làmbí ghɔ́ Ndùlá gə̀   táa yìwìŋ
       Lambi and Ndula go:PFV to market
       'Lambi and Ndula went to the market (together).'
    b Làmbí nə̀ Ndùlá gə̀   táa yìwìŋ
       Lambi and Ndula go:PFV to market
       'Lambi and Ndula went to the market (together or independently).'

Ghɔ́ also expresses the comitative, is used only with animates, and means literally 'in the hands of'. In (5a) *ghɔ́* expresses group coordination while *nə̀* in (5b) is indifferent to the group–separate distinction. Another language where the comitative expresses group coordination is Aymara (Aymaran, South America; suffix *-mpi*, in coordination it is added to both coordinands), whereas *-sa...-sa* expresses separate or distributive coordination (Ebbing 1965: 204). Interestingly, separate coordination is used in natural coordination with generalizing function: *uru.n.sa aruma.n.sa* 'day.GEN.and night.-GEN.and > night and day' (Mark 5: 5). This is evidence that the distinction between group and separate coordination has little to do with natural vs. accidental coordination.

It seems that comitatives generally have an affinity for group coordination.[4] This is the case even in English, where the comitative *with* as in *John went to the market with Mary* cannot express separatedness. The difference here to

Babungo and Aymara is that the comitative marker in English is not commonly used in coordination, but only in comitative constructions where there is a hierarchical relationship between the arguments. Comitative constructions are hierarchical not only in form but also semantically. In comitative constructions, the participation of the comitative argument is dependent on the participation of the argument to which it is associated, whereas in coordination there is no such hierarchical relationship between the arguments. If I invite John and Mary to a party, Mary is invited even if John is not able to come. But if I invite John with Mary to a party, Mary is not invited if John is not able to come.

While there are specific strategies for the expression of group coordination, there are also specific strategies for separate coordination. In English, separate coordination can be expressed by summary conjunction *Both John and Mary went to the market* (see Section 2.2.1 and Payne 1985*b*: 17–22), by coordination with an emphatic coordinator *John AND Mary went to the market*, and by loose coordination *John went to the market AND Mary went to the market*. The former two strategies can also express coordination counter-to-expectation; thus loose coordination is probably the most unequivocal strategy for the expression of separate coordination in English. According to Harries-Delisle (1978), in Navajo, the construction N_1 *dóó* N_2 *V* means that N_1 and N_2 did V together, whereas N_1 *V dóó* N_2 *V* means that N_1 and N_2 did V separately (Navajo *dóó* 'and' means actually '(distant) from', being 'from' in a stative sense, but occasionally also 'near', 'with'). This is evidence that group coordination is tighter than separate coordination.

Group coordination is not necessarily natural. If John and Mary go together to the market, they need not be either partners or siblings. On the other hand, natural coordination is not necessarily group coordination; items that naturally belong together may be separated. This is the case notably in distributive contexts, as *Brother and sister went to different schools.*

Naturalness and group are combined in NATURAL COMITATIVES. Natural comitatives are comitatives that preferably or exclusively express preestablished companions, such as spouse or children. An example for a natural comitative is the Finnish comitative case, mostly restricted to use with a possessive suffix, *Hän tulee puoliso.ine.en* 'he come:PRS3SG wife.COM.his = he comes with his wife.' The Quechua (Quechuan) marker *-ntin*, which derives from a comitative marker *-nti* with the possessive suffix for the third person *-n*, expresses natural comitatives (in some dialects of Quechua, other forms of the possessive suffix are still possible; see example 6 below). In comitative constructions, one participant often remains unexpressed, and so the natural comitative may become a collective marker or a marker of associative plurals as, for example, Quechua *c'osa.ntin* 'husband and his wife' (*c'osa* 'husband'), *mama.ntin* 'mother and child' (*mama* 'mother'; Tschudi 1853).[5] Especially important for natural coordination are constructions with two natural comitatives because the two natural comitatives then have a coordinating relationship between them. Thus two natural comitatives together illustrate natural coordination. Often such constructions have a generalizing connotation as in (6):

(6) Huallaga Quechua (Weber 1989: 47):
Llapan.ni:.ta   wañu.chi.manqa   warmi.nti.:.ta
all.us.ACC   die.CAUS.FUT:3>1   woman.NATCOM.my.ACC
wamra.nti.:.ta.
child.NATCOM.my.ACC
'It will kill us all including my wife and children.'

To summarize, separate coordination tends to be expressed by loose coordination. Group coordination is akin to comitative constructions and coordination deriving from coordinate constructions is usually rather tight. Group and natural coordination, even if both are associated with tight coordination, are quite different from each other semantically. Natural comitatives can develop to become markers of natural coordination.

3.3.2 Intersective vs. non-intersective coordination

How many people are *a typologist, a mother of three children(,) and an organist*?[6] It could be one, a single person as in *My supervisor is a typologist, a mother of three children and an organist*. But depending on the specific situation it could also be two, or three persons. If different coordinands denote a single referent, this is INTERSECTIVE coordination. If all coordinands are referentially distinct this is NON-INTERSECTIVE coordination. In intersective coordination, A & B is the intersection of A and B (As & Bs are As that are at the same time Bs, not just all As and all Bs). Intersective coordination is semantically closely related to apposition.

Intersective coordination is preferably expressed by tight coordination. It usually has only a single article in English, as in *[he] had a constant companion and housekeeper in his sister* (Austen 1811/1994: 1). This means that natural coordination and intersective coordination may be very similar formally as they both tend to be expressed by tight coordination. Intersective coordination is, however, not usually natural coordination. In the example given above, it comes as a surprise that the same person has the different capacities or properties given in the coordinands of the intersective coordination. But before this issue is discussed further, let us introduce another important distinction in coordination.

3.3.3 Overlapping vs. non-overlapping coordination

In OVERLAPPING COORDINATION, the meaning of A and B overlap, but the meaning of the whole is not the intersection of A and B as in intersective coordination. Rather, it is the union of the meanings of A and B. Thus, in the example *Her mouth and chin were all burnt by the acid* (Maugham 1919/1965: 126), the body parts mouth and chin are not neatly distinct but rather denote a single continuous area of the body. The coordination refers to this bigger area and not to the intersection area of mouth and chin. As can be seen from single marking for definiteness in this example, overlapping coordination, like intersective coordination, tends to be associated with tight coordination. Figure 3.2 illustrates schematically the differences between non-overlapping, overlapping, and intersective coordination.

Overlapping coordination, as can be seen from the English example with a single possessive pronoun, tends to be expressed by tight coordination. Overlapping coordination is restricted to coordinands whose meanings have an area of contiguity without a clear borderline between them.

A favorable domain for overlapping coordination are qualities and abstract entities which often cannot be kept clearly distinct from each other. The frequent use of overlapping coordination may be a characteristic stylistic trait. It is abundant in Jane Austen's book *Sense and Sensibility* (1811/1994):

> ... I love to see children full of **life and spirits**; I cannot bear them if they are **tame and quiet** (119). We might trust to **time and chance** for the rest (143). ... if you do not like to go wherever I do, **well and good**, you may always go with one of my daughters (147). ... she thought it most **prudent and kind**, after some consideration, to say more than she really **knew or believed** (167 f).

If both an overlapping and an intersective interpretation are possible, it is usually the former that dominates. Thus, *my relatives and friends* will usually denote all the people that are my relatives or my friends, and not only the people who are both my friends and my relatives. (This is

non-overlapping   overlapping   intersective

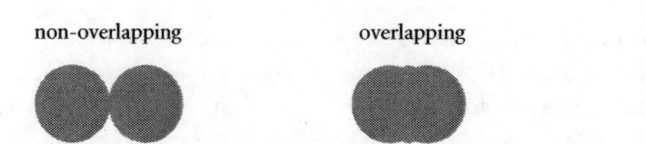

FIG. 3.2. Different semantic kinds of coordination

because overlapping coordination comes as less of a surprise than intersective coordination.) In *my friend and relative* there is, however, only a single referent and in this example the overlapping interpretation is excluded. Overlapping and intersective coordination merge in the case of maximally overlapping and maximally intersective coordination, that is, if both coordinands are synonyms. Coordination of synonyms is, however, not prototypical intersective coordination, given that the function of intersective coordination is limited to a small and exclusive set of possible references. In prototypical intersective coordination, the intersection between the coordinands will be small.

The difference between overlapping and intersective coordination can also be illustrated with adjectives. *Sweet-and-sour* is intersective. It applies to food that is both sweet and sour and not to food that is only sweet or only sour. In the case of *tame and quiet* or *prudent and kind*, on the other hand, there is no contrast between the coordinands, so there is no semantic opposition between *tame, quiet* and *tame and quiet* or between *prudent, kind* and *prudent and kind*.

In intersective coordination the semantic difference between the coordinands is focused, while it is backgrounded in overlapping coordination. Even if the coordinands are a pair semantically in intersective coordination, as in *She was mother and father to the child*, this is not really natural coordination because it is not coordination according to expectation and there is a strong tendency to stress the contrast between the coordinands formally (*She was both mother and father to the child, She was to the child mother and father at the same time, She was mother and father to the child*). This, somewhat paradoxically, sometimes causes intersective coordination to be closely associated formally with separatedness if it implies contrast.

Overlapping coordination is highly compatible with natural coordination, but not all cases of natural coordination are overlapping. In intersective coordination, however, there is a reduction of the extension of coordinands. Intersective coordination is rather similar in this respect to attributive constructions (NPs with dependent nouns, adjectives, or relative clauses) which reduces the semantic extension of a head.

3.3.4 *Contrast*

Another semantic factor that is highly relevant for the choice between a tight or a loose coordinate construction is CONTRAST. Loose coordination tends to be associated with a higher degree of contrast than tight coordination. This can be seen from the fact that adversative coordination, being coordination counter-to-expectation and highly contrastive, tends to be loose. In many languages, adversative coordinators can—or even must—form separate intonation units. Consider (7) from Toaripi:

(7) Toaripi (Brown 1968: 1):
Karu   rauapo   kotipe, a-   karu   foromai koti   kao.
people many   come   but   people all   come   not
'Many people came, but everyone did not come.'

The coordinator *a*-'but' has a hyphen after it in Toaripi orthography because it has 'a decided pause after it' (ibid.). The most common expression for 'but' after a negative clause in Bernese German (for Standard German *sondern*) is *nei* 'no' followed by an intonation break, as in *Nid dihr syt's de nämlech, wo redet, nei, der heilig Geischt* 'for it is not ye that speak, but the Holy Ghost' (Mark 13: 11). The same kind of cross-sentence adversative coordination is found in Tok Pisin:... *i no yupela yet bai i autim tok. Nogat. Holi Spirit em bai i autim* id. (Mark 13: 11), that is, what is one sentence in English are three sentences in Tok Pisin. But even in literary West European languages, adversative coordinators are often followed by a pause, if they are spoken: *but-*.

If we go back to example (1) above, the most neutral way of expressing a coordination between two concepts so different as, for example, university and sausages is adversative coordination, even if the two are not to be contrasted with each other: *The city of Göttingen is famous for its university, but also for its sausages.* Non-contrastive coordination is closely associated with overlapping coordination, since, if two items are overlapping (*the mouth and chin*), there is very little contrast between them.

The effect of different degrees of contrast between the coordinands on the degree of tightness in coordination can be exemplified by two Basque examples from the UDHR. In both examples there is a coordination of the two nouns *gizon* 'man' and *emakume* 'woman'. In *gizon.ek eta emakume.ek* 'man.-ERG:PL and woman.ERG:PL = Men and women [have the right to marry and to found a family]' (UDHR 16; 1), there is an overt coordinator *eta* 'and' with no group inflection, whereas in *gizon-emakum.ek* 'man-woman.ERG:PL = Everyone [has the right to recognition everywhere as a person before the law]' (UDHR 6), there is maximally tight coordination (a co compound with single marking for inflection). There is a semantic difference parallel to the formal difference. In the tight case, *gizon-emakume* 'man-woman' is equivalent to 'everyone, everybody'. The explicit mention of men and women is not really necessary and is actually a specific feature of the Basque text of the UDHR. In the looser case, however, the equal rights of men, on the one hand, and women, on the other, are at issue, and there is a considerable amount of semantic contrast between the coordinands.

Generalization in coordination, as it occurs in 'man-woman > everyone', is usually associated with a low degree of contrast in coordination. This entails that generalizing coordination is especially prone to being expressed by tight coordination, and we will see in Section 5.2.2 that generalizing co-compounds are actually the most widespread type of co-compound cross-linguistically.

The preservation of a minimal amount of contrast in coordination has its formal counterpart in the lack of unstressed (enclitic) or empty coordinands. Unlike co-compounds, the coordinations of phrases affords a certain minimal semantic contrast between the coordinands. Coordinands, if not necessarily emphatic, are usually at least stressed, and even tend to have a parallel focus structure (Jacobs 1988: 100 f). Thus, in most languages it is not permissable to coordinate clitic pronouns (in French, not clitic *tu et je, but toi et moi). Wherever there are co-compounds of pronouns they are not simply a coordination of pronouns semantically. Thus, Tok Pisin *yumi* is the inclusive first person pronoun 'we (incl.)' and not 'you *and* me'.[7] Co-compounds of personal pronouns may also have a figurative sense as in the following examples. In the Turkish example (8), the adjectivized personal pronouns for I and you together have the meaning 'be familiar with each other'. In the Mordvin example (9), the possessive pronouns my and thy (the genitive forms of the pronouns for I and you) together have the meaning of 'possession':

(8) Turkish (MTK 106)
...sen.li   ben.li   ol.muş.lar.dı.
you.PROP   I.PROP   be.EVID.3PL.PST
'[When they said goodbye to each other in front of the door after two hours,] they seemed to be already quite familiar with each other.'

(9) Erźa Mordvin (Abramov 1973: 226)
Orteĺ.se   eŕam.sto   veśeme.ś   t'eje.v.i   vejse,
guild.INESS   live.CONV   all.DEF   do.RFL.PRS3SG   together,
moń-toń —   aras.t'.
I:GEN-you:GEN   NEG:EX.PL
'Living in the guild everything is done together, there is no mine and thine.'

In these two examples there is generalization that reduces the contrast between the coordinands. This also holds for a very similar case from Kâte, where the co-compound consists, however, not of personal pronouns, but of verb forms that are inflected for person: *na.zaŋ ga.zaŋ e.râ* 'to_me.say to_you.say do.CONV = saying among themselves' (Haiman 1985: 77). Consider also the German figurative expression *mir nichts, dir nichts* 'to_me nothing to_you nothing > just like that'.

It follows from this that a lack of contrast is a characteristic feature of co-compounds. Generally, looser coordination tends to be associated with a higher degree of contrast, and tighter coordination with a lower degree of contrast.

3.3.5 *Non-exhaustive vs. exhaustive listing coordination*

In NON-EXHAUSTIVE LISTING COORDINATION some coordinands are implicit. In English this may be rendered by *for instance A and B*. In languages such as Kanuri, Japanese, and Koasati (Haspelmath forthcoming), there are distinct coordinators for non-exhaustive listing. In Kanuri (Lukas 1937: 16), the associative plural and collective marker *-so* (*férò.so* 'the girl and her people') may be used as a non-exhaustive listing coordinator (added to both co-ordinands: *-so...-so*) in contrast to the exhaustive listing coordinator (*-(C)à...-(C)à*) that falls together formally with the proprietive *-(C)à*.

Non-exhaustive listing coordination is sometimes natural coordination, notably in such cases where coordination is used to express collectivity in such collocations as *pots and pans* (cooking utensils), *shirts and trousers* (clothes), that is, where it expresses sets that are defined by the common properties of the coordinands. Unlike such collectivity coordination, the coordinands in non-exhaustive listing coordination are not necessarily closely related semantically. Non-exhaustive coordination is akin to enumeration (Section 3.3.9) as enumeration is often non-exhaustive. In contrast to collectivity coordination like *pots and pans*, it is not necessarily natural coordination. Neither non-exhaustive listing nor exhaustive-listing coordination seem to be especially associated with tight or loose coordination.

3.3.6 *Disjunction*

In the affirmative, DISJUNCTION is less informative than conjunction (Horn 1989). *I see a house and a tree* contains more precise information than *I see a house or a tree*.[8] Disjunction is thus a useful means of expression if there is only insufficient evidence for a particular state of affairs, and in the affirmative it often has the implicature that the speaker has insufficient evidence (see also Grice 1989: 46). This is also the reason why the coordinator for 'or' in many languages grammaticalizes from expressions of epistemic possibility (notably adverbs meaning 'perhaps', as in Toaripi *varo* (placed at the end of phrases and clauses) 'perhaps',... *varo*... *varo* 'or'; Brown 1968: 297). Disjunction may convey not only little, but also misleading information. (With exclusive 'or', one coordinand is certainly false. With inclusive 'or', one coordinand is possibly false. The distinction between exclusive and inclusive is, however, of little importance in a situation of restricted evidence, and comes into play only if it is known beforehand that only one alternative can be true.) Put differently, disjunction (in the affirmative) is used in cases where Grice's (1975) second maxim of quality 'Do not say that for which you lack adequate evidence' overrules the first maxim of quantity 'Make your contribution as informative as is required'.

In the negative, just the opposite holds, with disjunction being more informative than coordination because it excludes more possible variants than coordination. In *I don't see a house or a tree* the state of affairs is clear, while in *I don't see a house and a tree* there are three possible logical situations. Thus, disjunction in the affirmative and conjunction in the negative have much in common, as they can both be used to indicate lack of evidence.

Disjunction in the affirmative, and conjunction in the negative, can even be used as a pure marker for uncertain evidence if there is no real choice between two coordinands. This is the case notably if the second coordinand is a dummy element such as *something* or *things*. Many examples of this kind are found in Agatha Christie's (1972/1993) detective story, *Elephants can Remember*, in which old people are asked to remember what happened a long time ago: *You know, he couldn't pass an exam and things at the earlier school he was at—prep school or something* (ibid.: 103).

The low degree of informativeness of disjunction is in line with its frequent use in questions. The tight relationship of disjunction and question can be seen from the fact that some languages have a specific coordinator for the expression of disjunction in questions (Finnish *vai*, in the affirmative *tai*), and that in many languages the marker for yes/no-questions is identical with, or formally related to, the marker for disjunction (as in Latvian *vai* 'INT, or', Russian *-li* 'INT', *ili* 'or'). In questions, disjunction usually expresses the request for a choice while at the same time disjunction can limit the number of alternatives. Questions such as *How is he at school, good or bad?* indicate that there are only two expected answers. In such questions, the alternatives of the limited choice expressed by disjunction are often pairs of opposites.

Other favorable contexts for disjunction are generalization and distributivity. In general and distributive contexts, disjunction may express the varying element, and, as in the following example, the variation is often a natural pair: *I know something interesting is sure to happen... whenever I eat or drink anything...* (Carroll 1865/1994: 41).

To summarize: Disjunction tends to be associated with specific contexts, such as lack of evidence, question, negation, distributivity, and generalization.

As we have seen in this section, there are many cases in these specific contexts where disjunction is natural coordination and where it is rather tight coordination (with words used as coordinands rather than phrases or clauses). It follows from this that disjunction plays an important role for both natural and tight coordination.

3.3.7 *Explicative disjunction*

The intersection of coordinands exists not only in conjunction, but also in disjunction where there is no choice between two things, but only between two denominations of one thing. In this sense, intersective disjunction is a kind of metalinguistic disjunction (Haspelmath forthcoming). In practice, intersective disjunction is acceptable almost only if it is expected that the first coordinand is not easily understood by the audience (therefore: EXPLICATIVE DISJUNCTION). Thus, an example like *my brother or male sibling* is hardly ever found.

Some languages have special explicative disjunctions, such as Finnish *eli*, Estonian *ehk*, Latvian *jeb*, and Latin *sive, seu*. One might think that explicative disjunction is especially tight as its coordinands express completely the same thing, as in Latvian *neologisms jeb jaunvārds* 'neologism or new-word'. However, this is not necessarily the case, as the explicative coordinand can actually be very long as in (10) from Finnish, in which the second coordinand is a sentence containing a coordination with three coordinands:

(10) Finnish (book title)
      Ulkomaille matkustavan turvapassi, eli Kuinka palaan kotiin rentoutuneena, virkistyneenä ja terveenä
      'The security passport for the traveler abroad, or, How I will return home relaxed, strengthened and healthy'[9]

Explicative disjunction can also be used to establish an identity relationship between coordinands that are not naturally believed to be the same thing. This is the case in the philosophical slogan *deus sive natura* 'God or nature', in which the referential intersection is counter-intuitive (and directed against traditional beliefs). Explicative disjunction is thus somewhat akin to accidental coordination: a disjunctive relationship is established, either between expressions that are not well-known or between things that are not commonly believed to belong together. It is, therefore, not strange that explicative disjunction is usually overtly expressed and that some languages even have specific coordinators for explicative disjunction. In spite of its intersectivity, explicative coordination tends to be rather loose coordination. This is not, however, a general rule, and in Section 5.2.4 we shall meet with an example of an explicative co-compound.

3.3.8 *Repair and pseudo-repair*

Levelt (1983, 1989: 486) and DeSmeedt and Kempen (1987) observe that some types of retracting REPAIRS behave in a way similar to coordination (more precisely, to disjunction). The replaced and the replacing sequence behave syntactically like coordinands as in *Is the nurse—er—the doctor interviewing patients?* Repair is similar to (exclusive) disjunction that also consists of a true and a false coordinand.

If repair is a type of coordination, it is a type that lacks overt coordinators if the optional markers of hesitation, such as—*er*—in the example above, and explicit correction markers, such as *I mean*, are disregarded. As the lack of a coordinator may be a feature of tight coordination, the question arises whether repair is tight coordination, especially as the use of semantically closely related words is a frequent source of error in spoken language. But even if repair often lacks a coordinator and often has semantically closely related words as coordinands, it is not tight because there is usually a contrastive focus on the replacing sequence and because coordination in repairs is not preestablished.

Aside from real repair there is, however, also PSEUDO-REPAIR. It draws on the fact that the meaning of the first coordinand is not removed by repair if the coordinands are intersective or overlapping (*The doctor, the surgeon interviewed patients*). On the contrary, in these circumstances repair turns out instead to be a specification or reinforcement. Pseudo-repair is not only found in spoken language; it is often encountered in some elaborate styles of German. Nietzsche makes frequent use of triplets of pseudo-repair, such as *Ich bin zu neugierig, zu fragwürdig, zu übermüthig, um mir eine faustgrobe Antwort gefallen zu lassen.* 'I am too curious, too question-worthy, too overenthusiastic, to be content with a whopping big answer' (*Ecce homo*, 1999: 278). It becomes clear from this example that pseudo-repair need not be tight, even if it coordinates semantically closely related elements. Special emphasis is given here to the second coordinand, because the word is meant in its literal, not in its conventional meaning (which would be 'questionable'). The fact that one coordinand can be emphasized in this way shows that the coordinands have a rather high degree of independence from each other in spite of the lack of an overt coordinator. A further indication for looseness is the repetition of the adverb *zu* 'too' with each coordinand.

3.3.9 *Enumeration*

ENUMERATION often lacks coordinators cross-linguistically. Moreover, nouns in enumeration often do not have any non-relational marking, or have single non-relational marking if they function as a constituent in a sentence. Consider the following example from the UDHR: *and the right to security in the event of [unemployment, sickness, disability, widowhood, old age or other lack of livelihood] in circumstances beyond his control* (25; 1). This suggests that enumeration is tight coordination. On the other hand, the typical properties of enumeration might also be due to the fact that it is not really coordination. In fact, enumeration is not even really syntax (*one two three...* is not a sentence), which may explain its aversion to all kinds of relational marking. Even if enumeration sometimes has formal properties similar to natural coordination, it can be seen to be distinct from natural coordination by the fact that it usually has more than two coordinands, while natural coordination is typically limited to two. Enumeration is never univerbated (except for conventionalized names of enumeration, such as *ABC, alphabet, element*). If co-compounds occur in enumeration then they will clearly be the tighter structures. Consider (11) from Santali which contains an enumeration consisting of five co-compounds:

(11) Santali (Bodding 1925–29, 3: 24)
Ado unkin bakhra merom bhidi, ūṭ gadha,
then their:DU share goat sheep camel donkey
hati sadom, ṭaka kaudi, thari baṭi, joto.ko
elephant horse, rupee cowrie_shell brass_plate cup all.3PL
kol.at'.kin.a...
send.APPL.DU3.IND
'As the portion of these two children they sent along with them goats and sheep, camels and donkeys, elephants and horses, money, brass-plates and cups, all this...'

From the English translation, we may see that English binomials occur as tighter structures in enumeration. The tighter structure of the binomials is then confusingly marked distinctively by overt coordinators.

3.3.10 *Pseudo-coordination*

Coordination of verbs or verb phrases often has the function of temporal sequencing, where the coordinands occur in temporal order (and violations of that temporal order are very odd: see Grice's (1981: 186) example *He went to bed and took off his trousers*). That temporal sequencing is not proper coordination can be seen from the fact that sentences with subordinate clauses can often be exact paraphrases of temporal sequencing with coordination. Thus the sentence *I went to the store and bought a book* is almost equivalent to *I went to the store to buy a book* (at least in the factitive reading of the latter); here the second coordinand is not only temporally posterior, but there is also a final relationship between the events. Because of its subordinating properties, coordinate temporal sequencing is sometimes called PSEUDO-COORDINATION (Grover 1994). In pseudo-coordination we find violations of Ross' (1986: 98 f) COORDINATE STRUCTURE CONSTRAINT according to which, in transformational terminology, no coordinand or element contained in a coordinand may be moved out of the coordination (as in **The lute which Henry [plays Ø and sings madrigals] is warped*). In a non-transformational formulation this means that in coordination, elements outside a coordinate sequence must have scope over both coordinands and cannot apply only to one coordinand. This does not hold, however, in pseudo-coordination such as *This is the book that I went to the store and bought.*

As already mentioned, temporal sequence often implies final or causal relationships between events. In many languages there are, therefore, especially tight patterns for the expression of temporal sequence in which the events form a close unit, one of them being VERB SERIALIZATION, such as in (12) from Sranan:

(12) Sranan (Sebba 1987: 109)
Kofi naki Amba kiri.
Kofi knock Amba kill
'Kofi struck Amba dead.'

There is no agreed definition of verbal serialization. But most people would agree that it is characterized by verbs in (continuous or discontinuous) sequence 'which are not overtly marked for coordination or subordination with respect to each other' (Hyman 1975: 136).

In our context, it is important to note that temporal sequencing, which is closely related with coordination, can form very tight formal units which may lack any kind of relational marking. This sometimes makes it difficult to distinguish formally between serial verbs and co-compounds, a characteristic of which is that they also lack relational markers (see Section 4.4.2 for further discussion).

3.3.11 Conclusions

Various kinds of coordination are associated with tight coordination (even if the correlations are sometimes weak). Besides natural coordination these are, notably, group coordination, intersective coordination, enumeration, and pseudo-coordination, all of which are distinct from, or at least indifferent to, natural coordination.

Other semantic kinds of coordination were found to be highly relevant for natural coordination in that they apply to a subpart of it (overlapping, non-exhaustive listing coordination, and disjunction) or to co-compounds rather than to phrase-like tight coordination patterns (minimal contrast). In Chapter 5 we shall see how all these semantic factors come together in co-compounds.

3.4 Conclusions

It would go beyond the scope of this study to develop a detailed theory of all aspects of tightness in coordination.[10] The main topics, natural coordination and co-compounds, made it necessary to concentrate on the tight end of the tight–loose coordination continuum. It was shown in Sections 3.1–3.3 that it is not always possible to rank instances or patterns or semantic subtypes of coordination according to tightness, particularly because many patterns and semantic kinds of coordination have only weak correlations with tightness. From this, one might be inclined to think that tightness in coordination is only a phantom occurrence and/or not relevant at all. But even if instances, patterns, and semantic subtypes of coordination cannot always be ranked unequivocally according to tightness, it is undeniable that coordinate sequences may vary greatly in tightness. Coordination is the construction having the highest possible variation in the degree of tightness. Coordinands may be sentences (that is, coordination may go beyond the upper limit of syntax) and they may be parts of words (that is, coordination may go beyond the lower limit of syntax).

Tight and loose coordination do not simply form two clear-cut classes that are opposed to each other. Languages do not have just one construction for tight coordination and another for loose coordination. The various patterns for rather tight and rather loose coordination that may be found across languages are usually covert (in the sense of Whorf) and may be limited to very specific contexts. This suggests that the development of different marking patterns for tighter and looser types of coordination is not goal-directed. Different patterns arise because various non-relational and relational markers have different scope, this scope representing an aspect of their degree of grammaticalization. Since each marker can have its own degree of grammaticalization, and as each marker can even have different degrees of grammaticalization in different functions, there is no reason why different markers in different functions should behave the same way within a given pattern of tight coordination. Put differently, a large number of specific tight coordination patterns emerging through scope reduction in the grammaticalization of individual markers leads to disorder (or, more technically, to an increase in entropy) and not to class formation. An endless range of different marker-specific and function-specific patterns may arise, none of which is really a clear-cut class.

In the next chapter I shall claim that co-compounds form classes. If I am right, it follows that the evolution of co-compounds is something fundamentally different from the evolution of specific tighter patterns of coordination, even if co-compounds typically evolve from tight patterns of coordination (Section 7.2.1). The result of the former development is a class; the result of the latter is a number of particular marker-specific patterns which do not necessarily form classes.

Notes

[1] Some languages have specific coordinators for looser coordination. An interesting case is Toura *leni* (vs. tight *ni*); Bearth (1971: 132). However, it is also common in European languages to use specific coordinators for looser coordination (for example in English *as well as*, Swedish *samt*, German *sowie*, Estonian *ning*), especially if a tighter coordination is contained in a looser one, as in Swedish *hälso- och sjukvård samt social omsorg* 'health and "sickness" care as well as social welfare'.

[2] The difficulty of defining co-compounds in Turkish formally derives from (a) the large number of different formal patterns and (b) the low frequency of co-compounds, which is why they do not clearly emerge as a lexical class. ABx and A Bx represent co-compounds, A *ve* Bx clearly not; I am not sure about the pattern Ax Bx, it has been included in Section 6.2.

[3] The distinction is similar to that between collective and distributive coordination which is sometimes made in the literature, with the difference that distributive coordination is the stronger (or marked) case, whereas in the group–separate distinction, group is the stronger interpretation.

[4] An interesting example from Russian (Kopčevskaja-Tamm and Šmelev 1994: 215 f) may serve as a further illustration for the close relationship between comitative and group coordination. In Russian, coordination of two denominal adjectives has a preferably separate (distributive) interpretation: *Aleš.in.y i Maš.in.y deti* 'Alyosha.ADJ.PL and Masha.ADJ.PL children = Alyosha's and Masha's children' (they have no common children). In order to express the fact that something is related to two common possessors, a comitative construction can be used: *Aleš.in.a s Maš.ej stat'ja* 'Alyosha.ADJ.SG:F with Masha.INST article = Aljosha and Masha's paper'. See also Dalrymple et al. (1998) for some rare distributive uses of the Russian comitative construction.

⁵ Here are two more examples of natural comitatives. The Takelma (Penutian) 'dual' -*dīl* occurs as an associative dual marker (Sapir 1922/1969: 249). Interestingly, the 'dual' suffix -*dīl* is attested most often with kinship terms (*sgisi gūxdagwadīl* 'coyote with his wife') in the texts (Sapir 1909: 17).

In Udihe (Tungus) the comitative postposition *mule* (with animate nouns) 'presupposes a close "inalienable" association between two participants, which must constitute a "natural" pair: a husband and wife, a mother and son, cf.: *ogbö eni mule* "elk with female"' (Nikolaeva and Tolskaya 2001: 412). *Mule* is also lexicalized with a closed class of nouns meaning a close symmetric relationship between two or more people, such as *gagda-mule* '(married) couple' (*gagda* 'the other'), *xunazi-mule* 'sisters' (*xunazi* 'sister') as a kind of associative dual/plural marker (ibid.: 163). Generally, lexicalized forms of natural comitatives (as in Quechua and Udihe) are closely related to dyad constructions (Section 6.6.5). Evans (2003: 63 f) argues that proprietive and dyad constructions deriving from proprietives behave quite differently syntactically. The same argument applies to natural comitatives and their lexicalized counterparts as in Udihe and Quechua.

⁶ If we disregard the fact that punctuation helps to clarify meaning.

⁷ What Cysouw (2003: 166–84) discusses under 'compound pronouns' seems to represent inclusory coordination: {A,B,C} and {B} yields the set {A,B,C} (Haspelmath forthcoming; Cysouw's term is 'incorporative').

⁸ According to Wisniewski and Murphy (1989: 247), superordinate level concepts have the same effect as low informativeness.

⁹ Book titles are a favorable context for explicative disjunction. Here is another example from English: *The death of hockey, or, How a bunch of guys with too much money and too little sense are killing the greatest game on earth.*

¹⁰ For example, one might find that Harries-Delisle's (1978) 'coordination after regrouping' (or in a non-transformational framework: coordination with a continuous sequence) is tighter than 'coordination without regrouping' and gapping (or in a non-transformational framework: [condensed] afterthought coordination, discontinuous coordination); see also Brettschneider (1978: 251 ff).

4

Co-compounds as a Lexical Class Type

The traditional treatment of co-compounds within morphology as a pattern of word formation (Section 4.1) has many shortcomings. The traditional strict division of looser and tighter constructions into syntax and morphology presupposes a classical definition of the word which is at once the maximal unit of morphology and the atom of syntax. Linguistic evidence speaks against such a strict borderline between morphology and syntax because many constructions have both morphological and syntactic properties (Section 4.2). In most languages, co-compounds are intermediate between syntax and morphology and a strict insistence that compounds can only be purely morphological entities would exclude from the discussion most of what are considered in this monograph to be co-compounds. I will therefore advocate an alternative approach to co-compounds, the lexical class approach (Section 4.3). Co-compounds are thus considered to be a functional–formal class analogous to grammatical classes and, even if they represent tight, word-like constructions, they need not always be words. The next step is then taken to explore the differences between grammatical classes and lexical classes. One of the advantages of the lexical class approach to compounds is that it can account for formal non-distinctiveness between compounds and syntactic constructions. In Section 4.4 some cases of non-distinctiveness between co-compounds and other types of compounds and syntactic constructions will be discussed.

4.1 The traditional morphological (and indirectly syntactic) approach to compounding

Traditional morphology treats the notions of co-compound and sub-compound as tertiary in the sense that they are defined in terms of the primary notion of word via the secondary notion of compound. Co-compounds are thus considered to be a subcategory of compounds and compounds to be a subcategory of words. This approach, even if time-honored, is not unproblematic, especially because (a) the concept of word is often taken for granted as a kind of axiomatic entity, (b) the criteria for the three levels are different (words being necessarily distinct in form from phrases, but co-compounds and sub-compounds may differ only in meaning; see Section 4.4 below), and (c) syntactic and indirectly syntactic criteria are adduced to define compounds and co-compounds in spite of their allegedly pure morphological nature. As point (a) will be addressed in Section 4.2 below, let us deal here with point (c).

Interestingly, in defining compounds, reference is often made to syntactic or syntax-like processes. Consider the following two definitions: Spencer (1991: 309), 'compounding... is prototypically the concatenation of words to form other words' and Anderson (1992: 292), 'It [compounding] consists in the combination of (two or more) existing words into a new word ...'. These definitions suggest that compounds may have a syntactic structure internally.

In the traditional subclassification of compounds, it is not morphological criteria that are crucial, but semantic and indirectly syntactic ones. The description of compounds in modern linguistics is ultimately based on the work of Old Indian grammarians of Sanskrit, who distinguished three major types of compounds they named by examples of the type: TATPURUSHA (sub-compounds; *tat.puruṣa* 'this-servant > the servant of this (person)'), BAHUV-RIHI (also exocentric compounds, possessive compounds; *bahu.vrīhi* 'much-rice > a person having much rice'), and DVANDVA (co-compounds; *dvaṃ.dva* 'two.two > pair') (see Wackernagel 1905, Thumb and Hauschild 1959). In Sanskrit, and ever since, it has been common to describe compounds indirectly, that is by describing their syntactic paraphrases. Thus, tatpurushas are those compounds whose first part is an oblique case in the paraphrase (the genitive in *bhū.pati* 'earth.lord > king' and the ablative in *caura.bhaya* 'thief.fear > the fear of thieves'). Pāṇini defines co-compounds by the formula *ca-arthé dvaṃdváḥ* '(the) and-denoting (is the) dvandva' (Pāṇini 2.2.29; Katre 1987: 135).

The frequent classification of compounds according to the word class of their parts (for instance, as N–N compounds or V–N compounds) also testifies to the indirect syntactic analysis of compounds.

To summarize, syntactic notions are omnipresent in the treatment of compounds even in non-generative approaches. This should be reason enough to reconsider the question whether compounds are really words.

4.2 Are (co-)compounds really words?

From the traditional morphological view that compounds are words, it follows that the definition of compounds is inseparably tied to the definition of word. Spencer (1991: 309) makes this explicit: 'in looking at compounding processes we are looking albeit perhaps obliquely, at the problem of how to define the notion of "word"', though it is well-known that it is often impossible to distinguish compounds from phrases: 'we have often no satisfactory, unequivocal way of distinguishing between a compound word and a phrase' (ibid.). In an inspiring paper, Spencer (2003) has now given up the traditional view that all compounds are words by claiming that N N compounds and N N phrases in English have exactly the same structure.

The idea of the word as a clear-cut linguistic category is imposed on linguistics by Modern European writing systems (see Linell 1982: 83). But even in writing systems where words are usually distinguished by spaces from sequences of words, there are intermediate cases between words and sequences of words which may be indicated by hyphenation. Interestingly, co-compounds are hyphenated in many orthographies, which already suggests that they are intermediate between syntax and morphology.

In this section we shall address the question whether it is reasonable to consider co-compounds, and compounds in general, simply as words.

4.2.1 What is word? Laying out the problem

We have to deal here with two basic questions. The first is, what are words?; the second, how is the notion of word relevant for the cross-linguistic definition of co-compounds and other types of compounds?

When addressing the question of what a word is we can, first of all, take for granted that there are linguistic entities in many languages which are undoubtedly words, such as English *house*, *green*, and *read*, and it is also clear that all languages have entities which are other than words (henceforth: non-words), representing larger or smaller units, such as English *the green house* and /r/. Neither will I argue here against the universality of word. I agree with Dixon and Aikhenvald (2002: 32) that it does seem likely that every language will have words. From our point of view, however, this is not the relevant problem. The real issue is whether all linguistic entities in all languages can be clearly classified as either words or non-words. In the discussion of borderline phenomena like clitics, compounds, and case, the relevant question is this one.

Now, in the same way as it is obvious that most or even all languages have words, it is obvious that in most or even all languages there are some entities for which it is not immediately clear whether they are single words or sequences of several words. In spite of the long-standing tradition that there are only words and non-words, those who think the distinction between word and non-word is discrete carry the burden of the argument. They would have to show, for instance, that the difference between case and adposition is a clearly discrete one with cases always being word affixes and adpositions always being independent words against, for instance, the evidence presented in Kilby (1981).[1]

Given a quite large and troublesome residue of unclear cases from a great many languages, there are basically two approaches to the problem, if we do not want to assume a priori that the distinction must be discrete (this is not an option for empirical linguistics). One is to rescue the notion of word as a discrete entity by deconstructing it, that is, by showing that the troublemakers are words on one linguistic level and non-words on another level. If this direction of research is unrewarding, the other option is to accept that the distinction between word and non-word is not a discrete one; put differently, that words and phrases are prototypes with fuzzy boundaries. But it must be stated right from the beginning that the deconstruction approach will be successful only to the extent that it can come up with discrete entities on the different levels.

4.2.2 *Deconstructing the notion of word*

Different approaches have proposed various subdivisions of the notion of word. A favorite approach distinguishes the phonological word (also PROSODIC WORD) from the morphological/syntactic-word (also GRAMMATICAL WORD). Prosodic phonology (see, for instance, Nespor and Vogel 1986, and Hall 1999 for an overview) has developed a sophisticated theory of discrete prosodic units and is undoubtedly a promising field of research. For our purposes, however, it is largely irrelevant because it does not group co-compounds into consistent exclusive discrete groups to distinguish them clearly from other phenomena, neither in individual languages nor cross-linguistically. Recall from Section 1.1.1 that some Georgian co-compounds have single and some have double stress, thus subdividing Georgian co-compounds into two different prosodic classes of entities. In Mandarin, some co-compounds have tone neutralization on the second part, while the majority do not (*dōng.xi* 'east.west > thing' vs. *dōng-xī* 'east-west > east and west', *lái.wang* 'come.go > dealings, contact' vs. *lái.wǎng* 'come.go > come and go'). According to Nespor and Vogel's (1986: 110–15) typology, compounds in Modern Greek, including co-compounds, are single prosodic words, while in most other languages compounds consist of sequences of prosodic words. Note also that the technical term prosodic word in prosodic phonology is quite different from the intuitive idea about what words might be in many languages, so that one might ask whether the prosodic word is still a kind of word. But non-isomorphism between different kinds of word is desirable for the deconstruction approach. On the other hand, if the different kinds of word were mostly coextensive, there would remain little legitimation for deconstruction.

Similarly, Dixon and Aikhenvald (2002) make a distinction between the phonological and the grammatical word. Their phonological word is similar to, but not exactly identical with, the prosodic word in prosodic phonology (ibid.: 13–18; see also Hildebrandt forthcoming). For the grammatical word they give the following definition: 'A grammatical word consists of a number of grammatical elements which: (a) always occur together, rather than scattered through the clause (the criterion of cohesiveness); (b) occur in a fixed order; (c) have a conventionalized coherence and meaning' (ibid.: 19). Note that phonological/prosodic criteria are lacking from this definition as required for the methodology of the deconstruction approach; criteria of one level cannot be adduced for the definition of another kind of word on another level. Below we will show that none of the three criteria for Dixon and Aikhenvald's grammatical word fits co-compounds (Sections 4.2.3 vi, vii, i).

A further step of deconstruction is made by DiSciullo and Williams (1987). According to these authors, words should be considered as purely morphological and syntactic entities which do not fall together in extension with lexemes (or listemes, as they call them). They hold that many listemes are phrases, notably idioms and other fixed expressions (NP: *the Big Apple*, PP: *in the dark about NP*, S: *the cat has got NP's tongue*) and that many morpho-syntactic words which can be generated by morphological rules are not listed in the lexicon (such as potential words with the suffix *-ness* in English). According to DiSciullo and Williams lexemes and morpho-syntactic words just happen to coincide in many cases because in the hierarchy morpheme > word > compound > phrase > sentence, the items to the left are more frequently listed in the lexicon than the items to the right.

One thing which becomes clear from reading DiSciullo and Williams (1987) is that it is hardly possible to define the word in a classical definition at the same time as a morpho-syntactic word and as a lexical word. DiSciullo and Williams (1987) sacrifice the lexical dimension in order to maintain a classical definition on the syntactic and morphological levels. This does not really work either, as we shall see below. Let us first state that the authors have a very simplistic concept of the lexicon: 'If conceived of as the set of listemes, the lexicon is incredibly boring by its very nature. It contains objects of no specifiable type (words, VPs, morphemes, perhaps intonation patterns, and so on), and those objects that it does contain are there because they fail to conform to interesting laws' (ibid.: 3).[2]

There is growing evidence in linguistics that there exist a great variety of phenomena that are intermediate between words and phrases, both from a lexical and from a syntactic-morphological point of view. Many approaches are surveyed in Wray's (2002) monograph on formulaic language. These phenomena, which, so to speak, fall between words and phrases, may be described in many different ways and require an emergent model of the lexicon (Bybee 1998). Let us here briefly mention two relevant domains that cannot, however, be sharply divided from each other: lexicalized phrases and collocations.

LEXICALIZED PHRASES (or short lexphrases), described for Swedish by Anward and Linell (1975/76), are expressions with some clearly syntactic properties (they seem to consist of syntactic constituents) which form semantic units of their own (their meaning being not purely compositional), and which typically deviate in one or another way from prototypical phrases in form, in that they have some properties rather more characteristic of words than of phrases (such as specific intonation patterns). An example for a lexicalized phrase from Swedish is *sparka boll* 'kick ball' (with a single main stress on *boll*). This sequence deviates from a purely syntactic structure in that the noun *boll* has no article, and by its having a single main stress (connective prosody). Furthermore, *boll* cannot be referential as real direct objects can: **Vi sparkade bóll på gården, och plötsligt blev vi av med den.* '*We kicked ball in the yard and suddenly we lost it.' If ball has to be referential, the noun must have an article and there must be another lexical main stress on the verb: *Vi spárkade (på) en bóll på gården, och plötsligt blev vi av med den.* 'We kicked (on) a ball in the yard and suddenly we lost it.' The lexphrase *sparka boll* is an example of inceptive object incorporation (noun stripping in terms of Miner 1986) that is still somewhat on the syntactic part of a word–phrase scale. But there is no clear boundary between lexicalized phrases and compounds. Anward and Linell (1975/76: 102) conclude that (my translation):

'Compounds have ... the same properties as lexicalized phrases, although to a stronger degree.' Many bare binomials in West European languages, such as *brother and sister, kith and kin*, etc. (see Sections 1.1.3 and 2.3.3 above) are typical examples of lexphrases.

COLLOCATIONS are a domain between phrases and words identified in corpus linguistics. They are combinations of words frequently occurring together in a phrase, while other combinations, which should be equally good, sound odd. A collocation in English is, for example, *large number* (which, according to Biber et al. 1998: 47, is much more common than *great number*). Almost any word has other words with which it typically collocates; typical collocates for *hard* are *work, facts,* and *evidence* (see also Wray 2002: 6f, 51f, and passim).

Brettschneider (1978: 139), referring to work by Seiler and Benveniste, notes (my translation): 'Between the level of word and free syntactic combination there is the area which is characterized by restricted syntactic combination and semantic constriction.' He mentions instances of tight coordination in German which contain words with no meaning of their own that occur only in these collocations: *klipp und klar* '? and clear > in no uncertain terms' and *mit Kind und Kegel* 'with child and ?[3] > with kith and kin.' Such examples cannot be accounted for by morphological rules and they cannot be generated by syntactic rules either. Thus, the biggest obstacle to a classical definition of the word is that there are many phenomena which are intermediate between the word and the phrase. Consider also the phrasal affixes discussed in Section 2.4.3 above.

Thus, we may conclude that the deconstruction approach, even if probably justified as far as prosody is concerned, does not offer discrete notions on the syntactic, morphological, and lexical levels. Word, affix, and phrase are thus best considered to be prototypical notions and as such do not make it possible to define marginal phenomena like compounds, lexphrases, clitics, and case in terms of word, affix, or phrase in a classical definition; all of these phenomena tend to fail to be prototypical words, affixes, or phrases in most languages. Actually, there are some exceptions, co-compounds in Modern Greek being unequivocally words, but this is not very helpful for a cross-linguistic definition of co-compounds.

On the other hand, if word and phrase are prototypical notions, they remain highly relevant for the definition of co-compounds, not in the sense that all co-compounds would be words, but rather that co-compounds generally are word-like, that is, exhibiting many properties characteristic of words in contrast to phrase-like tight coordination (Section 1.1.3). Let us now discuss different criteria for 'wordhood'.

4.2.3 *Criteria for the 'wordhood' of compounds (with special reference to co-compounds)*

In this section we will consider different properties characteristic of words all of which are relevant for a prototypical definition of the word. None of these properties may serve, however, as a necessary and sufficient criterion for a classical definition of words which would also encompass compounds, and especially co-compounds. While criteria from all levels are considered, phonological and prosodic features are treated only briefly in (ii), because co-compounds are certainly not prosodic words in most languages (see above).

(i) *Semantic criteria for compounds* Some authors hold that compounds can be defined by a semantic criterion, such as non-compositional, unitary, or inherent, or, put differently, that it is possible to tell if something is a word or a phrase solely by looking at its meaning.

The feature 'NON-COMPOSITIONAL' is advocated, among others, by Brugmann for compounds in general and by Feng for co-compounds in Classical Chinese. Brugmann (1900/1981: 138f) holds that 'The real beginning of the process that we call compound formation is always a *modification* of the meaning of the syntactic collocation' (my translation, emphasis in the original). According to Feng (1998: 204), 'the most effective criterion for identifying compounds in Classical Chinese is the semantic one'. He claims that *ju-ma* 'carriage-horse' is no compound when it means 'carriage(s) and horse(s)', but is a compound when it means just 'carriage'. Other authors, however, deny the pervasive role of the semantic criterion; as Anderson (1985: 44) puts it for Mandarin Chinese, the 'degree of lexicalized meaning is often suggestive of the unitary nature of a compound, but cannot be taken as absolute: on the one hand, there are compounds (such as *jī-dàn* "chicken-egg:chicken's egg") whose meaning is entirely compositional; and, on the other, there are phrases with idiomatic sense (such as *yòng shuǐ* "use water: urinate") which are not compositional.' It has been pointed out repeatedly that if non-compositional meaning is the defining criterion for compounds, then compounds cannot be separated from idioms (Bauer 1978: 52ff for a discussion).

Another semantic feature, 'UNITARY', has been advocated by Anderson (1985: 50) for Mandarin Chinese co-compounds (but not for other types of compounds). He observes that co-compounds in Mandarin cannot express every kind of conjunction or disjunction, but have a kind of unitary meaning. This corresponds more or less to what I call natural coordination. 'Unitary' meaning or natural coordination, even if it is undoubtedly a very important characteristic of co-compounds, cannot serve to distinguish co-compounds in all cases from ordinary coordination; put differently, it may be part of a prototypical definition of co-compounds, but not of a classical definition.

A further candidate for a general semantic feature of compounds is 'INHERENT', which is advocated by Bauer (1978: 69ff) and fits best for Adj-N compounds. Adj-N compounds can be used together with a predicate that is limited to the present and that contradicts the inherent adjective in the compound, as in Danish *Rødvinen er lilla* 'the red wine is lilac'. We have seen earlier (Section 1.1.2) that inherence is highly relevant for natural coordination, but also that there may be different degrees of inherence. 'Inherent' is thus no better than 'unitary' for the definition of compounds. Of course, these semantic properties are important characteristics, at least for some compounds, but are not criteria for defining compounds in a classical definition.

To summarize: Even if the semantic component cannot be underestimated in the study of compounds, it is not possible to define compounds in a classical definition solely by means of a semantic feature. But it is certainly true that a characteristic property of many types of compounds (as part of their prototypical definitions) is that they form conceptual units semantically.

(ii) *Conventionalized prosodic patterns* Compounds tend to have conventionalized prosodic patterns (Haiman 1994: 16). A well-known example of a feature of compound prosody is single stress on one of the parts of the compound. Thus, sub-compounds in Germanic languages tend to be stressed only on the first part of the compound (English *bláckbird* in contrast to the phrase *black bírd* 'a bird that is black'). Sometimes, a conventionalized prosodic pattern is distinctively marked only under certain conditions. In Mandarin Chinese, contrastive stress can only fall on the final part of a compound, even if the first part is contrasted (Anderson 1985: 41).

The presence of a single main stress in compounds, however, which may also be called 'deaccentuation', is not a sufficient criterion for compoundhood. Lexicalized phrases can have a single main stress as well. In Swedish, not only compounds, but also lexicalized phrases have connective prosody (Swedish *sammanfattningsaccent*; see Anward and Linell 1975/76). Usually, lexicalized phrases have a final main stress (*varm kórv* 'warm sausage = a specific dish') and compounds an initial one (*vármkorv* 'a sausage that can be prepared as *varm kórv*), in contrast to phrases with two main stresses (as in *várm kórv* 'any warm sausage'). There are also, however, some compounds with a final stress (*tjugotré* 'thirty-three', *sydväst* 'southwest'. These happen to be mostly appositional, intermediate-denoting, fusional, and relational compounds in Swedish; Section 1.1.2). According to Spencer (2003), the distinction between left-stress and right-stress is notoriously difficult to apply in English. Consider such examples as *apple píe* vs. *cárrot cake*. Spencer therefore proposes 'that stress patterns are in many cases determined by (admittedly vague) semantic "constructions" defined over collections of similar lexical entries.'

It is often characteristic of co-compounds that they retain the stress on both elements, often indicated by hyphenation in orthography.

To summarize: Although different types of compounds in different languages tend to have different characteristic prosodic patterns, there are usually compounds that deviate from these patterns so that there is no generally typical compound prosody. On the other hand, lexicalized phrases can have prosodic patterns similar to compounds. Conventionalized prosodic patterns are thus a characteristic property of compounds but not a necessary and sufficient criterion for compoundhood.

(iii) *Compounding forms and clippings* Stem or compounding forms are characteristic for some compounds, such as Swedish *flask.hals* 'bottleneck' (the corresponding free form of the first part being *flaska*). The German traditional literature distinguishes between proper and improper compounds (*echte* and *unechte Komposita*), the former having stem form, the latter word form in the first component of compounds. The situation is, however, more complicated as has been pointed out by Brugmann (1900) since there are compounds with internal pseudo-inflection, such as German *Schwan.en.gesang* 'swan.?.song > swan song' where *-en* is not a possible inflectional ending of *Schwan*). Compounding forms are often shorter than corresponding words; shorter forms of words are, however, not necessarily compounding forms, but can be abbreviations (such as *doc* for *doctor*).

Clippings comprise a specific kind of reduced forms in compounds. In contrast to compound stems, clippings are reduced forms of words that have a certain maximal phonotactic structure. In Tibetan (Beyer 1992: 92ff), parts of compounds tend to be reduced to one syllable. As Tibetan roots usually consist of just a single syllable, this means that words in most cases lose their derivational and inflectional suffixes, if they had any, when they enter into compounds: for example, *gaŋs dkar-po* 'glacier white' > *gaŋs dkar* 'glacier white = white glacier', *dkar-po'i zas* 'white'GEN food' > *dkar zas* 'white food'. If roots of parts of compounds are, however, longer than one syllable (notably in loanwords), or if parts of compounds are already compounds, the same process of clipping may apply: *paṇ-chen* < *paṇḍita chen-po* 'scholar great =

great scholar' or *yon-mchod* < *yon bdag daŋ mchod gnas* 'lay patron and religious master' (*yon-mchod* is a co-compound, *daŋ* 'with, and' being the comitative postposition which also expresses coordination). Clipping may lead to very strange co-compounds, such as *bza' mi* 'eat man > men and women' (UDHR 16; 2). Its first part derives from *bza' ba* 'eating, eater > "non-productive" members of the family, children and/or wife'. In *bza' mi* the first part is clipped and sharpened first to 'wife' and then to 'women' in the particular context.[4]

To summarize: There are different kinds of formal deviations of parts of compounds from the free words to which they correspond: compounding forms and clippings (which cannot always be clearly kept distinct from each other). If such modified forms occur only in compounds, they are distinctive features of compounds and can be sufficient criteria for compounding. In most languages, however, they are not a necessary criterion for compounding as there are many compounds that have no modified forms of words that occur only in compounds.

(iv) *Bound stems* In morphology a distinction is often made between free and bound morphemes. A free morpheme may occur in isolation; a bound morpheme needs another morpheme to attach to. One might therefore assume that any structure containing a bound stem, such as *cran-* in *cranberry*, is a compound. This assumption, however, is problematic in several respects. First, typical bound stems may sometimes occur freely, such as English *psycho*. Secondly, bound elements are not restricted to compounds. In many tight coordinate sequences there are 'cranberry-words', words that occur only in collocation with certain other words, for example, English *to and fro*, *kith and kin*, Swedish *si och så* 'so and so', Estonian *nii ja naa* 'so and so'.

Neither does it solve the problem if we distinguish between free-bound vs. versatile-restricted (Chao 1968: 155), where restricted is applied to forms occurring only when one or a very small number of other forms occur in a near context (lexical bound rather than morphologically bound). It is true that *kith* lexically relies on *kin*, but it is not free in its syntactic position to occur anywhere in the neighborhood of *kin* and does not differ in this respect from *cran-* in *cranberry*. Similarly, Mordvin *pakams* 'walk' is not just lexically restricted, it occurs only (a) in the co-compound *jakams-pakams* 'walk-walk > walk' and (b) in parallelism (see Section 1.1.5) in the second variegated line in exactly the same position and form where there is *jakams* in the first line.

We may therefore conclude that bound elements are neither a necessary, nor a sufficient criterion for compounding.

(v) *Word slots* It is characteristic for derivation and compounding that, in contrast to syntactic constructions, they represent patterns which mostly have word slots rather than phrasal slots. One might therefore be tempted to define compounds as words that have at least two word slots, but no phrasal slots. Thus, in *dog-house* there is a single word in the dependent slot; *our-dog-house meaning 'house of our dog' with a phrase *our dog* in the dependent slot is, however, impossible. Unfortunately, compounding and derivation often allow for more than one word in a slot. Consider Bloomfield's (1933: 228) example *wíld ánimal house* (consisting, according to Bloomfield, of a phrase *wíld ánimal* without deaccentuation and a compound member *house* with reduced stress). Haiman (1994: 13) gives more extreme examples with cliché phrases, such as *a dog-doesn't-return-the-other-dogs'-phone-calls world.* For co-compounds it seems, however, that such complex parts do not occur. Generally, word slots are the rule, even if complex parts occasionally do occur.

However, restriction to word slots is not a sufficient criterion for compounding, as there are many lexicalized phrases that do not allow more than a single word in a position; consider Swedish **Vi sparkade röd boll igår kväll* '*We kicked red ball yesterday evening' (Anward and Linell 1975/76: 87). Some bare binomials do not allow attributes that are common to both parts. Thus, the German binomials *Ebbe und Flut* 'the tide', *Pfeil und Bogen* 'bow and arrows' cannot take any attributes.

(vi) *Continuity* Complex words are usually considered to be units where the parts may not be interrupted by syntactic constituents. Here we will discuss some possible exceptions.

The question of whether or not verbs with separable prefixes in German (*abkaufen, er kauft mir das ab*) are compounds was the source of a dispute between Brugmann (1900) and Paul (1903). According to Brugmann (1900: 136) continuity is not a necessary property of a compound. Paul disagrees and claims that the discontinuous structures that are considered compounds by Brugmann are at an intermediate stage between compounding and syntax.[5] Clearly, the idea of an intimate connection between the parts lies at the very heart of the notion of compound. So one way of resolving the question is to exclude discontinuous sequences from compounding right from the start. However, if the question is addressed empirically, things are not as easy as that. (Consider also that some languages have discontinuous or 'bipartite' stems (Bickel and Nichols forthcoming), so why shouldn't there be any discontinuous words if there are discontinuous stems.) In numerous languages there are discontinuous structures that have many characteristic properties of compounds. Discontinuous candidates for compounds are not restricted to verbs with directional elements. Another case in point is the lexicalized combination of serial verbs, as they occur in some West African languages, which are discontinuous if the direct object is placed between the two verbs, as in Ewe: *dó ámè kpɔ́* 'follow person see > test somebody', *xɔ nya se* 'accept word hear > believe something' (Westermann 1930: 86). Such sequences of verbs are not co-compounds as there is no natural coordination between the two verbs. The idiosyncratic meaning of the verb combinations suggests that this is compounding (or at least is closely related to compounding) in spite of the discontinuity of the parts, particularly because these verb combinations may exhibit specific behavior in inflection (ibid.: 87).

Discontinuity is also relevant for co-compounds, as some South East Asian, South Asian, and Meso-American languages (such as Hmong, Khasi, Karen, Sochiapan Chinantec) have discontinuous structures that behave like typical co-compounds in all other respects, so that it seems wrong to exclude them from classification as co-compounds just because of their discontinuity. (It would be like saying that *more beautiful* is not a comparative because it consists of two words.) In White Hmong (see also Sections 1.1.1 and 6.5) co-compounds can either be continuous or non-continuous without any change of meaning. Non-continuous co-compounds are of the structure ACBC or CACB, where a lexical or a grammatical (such as a classifier) element C is repeated after or before each member of the compound. Examples (1a–c) contain the synonymic co-compound *teb chaws*[6] in continuous (1a) and discontinuous (1b, 1c) form. In (1b) the co-compound (in boldface) is interrupted by a classifier, in (1c) by a proper noun.

(1)   White Hmong (Bisang 1988: 36, 56, 37)
    a Kuv pom ib   lub   **teb**   **chaws** zoo   kawg!
       I   see   one CL   **land** **land**   good very
      'I have seen a beautiful country.'

    b Kuv lub **teb**   lub   **chaw** kub   nyiab   cig
       I   CL   **land** CL   **land**   burning burned catch_fire
       liab tib vog.
       red   one everywhere
      'My land was everywhere in red-hot fire.'

    c Tab sis yog Yawm Pus **teb**   Yawm Pus **chaw**.
       But   his   Y. P.   **land** Y. P.   **land**
      'But the land belongs to Yau Pu.'

In Sochiapan Chinantec (Foris 2000: 44–53), co-compounds ('binomials' in Foris' terminology) of nouns, adjectives, adverbs, and verbs can have the structure CACB, C being an element with grammatical or lexical function:

cii^L $?la?^{MH}$ cii^L $nai?^M$ 'DIM cricket DIM grasshopper > hopping insects', $cá^M$ ku^M $cá^M$ $huẽ?^M$ 'person just person large:ANIM > mighty, powerful person (e.g. God)' (also continuously $cá^M$ ku^M $huẽ?^M$ 'person just large:ANIM > id.'; discontinuity is not obligatory if C is ku^M 'person'; the longer form conveys a stronger sentiment), $tiá^M$ $?á^H$ $tiá^M$ $ŋá^{HL}$ 'not step_on:TRNS:INAN:- FUT not pass_by:TRNS:INAN:FUT:3 > not go through (experiences)'. According to Foris, 'binomial verbs', as in the latter example, function as single lexemes phonologically (the first part usually undergoes the phonological modification of a normal nonfinal syllable) and semantically (they usually express intensitiy, iterativity, persistence, or complete-affectedness of an action), but as separate words syntactically (the innermost prefix or adverb is obligatorily repeated with the second base). Foris makes a distinction between 'coordinate compounds' that can only be nouns (such as $?ŋá^H.má?^L$ 'forest.mountain > world', $kua?^H.uõ^M$ 'gourd.plate > gourd bowl, crockery', $kua?^{MH}$ undergoes tone simplification, $hŋii^M.mu^H$ 'vein:1PL/3.bone(mu^{LM}):1PL/3 > body') and binomials and lists some criteria for the distinction. In my view, both are to be classified as co-compounds, since Chinantec coordinate phrases require a coordinator, such as $?i^L$ 'and' or hi^L 'also, and' (ibid.: 45).

It must be emphasized that in discontinuous compounds the positions of the parts are not free. In Lehmann's (1985) terms, discontinuous compounds exhibit a high degree of fixation, where there is no or little variation in the syntactic position of the elements. Thus, the parts of the German discontinuous verbs occur in the second and in the final position of the clause, the parts of the Ewe V V compounds occur in front of and after the object, and the Hmong discontinuous co-compounds occur only in structures of the type ACBC or CACB (if a lexical or a grammatical element is repeated).

We may conclude that from an empirical point of view continuity is a characteristic, but not a necessary, property of compounds, although there are hardly any compounds whose parts can occur freely in any position of the clause.

(vii) *Fixed order* As word order is usually fixed in syntactic constructions with head and dependent in noun phrases, the criterion of fixed order plays only a minor role for sub-compounds.[7]

In co-compounds, the order of elements is often fixed despite the absence of any head-dependent relationship. In compounds with terms denoting persons of the opposite sex, there is usually a preference for either female–male (Sanskrit, Hmong, Georgian) or male–female (Vietnamese, Uzbek, Mordvin), although there may be single co-compounds that deviate from the dominant order, as in Vietnamese *vợ-chồng* 'wife-husband' and *đào kép* 'actor-actress > the cast' (Nguyen 1995). Fixed word order is, however, not an exclusive property of co-compounds in contrast to coordination. Most languages have a preferred word order in the natural coordination of males and females. In West European languages there is a preference for male–female order, except for a few combinations such as *bride and bridegroom* and *ladies and gentlemen*. Malkiel (1959), Cooper and Ross (1975), and Lambrecht (1984) observe that there are strong preferences for word order in binomials in many West European languages. For Lambrecht (1984) irreversible binomials are even a specific subtype of binomials. On the other hand, order need not necessarily be fixed in co-compounds. Lezgian has both *dide-buba* 'mother-father' (the more frequent order) and *buba-dide* 'father-mother' for '> parents' (see also Talibov and Gadžiev 1966; for other languages see Map 6.2 in Chapter 6). Thus it follows that fixed order is certainly neither a sufficient nor a necessary criterion for co-compounds.

(viii) *Conclusion* Compounds cannot be clearly defined morphologically and I fully agree with Bauer (1978: 54) that 'despite a plethora of definitions of the compound, there is no really satisfactory definition with which to work.' If there are no properties of compounds which would define them clearly as words, this does not mean that compounds would not have characteristic features. All the features that we have discussed in this section are characteristic for at least some types of compounds in some languages. But the exact extension of single features is not the same; there are many cases where single features do not apply to all compounds, or where they also apply to structures that are not compounds.

Most important is that compounding is not confined to morphology. It is true that all compounds, including co-compounds, have some word-like properties and that in a few languages, co-compounds are unequivocally words, but many co-compounds also have some properties that are characteristic of phrases (compositional meaning, two word stresses, internal inflection, word form of parts rather than stem form, discontinuity, somewhat free order of parts). This means that drawing a strict borderline between purely morphological compounds and the rest of the phenomena exhibiting some properties of words would be completely artificial, and is in fact not possible. Moreover, it would leave us without a method for describing all the phenomena that are intermediate between morphology and syntax. What we need, therefore, is a completely different approach to co-compounds.

4.3 An alternative approach to co-compounds: lexical classes

In the previous section we have seen that co-compounds, like other types of compounds, cannot simply be considered as words because many compounds also have some syntactic properties and there are often no clear criteria to decide whether compounds are morphological or syntactic structures. A different approach is needed. I propose to consider co-compounds as a CROSS-LINGUISTIC FUNCTIONAL–FORMAL CLASS TYPE directly, without the intermediation of the notions word and compound. In analogy to GRAMMATICAL CLASSES, co-compounds are viewed as language-specific classes which have cross-linguistically recurrent semantic and formal properties. A grammatical class is the set of all forms in a language that are characterized by a certain GRAM (Bybee and Dahl 1989, Dahl 1985)[8], and a grammatical class type is characterized by the common cross-linguistic properties of the language-specific classes belonging to that cross-linguistic class type. Many grammatical class types can have either morphological (synthetic, bound expression) or syntactic (analytic, periphrastic expression) formal realization. English has an analytic future (*I will go*), whereas French has a synthetic future (*j'irai*). English has a synthetic plural (*shoes*), whereas Tagalog has an analytic plural (*mga sapatos*) with a plural word (Dryer 1989b). There is no need to refer to the notion of word for the description of grammatical classes, even if it is characteristic for grammatical classes to be represented by tight sequences. In the same vein, for the description of co-compounds, the distinction between morphological and syntactic structures is only of secondary importance, even if it happens to be the case that co-compounds are generally very tight (word-like) structures.

Co-compounds, however, are not a grammatical, but a LEXICAL CLASS TYPE. In contrast to representatives of grammatical classes which are typically INFLECTIONAL FORMS (the notion of inflection is used here in a wider sense to include all forms that occur in grammatical paradigms, be they synthetic or analytic), representatives of lexical classes are LEXEMES. Put differently, in spite of common semantic and formal properties in lexical classes, the distribution of the representatives of a lexical class is highly idiosyncratic and the meaning of the individual representatives often not fully compositional. Thus many representatives of lexical classes must be learned individually, in contrast to grammatical forms whose meanings are fully predictable from the meaning of the gram and the meaning of the lexeme (for exceptions to the latter, such as pluralia tantum, see below). We may define lexical classes tentatively as functional–formal classes which exhibit considerable lexical idiosyncrasy. This does not mean, however, that all representatives of lexical classes are lexicalized to the same extent. Lexical classes also contain items that are fully compositional and need not be learned individually. Lexical classes, therefore, always have a Janus-faced character, with both idiosyncratic and regular properties at the same time.

Like grammatical classes, lexical classes are not cross-linguistically universal in the strict sense that they would be represented in all languages (Dahl 1985: 31f), but neither are they phenomena restricted to individual languages, since their meanings, and to some extent also their formal patterns, are very similar in the different languages where they occur. An important difference from grammatical classes is that they are not typically obligatory in certain syntactic environments and under certain semantic conditions, and do not cluster into grammatical categories, such as tense, aspect, mood, voice, case, number, definiteness, etc. But this does not mean that lexical classes are always less frequent in language use than grammatical classes. Even more than for grammatical classes, text frequency is an important measure of the degree of development of a lexical class and an important measure of cross-linguistic variation. Frequency can be measured in different ways, notably by numbers of TOKENS (that is, all occurrences of a class) or by number of TYPES (the number of different lexical items that occur as representatives of a class; see Bybee and Thompson 2000). It is characteristic of grammatical classes that they have a high type frequency insofar as their lexical slot can be filled by almost any word of a word class. This is not the case for lexical classes (see below).

Lexical classes are not to be confounded with WORD CLASSES, such as nouns, verbs, and adjectives, which are also termed parts of speech, and lexical categories. It is true that word classes also have lexemes as their representatives, but word classes are much more comprehensive than lexical classes. Any word belongs to a word class, even words that have no specific morphological marker. Moreover, word classes are always syntactically relevant in that certain slots in certain syntactic constructions must be filled by a member of a certain word class. In contrast, lexical classes are not syntactically relevant. There may, however, be possible intermediate cases between lexical classes and word classes, such as transitive verbs in Tok Pisin which have a morpheme -*im*.

Examples of typical lexical classes are the middle, causatives, diminutives, agent nominals, light verb constructions, and verbs with directional markers. Let us first look at the middle voice as described by Kemmer (1993). Many of the properties that she ascribes to the middle are characteristic for lexical classes in general, so that the middle can be considered as a kind of model for a lexical class type, even if it is traditionally wrongly classified as a grammatical class (as a voice like active and passive).

4.3.1 *The middle as a typical example for a lexical class type*

According to Kemmer (1993: 3) the middle is a 'coherent, although complex, linguistic category' which 'although without fixed and precise boundaries, nevertheless has a clearly discernible semantic core' (ibid.: 3). The meaning of the middle consists of a network of INTERRELATED SEMANTIC SUBTYPES that can be represented on a semantic map, or put differently, there are various interrelated situation types for which the middle is typically used. Kemmer distinguishes among others the following situation types: grooming or body care ('wash', 'dress', 'shave'), nontranslational motion ('turn', 'bow'), change in body posture ('sit down', 'lie down'), indirect middle where the actor is also the recipient ('acquire', 'ask for oneself', 'take for oneself'), naturally reciprocal events ('meet', 'embrace', 'wrestle'), emotion middle ('be angry', 'grieve', 'complain'), and spontaneous events ('grow', 'recover'). However, whether a concrete verb in a concrete language that—unlike English—has a fully developed middle belongs to this lexical class cannot be predicted. In all situation types that are typical for the middle, the occurrence or non-occurrence of the middle marker is HIGHLY IDIOSYNCRATIC. Kemmer mentions the example of German middles *sich hinsetzen* 'sit down' and *sich hinlegen* 'lie down' beside the non-middle *aufstehen* 'stand up' in the semantic subtype of change in body posture. Even clearer examples of idiosyncrasy are two Russian verbs of change in body posture that belong to the middle in the imperfective aspect (*sadit'sja* 'sit down', *ložit'sja* 'lie down'), but not in the perfective aspect (*sest'* 'sit down', *leč'* 'lie down'). This is a clear difference to grammatical classes where the inclusion in a grammatical class is largely predictable and is, in any case, not dependent on the lexicon (except for lexicalized grammatical forms, such as pluralia tantum, which will be discussed below).

This does not mean, however, that the evolution of lexical classes is completely distinct from the evolution of grammatical classes. This can be seen from the fact that different grammatical classes may develop from the lexical class middle, notably the passive (as in Russian). There are also areas within the lexical class of middle verbs, such as the logophoric middle (Icelandic *Hann telur sig vera sterkan* 'He believes that he is strong'; Kemmer 1993: 85), which are not very idiosyncratic and which closely resemble grammatical classes.

Even if many middle verbs are lexemes with idiosyncratic behavior, middle verbs, in general, are not just lexemes that are completely independent in the lexicon from corresponding non-middle verbs. There is sometimes a degree of synchronic variation for specific lexemes, whether lexical class is used or not. This may also be called VACILLATION WITHIN CONCEPTS. For the middle, this means that some verbs may or may not have a middle marker, with little or no difference in meaning, such as for 'boil' and 'melt' in French: *(se) bouiller* and *(se) fondre* (ibid.: 21). This suggests that lexical classes are PARTLY AUTONOMOUS OF THE LEXICON, as the lexicon does not fully control where they occur and where they do not.

A further characteristic phenomenon that occurs in lexical classes are TANTUM-FORMS, lexemes of the class that have no unmarked counterpart (usually called deponents, as far as the middle is concerned). Thus the Latin middle[9] *obliviscor* 'forget' has no corresponding non-middle verb.

According to Kemmer, the middle is expressed by a 'LIGHT FORM' that has a corresponding 'HEAVY FORM' which is the reflexive construction (as *he sees himself*). The 'light form' tends to be tighter—it is often morphological—than the 'heavy form', the 'heavy form' usually, but not always, being a syntactic construction. The 'heavy form' is more widespread cross-linguistically than the 'light form'; put differently, there are more languages that have reflexive constructions than languages with a middle, and languages with a middle always also have a reflexive. Kemmer distinguishes three kinds of relationships between 'light forms' and 'heavy forms': ONE-FORM SYSTEMS, TWO-FORM COGNATE SYSTEMS, and TWO-FORM NON COGNATE SYSTEMS (ibid.: 24 ff). German is an example of a language with a one-form system of the 'light' and 'heavy forms', where there is a formal non-distinctiveness between middle and reflexive (*Er sieht sich* 'He sees himself' and *Er wäscht sich* 'He washes'). An example of a two-form cognate system is Russian (*On vidit sebja* 'He sees himself' and *On umyvaetsja* 'He washes'). An example of a two-form non-cognate system is Finnish (*Hän näet itseään* 'He sees himself' and *Hän peseytyy* 'He washes').

We may add some other properties characteristic of the middle—also typical of other lexical classes—that are not emphasized in Kemmer (1993). Middle verbs interact in specific ways with corresponding non-middle verbs in the lexicon, which is partly what causes their idiosyncratic behavior. Middle verbs strongly interact with the valency patterns of verbs. Thus, German *klagen* 'complain, go to court' is intransitive and does not occur with a middle marker. The transitive verb *beklagen* 'lament', however, combines with the middle marker: *sich beklagen* 'complain'.

A further property of the middle, and many other lexical classes, is that it is often unclear whether it exists in a language or not. This is not the case for languages where it is omnipresent, such as Latin, Russian, and French, but for languages where it is not common, such as English. It is clear that *He sees himself* is reflexive, not a middle; but what about *The computer lends itself to many different uses?* Lexical classes can be identified clearly only if they have become a prominent phenomenon in a language. This property is not exclusive for lexical classes, however. In the same way it is not possible for weakly developed grammatical classes to decide whether they are already instances of grammatical classes or not.

Lexical classes may have SEVERAL COEXISTENT FORMANTS that are not generally opposed to each other in meaning and that sometimes can be interchanged without any shift in meaning. Thus, the middle in Finnish has the two formants *-UtU-* and *-U-* (*U* is either *u* or *y* depending on vowel harmony), as in *kehittyä, kehkeytyä* 'develop intr.' (The formation of Finnish middle verbs is highly idiosyncratic.) However, this feature is not exclusive to lexical classes but also occurs in grammatical classes; consider the parallel English past forms *thrived* and *throve*. Generally, the existence of more than one formant is more characteristic for grammatical classes than for lexical classes. As the meaning of grammatical forms is purely compositional, and as fully developed grammatical classes are often obligatory under certain syntactic conditions, the existence of different formants or even suppletion does not render it difficult to decide whether grammatical forms with different formants belong to the same grammatical class or not (for instance, the weak and strong past in English). For lexical classes, because they do not have a purely compositional meaning and because they do not have obligatory contexts of use, it is always difficult to decide whether forms with different formants belong to the same lexical class or to different lexical classes because, due to their higher degree of semantic heterogeneity, lexical classes cannot have the same formal heterogeneity as grammatical classes.

To conclude this subsection, let us summarize some characteristic properties of lexical classes into a provisional, non-exhaustive list:

(a) a clearly discernible semantic core, with all representatives of a lexical class belonging to a network of interrelated semantic types;
(b) idiosyncratic, lexicalized (that is, not generally predictable) fixation of use for many representatives;
(c) vacillation within lexemes;
(d) tantum-forms;
(e) corresponding 'heavy forms' that are not lexicalized, or are less lexicalized, and that tend to be cross-linguistically universal;
(f) clashes and interactions with other lexical classes;

(g) the possible coexistence of several formants;
(h) greater difficulty in delimiting a lexical rather than a grammatical class.

4.3.2 *More examples of lexical class types*

Given the Janus-faced nature of lexical classes, the best way of learning more about their nature is cumulative evidence. Let us therefore briefly consider some further examples of cross-linguistically recurrent lexical classes.

DIMINUTIVES[10] are frequent, for example, in German, Italian (see Dressler and Merlini Barbaresi 1994), Latvian (Rūķe-Draviņa 1959), Mordvin, Eastern Ojibwa (*eškotē.ns* 'fire.DIM > match'; Bloomfield 1956: 69), and Ewe. Diminutives are, in a way, an untypical lexical class as they have a very high type frequency (in languages with diminutives most nouns can take diminutive affixes although some nouns rarely do so either for formal (German *?Kuhchen/ ?Kühchen* 'little cow') or semantic reasons) and as they need not necessarily be lexical. They can have a pure discourse function, as in child-directed speech (see Rūķe-Draviņa 1959: 25 ff for Latvian). Nevertheless, many diminutives are lexicalized; consider the following German examples: *Männchen* 'man:DIM male (animal), *Frauchen* 'woman:DIM > Mummy (of a dog)', *Früchtchen* 'fruit:DIM > troublemaker'. Interestingly, lexicalization does not always preempt diminutives from being applicable in non-lexicalized functions. Moreover, many diminutives are lexicalized only in specific contexts, *Kätzchen* usually being just a little cat, but in the case of a willow tree, a pussy willow. Furthermore, diminutives that are not yet lexicalized are potential contextual lexemes (*Lämpchen* 'small lamp' may be a very specific kind of small lamp, depending on the context). Some diminutives are tantum-forms, as are the German *Veilchen* 'violet' and *Kaninchen* 'rabbit'. Other examples, such as *Eichhörnchen*, are almost tantum-forms (*Eichhorn* id. is very rare) and can be said to be highly locally unmarked. Such tantum-forms are not distributed at random across the lexicon; they cluster in groups of nouns with specific meanings (in German small animals with positive connotation, such as *Eichhörnchen*, *Kaninchen*, *Meerschweinchen* 'guinea pig') even if it cannot be predicted from the meaning of a noun whether it is a diminutive tantum or not. In spite of their idiosyncratic behavior, diminutives have many cross-linguistically recurrent characteristic properties, or, as Taylor (1989: 144) puts it: 'there is considerable agreement across different languages with regard to the kinds of meaning that can be conveyed by the diminutive.'

It is well-known that diminutives not only indicate small size, but the construction of a noun with an attributive adjective 'little' or 'young' (alternatively with a noun meaning 'child') can be considered to be the corresponding 'heavy form' to diminutives (neither does *little N* in English always mean small size). In German and other European languages that have derivational diminutives, there is a two-form non-cognate system between heavy and light forms. In Ewe, where diminutives are compounds with a second part *vi'* 'child', there is a two-form cognate system. For a semantic map of diminutives in Ewe, see Heine et al. (1991: 87).

In many languages, diminutives can have several formants that are freely interchangeable as long as there is no lexicalization. Thus, German has *-chen* and *-lein* (which originate from different dialect areas), as in *Bäumlein* 'little tree', *Bäumchen* id., but *Männlein* can be just a 'little man', not a 'male (animal)'. *Fräulein*, on the other hand, is lexicalized for 'Miss' (this lexeme has become obsolete in the last twenty years) and is completely distinct in meaning from *Frauchen* 'Mummy (of a dog)'.

An example of a lexical class which is often not derivational is the LIGHT VERB WITH SPECIFIER CONSTRUCTION, that is, verbs with very general meanings, such as 'do', 'take', 'hit', etc., are combined with a specifier that may belong to different word classes (nouns, verbs, or a word class of its own) in different languages. In Kaugel (Blowers and Blowers 1970), 'teach' is 'instruction give': *máne ti.kí.ru* 'instruction give.PRS.1SG > I am teaching'. Other examples are *mími te.ké.ro* 'make do.PRS.1SG > I am making something', *ápu to.kó.ro* 'ride hit.PRS.1SG > I am carrying on the shoulders', *káro li.kí.ru* 'cut take.PRS.1SG > 'I am cutting', *égele te.ké.mo* 'hunger do.PRS.3SG > I am hungry.' For the light verb slot there is a restricted number of very general verbs, such as 'hit', 'take', 'do', 'speak', 'be'. As can be seen from the examples, the meaning is not compositional and is sometimes highly idiosyncratic. The light verb with specifier construction is not rare cross-linguistically and is found in many Eurasian languages, such as Basque, Persian, and Turkish (Turkish *devam etmek* 'continuation do > continue', *iman etmek* 'believe(N) do > believe'). The light verb with specifier construction in Lezgian is highly instructive: the combination of noun/adjective + *awun* 'to do' (only *awun* 'do' and *x̂un* 'be, become' occur as light verbs) occurs in a full and in a reduced form; the full (analytic) form *k'walax awun* 'work do > to work' has the corresponding reduced (synthetic) form *k'walax.un*, where the light verb is reduced to a mere suffix. In many cases, the full forms and the reduced forms occur side by side with no difference in meaning or in use (see Haspelmath 1993: 178–83 for more details). Similarly, in Turkish some light verb combinations with *etmek* are written as one word (Lewis 1967: 154).

A lexical class which can be both morphological and syntactic is VERBS WITH DIRECTIONAL MARKERS, such as the phrasal verbs in English (*go up, go out, slow down*, etc.) and the verbs with directional prefixes in Russian, Latin, and Georgian. An intermediate case between morphology and syntax are the separable prefixes in German (see Section 4.2.3.vi above). Closely associated with verbs with directional particles are verbs with directional auxiliary verbs, such as are found in Vietnamese and other South East Asian languages (see Wälchli 2001b for a cross-linguistic consideration of directional particles, affixes, and auxiliaries).

For a discussion of LIGHT 'AGAIN' (also called repetitive), a lexical class type expressing non-emphatic 'again' (such as English re-), in a sample of 100 languages see Wälchli (forthcoming).

A type of compound which can clearly be considered a lexical class is NOUN INCORPORATION as described by Mithun (1984), who distinguishes four functions of noun incorporation that, according to her, fall into an implicational hierarchy, such that a higher function can be present in a language only if the lower functions are present as well (Table 4.1).[11]

Noun incorporation has cross-linguistically recurrent functions (or semantic types) among which some tend to occur in weakly incorporating languages, while others tend to occur only in highly incorporating languages. What characterizes a high degree of noun incorporation is not only the presence of specific functions that are not present at lower degrees, but also a higher frequency of functions that occur in weakly incorporating languages. Thus, in Huahtla Nahuatl (has functions I–III), function I in many cases provides the pragmatically unmarked means of expressing a fact such as closing a door, since door-closing is a common action. An unincorporated equivalent 'would suggest that the actor "closed the door in such a way that it cannot be opened, or that the closing of the door was in some other way

TABLE 4.1. The functions of noun incorporation

Functions (and maximal stages of development)	I Lexical compounding >	II Manipulation of case >	III Manipulation of discourse structure >	IV Classificatory noun incorporation >
Languages that have reached this maximal stage	Oceanic languages, some Mayan languages, Lahu, Nisgha, Comanche	Tupinambá, Yucatec Mayan, Blackfoot	Huahtla Nahuatl, Chukchee	Caddo, Mohawk

Source: Mithun (1984)

unusual" ' (ibid.: 860). This suggests that function I occurs more frequently in Huahtla Nahuatl than in languages which have only function I. It is also important to note that noun incorporation cannot be defined strictly in terms of morphology, especially in languages with a low degree of noun incorporation, as it is not always fully clear whether it is morphological or syntactic (see also Miner 1986).[12]

It is not possible in this subsection to provide an exhaustive list of possible lexical classes, nor can this chapter present a satisfactory survey of lexical classes. But it should be clear that there are a large number of lexical classes around still waiting for a typological treatment.

4.3.3 Co-compounds as a lexical class type

Like the classes discussed above, co-compounds are an instance of a lexical, not a grammatical class. This can be seen from the following properties of co-compounds, among other things.

Co-compounds are highly idiosyncratic. Even if they have prototypical lexical domains, where they are recurrently found in co-compounding languages, such as 'parents', 'siblings', 'people', 'face', 'animals', 'clothes', 'belongings', 'food', etc., it cannot be predicted which concepts are expressed by co-compounds in a particular language. Table 4.2 serves as an illustration of this idiosyncrasy. It indicates in which of five moderately and highly co-compounding Asian languages some selected collective and abstract concepts are expressed by co-compounds in the translation of the Universal Declaration of Human Rights. Note that the three languages on the left-hand side of the table are closely related.

TABLE 4.2. Some concepts above the basic level of conceptualization in the text of the UDHR in several co-compounding languages

	Kazakh (Turkic)	Uzbek (Turkic)	Kirghiz (Turkic)	Khalkha (Mongolian)	Vietnamese (Austroasiatic)
'food'	−	+	+	+	−
'clothing'	−	−	+	+	−
'housing'	−	+	+/−	+	−
'sickness'	+	−	−	−	+
'family'	−	−	+	+	+
'property'	−	+	−	+	+
'religion'	−	−	−	+	−

(+: co-compound; −: no co-compound)

Vacillation is very common in co-compounds. For example, in most languages with co-compounds, 'parents' can be expressed by co-compounds, but while *t'et'a.t-ava.t* 'father.PL-mother.PL' is the only conventionalized expression for 'parents' in Mordvin, Georgian has a non-compound expression *mšoblebi* for 'parents' that is more common than *ded-mama* 'mother-father > parents' (see Map 2 in Chapter 6 for a survey for 'parents').

The corresponding 'heavy form' for co-compounds is coordination (or more precisely, phrase-like tight coordination). There are one-form cognate systems, where co-compounds and coordination are not formally distinct (Section 4.4.3), and there are perhaps also two-form non-cognate systems (Modern Greek co-compounds may have derived from bahuvrihi compounds). The usual case seems to be represented, however, by two-form cognate systems (see Section 7.2.1 for a discussion of these points).

Co-compounds interact strongly with the structure of the lexicon and with other lexical classes. For example, whether there is a co-compound for 'brother(s)' depends to a large extent on whether there is a single word for 'brother' (as in Georgian, Lezgian, Hindi), and whether there are special words for 'elder brother' and 'younger brother' (as in Mordvin, Khalkha, Uzbek, Mandarin) that are combined to form a co-compound 'brother(s)'.

The coexistence of several formants adapted for compounds means the coexistence of several formally different compound patterns. This occurs frequently with co-compounds. Variation is possible with different kinds of non-relational marking and in prosodic patterns. Thus, Mari has both *at.at-av.at* 'father.also-mother.also > parents' with double additive focus particles and *ata-ava* 'father-mother' without any marker.

Of course, these few remarks do not complete the description of co-compounds as a lexical class type. Chapters 5–7 will illustrate the lexical class character of co-compounds in more concrete terms.

4.3.4 *Reconsidering lexicalization and the lexicon*

For a better understanding of the notion of lexical class we have to reconsider the structure of the lexicon and the nature of lexicalization. In my view, the widespread dictionary-metaphor concept of the lexicon, according to which it is a static list of lexemes (or listemes), is wrong insofar as it presupposes that the lexicon is more or less unchangeable and, in its mental representation, is exclusively a long-term or permanent lexicon. I do not deny that the speakers of a language—and in a metaphorical sense, language communities—have a long-term lexicon, but while such long-term lexica exist, there exist also short-term lexica. A SHORT-TERM or TEMPORARY LEXICON, however, is not a lexicon of a language community, but of more restricted discourse situations.[13] Each speech situation can have its individual short-term lexicon. If I am discussing impractical wedding presents with my hairdresser, he might introduce a Ming vase as an example, with the *Ming vase* then coming to mean more generally 'impractical present' in the specific short-term lexicon of our conversation. If I am speaking to somebody else, however, I cannot presuppose the meaning 'impractical (wedding) present' for *Ming vase*. Maybe my hairdresser will recall our conversation when I go to see him next time and, if we happen to talk about impractical wedding presents again, he might still understand *Ming vase* as 'impractical wedding present'; but certainly I would not presuppose that after a year's time he will still have maintained this lexeme.

There are also more general kinds of temporary lexica that are somewhere between the short-term lexicon of a single conversation or a single text and the long-term lexicon of a language community. In Bernese German it may happen that the word *Wanderpriis*, which means 'challenge trophy', is used in the sense of 'impractical wedding present'. This word in this sense is certainly not part of every native Bernese speaker's lexicon and is not included in any dictionary of Bernese German. It has to be located somewhere on a scale between the extreme poles of the temporary and the permanent lexica of Bernese German.

Interestingly, both *Ming vase* and *challenge trophy* are compounds and this is not mere coincidence.[14] Sub-compounds in Germanic languages are one of several devices that form lexemes of temporary lexica, which is perhaps their most important function in language use. Speakers are well aware that many lexemes are restricted to specific discourse communities (a given family, a village, readers of a particular book, fishermen, physicians) which share a certain common ground (Clark 1996: ch. 4; also ibid.: 79 regarding compounds). New lexemes always start in the short-term lexicon of small discourse communities, from where they eventually spread (to be used increasingly often by more and more speakers).

This leads us to a dynamic conception of the lexicon. The lexicon of a language community is on a scale ranging from the temporary lexica of individual texts and individual conversations to the permanent lexicon as it is presented in dictionaries.[15] The dynamic model of the lexicon leads us also to a new view about lexicalization. A lexeme of a temporary lexicon is not yet lexicalized.[16] Lexicalization consists essentially of two different, but often associated processes: DRIFT TOWARD THE PERMANENT LEXICON and DEMOTIVATION. Temporary lexemes may drift toward the permanent lexicon if they happen to be used increasingly often by ever more speakers. The cost of becoming more permanent is, however, the loss of context sensitivity because the extension to more contexts of use encourages the loss of context restrictions. Contextually dependent temporary lexemes tend to be motivated in the sense of de Saussure (*relativement motivé*, 1916: 187), insofar as they are not fully arbitrary, but somehow consist of or derive from permanent lexemes. As lexemes become more permanent (and less context-dependent) their motivation becomes unnecessary, which may lead to demotivation; words then become dissociated from the parts of which they consist etymologically. Like the drift of lexemes toward the permanent lexicon, demotivation of lexemes is a gradual process. Thus English *lord* (< *loaf-ward*) is completely demotivated, *nostril* (< *nose-thrill 'nose-hole') is almost completely demotivated (except that it retains a vague phonological similarity with *nose*) and *elbow* is on the way out of the class of sub-compounds (as its first part *ell* is not a common word in English any more).[17]

For lexical classes, the two aspects of lexicalization have diametrically opposite effects. The drift toward the permanent lexicon of lexemes belonging to a lexical class leads to an increase of the token frequency of that lexical class, thereby contributing to a higher degree of entrenchment of that lexical class in a language. Demotivation of lexemes from a lexical class contributes to the decline of a lexical class. A lexical class whose most frequent and most permanent lexemes are demotivated loses ground.

A lexical class is a salient phenomenon in a language if it has both high type and high token frequency. For a high type frequency, it is essential that a lexical class be productive in the temporary lexica of that language, in that new representatives of it are constantly formed in discourse. For a high token frequency, it is essential that some representatives are used all the time, that is, that some lexemes in that class have come a long way toward the permanent pole without being dissociated from it. This leads to the Janus-faced nature of well-established lexical classes which are both highly idiosyncratic (because of their lexicalized representatives) and highly productive (because of their temporary representatives).

The dynamic concept of the lexicon proposed here necessitates a differentiated view about the notion of morphological productivity. A lexical class may be highly productive in temporary lexica and be rather unproductive in the permanent lexicon. Actually, what is called productivity is a complex of at least two completely different phenomena only weakly related to each other: the frequency of formation of new lexemes according to a certain functional–formal pattern in temporary lexica, and the drift of these lexemes toward the permanent pole of the lexicon. New lexemes and new meanings of existent lexemes always start their development in the temporary lexicon. (Recall de Saussure's saying that nothing is in *la langue* which has not been previously in *la parole.*) Most lexemes in short-term lexica are, however, highly context-dependent, and are understood properly only in a specific context, which makes it rather difficult for them to become permanent.

Neither can opacity or transparency of certain representatives of lexical classes be treated properly in a static model of the lexicon. Many compounds are context-dependent, being transparent in a specific situation and opaque out of context. Thus a *straw tour* may be a fully transparent compound in the situation of biking holidays where you sleep in barns on straw instead of in hotels. Without this context you can hardly understand what is meant. Representatives of well-entrenched lexical classes range from contextually non-transparent lexemes of the general long term to fully context-dependent occasional formations.

4.3.5 *Differences and similarities of lexical and grammatical classes*

Besides syntactic generality which is characteristic of grammatical, but not of lexical classes, there are at least three dimensions in which lexical and grammatical classes typically differ.

1. LEXICALIZATION: Lexical classes begin to lexicalize much earlier in their evolution than grammatical classes. On the other hand, lexical classes, unlike grammatical classes, develop discourse functions (functions that are largely independent of the lexemes to which they apply) only at later stages of their evolution.
2. DOMAIN OF COMPETITION: Grammatical forms (representatives of grammatical classes) compete with forms of the same lexeme, whereas lexemes (representatives of lexical classes) compete with other lexemes (which are often not etymologically related).
3. SPECIFIC MEANING: Representatives of lexical classes typically have specific meaning ('a specific kind of X') with the consequence that the meaning of the whole is not fully compositional. This makes representatives of lexical classes an ideal means of expression for temporary lexemes. Specific meaning is not characteristic of grammatical classes in the same way.

In the rest of this section, I will concentrate on the first (and most important) dimension: early vs. late lexicalization. As was pointed out above, lexical classes typically consist of lexemes (be they permanent or temporal), and grammatical classes of inflectional forms.[18] Inflectional forms of a lexeme typically have identical lexical meaning and cluster into a paradigm. The distinction between lexical and grammatical classes, however, is not as simple as that and there are many problems with the notions of lexemes and inflectional forms.

One problem with inflectional forms is that paradigmaticity is fully developed only with grammatical classes that are already highly grammaticalized. Similarly, lexicalization in lexical classes is prominent especially in highly developed lexical classes, and as we have seen in Section 4.3.3, lexemes in lexical classes never exhibit full lexicalization, which would imply demotivation, thus removing lexemes from lexical classes.[19]

Even more problematic is that some inflectional forms look as if they were lexemes. This is the case for the so-called pluralia tantum or lexical plurals, words that occur only in the plural or that have a different meaning in the plural than in the singular (English *scissors*, Lithuanian plural *ratai* 'cart' vs. singular *ratas* 'wheel'). Similarly, in lexical classes, and especially in highly developed lexical classes, there are areas that are not—or almost not—subject to lexical restrictions and are not lexicalized at all, as in the logophoric middle and diminutives with discourse function (see above). The fact that lexical classes may have affinities to grammatical classes can already be seen from the fact that parts of lexical classes may become grammatical (passive from middle, plural from collectives, imperfective aspect from iterative).

To summarize, the difference between lexical and grammatical classes is most manifest at a medium level of their development when their characteristic features, entrenchment in the lexicon and paradigmaticity, are fully developed but they have not yet acquired features that are characteristic of the other (the grammatical or the lexical) type of classes.

From what we have found, it seems that there is no fundamental difference between grammatical classes and lexical classes as mixed cases are not rare, that is, classes that are predominantly grammatical and partly lexical, or the other way round. We might say that there is a continuum between grammatical and lexical classes, but this would not help us understand what really lies behind them.

To understand what makes the difference, we have to look at what happens diachronically in lexical and grammatical class formation. Let us look first at highly advanced stages of grammatical classes for which characteristically there are many cases of local unmarkedness. Remember from Section 2.1 that local markedness is the relative frequency of an expression in a specific domain; the plural *feet*, for example, is more frequent in English than the singular *foot* and is, therefore, locally unmarked. Local markedness is highly variable cross-linguistically for a grammatical class type, such as plural. Locally unmarked plurals occur especially in languages with highly grammaticalized plural classes, where plurals (of nouns) generally have a high token frequency. This becomes readily apparent even if only a few examples in parallel texts are considered. Table 4.3 lists the proportion of plural forms in

TABLE 4.3. Local (un)markedness of the plural of 'foot' in some unrelated languages

	Number of plurals	Total occurrences	Type of plural formation
English	4	5	Irregular
Maltese	2	3	Irregular
Songhai	3	5	Irregular
Tamil	2	4	Agglutinative
Turkish	2	5	Agglutinative
Mari	0	5	Loosely agglutinative
Bahasa Indonesia	0	5	Reduplicative
Vietnamese	0	5	Plural word

eight unrelated languages for the word for 'foot' from five places in the Gospel according to Mark (5:22, 6:11, 7:25, 9:45, 9:45), of which only one clearly refers to single foot.

While the plural of 'foot' is locally unmarked in English, it is clearly the singular that is locally unmarked in Vietnamese, Bahasa Indonesia, and Mari. It does not come as a surprise that there is a correlation between the existence of clashes between structural and local markedness (see Section 2.1; cases where the structurally marked plural is more frequent than the singular) and the type of plural formation. Irregular plural formation seems to be characteristic for languages where such markedness clashes are frequent, while loose strategies for plural formation, such as plural words and full reduplication, seem to be characteristic of plural classes with little or none of such clashes. Agglutinative plural formation is intermediate.[20]

What is important in our context is that the existence of cases of local unmarkedness of plurals is the precondition for the lexicalization of plurals. Locally unmarked forms may become lexicalized. If the relative frequency of a form approaches 100 per cent, it may become a tantum-form. A typical example of lexicalized forms of a grammatical class are pluralia tantum, which are especially frequent in the Baltic languages, Latvian and Lithuanian, and which also occur in many other languages with a highly developed plural gram (most Indo-European languages, Semitic languages), but not in languages with a weakly grammaticalized nominal plural gram. Typical domains for pluralia tantum in Latvian are vehicles and musical instruments (like other objects that consist of several parts). But while *rati* 'cart', *ragavas* 'sled', *klavieres* 'piano', *ērģeles* 'organ', *bungas* 'drum', and *durvis* 'door' are lexical plurals in Latvian, *vilciens* 'train', *ritenis* 'bicycle', *vijole* 'violin', and *logs* 'window' are not. In spite of the idiosyncratic distribution, preferred domains for lexical plurals are cross-linguistically recurrent. (For further discussion of pluralia tantum in European languages see Koptjevskaja-Tamm and Wälchli 2001: 629–37.)

Tantum-forms develop in most different grammatical classes, but only if they are highly grammaticalized. Examples are possessiva tantum, inalienable nouns which must have a possessive affix (as in Navajo '*a-kee*' 'someone's-foot'; Young and Morgan 1980: 10); definita tantum, words that occur only in the definite form, such as Hössjö Sydvästerbotten Swedish *möyja* 'bride:DEF' (Larsson and Söderström 1980), and perfecta tantum, perfects which have no corresponding present forms, such as Latin *odi* 'hate' and *memini* 'remember'.

It appears that what happens in lexical class formation is very similar to lexicalization in highly grammaticalized grammatical classes. In lexical classes there are many representatives which exhibit local unmarkedness in their lexical domain of use. For instance, for 'squirrel' in German the diminutive *Eichhörnchen* is locally unmarked in contrast to *Eichhorn* (very rarely used; the English word is etymologically a diminutive as well). In English most phrasal verbs with 'redundant' verb particle, such as *cool down, queue up,* and *cover up,* are locally marked with respect to their corresponding simple verbs (*cool, queue,* and *cover*). *Calm down,* however, occurs more often than *calm* according to Hampe (2002: 115) and is locally unmarked in English. In other languages, corresponding inchoative verbs with local affixes or particles may be more frequent or may even be the only possible variant. In German the verb for 'calm down' *(sich) beruhigen,* which always has a prefix, is not only locally unmarked, but is in fact fully lexicalized. A co-compound 'father-mother' is lexicalized if it becomes the most frequent (normal) expression for 'parents.' The difference between lexical and grammatical classes, then, is essentially that the former have never been grammatical when they start to become lexicalized. However, local unmarkedness of forms of a grammatical class begins only if the class has already spread to a high number of lexemes, ideally to all lexemes of the word class or word classes with which it is typically associated. This would mean that a perfect tantum develops only if all (or at least most) verbs form perfects. This would permit grammatical classes to be graded in their degree of 'grammaticalness', the (nominal) plural being less grammatical than the (verbal) past because plurals typically are restricted to countable nouns, whereas in languages with fully grammaticalized past grams, usually all verbs have a past form.

In lexical classes, however, local unmarkedness in certain lexical domains begins at a very early period of development, usually at a time when the class has not yet spread to many lexemes of a certain word class. There are different degrees of 'lexicality' of lexical classes. Diminutives are an example of a lexical class which may reach a high type frequency within a word class, therefore having more affinities to grammatical classes than other lexical classes.

We may conclude that grammatical classes first tend to acquire a high type frequency before they eventually start to become lexicalized, and that lexical classes first tend to lexicalize before they eventually acquire a high type frequency. It remains to add that what distinguishes word classes is both a high degree of lexicalization and a maximal type frequency. Ideally, then, a word class would consist exclusively of tantum-forms (of lexemes that may belong only to one word class) and comprise all lexemes that have a certain discourse function.

It has become clear in this section that the difference between grammatical and lexical classes is not a strict one. Some grammatical classes have areas that behave very much like lexical classes, such as pluralia tantum; some lexical classes have some properties of grammatical classes, such as diminutives. This is more evidence that what is traditionally interpreted as patterns of word formation are actually lexical classes, these being functional–formal classes of a kind similar to grammatical classes which can manifest themselves either syntactically or morphologically, and are very often intermediate between syntax and morphology.

Finally, we must address the question of the psycholinguistic nature of lexical classes. From a generative perspective, a lexical class does not represent a single phenomenon, there is no single rule by which all representatives of a lexical class can be produced. Some representatives are idiosyncratic and well-entrenched in the lexicon and will always be retrieved as prefabs from memory; others will be produced spontaneously, be it by a rule or by analogy to well-entrenched representatives. A third group can either be retrieved from memory or produced spontaneously. As a coherent phenomenon of its own, a lexical class emerges only in texts, not in the act of language production. Thus, lexical classes are an argument that linguistic competence is not simply rule-governed language production, but relies on a large knowledge about previously uttered text (see also Section 7.4).

4.4 The form of co-compounds and the problem of formal non-distinctiveness

From the traditional perspective, where all (co-)compounds are words, it is presupposed that there is always a formal difference between words and phrases, but there need not always be a formal difference between different types of compounds. However, in the lexical class approach (Section 4.3), where co-compounds are considered as a more fundamental notion than compounds, the problem of formal non-distinctiveness poses itself not only for words vs. phrases, but also for co-compounds vs. other types of compounds. Co-compounds have a strong tendency to be formally non-distinct from other linguistic phenomena, because they tend to lack any kind of formal marking. This highly restricts the validity of form as a delimiting criterion for co-compounds. Put differently, class membership may sometimes be covert in the sense of Whorf (1945/1956). There are, however, always some languages where class membership is formally transparent.

A fundamental criticism of the approach of viewing linguistic categories as distinct if, and only if, they are distinct formally, derives from Croft's work (2001: 65–83) on word classes. There are always some formal criteria by which larger classes (lumping) or smaller classes (splitting) can be formed.

The approach taken here is that co-compounds, like any cross-linguistic class or construction type, have a semantic prototype with properties on three meronomic levels, such as was pointed out in Section 1.1.2. If, in a language, there is a class of phenomena that corresponds to this semantic prototype, complying at the same time with the formal prototype of co-compounds (tight pattern consisting of at least two parts, ideally without any relational marking) and used in those domains where co-compounds typically occur, then this class can be identified as a class of co-compounds in that language, irrespective of whether it is formally distinct or non-distinct from any other class whose semantic properties contradict the semantic prototype of co-compounds. This approach implies that it may not be clear in all cases whether or not a certain class exists in a particular language. Classes are emergent, and not all classes are equally well established. A weakly developed class of co-compounds will be more difficult to identify than a well developed one. A class is stronger the more frequently it appears in texts (in terms of both type and token frequency), the more unambiguous representatives there are (such that they cannot be taken for representatives of another class or construction), and the more that class has prototypical domains of use.

Let us now look at some cases of formal non-distinctiveness.

4.4.1 Distinguishing co-compounds and sub-compounds

Co-compounds are clearly distinct formally from sub-compounds only in some languages. They may be distinct from sub-compounds by double marking, as in Mordvin (Section 1.1.1) and Vedic (Section 7.2.1). Co-compounds are, of course, also a formal pattern of their own if there are no sub-compounds, as is the case for Lezgian (Haspelmath 1993: 107).

In some other languages, however, co-compounds are formally identical with sub-compounds. This is notably the case if both sub-compounds and co-compounds are formally unmarked, as in Mandarin and Vietnamese.

Aside from clear cases of formal difference and clear cases of formal non-distinctiveness, there are also many languages where co-compounds can only occasionally be clearly distinguished from sub-compounds. Thus, in Hmong, co-compounds and sub-compounds can look very much the same, but only co-compounds can be discontinuous (Section 4.2.3.vi). In Avar, some sub-compounds have a genitive marker on the first part (Saidov 1967: 724) and are obviously formally distinct from co-compounds.

Modern Greek co-compounds often have a different gender than the words represented in their parts; in this respect they go together with bahuvrihi compounds, but certainly not with typical sub-compounds, where the gender of the head is normally the gender of the compound.

For Kannada, Sridhar (1990: 283 f) lists a number of partial differences between co-compounds and sub-compounds: co-compounds do not permit optional omission of the final vowel of the first part; in sub-compounds the initial vowel of the second part is often voiced; there is a pause juncture between the parts of co-compounds (I take the presence of pauses to be a partial difference); and the word-final -*a* in Sanskrit loanwords in the first part of compounds is 'nativized' to -*e* only in co-compounds.

Even in languages where co-compounds are normally distinct in form from sub-compounds, there may be some co-compounds which are not formally distinct. Thus, in Mordvin, there are some few co-compounds, especially figurative and highly lexicalized ones (*ul'i-paro* 'exists-good > possession'), which have no double marking. Thus, in considering whether or not co-compounds and sub-compounds are distinct from sub-compounds in form, we are confronted with Croft's (2001) lumping-or-splitting problem. It is almost always possible to find at least one co-compound that is non-distinct from another type of compound or coordination or, in the opposite case, to find at least one co-compound which is formally distinct.

But even where co-compounds and sub-compounds in various languages are non-distinct in form (completely or at least partly), we cannot deduce from this that there would be an intimate relationship between co-compounds and sub-compounds. Compounds and sub-compounds are typically non-distinct in form if they lack positive formal characteristics. And it happens to be typical for both co-compounds and sub-compounds that their formal properties tend to be purely negative. Thus, in the case of co-compounds and sub-compounds, a common form cannot be taken as evidence for a common diachronic origin (Section 1.3.2.iii). There is evidence from Sanskrit (Section 7.2.1) that co-compounds and sub-compounds which have basically the same form can have different diachronic origins. There is also evidence from typology that no universal cross-linguistic relationship exists between co-compounds and sub-compounds (Section 6.6.3). Accordingly, we may conclude that co-compounds and sub-compounds may be clearly distinct from each other even if they have exactly the same form in some languages, given that their meanings are different.

4.4.2 *Distinguishing co-compounds and serial verbs*

Some authors include verbal co-compounds under serial verb constructions (for serial verb constructions see Section 3.3.10, Durie 1997, Sebba 1987, 1994, Bisang 1986, 1992, 1995, Lord 1993, and Aikhenvald 1999).

Durie (1997: 337) discusses verbal co-compounds in Khmer under the label 'synonymic serialization'. He gives the example (2) below (the co-compound is given in boldface, my emphasis), which also contains several cases of more prototypical verb serialization (verbs are in italics):

(2) Khmer (Durie 1997: 337)
```
...?auj      niəŋ           ?ɛɛt  joo?  tγw  pɔnlɛəh       pɔnlɔət       sbae?
give         young.woman    Eet   take  go   skin          skin.serpent  skin
caol
throw.away
```
'[Now the middle part of the body] (he) gave to Eet to skin.'

According to Durie, '*Synonymic serialization* is the combining of verbs that are closely related in meaning, usually near-synonyms, but sometimes antonyms ("enter–exit"), with identical argument structures, and the two verbs are not ordered either causally or temporally.' Bisang (1992: 49) considers such examples as Mandarin *jū-zhù* 'dwell-life > dwell' and *lái-wǎng* 'come-go > come and go' as instances of a specific subcategory of serial verbs which he calls 'lexical juxtaposition'.

Now, the question is not whether these verbal compounds are either co-compounds or serial verbs, since without doubt they fall under the lexical class type of co-compound, as understood here. Similarly, they also fall under verb serialization, where this is defined, as it usually is, in a purely form-oriented way, as a sequence of two (or more) verbs in a clause without any marker of subordination or coordination. Whether it is useful to classify verbal co-compounds together with more prototypical kinds of serial verbs is another question, there being several possible lines of argument that they should not be considered as closely related phenomena.

Another question is whether it would not be useful to add some kind of semantic characterization to the definition of serial verbs. Durie (1997) takes an important step in this direction. He identifies a cause–effect relationship in many different kinds of serial verb combinations, including some grammaticalized types, such as causative, goal/benefactive, motion, and instrumental serialization. This opens the way to considering serial verbs as a functional–formal class with characteristic formal and characteristic semantic properties, which, in contrast to co-compounds, do not express coordination per se. The two (or more) parts of a serial verb construction are usually not on the same hierarchical level. One verb will be strongly grammaticalized or there will be some manner of subordinating relationship between the parts, such as in resultative verb constructions where the second verb expresses the result achieved by the event expressed by the first verb.

Another line of argument against classifying verbal co-compounds together with typical serial verb constructions derives from typology. Verbal co-compounds are not characteristic for all languages with serial verbs. Unfortunately, it is not easy to test whether there is any typological relationship between serial verbs and verbal co-compounds, because both serial verbs and co-compounds represent continuous variables, that is, there are very few languages which have many of them and there are many languages which have very few of them. As it happens, both serial verbs and verbal co-compounds are highly frequent in Sinitic[21] and South East Asian languages.[22] There are also some other languages where both phenomena occur with at least moderate frequency, as in Tok Pisin, Sentani, and Santali. Verbal co-compounds, however, are not common in the West African area of serial verb languages (Ewe, Yoruba, Ijo, etc.), while some other typical serializing languages have co-compounds only to a small extent (Yabem, see Section 6.3.8, and Haitian Creole, *alé vini* 'go come > going and coming', Mark 6:31). However, verbal co-compounds are also frequent in many languages which are not typically serializing, such as Avar, Hunzib, many Uralic languages, and Sochiapan Chinantec (see Foris 2000: 50, n. 25 who points out crucial differences between serial verbs and verbal co-compounds, 'binomial verbs' in his terminology).[23] After all, verbal co-compounds correlate much better typologically with nominal co-compounds than with typical serial verb constructions. It is possible that there are a few languages that have only verbal co-compounds and no nominal co-compounds (possibly Haitian Creole and Yabem), but verbal co-compounding remains very restricted in those languages (to generalizing verbal co-compounds; Section 5.2.2).

However, the most important argument against viewing verbal co-compounds as serial verbs comes from languages with verbal co-compounds which have a developed morphology for infinite verbs, as in the case of Mordvin. Here, verbal co-compounds can occur with both finite and infinite verb forms: *śim.ś-jarsa.ś* 'drink.PST3SG-eat.PST3SG' and *śim.ems-jarsa.ms* 'drink.INF-eat.INF'. It is not in the spirit of the notion of serial verbs to include sequences of infinite verb forms, even if some form-oriented definitions of serial verbs are so broad that they include even sequences of infinite verbs, as long as these are not overtly marked for subordination *in respect to each other*. After all, verbal co-compounds have a high degree of affinity for infinite verbs. In some languages, verbal co-compounds are almost absolutely restricted to infinite verb forms (as in Chuvash) or are always deranked (as in Kâte; see Pilhofer 1933: 96). I have not come across any language that has both infinite verb forms and verbal co-compounds restricted to finite verbs.

A further argument against considering verbal co-compounds as serial verbs is that some verbal co-compounds are in conflict with an important partial cover meaning of serial verb constructions: temporal sequencing. The aspect of temporal sequence of paired activities in natural coordination may be so insignificant in some verbal co-compounds, that it may be 'wrong' (*hysteron proteron*), as in Mordvin *vid'ems-sokams* 'sow-plow > work on the fields'.

4.4.3 *Distinguishing co-compounds and coordination*

One major advantage of the lexical class approach to compounds is that it allows for 'one-form systems' in Kemmer's (1993) terminology, or, put differently, for formal non-distinctiveness of compounds and phrases. Let us illustrate this point first in the case of sub-compounds.

Table 4.4 lists in English, Mari, Czech, and Bahasa Indonesia some designations for body parts which may be considered subordinate concepts (or at least less basic concepts than 'head', 'eye', 'nose', 'tooth', 'hand/arm', 'foot/leg', 'back', 'bone'). As was pointed out in Section 1.3.2.i, subordinate concepts are a favorable domain for sub-compounds. Body parts were chosen for this example because of their universality across different cultures.

In Mari, all ten forms are clearly compounds (at least one of which is a cranberry-compound). In English, there is one clear compound, *backbone*, a former compound which has been fully lexicalized out of the class of co-compounds, *nostril* (see Section 4.3.4 above), and an intermediate case, *elbow*, which is on the way out of this class. Synchronically, there is thus one, or perhaps two, sub-compounds in English. For Czech it seems that there are no compounds at all, since nine forms are certainly not compounds (they contain only one lexical root) and the remaining one looks formally like a phrasal sequence of an adjective and a noun ('nose:ADJ hole'). In Indonesian, five forms consist of two lexemes and appear to be good candidates for compounds, but they happen to be formally identical with phrases comprised of an dependent noun and a head noun. This suggests that Indonesian has a lot of N N items in contexts where other languages have sub-compounds.

TABLE 4.4. Some body parts in English, Mari, Czech, and Bahasa Indonesia

English	Mari	Czech	Bahasa Indonesia
skull	*vuj.gorka* 'head.bowl'	*lebka*	*tengkorak*
brain	*vuj.doryk* 'head.cream_cheese'	*mozek*	*otak*
tear	*šinča.vüd* 'eye.water'	*slza*	*air mata* 'water eye'
nostril	*ner.rož* 'nose.hole'	*nos.n.í dír.ka* 'nose.ADJ.F hole.DIM'	*lubang hidung* 'hole nose'
gums	*püj.šyl* 'tooth.meat'	*dáseň*	*gusi*
thumb	*kugy.varnja* 'big.finger'	*palec*	*ibu jari* 'father finger'
el.bow	*kyner.vuj* 'ell.head'	*loket*	*siku*
back.bone	*tup.rüdö* 'back.pith/axis'	*páteř*	*tulang punggung* 'bone back'
rib	*ördyž.lu* 'side.bone'	*žebro*	*tulang rusuk* 'bone side'
knee	*pul.vuj* '?-head'	*koleno*	*lutut*

If we take German, which is notorious for compounds, it has only four in the relevant contexts: *Nas.en.loch* 'nose.PL?.hole', *Zahn.fleisch* 'tooth.meat', *Ell(en)bogen* 'ell(PL?)bow', and *Rück.grat* 'back.ridge'. Thus, Indonesian has more N N items than some typical compound languages in the relevant contexts.[24] This means that there is a formal non-distinctiveness of sub-compounds and head-dependent noun phrases in Indonesian, in the same way as there is a formal non-distinctiveness between reflexives and middles in German or French. In the relevant semantic domain for sub-compounds (where I have selected just a small sample) there is an important frequently recurrent pattern based on the combination of two lexical items in Indonesian, in the same way as in Mari and German. The Czech Adj N construction might theoretically be of this type, too. The problem is that it is not as frequent as distinct compounds typically are in a language. Therefore, the Czech Adj N pattern cannot be unequivocally identified as a lexical class, or, put differently, if it is a class of compounds, this is so only to a much lesser extent.

There are no clear criteria where the exact border lies between 'heavy forms' with some weak inclination to lexicalization, and formal non-distinctiveness of 'heavy forms' and compounds. But as soon as there is a high frequency of lexicalization, as in Bahasa Indonesia, it is clear that a lexical class of sub-compounds exists in a particular language.

Even if there is formal non-distinctiveness between noun phrases and sub-compounds, as in Indonesian, the nature of the formal pattern cannot be completely disregarded. Note that there is no relational marking in the Indonesian N N pattern, this being a tight pattern, as is typical for compounds. Generally, we may say that the tighter the pattern with two lexical slots, the more likely it is to represent some type of compound (irrespective of the question whether it is, or is not, formally distinct from a syntactic construction).

Having discussed cases of formal non-distinctiveness between 'light' and 'heavy forms' involving sub-compounds, we can now return to the question of formal non-distinctiveness between co-compounds and phrase-like coordination. First of all, it is interesting to note that systematic formal non-distinctiveness between co-compounds and phrase-like coordination is rare, at least in written language. Many orthographies have specific devices to mark co-compounds (hyphenation) or phrase-like coordination (commas), which is very helpful when co-compounds must be counted for quantitative purposes (Chapter 6). This does not mean, however, that the whole discussion above about the dubious wordhood of co-compounds was useless. If co-compounds are distinctive from phrase-like coordination formally, this does not automatically entail that co-compounds are words. Co-compounds may have some phrasal properties while being distinctive from phrase-like coordination, as in the case of Mordvin, where usually both parts of co-compounds are inflected.

However, the essential feature of co-compounds is their frequent use in word-domains rather than being formally distinct from phrase-like coordination. Thus, if no formal difference is attested, it is nevertheless possible to identify a class of co-compounds. A case in point is Manchu, a language in which noun phrase coordination is usually expressed by simple juxtaposition, even if there are also overt coordinators, and in which co-compounds cannot be distinguished formally from asyndetic coordination (at least not in the traditional orthography and in its transliteration into Latin characters). Gorelova (2002: 381) gives example (3) with three co-compounds (pair words, in her terminology) which occur in a coordinate sequence:

(3) Manchu (Gorelova 2002: 381)
Adun ulha ulin aka jetere omire ele
herd domestic_animal property thing meal drink all
hacin baitalan gemu bi.
various thing_in_daily_use everything exists
'Domestic animals, property, meals and drinks, various things in daily use, everything there is.'

The three co-compounds, *adun ulha* 'herd domestic_animal', *ulin jaka* 'property thing', and *jetere omire* 'meal drink', are clearly identifiable because of the close lexico-semantic relationship between their parts. We see from this example that co-compounds do not need any formally distinctive pattern in order to be identifiable. This does not mean that co-compounds can be kept distinct from phrase-like coordination in every particular case in languages with formal non-distinctiveness, but if they occur with appropriate frequency in typical co-compound domains, they can.

A similar situation exists in Khalkha Mongolian. While the orthography allows us to distinguish between nominal co-compounds (with space between the parts) and phrase-like nominal coordination (a comma between the coordinands; both co-compounds and phrase-like coordination use group inflection) no graphemic distinction is made between verbal co-compounds, verbal coordination, temporal sequencing, and some grammatical TMA-constructions, in all of which non-final verbs are converbs. Two kinds of converbs can appear in verbal co-compounds, the imperfective converb on -*ž/č* and the converb with the marker -*n*, similar in meaning to the imperfective converb. Consider example (15) in Chapter 6, where three verbal co-compounds occur in sequence (*er.ž survalžl.ax, ol.ž ašigl.ax, tügee.n delgerüül.ex* 'seek.CONV interview.INF, find.CONV use.INF, distribute.CONV distribute.INF = seek, receive, and impart'), anticipated here for convenience. I doubt whether all languages that distinguish co-compounds in orthography also distinguish them prosodically in spoken language. Hyphenation, rather than reflecting prosodic differences, reflects lexical differences; co-compounds are marked graphically because they form a systematic complex in the lexicon; put differently, because they represent a lexical class.

From the Khalkha example, we can see that co-compounds do not necessarily lack overt markers for coordination. Usually they do, but this is not a necessary characteristic. If a tight coordination pattern with overt coordinators frequently occurs in typical lexical domains, this is co-compounding. An unclear case is represented by N-*u* N in Tadzhik (and, similarly, in Persian). Tadzhik has two 'and'-coordinators, *va* (borrowed from Arabic) and -*u*. At least in some texts -*u* is found especially in natural coordination. It is not clear to me whether -*u* and Persian -*o* generally express natural coordination, since Persian -*o* is generally more common than *væ* in informal speech (Mahootian 1997: 72). In the Tadzhik version of the Gospel according to Mark, -*u* occurs most often in contexts where English and also languages with co-compounds have phrase-like coordination rather than co-compounds (I counted twenty-four tokens), while there is a minority of examples (I counted ten) where the N-*u* N pattern occurs in contexts where English has a single word (*mol.u mulk* 'property.and property > possessions', 10:22). Tadzhik N-*u* N is thus on the verge of representing a co-compound pattern, but if it is one, it is non-distinctive from phrase-like coordination.

However, there may be also distinctiveness between a tighter and a looser pattern of phrase-like coordination, where the tighter pattern does not represent co-compounds. In languages where a formal difference can be made between juxtaposition in natural coordination and coordination with an overt coordinator in ordinary noun phrase coordination, it is not always easy to decide whether or not the juxtaposition represents co-compounds. In order to identify co-compounds, it must be clarified that they occur in typical word-domains, which is not always evident in distinctive juxtaposition for natural coordination. Languages such as Diyari (Pama-Nyungan) and Hopi (Uto-Aztecan; Malotki 1979: 388, sentence 18.) are examples in question. In Diyari (Austin 1981: 231f), the coordinator *ya* in nominal coordination can be omitted only for pairs of human beings (especially kin terms) of the same generation, most usually of the opposite sex as in *ŋandi.yali ŋapiṛa.li* 'mother.ERG father.ERG' and *pinadu wiḻapina.li* 'old_man old_woman.ERG'. There may also be either single or double marking for case. It is true that pairs of relatives are a nuclear domain for co-compounds, but the examples given in Austin (1981) do not allow the conclusion that Diyari does, in fact, have a fully developed class of co-compounds.

4.5 Meronomic structure

The approach of describing co-compounds as functional–formal classes on a par with definiteness, future, diminutive, etc. as chosen here cannot account for their specific formal properties, notably for their being compounds. Therefore, we have to deal here briefly with another essential feature of co-compounds, their specific MERONOMIC STRUCTURE (part–whole structure). Many functional–formal classes do not have exclusive characteristic meronomic structure cross-linguistically. Co-compounds, however, have a very characteristic form. Unlike most other functional–formal classes they represent two-slot patterns (Section 2.1) with two free lexical slots, this being the essential feature they share with other types of compounds. Of course, the form of co-compounds is not universally unique; as we have seen in Section 4.4, in many languages they are not formally distinctive from other types of compounds and sometimes not even from phrase-like constructions. But it is essential to note that co-compounds universally have this specific meronomic property that they minimally contain two lexical slots (parts) and that this meronomic structure is a necessary condition for co-compounds since their meaning, natural coordination, as described in Section 1.1.2, necessarily relies on the notions of parts and whole. Moreover, since the lexical slots of co-compounds are not in a hierarchical semantic relationship, their semantic equality is often represented formally, for instance, in a tendency toward inflection harmony (Section 1.1.1), discontinuous structure with a repeated element ACBC/CACB (Section 4.2.3.vi), or alliteration (Section 5.2.6). These are just tendencies, however, instantiated recurrently in particular languages, not universal properties. In Chapter 5 we will further explore the specific semantic relationships between parts and whole in various types of co-compounds.

Even if compounds, among functional–formal classes, have a specific meronomic structure, I doubt whether they can be defined simply in meronomic terms. Compounds share their specific meronomic properties with phrase-like two-slot patterns. The best tentative definition of compounds I can come up with therefore relies on two spheres: compounds are the sum of all different lexical classes with the specific meronomic property that they minimally contain two free lexical slots.

To summarize, my approach to compounds differs essentially in the following points from the traditional approach. It is functional rather than formal. Form, meaning, and especially use (domain and frequency) are considered together in their interplay. It proceeds bottom-up and considers co-compounds, sub-compounds, etc. as basic and compounds as secondary, while the traditional approach is top–bottom. Finally, it is typological; co-compounds are considered first of all as a cross-linguistically recurrent class type rather than an individual phenomenon in an individual language.

4.6 Conclusions

In traditional morphology co-compounds are tertiary concepts, indirectly defined by way of two intermediate concepts: word and compound. In this chapter I have developed a different approach to co-compounds which treats them as being a more basic notion than compounds. Co-compounds are viewed as a functional–formal class type in a way similar to grammatical class types, such as future, plural, and passive; they need not necessarily be realized as words.

However, co-compounds are not grammatical classes, but lexical classes, like many other phenomena traditionally treated in derivation and compounding. A major part of the chapter has been devoted to the question how lexical classes differ from grammatical classes, and it was shown that the differences tend to be a matter of degree. This is a further argument for grammatical and lexical classes to be treated within a similar framework.

If co-compounds are considered functional–formal classes, there need not always be a formal difference between a class of co-compounds in a particular language and other lexical classes and constructions in that language. Thus, we can identify several cases of formal non-distinctiveness, as between co-compounds and sub-compounds, between co-compounds and serial verbs, and between co-compounds and coordination.

Notes

[1] Bickel and Nichols (forthcoming) distinguish between words and 'formatives'; formatives are morphological entities that cannot require or undergo agreement, and cannot head phrases. Cases are formatives, adpositions are words. In my opinion this does not solve the problem since (a) many languages lack head and dependent marking, so that we often lack criteria to decide, (b) for some case markers, like the Estonian comitative, it is not clear whether they actually consist of two markers (genitive + comitative), leaving us with the choice between one case formative or case plus adposition, and (c) the authors speak of 'agreeing case' which violates their definition of cases as formatives.

[2] Interestingly, DiSciullo and Williams (1987) implicitly convey evidence against their own claim that the lexicon is unstructured, if they speak of English phrasal verbs, such as *look up, throw up*, which they mention as examples for listed syntactic objects, as a system or as a construction (ibid.: 5 and 6).

[3] Etymologically 'illegitimate child'.

[4] Clippings in compounds are also characteristic of American Sign Language (Liddell and Johnson 1986, Klima and Bellugi 1979: ch. 9).

A kind of clipping is also found in Russian 'stub' compounds (most of which are typical Soviet words) such as *zapčast'* 'spare part' < *zapasnaja čast'* 'in_stock part > id.' (Spencer 1991: 346).

[5] Of course, it is problematic to consider the German verbs with separable prefixes as compounds anyway, because separable prefixes are a closed class of local adverbs, whereas compounding typically involves words or stems belonging to a productive word class, such as nouns and verbs.

[6] The final consonant letters *b, d, g, j, m, s, v* (and zero) indicate tones. *-s* in *chaws* is caused by tone sandhi. After high tones (*b, j*), among other things, zero (middle level tone) may become *s* (low level tone).

[7] Fixed order may be relevant if the word order in noun phrases is free, as in Tagalog. The elements in Tagalog noun phrases may occur in any order and are linked by *-ng* (after consonant or *n*) or *na* (after consonant), thus 'a rich child' is either *anak na mayaman* 'child LINK rich' or *mayama.ng anak* 'rich.LINK child'. In compounds, there is still overt linking after consonant or *n* (*ng*), but not after other consonants

(zero) and the order is fixed: head-dependent, *anak-mayaman* 'child-rich > a person born to wealth', *baro.ng-pamparti* 'dress.LINK-party > party dress' (Schachter and Otanes 1972: 107–11).

While spoken languages tend to have fixed order in compounds with respect to head and dependent, in signed languages this is not the case to the same extent. The different location of the signs in the signing space may be more important than the head-dependent relationship. In Swedish Sign language 'rat', which is expressed by a bahuvrihi compound of the signs TOOTH-YELLOW, has the order head-dependent, in spite of the preferred order dependent-head in such compounds, because the sign for TOOTH is signed in a higher position than that for YELLOW and signs with higher location tend to precede signs with lower location in compounds (Wallin 1983).

[8] Bybee and Dahl (1989) use the term gram as a shortening for grammatical morpheme, under which they include also periphrastic expression and such marking strategies as reduplication, stem change, and ablaut. Consider also that a single gram may be realized by completely different marking strategies (the past in English may be marked by a suffix or by ablaut).

[9] The middle in Latin is traditionally called passive as the passive and the middle in Latin are not formally distinct.

[10] For an excellent cross-linguistic survey see Jurafsky (1996) who does, however, downplay the idiosyncratic component of diminutives.

[11] Noun incorporation is sometimes viewed as a process on a par with compounding (Bybee 1985), sometimes as a kind of compounding (Sapir 1911/1990, Anderson 1985: 55).

[12] In Southern Tiwa, incorporation is obligatory under certain fully syntactic conditions. This might represent a case of grammatical incorporation (see Frantz 1990 and the literature given there).

[13] Cf. also Anward and Linell (1975/76: 116; my translation): 'Many syntactic expressions are on the verge of, have the preconditions for, lexicalization; some of them are temporarily lexicalized (in individual "conversations"), and part of them may continue to be lexicalized permanently.'

[14] For convenience I have chosen to exemplify temporary lexemes here with new meanings to already existing lexemes. The same point could, of course, also be made with completely new forms, even if you never know in which temporary lexica the 'new' forms already exist or existed.

[15] But even the permanent lexicon is not really 'permanent' as it changes diachronically. Its most stable component is the base vocabulary that historical linguists reconstruct for proto-languages which usually happens to denote items that are highly frequent in all kinds of discourse or that are not responsive to cultural changes, such as the concepts represented on the Swadesh list (Samarin 1967: 220ff). We know from the limitations of the historical-comparative method that even this most permanent lexicon is not really permanent either.

¹⁶ Not every collocation of morphemes or words is a temporary lexeme. A lexeme, even a temporary one, must express a kind of conceptual unit, which explains why lexical classes are predestined for the expression of temporary lexemes. Lexical classes, like sub-compounds, co-compounds, noun incorporation, diminutives, etc., typically express conceptual units.

¹⁷ But note that even fully transparent compounds, such as *Rice Krispies*, can have reached a considerable degree of demotivation (Wray 2002: 3).

¹⁸ In my understanding, neither lexemes nor inflectional forms are restricted to morphology. That is why I avoid the term 'word form', which is in use as an alternative for inflectional form (Haspelmath 2002: 13).

¹⁹ In a similar way grammatical classes actually represent incomplete grammaticalization, since the last stage in grammaticalization is the complete loss of distinctive marking (Dahl 2001).

²⁰ The singular–plural ratio cannot, of course, be directly predicted from the way plurals are formed. Plural formation in English, for example, is mostly agglutinative (*-s*) even if there are many cases of local markedness.

²¹ For Chinese, there seems to be some diachronic evidence that co-compounds and resultative verb compounds (which are instances of cause–effect serialization) developed at different stages diachronically (Feng 1998: 246).

²² It is also characteristic of these languages that they can have juxtapositional coordination of verb phrases with objects which fall under the formal definition of serial verbs, but which are rather untypical for serial verb constructions from a semantic point of view, such as Mandarin *tā tiāntiānr xiě xìn huì kè* 'S/he everyday write letters receive callers = He writes letters and receives callers every day' (Bisang 1995: 146).

²³ Motion verbs are illustrative examples for making clear the difference between verbal co-compounds and serial verbs. Typical co-compounds of motion verbs are generalizing (frequentative, habitual), such as 'come-go > go and come repeatedly', 'ascend-descend > go up and down repeatedly'. In serial verbs, the two verbs either have a different function (manner and path, path and deixis) or are two different, but not opposite, components of a complex motion such as in the following Zoque example with root serialization: *qui'm.dʌjcʌy.u barco'.ojmo* 'ascend.enter.COMPL boat-LOC > he climbed into the boat' (Mark 6:51).

²⁴ It is clear that more examples are needed to prove this in a statistically significant manner.

5

A Semantic Classification of Co-compounds

In this chapter, a semantic classification of co-compounds is introduced based on the semantic relationship between the parts and the whole (Sections 5.1–5.2). In Section 5.3 contextual sharpening in co-compounds is addressed and in 5.4 I discuss some types of compounds that are closely related to co-compounds. Finally, Section 5.5 considers how specific contexts may favor the use of non-conventionalized co-compounds.

Since it is always essential to examine co-compounds in their functional contexts, I concentrate on texts (original ones where possible) chosen from a number of moderately co-compounding languages of Eurasia, primarily Erźa Mordvin, but also Chuvash and Georgian. The texts are mainly from literary fiction, the major sources for examples being two Erźa Mordvin novels (D = Doronin 1993, A = Abramov 1973), a Chuvash reader (TL = Xlebnikov 1993), and a Georgian reader (Hewitt 1996). In these texts, the frequency of co-compounds is higher than in texts from West European languages, but much lower than in texts from East and South East Asian languages (Chapter 6). In East and South East Asian languages, we also find some specific co-compounds that do not appear in moderately co-compounding languages, motivating the discussion of examples from languages such as White Hmong, Vietnamese, and Khalkha in some sections of the chapter. The study of the contextual motivation of co-compounds—one of the major aims of the chapter—is more profitably undertaken on moderately co-compounding languages, as the threshold for using co-compounds is higher there, making it easier to investigate contextual factors in specific passages. It was also convenient, on occasion, to discuss examples taken from other languages in addition to those already selected. Generally, a bias toward Eurasia could not be avoided. For co-compounds in other continents see the Appendix to Chapter 6.

5.1 The basis of the semantic classification

A semantic classification can only be an approximation because there are always several possible ways of classifying linguistic phenomena semantically. This follows necessarily from the nature of cover meanings (Section 1.3.2.ii). Furthermore, since semantic classifications concern linguistic entities that have both semantic and formal components, semantic classifications of linguistic phenomena are never purely semantic. Thus, a classification of compounds cannot do without the notions of parts and wholes of compounds, which remain basically formal notions, even if only their meanings are considered. Each of the several possible ways of semantically subclassifying a functional–formal class has advantages and disadvantages. Consider, for example, the excellent monographs by Kemmer (1993) and by Geniušienė (1987) on the middle/reflexive. Kemmer takes the meanings of middle verbs as wholes as the basis for her classification (see Section 4.3.1) and completely disregards the meaning of the verb stems from which middle verbs are derived; this entails that whether the corresponding non-middle verbs are transitive or intransitive is disregarded. Geniušienė, on the other hand, bases her semantic classification on the relationship between reflexive verbs and their corresponding non-reflexive verbs; consequently, her classification cannot cope with deponents.

Co-compounds can be classified semantically on the basis of: (a) the semantic relationship between the parts; (b) the semantic relationship between the parts and the whole; (c) the meaning of the whole (irrespective of the meaning of the parts); (d) the semantic relationship between the whole and the contexts in which co-compounds are is used, or a mixture of (a), (b), (c), and/or (d).

In descriptions of co-compounds in a given language, there is often a classification on the basis of (a) the semantic relationship between the parts. For Mandarin, Anderson (1985: 50) distinguishes compounds of synonyms, *yì-si* 'idea-thought > meaning'; compounds of antonyms, *cháng-duǎn* 'long-short > length'; and parallel compounds, involving grammatically similar, but non-synonymous elements, *fù-mǔ* 'father-mother > parents'. A major problem with such a classification are compounds of antonyms since, in most co-compounds whose parts are not synonymic, there will be some kind of antonymic relationship. Kononov (1960: 136) thus classifies Uzbek *ota-ona* 'father-mother > parents' (corresponds exactly to Mandarin *fù-mǔ*) as an antonymic compound.

Basis (c), the meaning of the whole, is not used because it is impracticable for a neat classification into types. If the meanings of the parts of a compound are completely disregarded, few criteria remain for an unequivocal semantic classification. Basis (d), the semantic relationship of the whole form and its context is not practicable for all co-compounds but does have to be taken into consideration for those co-compounds that are highly context-dependent (Section 5.5).

For my semantic classification of co-compounds, I choose (b) the semantic relationship between the parts and the whole. This basis of classification was implicit in Haspelmath's (1993: 108) description of co-compounds in Lezgian. According to him 'N$_1$ and N$_2$ may belong closely together as a pair' (ADDITIVE CO-COMPOUNDS) as in *buba-dide* 'father-mother > parents', 'they may represent two particularly salient members of a larger class' (COLLECTIVE CO-COMPOUNDS) as in *xeb-mal* 'sheep-cattle > domestic animals', 'they may have more or less the same meaning... so that the resulting compound has roughly the same meaning as N$_1$ and N$_2$,' (SYNONYMIC CO-COMPOUNDS), and 'in a few cases one member of such a co-compound does not occur independently' (IMITATIVE CO-COMPOUNDS) as in *ajal-kujal* 'child-IMI > child'. It must be emphasized right from the beginning that co-compounds consisting of the same parts may belong to different semantic types depending on how the meaning of the parts is related to the meaning of the whole. Thus, 'plate-spoon' can be additive '> a plate and a spoon, plates and spoons' or collective '> cutlery and crockery (including knives, forks, and cups)'. Let us now consider examples of the different types of co-compounds in turn.

5.2 The various semantic types of co-compounds

Table 5.1 lists the semantic types of co-compounds as discussed below and gives one example for each type.

5.2.1 *Additive co-compounds*

In a narrower sense, additive co-compounds denote pairs, each consisting of the parts A and B. In a broader sense, they denote sets exhaustively listed by A and B (possibly without the pairing of A and B). Let us begin the discussion with pairing additive co-compounds, which are clearly the prototypical ones, as they are found in more languages and also more frequently in texts. Examples include Mordvin *t'et'a.t-ava.t* 'father.PL-mother.PL > parents', Georgian *da-dzma* 'sister-brother', and *xel-p'exi* 'hand-foot'. The parts of pairing additive co-compounds are typically relational nouns, notably

TABLE 5.1. The various semantic types of co-compounds

Semantic type	Example
Additive co-compound	Georgian *xel-p'exi* 'hand-foot'
Generalizing co-compound	Khalkha *ödör šönö.güj* 'day night.without > day and night'
Collective co-compound	Chuvash *sĕt-śu* 'milk-butter > dairy products'
Synonymic co-compound	Uzbek *qadr-qimmat* 'value-dignity > dignity'
Ornamental co-compound	Erźa Mordvin (epic) *vel'e-śado* 'village-hundred'
Imitative co-compound	Khasi *krpaat krpon* 'pray IMI > worship'
Figurative co-compound	Vietnamese *giang hồ* 'river lake > adventurous'
Alternative co-compound	Erźa Mordvin *vest'-kavkst'* 'once-twice > once or twice'
Approximate co-compound	White Hmong *ob peb* 'two three > some'
Scalar co-compound	Old Uyghur *ulug.i kičig.i* 'big.its little.its > size'

kinship terms and body parts. Frequent instances include parts denoting clothes, as in Mordvin *ponks.t-panar.t* 'trouser.PL-shirt.PL > shirt and trousers'. Additive co-compounds can, however, also be verbs, as in Mordvin *śimems-jarsams* 'to drink-eat' (paired in persons, each of which eat and drink), *šlams-nardams* 'wash-dry > wash and dry one's body', *oršams-karśems* 'put_on_clothes-put_on_shoes > put on clothes and shoes'. In verbal co-compounds, pairing is sometimes less manifest. Thus, 'eat-drink' is not necessarily pairing with respect to the objects of the actions. In pairing additive co-compounds, A and B are either related to the same reference object (often a person) 'father and mother of somebody', 'eating and drinking by somebody', or A and B are CONVERSES (Cruse 1986: 231ff; A is the reference point for B and B for A) as Mordvin *t'et'a.t-ćora.t* 'father.PL-boy/son.PL', *mird.t'-ńi.t'* 'husband.PL-wife.PL', and 'guest-host' in (1) from Georgian:

(1) Georgian (Hewitt 1996: 153)
...t'it'o   k'at'xa   xel.ši   mi.s.c'.es
...each   goblet   hand.in   thither.IO:3.give.AOR3PL
st'umar-masp'indzel.s.
guest-host.DAT
'[Then they poured the vodka into goblets and] gave a goblet each into the hands of the guest and the host.'

BIPARTITE TOOLS such as Georgian *mšvild-isari* 'bow-arrow > bow and arrows' or Chuvash *xut-kărantaš* 'paper-pencil > paper and pencil' are also a kind of converse, where A and B are each other's reference points.

In Mordvin *ikel'e.t'-udalo.t (kudo)* 'in_front_of.PL-behind.PL (house) > a house with a front and back room, a house with five walls' and *vere.t'-alo.t' (kudo)* 'above.PL-below.PL (house) > a two-story house', there is an external reference point (house).

Examples for non-pairing co-compounds are Mordvin *skal.t-vaz.t* 'cow.PL-calf.PL > cows and calves' and *sivel'.t'-lovso.t* 'meat.PL-milk.PL > meat and milk'. They express collection complexes which are exclusively listed by the parts. Non-pairing additive co-compounds are less 'stable' than pairing ones. They often require contextual motivation (Section 5.5). Thus *skal.t-vaz.t* is used in a negative context in D 174: 'they do not allow to hold cows and calves'.

An important factor for lexicalization is whether a co-compound can be used generically. Mordvin *pat'a.t-jalaks.t* 'elder_sister-younger_brother' can only denote a collection complex of two siblings; it is not used to denote siblings in general (including pairs of elder brothers and younger sisters), in contrast to Vietnamese *anh em* 'elder_brother younger_sibling > siblings' which, however, is already a collective co-compound (elder sisters are not explicitly listed). Some additive co-compounds become collective co-compounds when used generically. Thus, Mordvin *ponks.t-panar.t* 'trouser.PL-shirt.PL' may be used both for the collection complex of a pair of trousers and a shirt worn by somebody (additive) and for clothes in general (the latter more rarely, as there is a separate word for 'clothes').

5.2.2 *Generalizing co-compounds*

Generalizing co-compounds denote general notions such as 'all', 'always', and 'everywhere', depending on whether they are item-, time-, or space-generalizing. Their parts express the extreme opposite poles of which the whole consists. Examples are Mordvin *či.ńek-ve.ńek* 'day.NEK-night.NEK > day and night', *t'ese-toso* 'here-there > here and there > everywhere', *pokš.ńek-viški.ńek* 'big.NEK-small.NEK > everybody'.

Generalizing co-compounds are rather widespread cross-linguistically. At least some of them, most typically 'here-there' and 'day-night', also appear in languages, such as Nanai and Tagalog, that do not have other co-compounds in texts. For Tagalog *araw-gabi* 'day and night' is the only co-compound mentioned in Bloomfield (1917), and it is also the only co-compound in the Tagalog translation of the Gospel according to Mark. On the whole, generalizing co-compounds seem to be more widespread cross-linguistically than additive co-compounds. A language with additive co-compounds is very likely to have some generalizing co-compounds, whereas the opposite seems not to be true.

In some languages generalizing co-compounds can have a special marker. In Mordvin -*ńek*, a morpheme of comitative origin (probably through the mediation of natural comitatives; Section 3.3.1), is added to both parts of time- and item-generalizing co-compounds (as in the examples given above). However, this marker is lacking in space-generalizing co-compounds, perhaps due to the fact that these are less prototypically generalizing and often have the meaning '> at some places' instead of '> at all places' (see below); such expressions often have local case markers (*seŕ.s-kel'e.s* 'height.ILL-width.ILL > in height and width').

In Mari, generalizing co-compounds often have double marking for possession, *jüd.žö-keč̣y.že* 'night.its-day.its > day and night' (Šketan 1991: 5). Besides, there may also be double marking with additive focus particles (*jüd.et-keč.et* 'night.also-day.also'), or both possessive affixes and additive focus particles (*jüd.ž.at-keč̣y.ž.at* 'night.its.also-day.its.also'; N. Gluxova, p.c.).

In Khalkha Mongolian, generalizing co-compounds are marked by the nominal negative marker -*güj*: *ödör šönö.güj* 'day night.without > day and night', also *šönö ödör.güj* id., *xögšin zaluu.güj* 'old and young', *tom žižig.güj* 'big and small', *dotor gadaa.güj* 'inside and outside'. Khalkha makes a distinction between *end tend.güj* 'here-there.without > everywhere' and *end tend* 'here-there > at some places'. We might consider them as two separate types: generalizing and indefinite. For simplicity, and because both generalization and indefiniteness are quantitative notions, I choose to treat them as a single type. In some co-compounding languages there are indefinite pronouns that are co-compounds, Mordvin *mińeń-śunoń* 'IMI-IMI > all kinds of, different kinds of' (a reciprocally imitative co-compound; see Section 5.2.6). The third possibility for a co-compound 'here-there' is to mean '> on both places/sides', in which case it is intermediate between additive and generalizing as in the following Georgian example: *Alazni.s akʻetʻ-ikʻitʻ napʼir.eb.zed*... 'Alazani.GEN hither-thither shore.PL.on = On both banks of the Alazani (river)' (Hewitt 1996: 157).

Space-generalizing co-compounds can be static or directional. Typical directional co-compounds are Mordvin *tʼej-tov* 'hither-thither', *mekev-vasov* 'back-long(ADV) > back and forth', *veŕev-alov* 'up-down > up and down'. In some languages there are also verbal generalizing co-compounds, such as in (2):

(2) Erźa Mordvin (Buzakova et al. 1993: 309)
Kuź.i-valg.i   mekš.ava   čuvto.ntʼ   kuvalma.
ascend:PRS3SG-descend.PRS3SG   bee.mother   tree.GEN:DEF   along
'The queen bee flies up and down around the tree.'

In Georgian the only existing inflected verbal co-compounds are generalizing and have the same verb root in both parts with opposite directional prefixes (see Section 2.4.3).

Very close to generalizing co-compounds are source-goal compounds, such as Mordvin *pe.d'e-pe.v* 'end.ABL-end.LAT > from end to end' (D 115) and Georgian (Hewitt 1996: 233) *t'avit'-p'examde* 'head.INST-foot.ADV:until > from head to foot', where generalization in a static situation is expressed pseudo-dynamically by means of a pseudo-source and a pseudo-goal (fictive motion, in the terms of Talmy 2000, I: ch. 2). Lambrecht (1984) has pointed out that corresponding expressions in English and German, such as *from top to toe* behave similarly as bare binomials, as they lack articles.

In extension from iterated reversives and iterated opposite directions, verbal generalizing co-compounds sometimes express iterative movement. The parts of the co-compound may then be synonymic, such as in Mordvin *čarams-veľams, veľams-čarams* 'turn-turn > twist and turn', *čekams-pokams* 'make the sign of the cross, pray < id.-IMI'. Verbal co-compounds are also used for the expression of unharmonious, shaky movements, such as in *nurśe.ź-pupoŕ.kśńe.ź* 'rock.CONV-stumble.FREQ.CONV > rocking and stumbling' (D 164). The examples discussed in the last part of this section are actually already synonymic and imitative co-compounds (see below) and show how generalizing and synonymic co-compounds may be related.

5.2.3 Collective co-compounds

There is no simple unequivocal way to define collective co-compounds because there are different relevant criteria which do not always agree, notably the following: (a) the parts do not exhaustively list the whole, (b) the whole comprises all meanings having the properties shared by A and B, and (c) collective co-compounds are co-compounds which denote collectives (Section 1.1.2).[1] Examples that meet all three criteria are Chuvash *sĕt-śu* 'milk-butter > dairy products', *erex-săra* 'vodka/wine-beer > alcoholic beverages', *xyr-čărăš* 'pine-spruce > conifers'. The explicitly listed elements are usually prototypical members of the superordinate concept. Moreover, the explicitly listed elements are often chosen in a way that they form functional units if paired (such as 'plate-spoon'), which testifies to the diachronic evolution of many collectives from additive co-compounds.

It is not possible to draw a clear boundary between collective and additive co-compounds if criteria (a) and (b) do not apply at the same time. Mordvin *penč.t'-vakan.t* 'spoon.PL-plate.PL' is clearly additive if it denotes a concrete pair of a spoon and a plate used together, and clearly collective if it denotes generally '> cutlery and crockery', but remains intermediate if it denotes an unordered accumulation of plates and spoons (but no knives, forks, cups). Similarly, *ponks.t-panar.t* 'shirt.PL-trouser.PL' is additive if it denotes a shirt and a pair of trousers worn by the same person, collective if it denotes unpaired clothes in general, but intermediate if it denotes an unpaired accumulation of shirts and trousers or the clothes worn by a person including other clothes, such as a coat. There are also cases which systematically meet (a) and fail to meet (b), for example, co-compounds denoting '> face', such as White Hmong *ntsej muag* 'ear eye > face', Avar *ber.k'al* 'eye.mouth > face' (eyes, ears and noses belonging to a face always belong to an ordered set, but two of them cannot exhaustively list the whole), or Mordvin *kudo.t-kard.t* 'house.PL-stable.PL > farmstead'.

Criterion (c) considers only the meaning of the whole and applies to those co-compounds that denote collectives (similar to the German collectives and hyperonyms with *Ge-*, such as *Geschirr* 'crockery', *Gewand* 'cloth', *Gesicht* 'face', *Gehöft* 'farmstead'; this parallel has to be considered with caution, given the idiosyncratic distribution of lexical classes in the lexicon). In Chuvash there are many co-compounds that denote collectives which are synonymic (Section 5.2.4), ornamental (5.2.5), or imitative (5.2.6) in a classification according the semantic relationship of the parts and the whole. Examples for imitative co-compounds denoting collectives are the following (phonologically similar sequences are underlined; the second part glossed as IMI does not mean anything): *vyl'ăx-čěrlěx* 'cattle-IMI > cattle, domestic animal', *kajăk-kěšěk* 'bird-IMI > birds, fowls' (German *Geflügel*), *šăm-šak* 'bone-IMI > bones, skeleton, body' (*šak* 'fish basket'; German *Gebeine*).[2] An interesting example is also Mari *küč.an-püj.an* 'claw.PROP-tooth.PROP > wild animals (literally: having claws-having teeth)' (N. Gluxova, p.c.), as neither of the parts is used to denote a particular species of wild animal; the set is not formed by non-exhaustive listing of possible members, but by listing characteristic properties of the members.

To summarize, there are few collective co-compounds which meet all relevant criteria, while there are many which are closely related either to additive co-compounds or to synonymic, ornamental, and imitative ones. Wherever it is necessary to distinguish collective co-compounds sharply from other types in this study (for quantitative purposes), I understand the class in the narrowest sense possible, where all cases that can be classified as additive, synonymic, ornamental, or imitative are not counted as collective cases, except where otherwise indicated. Thus, criterion (c) is to be disregarded because it characterizes the meaning of the whole rather than the semantic relationship between the parts and the whole.

Collectives are a specifically nominal domain. Verbs rarely denote collective notions. At first glance, (3) from Meithei with a co-compound 'sleep-eat' seems to be an exception to this, but consider the nominalization markers on the verbs and the 'nominal' meaning of the whole '> basic comforts':

(3) Meithei (Chelliah 1997: 275)
əy.khoy.di tum.bə   čá.bə   čə́ŋ.lək.t.e.
I.PL.DLMT   sleep.NOML eat.NOML   enter.DISTAL.not.ASRT
'Our basic comforts were not a consideration.'

5.2.4 Synonymic co-compounds

In SYNONYMIC CO-COMPOUNDS the parts A, B, and the whole C all have the same or almost the same meaning (there is no contrast in meaning between A, B, and C, and A and B are not at opposite poles). Examples are Chuvash *uj-xir* 'field-field > fields', Mordvin *trams-kastams* 'nourish-bring_up > bring up', *vel'ams-čarams* 'turn-turn > twist and turn'. In spite of this simple characterization, synonymic co-compounds are not a homogenous type. They may have affinities either to collective, to additive, or to generalizing co-compounds.

We will first discuss different kinds of synonymic co-compounds that are related to collective co-compounds. In languages where collective co-compounds dominate, such as Chuvash, some (nominal) synonymic compounds are clearly related to collective co-compounds; Chuvash *uj-xir* 'field-field > fields' (German *Gefilde*), *jumax-xalap* 'story/talk-story/talk > conversation/talk' (German *Gespräch*), *jură-kĕvĕ* 'song-motif/melody > songs' (German *Gesang*), *sasă-čĕvĕ*, *sas-čĕv* 'sound-sound > sound' (German *Geräusch*), *văj-xal* 'force-force > force', *xĕn-xur* 'pain-bad_luck/want > want/need', *tujăm-sisĕm* 'feeling-feeling > feeling (German *Gefühl*)'. All these examples are classified as collectives (*sobiratel'nye*) in Skvorcov (1982). To understand the transition from collective to synonymic co-compounds, one has to distinguish between mixed and homogeneous collection complexes. Synonymic co-compounds, in contrast to collective and additive co-compounds, express homogeneous collection complexes in which (ideally) every element contained in them can be referred to by both parts of the co-compound. This explains the affinity of synonymic co-compounds with plurality, even if there is no language in which synonymic co-compounds have developed to a fully grammaticalized plural. However, for some lexemes it comes close. In Vietnamese, the synonymic co-compound *mồ-mả* 'grave-grave > graves' is used predominantly for plural, and a simple form used for singular reference (without exception in the translation of the Gospel according to Mark). Similarly, *bạn hữu* 'friend friend > friends' is used especially for plural reference.

In some languages with moderate-to-high levels of co-compounding, abstract notions are often expressed by synonymic co-compounds, as exemplified by Uzbek and Khalkha: Uzbek *qadr-qimmat* 'value-dignity > dignity', *azob-uqubat* 'pain-torture > torture', *sihat-salomatlik* 'health-health/security > well-being', *sabr-bardosh* 'patience-patience > tolerance', *ahloq-odob* 'morals-sense_of_tact > morality'; Khalkha *šašin šütleg* 'religion-faith > religion', *üzel bodol* 'view-thought > opinion', *gem buruu* 'vice/guilt-false/guilt > guilt', *uls tör* 'state/people-government/state > politics', *xüsel zorig* 'wish/will-courage/willpower > will', *jas ündes* 'bones-root/base/nation > nationality' (all examples from the UDHR). There is reason to believe that abstract synonymic co-compounds develop after the model of collective co-compounds, since both collectives and abstracts denote terms above the basic level of lexical categorization and lack 'shape', and derivative collectives, such as the German collective, can also express abstracts.

Additive co-compounds that express overlapping coordination (Section 3.3.3 above) come close to being synonymic co-compounds. Such a case is 'mountains-hills'. The concepts hills and mountains are not as clearly distinct as the concepts fathers and mothers or hands and feet. To say that there are mountains in a region is almost tantamount to saying that there are mountains and hills in a region. In the Georgian example given below, the major function of the co-compound 'mountain-hill' is to add emphasis (it is synonymic rather than additive).

(4) Georgian (Hewitt 1996: 171f)
Rač'a mt'a-gor.iani adgili.a...
Rač'a mountain-hill.ADJ place.is...
'Rach'a is a place of mountains and hills; [here, without considering the local conditions, it is certainly difficult to implant every kind of technology.]'

A similar case is Mordvin *pŕa.so.st-tarad.so.st* 'head/treetop.INESS.their-branch.INESS.their > with their tops and branches (of trees)' (D 52).

In verbs, it is often difficult sharply to distinguish additive from synonymic co-compounds. Consider (5) from Mordvin with two co-compounds with semantically overlapping parts 'tug-pull' and 'lick-smack':

(5) Erźa Mordvin (D 63)
Nockovt.ń.i.t'-tark.ś.i.t' ej.se.st,
tug.FREQ.PRS.3PL-pull.FREQ.PRS.3PL PP.INESS.POSS3PL
nol.ś.i.t'-ćamka.j.i.t'...
lick.FREQ.PRS.3PL-smack.FREQ.PRS.3PL

'They [wolf cubs] tugged and pulled at them [teats], licked and smacked, [but their bellies did not become full. The teats were empty.]'

Sometimes there seems to be a part–whole relationship between the parts of a synonymic co-compound, as in example (6) from Lezgian:

(6) Lezgian (Haspelmath 1993: 453)
Tamu-tara   peš   aqʰaj.na   q'ud   pad   qacu
forest:ERG-tree:ERG leaf open.AOR   four   side   green
x̂a.nwa.j.
become.PF.PST
'[It was the time of spring.] The forest made the leaves shoot, the environment had become green.'

Contextually, 'forest' and 'trees' are, however, synonymic. The use of the co-compound 'forest-tree' in (6) is expressive, as is 'four side' which actually means 'all sides'. The generalizing connotation of the co-compound (spring breaks through everywhere) is not expressed in the more rational English translation.

Groups of verbs that often form synonymic co-compounds in Mordvin, especially in the novel of Doronin, are verbs of checking and testing, and verbs of tidying and arranging; for example, *onkst.ń.ems-lovo.ms* 'measure.FREQ. INF-count.INF', *lad.ś.ems-valakavt.ń.ems* 'rearrange.FREQ.INF-smooth_out. FREQ.INF > rearrange'. Generally, inchoative verbs are often co-compounds in Mordvin: *trams-kastams* 'nourish-bring_up > bring up', *tejińgadoms-alkińgadoms* 'become_narrow-become_low'. It is very likely that these synonymic or near-synonymic co-compounds consisting of verbs of checking, verbs of arranging, and inchoative verbs are an extension of generalizing verbal co-compounds.

Synonymic co-compounds may thus develop from collective co-compounds (Chuvash *jură-kĕvĕ* 'song-motif/melody > songs'), from additive co-compounds (Mordvin *prasost-taradsost* 'their treetops and branches'), and from generalizing co-compounds (Mordvin *vel'ams-čarams* 'turn-turn >-twist and turn'). Different groups of synonymic co-compounds may therefore emerge in various languages at different stages of development. In Chuvash synonymic co-compounds developed mainly from collective co-compounds. In Mordvin synonymic co-compounds developed from generalizing and additive co-compounds.

A specific and rare group of synonymic compounds are the explicative co-compounds, in which there is an explicative 'or'-relationship between the parts (see Section 3.3.7 for explicative disjunction). These occur in the Mordvin translation of the Gospel according to Mark, where the co-compound *undoks.ost-koŕon.ost* 'root.their-root.their' is consequently used to denote 'root(s)'. The normal word for 'root' in Erźa Mordvin is *koŕon*. As this is a borrowing from Russian, some authors instead use the word *undoks*, meaning, rather, 'hollow space in a tree'. (*Undoks* is explained in the glossary as Russian *koren'* and as Mordvin *koŕon*.) So, in *undoks.ost-koŕon.ost* the second part explains that the first part means 'root'.

5.2.5 Ornamental co-compounds

Ornamental co-compounds contain a semantically empty part that does not contribute to the meaning of the whole and may even be misleading. Examples are Mordvin (in the traditional ritual language) *vel'e-śado* 'village-hundred[3] > village', *viŕ.ga-ukštor.ga* 'forest.PROL and maple.PROL > through the forest' (see example (3b) in Chapter 1).

The following examples from White Hmong show how a collective co-compound can become an ornamental one. The co-compound *xyoob ntoo* 'bamboo tree' is used collectively in the sense of 'major forms of vegetation' parallel to 'rodents-birds > (smaller wild) animals' in the passage, 'Do not kill animals and birds for your pleasure; for every one has also one life and does not wish to die. Do not cut down bamboos or trees for your pleasure, but only those that you really need.' (Mottin 1980: 86, Bisang 1988: 94). In (7) below, however, 'bamboo-tree' (discontinuous, in boldface) refers to a single tree, not to bamboos and trees. As 'tree' happens to pair with 'bamboo' in Hmong (in collective contexts originally), 'bamboo-tree' is used in Hmong instead of the simplex 'tree' when there is a need for emphasis (note also the reduplication of the verb) as here in the generalizing context (see Section 5.5.3):

(7) White Hmong (Mottin 1980: 24, Bisang 1988: 40)
Ces kam kam ceg **xyoog** ceg **ntoo** lov
Then fight fight branch **bamboo** branch **tree** break
tag.
completely.
'[Now Yau Pu left the younger brother alone and fought with the older brother in the treetop.] They fought and fought that all branches of the tree fell down.'[4]

There is no abrupt transition between collective and ornamental co-compounds. Consider the Khalkha example *navč naxia* 'leaf bud/young_ shoot > leaves, foliage' which is collective (or even additive) in spring (see the example in Vietze 1969: 122), but ornamental in autumn. Chuvash *šěr-šyv* 'land-water > land' may sometimes be interpreted as generalizing or additive, but in *šěr-šyv tipsen* 'when the land dries up' (Skvorcov 1982: 414) it is ornamental. Ornamental co-compounds occur predominantly in texts with a high frequency of co-compounds.

5.2.6 *Imitative co-compounds*

In imitative co-compounds, one part is a cranberry-word, which has no meaning (not even a misleading meaning, as in ornamental co-compounds). Typically the whole will have the same meaning as, or be a collective of, the meaningful part, while the meaningless part (glossed as IMI) is in most cases phonologically similar (by rhyme, alliteration, or assonance) to the meaningful part (thus, the name imitative). Examples are Turkish *çoluk çocuk* 'IMI child > wife and family' and *sıkı fıkı* 'close IMI > intimate' (Lewis 1967: 236).

There are also imitative co-compounds with two meaningless parts which may be called reciprocally imitative co-compounds, where each part phonologically imitates the other: *allak bullak* 'IMI IMI > topsy-turvy', *abuk sabuk* 'IMI IMI > nonsensical'. Reciprocally imitative compounds seem to be widespread cross-linguistically in certain domains (notably chaos and disorder).[5] At least some of them are double ideophones (Section 5.4.4) and there is reason to believe that they are quite different from simple imitative co-compounds; they are not associated with synonymic and collective co-compounds and they have a wider cross-linguistic distribution. In this section, I concentrate on simple imitative co-compounds.

Imitative co-compounds are especially frequent in some Austroasiatic languages, such as Khasi and Khmer. In both languages, alliteration[6] is very prominent (Ourn and Haiman 2000, Jacobs 1979/1993 for Khmer). Consider (8) from a Khasi mythic tale (imitative co-compound in boldface, a synonymic discontinuous co-compound is underlined):

(8) Khasi (Rabel 1961: 149, 156/7)
 ...ban <u>dem</u> ban ŋu' bat ban **krpaat krpon** na ka
 ...to <u>bow</u> to bow with to pray IMI of DEF:F
 bnta 'uu khuon.bnriw
 share DEF:M child.human
 '[The cock promised to go before the Lord] in order to worship and to speak on behalf of man.'

In (8) there is first a discontinuous synonymic co-compound (underlined), then a continuous imitative co-compound (boldface). Imitative co-compounds cannot always be sharply distinguished from synonymic and ornamental co-compounds; consider, for example, Khasi *ka laj ka let* 'DEF:F mistake DEF:F transgression/wrongs > the mistake'. Co-compounds generally have a tendency to develop phonological similarities between the parts (probably because co-compounds that happen to have phonological similarities between the parts tend to be used more frequently). An example in point is Turkish *kanlı canlı* 'having blood and life > robust' (Lewis 1967: 236). On the other hand, phonological similarity between the parts can compensate for a lack, or a lower degree, of semantic similarity between the parts. 'Blood' and 'life' make a better pair in Turkish as the words happen to be phonologically similar. Imitative co-compounds show that the formal component cannot be completely disregarded in a classification of co-compounds. While consideration of the semantic relationship between the parts is most important, formal similarity in co-compounds can compensate for lacking semantic similarity. Sound symbolic processes, such as alliteration and ablaut, are very common in both co-compounds and phrase-like tight coordination. Languages that do not have ablaut in other forms may show ablaut in co-compounds, as in Mordvin (mostly *u-a*) *lušmo.t-lašmo.t* 'valley.PL and canyon.PL', *lutk.t-latk.t* id., *nuč̌k-nač̌k* 'criss-cross', *tult-talt* 'pretext' (see also Pott 1862: 65–9).

Very complex co-compounds consisting partly of analyzable and partly of unanalyzable parts can be found in ritual texts in Kiranti (Sino-Tibetan) languages. In Mewahang oral ritual texts (Gaenszle 1998), co-compounds (Gaenszle's term is binomials) typically consist of two three-syllabic parts, the last syllable of each being identical. For instance, the ritual expression for 'birds' is *chechoŋwa dochoŋwa* (the normal word for 'bird' being *choŋwa*), while the prefixed syllables *che-* and *do-* have no identifiable meaning. Gaenszle, using a notation developed by N. J. Allen for 'binomials' in Rai languages (Kiranti), represents the relationship between the ritual form and the ordinary form in this example as aB.cB. Capital letters (A, B, C) symbolize 'free-standing words' of the ordinary language. Small letters (a, b, c) symbolize non-identifiable elements and (s, t) affixes from ordinary language. Underlined are elements that represent the global meaning (or an approximation) of the expression. The matter is complicated because some elements are only diachronically transparent. Thus, *situluŋ thuŋmaluŋ* 'stones' is represented by a*B.C*B, **luŋ* 'stone' being a common Kiranti root, but not the usual word for 'stone' in Mewahang. The need for such a complicated notation system testifies to the many ways in which co-compounds that contain partly analyzable and partly unanalyzable parts can be structured in the Mewahang ritual language.

Phonologically similar parts occur not only in co-compounds, but also in phrase-like tight coordination patterns, such as binomials in Germanic languages. They are especially frequent in Old Germanic poetry where their use is favored by the principles of verse structure: Old English *wicga ond wæpna* (GEN.PL) 'saddle-horses and weapons', *bearnum ond bróðrum* (DAT.PL) (Heyne 1888: 1046a and 1075a).

To summarize, although co-compounds with phonological similarities of their parts seem to occur in all languages that have co-compounds, and while reciprocally-imitative compounds in certain restricted domains are omnipresent cross-linguistically, there are nevertheless very few languages where imitative compounds are frequent, as is the case for some Austroasiatic languages, such as Khmer and Khasi.

5.2.7 *Figurative co-compounds*

In figurative co-compounds C belongs to another domain than A and B. Examples are Mordvin *piže-ožo (vajgeľ.se)* 'yellow-green (voice.INESS) > (with a) shrill/angry (voice)', Chuvash *xura-šur* black-white > [see] (much) harm'. Figurative co-compounds in Mordvin and Chuvash typically favor certain collocations ('yellow-green' with 'voice' and 'black-white' with 'see'). The transition between metonymy and metaphor is fluent; Mordvin *kišť'ems-morams* 'dance-sing > be happy' can be used either in a situation involving singing and dancing (metonymy) or in a situation where there is no singing and dancing (metaphor). In other figurative co-compounds, such as Mordvin *pijems-paloms* 'cook-burn > suffer pain; be excited', the parts are hardly ever to be taken in their literal meaning. For the development of metaphor by intermediation of metonymy see Heine et al. (1991, ch. 3).

In central Eurasian languages, figurative co-compounds are rather infrequent except for co-compounds of body parts (as is well-known, body part terms generally tend to be extended metaphorically). Examples include the following:

(9) Erźa Mordvin: figurative co-compounds from body parts
 pŕa.ń-polda.ń (śind'e.ź) 'head.GEN-ancle.GEN (break.CONV) >
  headlong, head over heels'
 pŕa.t-piľ'g.t' (čavoms) 'head.PL-foot/leg.PL (beat) > writhe with pain'
 langa-pŕa.va 'surface/back_of_animal:PROL-head.PROL >
  somehow'

Figurative co-compounds often express extreme qualities (see also Section 5.5.2 for the role of emphasis). Emphasis may also be associated with less conventionalized figurative uses of body parts in co-compounds, which is evidence for a continuous transition from non-figurative to figurative co-compounds:

(10) Erźa Mordvin (D 29)
... avol'a.żev.s.t' ked'.se.st-pŕa.so.st.
wave.INCH.PST.3PL hand.INESS.their-head.INESS.their
'They made vehement signs of refusal (when offered horsemeat).'

Figurative co-compounds can also express abstracts, as in (11) from Chuvash with a co-compound consisting of two verbal nouns *laru-tăru* 'sit.VN-stand.VN > sitting-standing > state (of affairs)':

(11) Chuvash (TL 138)
Politkomissar śĕr-šyv.r.i   lar.u-tăr.u   śinčen mĕn
Politcomissar land-water.LOC.its sit.VN-stand.VN   about   what
pĕlter.et?
proclaim.PRS3SG
'What does the politcommissar announce about the state of the country?'

Figurative co-compounds are more frequent in East and South East Asian languages than in the moderately co-compounding languages of the Volga basin. Here are some conventionalized examples from Mandarin Chinese *yún.yŭ* 'cloud rain > - sexual intercourse (the sport of cloud and rain)', *yŏng.yuè* 'skip. leap > enthusiastic (< leap, jump)', *máo.dùn* 'spear.shield > contradictory, inconsistent; contradiction' (Chao 1968), and Vietnamese *ảnh-hu'ở'ng* 'shadow/image-echo > influence', *giăng-hoa* 'moon-flower > flirtation, ephemeral romance'.

Figurative co-compounds are common in Vietnamese folk poetry. A major function of the traditional Vietnamese alternate chants of boys and girls from which (12) is taken (co-compound in boldface; see Nguyên 1933) is to sound out whether a particular singing partner is a potential partner for marriage. If the real subject of interest is addressed in an indirect (metaphorical) way, nobody loses face in the case of failure. Singing partners have to prove their wit and skill by spontaneously producing elaborate parallel verses. (This is an impressive example for ritualization in language in the sense of Haiman 1994.)

(12) Vietnamese (Cordier 1914: 33, 29)
Anh   tuy   là kẻ   **giang hồ**...
Elder_brother(=I)   though be person **river lake**
'(He:) Though I am a person who travels along rivers and lakes (Though I am a merchant and adventurer).'

In some cases, only one part of a co-compound is figurative; the whole is then rather an ornamental co-compound, as in White Hmong *ua tsov ua rog* 'do **tiger** do war > do war'.

In contrast to central Eurasia, where metaphor in co-compounds is infrequent, formal registers (poetry, prayer) in some Meso-American languages abound with a kind of word pair (often called couplets) that are instances of parallelism rather than co-compounds, even if the elements of Classical Nahuatl couplets are occasionally juxtaposed or even univerbated, as in *altepetl* 'city' < *a.tl tepe.tl* 'water hill' (*-tl* is a so-called absolutive used on unpossessed nouns). Lexicalized co-compounds are, however, very rare. Word pairs are more often separated by particles or occur in shorter or longer parallel segments. Even the few word pairs that can be considered as fully lexicalized often occur discontinuously. Couplets in Classical Nahuatl, in contrast to co-compounds in Eurasian languages, are almost always metaphorical. Most word pairs are directly associated with the ancient Aztec political or religious culture: *yn j.petla.tzin in i.cpal.tzin* 'DEF his.mat.HON DEF his.seat.HON > throne, government', *cujtlapil.lj ahtlapal.lj* 'tail.CL wings/leafs(tree).CL > the common people, subjects (in contrast to the head)' (Lehmann and Kutscher 1949, Bierhorst 1985). That the metaphorical couplets were essential to the Classical Nahuatl culture rather than deeply rooted in the Nahuatl language structure can be seen from the fact that almost none have survived in modern Nahuatl dialects. Metaphorical couplets, however, are still much in use in formal registers in Mayan languages and elsewhere in Meso-America. Consider the following example of Zinacantán Tzotzil from Bricker (1974: 369ff): *k'u yepal mi li' čamala* **hlumale**?/*mi li' čamala* **kač'elale**? 'How long have you been waiting here for my **earth**?/How long have you been waiting here for my **mud**?' 'Earth and mud' here stand metaphorically for 'arrival'. For a discussion of couplets in Meso-American languages, see Bricker (1974), Gossen (1974a, 1974b), Brody (1986), Edmonson (1971, 1973), Garibay (1953, 1961), and Bierhorst (1985). See also the Appendix to Chapter 6 for co-compounds in Meso-America.

5.2.8 *Alternative and approximate co-compounds*

In alternative and approximate compounds there is a disjunctive relationship between the parts. C is A or B, or, if approximate, some value which is close to A or B (while A and B will always be very close to each other). Examples include Mordvin *vest'-kavkst'* 'once-twice > once or twice', *kavto-kolmo* ' two-three > two or three', *mel'at-manit'* 'last_year-two_years_ago > one or two years ago', and Chuvash *pĕr-ikĕ* 'one-two', *ult-śič* 'six-seven'. As alternative co-compounds are typically used in contexts of a lack of evidence, or where the exact value does not matter, alternative co-compounds can rarely be sharply distinguished from approximate ones (see also Section 3.3.6). Thus, in most contexts, *vest'-kavkst'* 'once-twice' can also mean 'three times'. Alternative and approximate co-compounds are very common cross-linguistically. They occur even in West European languages where additive compounds are (almost) absent. Like generalizing co-compounds they are, however, very restricted in type frequency, mainly to numbers and periods of time, such as 'today-tomorrow', 'Saturday-Sunday > Saturday or Sunday', 'July-August > July or August'. Co-compounds for periods of time can, of course, also be additive. The same holds for Udmurt *nyl-pi* 'girl-boy', which can mean either '> child (a single child)' (alternative) or '> boy(s) and girl(s)' (additive), and Sentani *do-mijɛ* 'man-woman > human being' (alternative) or 'man/men and woman/women' (additive).

Certain combinations of numerals may be conventionalized to have the meaning of 'some' and are then clearly approximate and not alternative. In Hmong *ob peb* 'two three' means 'some (from 2 to 10)'. To express 'two or three' one has to use an explicit disjunction: *ob* CL *los peb* CL 'two CL or three CL':

(13) White Hmong (Mottin 1978: 177)
'Kuv muaj ob peb tug.'
I have two three CL
['And you, how many children do you have?'—] 'I have some (two-three) children.'

Lexicalized alternative co-compounds may be found even in weakly co-compounding languages such as Estonian (*enam-vähem* 'more-less > more or less, about'), Latvian (*daudz.maz* 'much-little > about'), and Lithuanian (*maž.daug* 'little-much > about'). The implication of a lack of evidence is so strong with alternative co-compounds, that there seems to be no language where only alternative and not approximate co-compounds are found.

Not all alternative co-compounds derive from disjunction. The Mordvin alternative co-compound *a t'eči-vandi* 'not today-tomorrow > today or tomorrow' obviously derives from a sentence with a negative conditional clause: '(if) not today (then) tomorrow'.

Approximate co-compounds come very close in their meaning to indefinite generalizing co-compounds of the type 'here-there > somewhere'.

5.2.9 *Scalar co-compounds*

Scalar co-compounds denote an abstract scale with opposite qualities A and B as extreme poles. A and B are adjectives, C is rather a noun (but the noun–adjective distinction is not very clear in some of the languages concerned).

Examples are Tibetan *srab-mthug* 'thin-thick > density', *skyid-sdug* 'happy-sad > luck, livelihood', Old Uyghur *ulug.i kičig.i* 'big.its little.its > size' (von Gabain 1950: 161), Khalkha *xaluun xüjten* 'heat cold > temperature', *orlogo zarlaga* 'income expenditure > budget', Tokharian A *kāryap pärko* 'loss profit', *tsopats mkältö* 'big small > size' (Aalto 1964: 75). Scalar co-compounds are characteristic of East and South East Asian languages with a high level of co-compounding.

In contrast to Tibetan, Khalkha, and Vietnamese, Mandarin has scalar co-compounds as the most usual expressions for such quality scales as 'length' or 'height'. In Vietnamese, Khalkha, and Tibetan other expressions are more frequent for these concepts. In Khalkha *urt bogino* 'long short' can be used in a question, as in:

(14) Khalkha Mongolian (Enkhtuvshin Dorjgotov, p.c.)
 Šireen.ij urt bogino (n') xed.ve?
 table.GEN long/length short (its) how_much.INT?
 'How long is this table?'

In a corresponding affirmative sentence only *urt* 'long/length' is used instead. In Tibetan scalar compounds may be used for specific poetic purposes as in (15) from the Gezar epic poem where a thrilling and uncertain horse race will reveal a divine decision:

(15) Classical Tibetan (Stein 1956: 285 III17a, Beyer 1992: 105f; see also Helffer 1977)
 rta-la **mgyogs-bul** zer ba de / nub-gcig rtsa-chu[7]
 horse-LOC **fast-slow** say:NOML SFP night-one grass-water
 bzaŋ-ŋan zer / pho-la **rgod-źan** zer-ba de / ñin-gcig
 good-bad say man-LOC **strong-weak** say-NOML SFP day-one
 rluŋ-rta **dar-rgud** yin.
 wind-horse **flourish-fall** is
 'What is called the speed of a horse / is the quality of one night's feed (grass-water); / what is called the strength of a man / is the flow (flourishing and fall) of one day's luck (wind-horse)'.

There is much evidence that scalar co-compounds develop from alternative/approximate co-compounds in direct and indirect questions. In Khalkha (14) some scalar co-compounds may occur in questions but cannot occur in corresponding affirmative clauses, while in the Classical Tibetan example above, the first and the third scalar co-compounds can be still interpreted as a kind of indirect question ('Whether a horse is fast or slow...whether a man is strong or weak'). Alternative co-compounds consisting of opposite

154   *A Semantic Classification of Co-compounds*

adjectives in questions do also occur in moderately co-compounding languages such as Mordvin which lack scalar co-compounds, as in (16):

(16) Erźa Mordvin (D 272)
  Koda   pand.i.t'   t'enk,   Jemel'an Spiŕidonič,
  How   pay.PRS.3PL   you:DAT   J. S.
  par.st'e-beŕań.ste.
  good.ADV-bad.ADV
  'How are you paid, J. S., well or badly?'

The function of the alternative co-compound in (16) is to restrict the number of possible answers to two. Moving farther eastward, such alternative co-compound tags become more common in questions about qualities. Consider (17) from Colloquial Tibetan:

(17) Colloquial Tibetan (Vollmann 1989/90: 18–19)
  ŋy: maŋ   nʲuŋ   kʰa ⁿdɛ   du?
  money   many   little how   EX
  'How many money is (there)?'

maŋ nʲuŋ may be used for '> mass, quantity' also in other, non-interrogative contexts. In Mandarin Chinese, finally, the normal interrogative 'how much' is an alternative co-compound: *duō.shao* 'much.little > how much?'

5.2.10 *Basic and non-basic co-compounds*

We may roughly classify the different types of co-compounds into BASIC (generalizing, additive, alternative and approximate, collective) and NON-BASIC types (synonymic, ornamental, imitative, figurative, and scalar). Basic types correspond better to the properties of natural coordination, such as defined in Section 1.1.2. Non-basic types do not ignore these properties fundamentally, but exhibit only some of them. The properties of natural coordination on three meronomic levels, as characteristic of co-compounds, are listed below. In contrast to phrase-like tight coordination patterns, in co-compounds there is no (or only minimal) contrast between the parts and co-compounds are typically used in word-domains:

- PART–PART: inherent coordination between parts, close lexico-semantic relationship between parts, parts belong to the same taxonomic level, no (or only minimal) contrast between the parts;
- PARTS–WHOLE: close lexico-semantic relationship between parts and whole, whole is superordinate in relation to parts, pair sharpening (Section 5.3) determines the meaning of the parts;

- WHOLE: whole expresses a conceptual unit typically of a word-domain, whole expresses a superordinate or plural concept

Non-basic co-compounds show only some semantic characteristics of natural coordination. In imitative co-compounds, we can speak of coordination only in analogy to other types. This is also the case for binomials with cranberry-words. *Kith and kin*, where *kith* has no meaning of its own, can be considered as an instance of coordination only because we know from other instances of coordination that the construction X *and* X has the cover meaning of coordination. We may then, by pair sharpening (Section 5.3), hypothesize that *kith* means something that is closely associated to *kin*. In the same way, imitative co-compounds can be interpreted as co-compounds in analogy to co-compounds of the basic types, especially as they retain some features of natural coordination (for example close lexico-semantic relationship between a part and the whole). So each non-basic type does not conform to the semantic prototype of co-compounds in some respects, but still conforms to it in others. What is problematic in figurative co-compounds is especially the parts–whole component (parts and whole belong to different semantic domains), while the part–part component tends to remain in conformance to natural coordination. It may even be the case that certain features of the semantic prototype are strengthened while others are absent. Thus, in synonymic co-compounds, only the most minimal semantic contrast imaginable is present between the meanings of the parts.

Thus, the idea behind the classification of semantic types into basic and non-basic is to show that the non-basic types are generally less prototypical than those of the basic types. But even within the basic types, some are more and some are less prototypical. The co-compound 'day-hour > all the time' is less prototypical than 'day-night > all the time'. Even co-compounds that share all the features of natural coordination can be ranked according to their degree of prototypicality insofar as these features differ. For instance, 'father-mother > parents' is more prototypical than 'father-son > father and son, male members of a family', because 'parents' is the tighter conceptual unit than 'male members of a family'. Accordingly, the former occurs in more languages and is usually more frequent in texts than the latter.

Prototypical co-compounds are thus the semantic nucleus of a functional–formal class of co-compounds. Non-prototypical co-compounds can be part of a lexical class of co-compounds only if there are also prototypical co-compounds. A similar situation exists in gender where phonological or morphological gender assignment occurs only if there is a nucleus of semantic

156   A Semantic Classification of Co-compounds

gender assignment (Corbett 1991: 63), even if the difference is more gradual in co-compounds than in gender.

Generally, less basic co-compounds profit in their interpretation from basic co-compounds. It is the basic co-compounds which establish a lexical class of co-compounds with its cover meaning of natural coordination. Less basic co-compounds which deviate in their meaning from prototypical natural coordination rely in their interpretation on the existence of this cover meaning, at least as far as they are not yet conventionalized.

It is important to note that the synchronic and diachronic semantic relationships between different semantic types of co-compounds do not coincide, which makes it impossible to draw *the* semantic map of co-compounds. Figure 5.1 is an attempt to represent the synchronic semantic relationships between the types. Basic and non-basic types are distinguished. The former are subdivided into connective and disjunctive, the latter into macro-synonymic (at least one part is a close synonym to the whole) and translational (the whole belongs to a domain other than that of the parts).

Diachronic semantic relationships do not coincide with synchronic semantic relationships, however those are represented in detail. For example, ornamental co-compounds can develop from additive co-compounds (Classical Chinese *ju-ma* 'carriage-horse > carriage'; Feng 1998: 215), or from collective co-compounds (White Hmong *xyoog ntoo* 'bamboo tree > tree'; see Section 5.2.5), with which they are not closely related synchronically. On the other hand, ornamental co-compounds—closely associated to synonymic co-compounds synchronically—cannot develop from synonymic co-compounds. As

Basic:	Connective		Disjunctive
	generalizing		
	additive		alternative
	collective		approximate
Non-basic:	Macro-synonymic		Translational
	synonymic		scale
ornamental	imitative		figurative

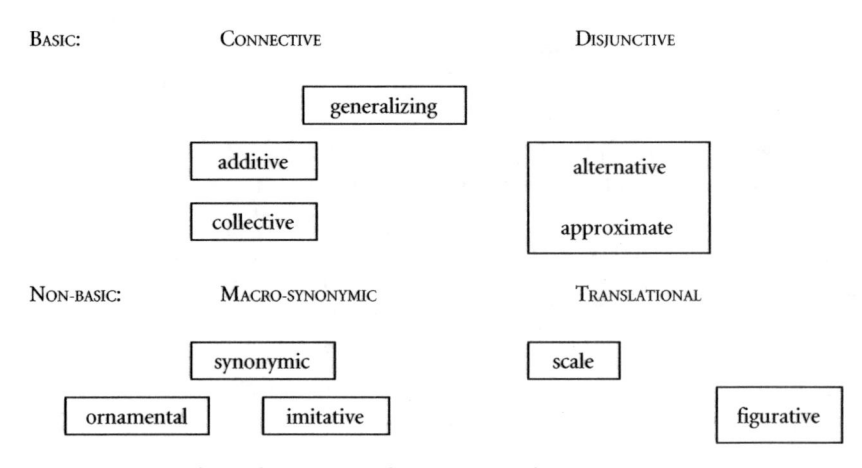

Fig. 5.1. Basic and non-basic types of co-compounds

many cases of diachronic relationships between different semantic types of co-compounds have been discussed in detail in various subsections of Section 5.2 above, let it suffice here to refer to the relevant passages in a non-exhaustive list:

- ADDITIVE > COLLECTIVE in cases, such as 'elder_sister-younger_brother' and 'plates-spoons', when specific use becomes generic use (Sections 5.2.1 and 5.2.3).
- GENERALIZING > SYNONYMIC in cases of cyclic events, such as 'twists-turns' (5.2.2).
- COLLECTIVE > SYNONYMIC if the meaning of the whole is collective and the parts–whole relationship synonymic (5.2.4).
- ADDITIVE > SYNONYMIC in cases of partial overlap, such as 'mountains-hills' (5.2.4).
- COLLECTIVE(/ADDITIVE) > ORNAMENTAL Hmong 'bamboo-tree' (5.2.6).
- COLLECTIVE(/ADDITIVE) > IMITATIVE 'fathers-old_fathers' > 'fathers-IMI' in Mordvin (5.2.3).
- ADDITIVE > FIGURATIVE Mordvin 'sings-dances' > 'be happy' (5.2.7).
- ALTERNATIVE > APPROXIMATE 'one-two' > 'some' in contexts of lack of evidence (5.2.8).
- ALTERNATIVE > SCALAR 'big-small' > 'size' in indirect questions (5.2.9).

With the exception of scalar co-compounds, which occur in the languages of Eurasia only at a highly advanced stage of co-compounding, there is no implicational hierarchy among co-compounds suggesting which semantic types occur first, as has been postulated by Mithun (1984) for noun incorporation (Section 4.3.2). Almost all types may occur to some extent at early stages of co-compounding. However, there seems to be a hierarchy of dominance and increase. Non-basic types of co-compounds (especially synonymic co-compounds) are the major increasing group where languages move from moderate to high levels of co-compounding, additive co-compounds are the major increasing group where languages move from a lower to moderate levels, while generalizing (and alternative) co-compounds tend to remain more or less constant. This hierarchy of increase GEN(ALT) > ADD > (COL >) SYN will be examined in Chapters 6 and 7.

There are several reasons for the lack of an absolute hierarchy, the most important being that all semantic types found in co-compounds (except maybe for scalar[8]) are already present in phrase-like tight coordination; for example Turkish *mal ve mülk* 'possession and possession > possession' for a synonymic binomial and English *kith and kin* for a imitative binomial. If synonymic co-compounds in South East Asia easily outnumber additive co-compounds, this means that the evolution of co-compounds cannot

158   A Semantic Classification of Co-compounds

simply consist of a formal transition from phrase-like tight coordination to co-compounds. During the evolution of co-compounds some semantic groups will become more, and some less, dominant, and, as will be shown in Chapters 6 and 7, this does not happen in completely unpredictable ways.

5.3 Contextual semantic sharpening in co-compounds

Most words and morphemes are polysemous, having a variety of different conventionalized and occasional meanings, although they mostly have only a single meaning in specific uses. The process by which the actual meaning of a word or morpheme is selected in a specific context was introduced as CONTEXTUAL SEMANTIC SHARPENING in Section 1.3.2.v. In co-compounds, different sharpening processes are at work, the most important of which is PAIR SHARPENING with the following directive: select or adapt the meanings of the parts of a co-compound in such a way that they pair. This means, notably, that the meanings of the parts are selected in a way that they are on the same hierarchical level and that they have the closest possible lexico-semantic relationship. Let us look at some simple examples of co-compounds from Erźa Mordvin in order to see how pair sharpening works:

- In the additive co-compound *t'et'a.t-ava.t* 'parents', *ava* means '1. woman, 2. mother'. Meaning 2. 'mother' is selected by pair sharpening because this meaning pairs with *t'et'a* 'father'.
- In the additive co-compound *t'et'a.t-ćora.t* 'father and son', *ćora* means '1. (young) man, 2. son'. Meaning 2. 'son' is selected by pair sharpening.
- In the generalizing co-compound *ejkakš.ńek-pokš.ńek* 'children and adults', *pokš* means '1. big (adj.), the big one, 2. adult (adj., noun), 3. eldest (of siblings), the eldest one'. Meaning 2. 'adult' is selected in the co-compound by pair sharpening.
- In the generalizing co-compound *či.ńek-ve.ńek* 'day and night', *či* means '1. sun, 2. day, 3. second component of abstract nouns, 4. homestead', *ve* means 'I 1. one, 2. only; II night'. The meanings 2. 'day' and II. 'night' are selected by pair sharpening.
- In the collective co-compound *kudo.v-či.v* '(toward) home', *kudo* means 1. 'house, 2. (front or back) room' (the meanings of *či* were given above). 1. 'house' and 4. 'homestead' are selected by pair sharpening. (The meaning 'toward' comes from the lative suffix -*v*).
- In the approximate co-compound *val-kavto* 'a word or two', *val* has the lexical meaning 'word'. This meaning is not close enough to *kavto* 'two' to form a co-compound with it. The meaning of *val* is sharpened to 'one word' and the meaning of *kavto* to 'two words'.

It is important to note that pair sharpening can only determine the meaning of the parts in co-compounds, not the meaning of the whole co-compound or the semantic relationship between the meaning of the parts and the whole. Thus, a co-compound whose part meanings have been sharpened to 'night' and 'day' may be either a generalizing co-compound '> (all) night and day' or an additive co-compound '24 hours'. Whether it is the latter or the former depends on the context or conventionalization.

The meanings of the parts of co-compounds after pair sharpening are not overlapping in the examples considered above. In many cases the resulting meanings of the parts are antonyms. It seems that whenever pair sharpening can lead to a pair of antonyms, it does.[9] It is therefore possible that a specific process of antonymic sharpening applies wherever possible in co-compounds along with pair sharpening. Let us now look at synonymic co-compounds where there is no antonymic sharpening, but where synonymic sharpening occurs together with pair sharpening.

In the discussion of synonymic co-compounds above we have presupposed a very broad understanding of synonymy that does not coincide with the traditional use of the term. In lexical semantics synonymy is notoriously problematic as there are virtually no synonyms in a strict sense (see Schuster 1995: 11–36 for a survey of different approaches). As an alternative, Cruse (1986: 88) proposes the term cognitive synonyms, words whose substitution never changes the truth value of any sentence (he gives the example *violin : fiddle*), but vary in stylistic differences. But even cognitive synonyms are rare and certainly do not cover the range of semantic flexibility that can be observed in synonymic co-compounds. We are therefore in need of a different concept of synonymy.[10]

That synonymy is a problem in co-compounds can be easily demonstrated by the confrontation of different synonymic co-compounds that have one component in common but differ in meaning, such as the following examples from Khalkha: *ajan žin* 'X—caravan > caravan (of people and animals across the desert)' and *ajan dajn* 'X—war > (military) campaign, march'. How can the same word *ajan* form synonymic compounds with two different words, *žin* 'caravan' and *dajn* 'war', that are certainly not synonyms?

In the Mongolian–Russian dictionary (Luvsandendev 1957), four meanings for the word *ajan* are distinguished: 1. *putešestvie* 'trip', 2. *karavan* 'caravan', 3. *poxod* '(military) campaign, march', and 4. *dal'njaja doroga* 'long way'. Now, in co-compounds there is generally pair sharpening with the meaning of the parts selected according to the directive to select or adapt the meanings of the parts of a co-compound in a way that they pair. Given the meaning 'caravan' for *žin*, the best candidate from the conventional meanings of *ajan* is

2. 'caravan'. Given the meaning 'war' for *dajn* the best candidate from the conventional meanings of *ajan* is 3. '(military) campaign, march'. After pair sharpening has taken place, a low degree of semantic contrast exists between the meanings of the pairs of the two co-compounds. When this occurs, that is, when there is a low degree of contrast between the meanings of the parts and if the meanings of the parts are overlapping, the synonymic sharpening in co-compounds may result in a complete CONTEXTUAL SYNONYMY of the parts of synonymic co-compounds. What is at issue here is not synonymy of complete lexical items (with all their meanings, called *Synonymie* 'synonymy' by Schuster 1995), but a contextual synonymy of words which have particular meanings in a specific context (called *Synonymität* 'synonymity' by Schuster). Complete synonymy is unimportant in natural languages (because almost non-existent), while contextual synonymy, the result of synonymic sharpening, is an important and frequent phenomenon in dynamic semantics.[11]

Synonymic sharpening makes it possible for the lexical meaning of parts in synonymic compounds to be quite different, as in (18) from Mordvin (from an epic poem):

(18) Erźa Mordvin (Šaronov 1994: 199)
Arś.i-čeńard.i   eś   jalga.tńe.d'e...
think.PRS3SG-mourn.PRS3SG own   comrade.PL:DEF.ABL...
'[The Tsar Tyushtya was on his way back with sorrow in his heart, he goes grieving.]
He thinks-mourns of/for his comrades: [how he could draw them out of the innards of the Snake-Mother, how he could save their white souls.]'

Arśems 'think, expect, plan, wish, try, dream' and *čeńardoms* 'rot, smolder, be in a bad mood, mourn, weep' are clearly not synonyms. However, in the specific context of this example, the contextual meanings 'think of (a defunct person)' and 'mourn' are more or less synonymic.

For ornamental co-compounds another facet of contextual semantic sharpening is relevant, elimination of superfluous meaning, which always occurs if polysemous lexemes are contextually sharpened. But while the number of possible meanings is usually reduced to one, it is reduced to zero in the meaningless part of an ornamental co-compound because none of the possible candidates fits a particular context. Thus, in Mordvin *vir̆.ga-ukštor.ga* 'forest.PROL-maple.PROL > across forest', the meaning of *ukštor* 'maple' is completely eliminated for being superfluous.

Of course, contextual semantic sharpening is most relevant for co-compounds which are not conventionalized. As soon as co-compounds are lexicalized with their specific meaning, contextual semantic sharpening need not apply for each occurrence individually because the meaning of the co-compound can be retrieved from memory.

The process of contextual semantic sharpening sheds a new light on cover meanings of two-slot patterns. In a dynamic semantic model, an important aspect of cover meanings of constructions are directives for the semantic sharpening of the lexical slots of the construction. Thus, in a construction for attributive possession, there will usually be meronomic sharpening (part-whole sharpening) if the possessor is inanimate, as in *the foot of a hill*, where *foot* must be a part of the hill and interpreted in a metaphorical sense; meronomic sharpening forces the metaphorical interpretation.

There is no room in this chapter to discuss contextual semantic sharpening in general. For our purposes, it is important to note only that contextual semantic sharpening is crucial for an understanding of how parts of co-compounds acquire their specific meanings, and as regards synonymic co-compounds, synonymic sharpening is indispensable.

5.4 Compounds that are closely related to co-compounds

In this section I shall consider some types of compounds that are closely associated with co-compounds, some of which were mentioned in Section 1.1.2.

5.4.1 *Appositional compounds*

In appositional compounds, A and B are referentially intersective (see intersective coordination in Section 3.3.2). *Wagon-restaurant* in French is a *wagon* and a *restaurant* at the same time. Often B refers to the specific function, as in French *bateau-pompe* 'ship-pump > fire boat'. Appositional compounds are not co-compounds since there is no natural semantic relationship between the parts A and B. A 'ship' and a 'pump' are quite different and these two words do not usually co-occur in coordination. It is true that there are also appositional compounds where a close lexico-semantic relationship exists between the parts, such as the adjectival compounds in German *süss.sauer* 'sweet-and-sour', *berühmt-berüchtigt* 'famous and ill-famed'. There is, however, no natural coordination in these cases (sweet food will usually not be sour, famous people are not always ill-famed). Furthermore, from a taxonomic perspective, appositional compounds are subordinate in respect to their parts, whereas co-compounds are superordinate, which accounts for the close semantic affinity between appositional compounds and sub-compounds. The appositional compound in French (*wagon-restaurant*) is often a sub-compound in English (*dining car*) and in German (*Speisewagen, Zugrestaurant*).

162 A Semantic Classification of Co-compounds

In French, there is a specific lexical class of appositional compounds. In some co-compounding languages, appositional compounds are treated formally in a similar way as co-compounds. In Mordvin, appositional compounds are hyphenated like co-compounds, śorma-peńaćamo 'letter-complaint > a letter of complaint'. The formal difference between appositional and (most) co-compounds in Mordvin is that the former have only single (final) inflection and not double harmonic inflection (including double plural marking). In Russian, co-compounds and appositional compounds look similar formally, but they tend to occur in different texts and genres. While co-compounds are almost absent from Standard Russian, appositional compounds are relatively common.

Appositional compounds and co-compounds come closest to each other in vocativic contexts as in (19) from Mordvin (see also example (43)):

(19)   Erźa Mordvin (D 169)
       Vaj,   pakśa-and.ića,   koda ton   kuvat'   uč.i.t'
       Oh,   field-nourish.NA,   how   you   long_time   wait.PST.2SG
       sok.ića.nt'...
       plow.NA.GEN:DEF
       'Oh, how long did you, field-nourisher, wait for the plower.'

The use of such appositional compounds in vocativic contexts belongs originally to a ritual context (prayer), and is often emotional (consider the use of the interjection: vaj). Typically for such appositional compounds is that the second part is purely epithetic (and therefore does not determine the compound in any way).

To summarize, appositional compounds do not usually express natural coordination and are thus quite distinct from co-compounds. There are, however, some areas where co-compounds and appositional co-compounds come close to each other in meaning, as in vocativic contexts.

5.4.2 *Intermediate-denoting compounds*

In intermediate-denoting compounds, the whole C is neither A nor B, but rather intermediate or hybrid between A and B. Typical examples are Classical Greek *andró.gun.os* 'man.woman.M:SG > hermaphrodite', English *southwest*, Russian *jugo-zapad* id., English *blue-green*, Russian *sero.željyj* 'gray.yellow > gray-yellow'. Intermediate-denoting compounds also occur in languages that typically lack co-compounds. Even if there is often a close lexico-semantic relationship between the parts in intermediate-denoting co-compounds, there is no coordination. Intermediate-denoting compounds sometimes have an approximate function, in which case they come close in their meaning to alternative or approximate co-compounds, such as in (20):

(20) Georgian (Hewitt 1996: 35)
Mas   ak'et'   ts' ots'xal-mk'vdar.i   var.
that:DAT   since   alive-dead.NOM   1SG:be:PRS
'Since then I have been a mere zombie (after dreadful experiences).'

In such cases it is difficult to decide whether there is a co-compound or a intermediate-denoting compound.

5.4.3 *Comparative (or figurative-appositional) compounds*

In the simplest cases of comparative compounds, B is compared with A, so that B is thus the same as A in a figurative sense: Modern Greek *thalassa ládi* 'sea oil > completely calm sea (the sea is like oil)'. That is why comparative compounds of this kind are very closely related to appositional compounds, which sometimes makes it difficult to decide whether a compound is appositional or comparative as in French *chou-fleur* 'cauliflower' (a cabbage which is at the same time a flower, or a cabbage that is like a flower?).

Like appositional compounds proper, comparative compounds are often used to establish an unexpected relationship. The Russian poet Mayakovski uses comparative compounds abundantly to establish unusual associative connections:

(21) Russian (Majakovskij 1969)
Professor,   snimite   očki-velosiped!
professor   take_off:IMP2PL   glasses:ACC:PL-bicycle:ACC:SG
'Professor, take off (your) glasses-bicycle!'

If it seems from these examples that comparative compounds go together with appositional compounds rather than co-compounds, comparative compounds may also be closely associated with co-compounds. Some comparative co-compounds, especially those used verbally, come close to synonymic compounds, as in pictorial contexts (Section 5.5.7). In (22) there is synonymic sharpening between the parts; the bell peals as if it would weep.

(22) Erźa Mordvin (D 6)
...veśe   vajgel'.se.nze   čav.ś-avard.ś   požarka.ń
...all   voice.INESS.its   beat.PST3SG-weep.PST3SG   blaze.GEN
bajaga.ś...
bell.DEF
'[Ding-dong! Ding-dong!] beat and wept the fire bell with full voice.'

We may conclude that some appositional, intermediate-denoting, and comparative compounds can come close to being co-compounds, notably if the function of the compound is not specification, but rather approximation; and that appositional, intermediate-denoting, and comparative compounds sometimes cannot be distinguished formally from co-compounds. However, languages that have appositional, intermediate-denoting, and comparative compounds need not necessarily have co-compounds (as in the case of French).

5.4.4 *Ideophones and ideophone compounds*

Ideophones (see Alpher 1994 for Australia; Tucker Childs 1994 for Africa; Emeneau 1969/1980 for South Asia) are uninflected words often of an onomatopoeic character (or at least with a phonologically deviant structure) which typically express salient events (sound, cry, gleam, beat, or rapid movement) and which tend to occur in one of the following contexts:

1 in isolation (as a sort of interjection)
2 (redundantly) in combination with verbs that express the same or a similar meaning
   Hixkaryána *nomokyatxkonà, àhpo* 'they_used_to_come, action_of_arriving' (Derbyshire 1977: 178)
3 in combination with verbs such as 'go', 'make', or 'say'
   English **Ding-dong** went the door bell.

Languages (and registers and styles within languages) may differ greatly in their frequency of ideophones (both in token frequency and type frequency, which is the number of events that can be expressed by ideophones). Thus, ideophones are more common in Hixkaryána than in English, and within English are most common in comic strips and vivid spoken narrative.

The reason why we have to deal with ideophones here is that they often cluster into pairs of ideophones or IDEOPHONE COMPOUNDS, such as English *ding-dong*, even in languages that have no or very few co-compounds. In languages with co-compounds, ideophone compounds behave very much like co-compounds. Consider (23) and (24) from Mordvin and Chuvash. The ideophone in (23) occurs in context 3. (with a verb 'do') and the ideophone in (24) in context 2. (with a verb of similar meaning):

(23) Erźa Mordvin (D 314)
      ...seźe.ź   pŕa   marto sandal'a.nzo   čikor-lakor
      ...tear.PTC:PASS head   with sandal.PL:POSS3SG   sound-of-squeaking
      t'ej.s.t'...
      do.PST.3PL

'[The woman walked on tiptoe, from which] her sandals with torn tips squeaked.'

(24) Chuvash (Skvorcov 1982: 119)
Păru   jăkălt-jakălt   sikkele.t.
calf   action_of_abrupt_jumping   jump.PRS3SG
'The calf romps around jumping.'

It is not always easy to distinguish ideophones from other word classes. In (25) from Georgian, there is an ideophone compound *t'qlaša-t'qluš.i* 'sound of cracking' which functions as a noun (the subject of a sentence with nominative case marking):

(25) Georgian (Hewitt 1996: 29)
... namet'navad   buer.eb.ze   da.ic'q'.o
... especially   butter_bur.PL.on   PREV.begin.AOR3SG
t'q'laša-t'q'luš.i.
sound_of_cracking.NOM
'[Rain came down in torrents on the ridges opposite; shortly around us, too,] it began to splatter and splutter [on the leaves of the trees and] especially on the butter-burs.'

Ideophone compounds are, however, not characteristic of all languages where ideophones and repeated ideophones are common. Udihe (Tungus) has many ideophones including ideophones with full reduplication, but very few ideophone compounds as the term is understood here: *čak-čik* 'striking fire', *geŋ-gem* 'motionless', *giŋ-gom* 'head up' (Nikolaeva and Tolskaya 2001: 947 and I. Nikolaeva, p.c.). In preverbs in Northern Australian languages (an open word class, a subclass of which has ideophone properties; Schultze-Berndt 2001), complex forms tend to be restricted to reduplication, whereas consonant or vowel alternations (being characteristic properties of ideophone compounds) are not typical (E. Schultze-Berndt, p.c.). Further cross-linguistic research of ideophone compounds is needed to investigate their relationship to co-compounds.

Ideophone compounds are closely associated with reciprocally imitative compounds (Section 5.2.6), even if the parts of ideophone compounds somehow have a meaning of their own. Ideophone compounds are certainly closely associated with co-compounds. It is, however, very unlikely that they play a major role in the development of co-compounds because of their marginal status in many co-compounding languages. There does not seem to be any correlation between the frequency of ideophones and the frequency of co-compounds in a language. If co-compound-like structures occur earlier in ideophones than elsewhere, this is only one of several 'progressive' features of ideophones. Another one is ablaut, which occurs in ideophones, both in typical ablaut languages (such as Georgian) and in languages that otherwise lack ablaut (such as Mordvin and Chuvash; see Section 5.2.6).

5.4.5 *Reduplication*

The traditional Sanskrit name for co-compounds (*dvaṃ.dva* 'two-two > pair') is a reduplication, which is reason enough to ask how co-compounds are related to reduplication. Co-compounds are associated with FULL REDUPLICATION (also word reduplication, reduplicative compounds, word iteration; see Stolz 2004), but not with PARTIAL REDUPLICATION (or affixal reduplication).[12] An example of the former is Tagalog *pantay-pantay* 'measured, uniform, regular', an example of the latter is Tagalog *nararapat* 'appropriate' from *marapat* id. (reduplication of the first syllable of the stem *dapat* 'worthy' [d > r /V_V], *ma-* and *na-* are prefixes). Figure 5.2 lists partial and full reduplication together with some less prototypical types of reduplication, aligned on a tight–loose reduplication scale.

In co-compounding languages full reduplication is often related in form and meaning to co-compounds. This is the case for distributive numerals and related distributive expressions, like in (26) from Georgian. In both distributive reduplication and co-compounds there is single case marking on the second part in Georgian:

(26) Georgian (Hewitt 1996: 33)
   ... džgupʻ-džgupʻ.ad   exve.od.nen   čʻitʻ.eb.i,
   group-group.ADV   swarm.IMPF.3PL   bird.PL.NOM
   šašv.eb.i ...
   blackbird.PL.NOM ...
   '... birds, blackbirds, clustered around them in groups...'

Distributive numerals like Swedish *två och två* 'two and two > two-by-two, by twos' suggest that reduplication in distributive numerals might at least

repetition of sentences	repetition of phrases	repetition of words (without connective prosody)	full (stem) reduplication (word iteration)	partial reduplication (affixal reduplication)	gemination of vowels or consonants
loose reduplication <--> tight reduplication					

FIG. 5.2. Different types of reduplication

sometimes derive from coordination. This is, however, not always the case, as can be shown in Mordvin distributive numerals. Mordvin distributive numerals and related distributive expressions have a genitive marker on both elements, as in *kolmo.ń-kolmo.ń* 'three.GEN-three.GEN = three each', *keskal.oń-keskal.oń* 'sack.GEN-sack.GEN = a sack each, in sacks'. There is reason to believe that this double marking derives diachronically from the single marking of the first part, as it still occurs as an alternative to double marking: *kepteŕ.eń-kepteŕ* 'in baskets' (D 123). It seems to me that this pattern evolved from a subordinate construction 'basket(s) of basket(s)'. This construction, with the same noun in the genitive for expressive augmentative purposes, is widespread in the languages of North Eastern Europe, as in Lithuanian *metų metai* 'years.GEN years = many years' (Ambrazas 1997: 478). Thus, there is reason to believe that reduplication in distributive expressions may develop from both coordinate and subordinate constructions. For the role of distributivity in co-compounds see Section 5.5.6.

We may conclude at this point that full (but not partial) reduplication is formally related to co-compounds and has some functions similar to some co-compounds (as in distributive contexts). There are, however, some important differences between full reduplication and co-compounds. Unlike co-compounds, full reduplication has only one free slot and is not coordinating, at least not in a narrow understanding of the term, and it does not necessarily derive from coordination diachronically. The most important reason, however, for viewing full reduplication and co-compounds as rather distinct phenomena is that there is no apparent typological correlation between the two. Full reduplication can be very common in languages that have almost no co-compounds.

5.4.6 *Echo-words*

Many co-compounding languages have one or several types of compounds in which B is a phonologically modified variant of A, or a pronoun which has the meaning 'A and the like, A and such stuff'. In South Asian linguistics such compounds are called echo-words and this name will be used here.

Echo-words are considered to be an areal phenomenon of South Asia (see Bloch 1934: 163 and Masica 1971: 189). The dominant echo-word patterns vary from language to language (Trivedi 1990). Most common is the replacement of an initial consonant or an initial CV-sequence in the second part, in Kannada, for instance, with *gi-* or *gī-*: *hallu-gillu* 'teeth and the like', *shēhitaru-gīhitaru* 'friends and the like', *āṭa-gīṭa* 'games and the like'. The process applies also to verbs: *ōḍi-gīḍīye!* (run:CONV-ECHO:CONT2SG) 'don't you run or something!' (Sridhar 1990: 285).[13]

In Turkic and Mongolian, and in many contact languages of Turkic (many languages of the Caucasus, some Finno-Ugric languages, Iranian languages, Armenian), there is a widespread type of echo-words in which the second part of the compound begins with *m-* (often called m-doublets), which often occur in negative contexts (Section 5.5.5.i):

(27) Turkish (MTK 72)
  Ben doktor moktor değilim.
  I doktor ECHO NEG1SG
  'I am not a doctor or the like.'

Although they seem to be characteristic of central Eurasian languages, echo-words are found elsewhere. They occur in co-compounding languages of New Guinea. In Sentani (Cowan 1965) there are echo-words with *m-* and *ha/sa-*: *hikoj-sakoj* 'swim:CONV-ECHO:CONV > tired out, exhausted'. In Kaugel (Blowers and Blowers 1970: 57f) there are echo-word specifiers (the word class that occurs with verbs to specify actions) whose second part usually is on *ma-*, *tópele-mápele tokóro* 'turning-ECHO I:hit > I am turning it around and around'.

In many languages (at least among the languages of Eurasia) echo-words are found predominantly in colloquial style. As Emeneau (1938a/1967: 43) puts it for Toda and other Dravidian languages: 'The impression gained is that, as in other Dravidian languages... [echo-words] are felt to be highly useful and racy forms, but somewhat too undignified to be used in literature, or in songs which may take the place of literature with an illiterate people' (1938a/1967: 41, 43; see Lewis 1967 for a similar statement about m-doublets in Turkish). In contrast to co-compounds with semantically empty components that cannot be derived by a simple rule (imitative and ornamental co-compounds), echo-words are unsophisticated forms and their effect is cheap. This is one reason why they—unlike co-compounds—are associated with lower registers. Like reduplication, echo-words are a pattern with only one free lexical slot. They are often treated as a kind of reduplication (see Pott 1862: 65–86). It seems to me, however, that the two phenomena should be kept apart, there being no strong typological correlation between them. Rather, such a correlation can be found between echo-words and co-compounds, even if the former may occur without the latter, as in Yiddish (echo-words with *shm-*).[14] Echo-words are very similar to imitative co-compounds.[15] What distinguishes the two is that the meaningless part in imitative co-compounds cannot be derived by a simple rule since they have a two-slot pattern.

Another possible way to form echo-compounds with the meaning 'A and/or something similar' is to have a pronominal B-part rather than a phonologically similar B-part. ('what' in Mordvin and Udmurt). Pronominal echo-words are akin to associative plurals. The reason why such cases as Mordvin *jam.t-mez.t'* 'soup.PL-what.PL > soup and the like' and *koŕon.nek-mez.ńek* 'root.NEK-what:NEK = with roots and everything, with all its roots' are considered as echo-words and not as associative plurals is that they formally behave exactly like co-compounds (double plural marking and double marking with *-ńek* as generalizing co-compounds).

In Mordvin there are also verbal pronominal echo-words where the second part is *t'ejems* 'to do', *učoms-t'ejems* 'wait-do > wait for a while'. In contrast to fully reduplicated verbs that express a repeated action, such compounds express delimitative aktionsart (similar to *po-* in Russian). They are typically found with everyday actions such as 'eat, drink, put on clothes, sleep, rest, wait' as in (28):

(28) Erźa Mordvin (D 35)
 Požar... Bojkasto orš.ńe.ś-t'ej.ś di—
 Fire quickly dress.FREQ.PST3SG-do:PST3SG and
 ušov.
 out(of_the_house)
 'Fire... He quickly put on some clothes and (ran) out.'

It may be assumed that pronominal echo-words derive from coordinate constructions, mainly disjunction for the nominal type (see Section 3.3.6; *prep-school or something*). For the verbal examples in Mordvin consider the 'to do'-second coordinand construction in Bernese German:

(29) Bernese German
 Er kompjüüterlet u macht.
 he computer:PRS3SG and do:PRS3SG
 '(A woman telling another one what her son is doing.) He is frequently occupied with a computer engaged in not clearly identifiable activities and having great fun with it.'

Not only pronominal, but also non-pronominal echo-words may grammaticalize as in the case of the 'plural action verb' in Kui and other Kondh (South-Central Dravidian) languages (see Steever 1993: ch. 5).

To summarize: Echo-words are very similar to co-compounds as they mainly occur in the same languages as co-compounds (at least in Eurasia) and as they are used in similar contexts as co-compounds (5.5.5.i), even if they (in contrast to co-compounds) are characteristic of low informal registers and have only one free lexical slot.

5.4.7 Affirmative–negative compounds

In affirmative–negative compounds, B is the negative form of A. (This means that affirmative–negative compounds are defined in terms of the relationship of the parts, not of the parts to the whole.) If A is a verb, the compound as a whole is often the predicate of an indirect question as in (30) from Tuva (or more rarely of a direct question):

(30) Tuva (Mark 15:36)
    ... Ilija.nyŋ   kel.ir-kel.bez.in   köör.dür.
    ... Elias.GEN   come.FUT-come.NEG:FUT.ACC   look.PST
    '... let us see whether Elias will come [to take him down].'

Such compounds obviously derive from disjunction in questions, similarly to scalar compounds (Section 5.2.9). As in reduplication and echo-words there is, however, only one free lexical slot in affirmative–negative compounds in contrast to co-compounds.

Affirmative–negative compounds usually occur if negation is affixal rather than free. But even languages which do not usually have affixal negation can have singular examples of affirmative–negative compounds: Latin *nolens volens*, English *willy-nilly*.

To consider affirmative–negative compounds as a group of its own makes sense only if they have a specific function, such as interrogation in affirmative–negative compounds of verbs. Affirmative–negative compounds of adjectives and participles, as in Sanskrit *kr̥tākr̥ta-*'done:undone > what has been done and what has not been done, done halfway' (Wackernagel 1905: 170), are either additive, generalizing, or intermediate-denoting.

5.4.8 Conclusions

None of the compounds discussed in this section are prototypical co-compounds, but all of them either have some properties in common with co-compounds or partly overlap with them.

Echo-words and affirmative–negative compounds occur with the same or often similar functions as co-compounds and also occur mostly in the same languages as co-compounds. The major difference between them and co-compounds is that they have only one free lexical slot. Similarly, full reduplication has only one free lexical slot, but in addition it has a typological distribution completely different from co-compounds and has only little functional overlap with co-compounds.

Appositional, intermediate-denoting, and comparative compounds express subordinate-level rather than superordinate-level concepts, and do not at all have the same typological distribution as co-compounds. There are, however, some areas of contiguity between the above types of compounds and co-compounds.

Of the compounds discussed above, ideophone compounds come closest to co-compounds; one reason for not considering them to be co-compounds is that they also occur in languages which typically do not have co-compounds.

5.5 Contextual motivation of co-compounds

In this section I shall consider co-compounds whose use cannot properly be understood if the context in which they occur is not taken into account. This is the case most notably for:

- non-basic co-compounds, where the whole has more or less the same meaning as one or both parts, insofar as they are not conventionalized in a language, and
- co-compounds of the basic types, which can be interpreted correctly only in the specific context where they are used.

An important question to ask here is why synonymic co-compounds exist at all. From a rationalist's point of view synonyms are completely useless. This position can be characterized by the following quotation from Ockham's *Summa Logicae*:

nominum synonymorum multiplicatio non est propter necessitatem significationis inventa, sed propter ornatum sermonis vel aliam causam consimilem accidentalem, quia, quidquid per omnia synonyma significatur, posset per unum illorum exprimi sufficienter, et ideo multitudo conceptuum tali pluralitati synonymorum non correspondet... (Ockham, Summa Logicae I, 3 (3) quoted after Ockham 1984)[16]

There are a number of different possible approaches to regarding the redundancy represented in synonymic co-compounds:

1. Redundancy occurs only if it is unavoidable. This is the view behind the homonymy and overshort words explanations for synonymic co-compounds in Mandarin Chinese (see Section 7.3 for discussion).
2. Redundancy occurs in discourse in a completely unpredictable distribution.
3. There are circumstances which favor the use of certain kinds of redundancy. These do not necessitate the use of redundancy; they just make it more natural for redundant expressions to occur.
4. If redundancy appears frequently in a certain context, it can be conventionalized (grammaticalized or lexicalized).

I take the position here that (3) and (4) and not (1) or (2) are the essential approaches for understanding the use of synonymic co-compounds. Put differently, I assume that redundant co-compounds, as far as they are not yet lexicalized, occur if there is some contextual semantic factor that favors their use. The reasoning behind this is that redundancy, while not wrong, is odd and that it occurs particularly if its odd effect is mitigated by contextual semantic factors, such as emphasis, generalization, contrast, or non-referentiality. This I call the CONTEXTUAL MOTIVATION of co-compounds. It is best illustrated in moderately co-compounding languages, such as Mordvin, where there are few lexicalized synonymic co-compounds and where there are no formal reasons (homonymy, overshort words) requiring the use of redundant co-compounds. Thus, the Mordvin synonymic co-compound *muśkems-lopavtńems* 'wash-wash > wash (clothes)' occurs only under specific conditions, notably generalization, as in 'She washes the whole day' (Buzakova 1993: 394), or non-referentiality in negation, such as '[the shirt] has not been washed for a long time' (D 239). It need not occur in generalizing and negative contexts; but, if it occurs, it occurs only in those or similar specific contexts.

However, it has to be kept in mind that lexicalization is a gradual process (Section 4.3.4). A certain co-compound in a language can be fully conventionalized in one specific register, but not in others (for example, Erźa Mordvin *eŕams.ašt'ems* 'live-be_located > live' needs no contextual motivation in fairytales and in epic poems where it is a completely normal expression. It is, however, not a normal expression for 'to live' in fiction or in colloquial Erźa Mordvin).[17] This makes it difficult to show that a certain context motivates the use of a certain co-compound at a certain place in a text. This is, however, not really necessary for the purposes of this section. What I would like to show here is that the use of redundant co-compounds is due either to contextual motivation or to conventionalization resulting from earlier contextual motivation. This means that both non-conventionalized and conventionalized co-compounds provide evidence for the important role of certain contexts in the use of redundant co-compounds, if they occur in these contexts in particular.

The same contexts that motivate the use of redundant co-compounds are also responsible for the use of co-compounds of the basic types that do not make sense when considered in isolation. Consider (31) from Mordvin with the co-compound *ukol.t-poroška.t* 'injection-powder', whose meaning is difficult to understand if considered out of context:

(31) Erźa Mordvin (D 338)
... eŕva ukol.ont'-poroška.nt'   mel'ga
every   injection.GEN:DEF-powder.GEN:DEF after
ard'.tńe.k.a   Kaćelaj.ev.
ride.FREQ.IMP2SG.PRT   Katselay.LAT
'[It is bad without a doctor,] (even) for every injection and powder one has to go to Katselay'.

At first glance, 'injection-powder' looks like an additive or a collective co-compound. But neither does it mean '> injection and powder (as a natural pair)' nor '> (minor forms) of medical treatment'. Rather it means here '> each, even the most basic form of medical treatment', where there is in the context both generalization (made explicit by *eŕva* 'every, each') and emphasis, without which the co-compound cannot be properly understood.

Let us now consider some relevant semantic contexts that may motivate the use of co-compounds one by one.

5.5.1 *Additive contextual co-compounds*

In Section 1.1.3 contextual binomials in German (Lambrecht 1984) were discussed. Interestingly, co-compounds of the additive type which are motivated in a similar way are extremely rare and play only a minimal role in the contextual motivation of co-compounds. A case in point is (32) from the Erźa Mordvin epic poem 'Mastorava' ('Earthmother'), where there are as many as two contextually motivated additive co-compounds, 'horse-falcon' and 'legs-wings', in the context of a race between a horse and a falcon:

(32) Erźa Mordvin (Šaronov 1994: 175)
L'išme.t'-karćigan.t   pel'ksta.kšn.i.t',
horse.PL-falcon.PL   argue.FREQ.PRS.3PL
Pil'ge.st-śolmo.st,   eś   pŕa.st   šna.kšn.i.t'.
leg.their-wing.their,   own   head.their praise.FREQ.PRS.3PL
'[Under the tree there is a brown horse with thin legs and large hooves with a comb-like front and a mane of silk. On the tree there is a bird, sits the big falcon.] Horse and falcon were arguing, praising their legs and wings, themselves.'

We may conclude that this context is of almost no importance for co-compounds.

5.5.2 Emphasis

Synonymic compounds may serve emphatic purposes. This function of co-compounds is iconic. A notion uttered twice in sequence with lexical variation is a reinforcement of that notion. Emphasis is higher degree, and degree applies to qualities. That is why co-compounds of adjectives are a favorable domain for emphasis. An already conventionalized case in Mordvin is *vid'e-paro* 'right/direct-good > real(ly)' where emphasis has been removed by inflationary use.

Emphasis is, however, also possible with nominal or verbal co-compounds. The quality to be emphasized is then implicit or expressed attributively ('big' in (33), 'powerful' in (34)):

(33) Georgian (K'Z 261)
Bolo.s, did.i t'xovna-mudar.is šemdeg...
end.DAT big.GEN asking_for-imploring.GEN after
'Finally, after big begging and imploring [he sold the penknife for three rubles and let him have it.]'

(34) Georgian (Hewitt 1996: 224)
...k'mari mis.i srul.up'lebian.i
...husband s/he:GEN.NOM all.authorized.NOM
bat'on-p'at'ron.i.a...
master/lord-feudal_lord.NOM.is...
'[In the family of a Mingrelian a woman is without any sort of right,] the husband is her all-powerful lord and master, [and as such the wife obeys him in everything without question.]'

The importance of emphasis as a relevant contextual factor for the use of co-compounds can also be seen from the fact that co-compounds tend to conventionalize in such domains where emphatic expressions are so common that they become devalued by inflationary use. This is the case for such emotional qualities as 'sad', 'sorry', and 'afraid'. Thus, in English, the expression *I am very sorry* is no longer very emphatic in spite of the overt marker for emphasis. In Vietnamese, a language which generally has a high frequency of co-compounds, emotional qualities such as 'anxious, afraid' and 'sad, sorry' are often expressed by synonymic or imitative co-compounds. In the Vietnamese translation of the Gospel according to Mark there are five tokens of co-compounds and only one simple word for the equivalents of *sorry, sorrowful, grieved, sad*: *buồn-rầu* 'sad-sad > sad' (6:26, 14:19, 14:34), *rầu-rĩ* 'sad-IMI > sad, depressed' (10:22), *buồn-bã* 'sad-exhausted > sad' (10:22). This means that, in this text, co-compounds are locally unmarked in the domain 'sad'. For *afraid, fear, frightened* co-compounds occur several times in the text, but are still less frequent than other expressions. (In the Mordvin, Mari, and Udmurt translations there are no co-compounds in these contexts.)

5.5.3 Generalizing context

While generalizing co-compounds (Section 5.2.2) express such notions as 'all, always, everywhere' by themselves, other co-compounds frequently occur in generalizing contexts, notably under the scope of quantifiers. Consider (35) from Georgian with a synonymic co-compound (for a Hmong example with an ornamental co-compound, see Section 5.2.5):

(35)   Georgian (Hewitt 1996: 107)
...q'vela   t'av.is.i   γone-šedzleba   k'ošk'.isa.t'vis
...all   head.GEN.NOM   force-ability/means   tower.GEN.for
mo.undomebi.a...
hither.use.PF3SG...
'[It would appear that a Svan] devoted all his might and means to his tower [so that at one and the same time it should emerge both beautiful and strong.]'

In (36) from Uzbek the generalization consists of a coordination of an imitative and an ornamental co-compound (note that there is single marking for number and possession):

(36)   Uzbek (Laude-Cirtautas 1980: 35)
...mahalla.ning   qari-qartang   va   još-jalang.lar.i...
...block.GEN   old-IMI   and   young-naked.PL.POSS3...
'[Around the tablecloth my father used to sit in a circle with] old and young of the quarter.'

Generalization is an important contextual motivation for co-compounds and is often connected with other contextual factors such as emphasis, contrast, and distributivity.

5.5.4 Contrast (in adversative sequences)

Expressions of contrast in English are *on the one hand...on the other hand*, however, in German *der eine...der andere* 'someone...the other', and in Classical Greek (where contrast is highly grammaticalized) *men...de*. All these have in common that two different things are contrasted as opposite poles. In languages with co-compounds, opposite poles, or one of two opposite poles, in contrast are often expressed by co-compounds. In (37) the opposite poles are 'seas-oceans' and 'bread crumb', in (38) 'sways-ripens' and 'rots' (in boldface).

(37) Erźa Mordvin (D 353)
Ińe.ved.t'-okean.t uj.t', śisem mastor.t juta.k
big.water.PL-ocean.PL swim.IMP2SG seven country.PL cross.IMP2SG
troks-kel'e.s...
across-width.ILL
'[It is said that a person cannot escape destiny.] You can cross seas and oceans, go across all (lit. seven) countries all over; [if the end of your life comes, you can choke on a bread crumb.]'

(38) Erźa Mordvin (D 187)
Anśak śe meźe.ś **limbakst.ń.i-keńeŕ.kšń.i**
only this what.DEF sway.FREQ.PRS3SG-ripen.FREQ.PRS3SG
pakśa.tńe.se...
field.PL:DEF.INESS
'Only this (the corn) that sways and ripens on the field, [remains on the fields during the harvest and rots during transport or during threshing on the threshing ground.]'

Contrast is typical of persuasive discourse. Both (37) and (38) have a persuasive function. Contrastive contexts are often generalizing at the same time, which again holds for both (37) and (38).

5.5.5 Non-referential contexts and restricted evidence

Domains which host non-referential entities or things not conceptually identified, such as negation, question, irrealis, and future, are popular areas for co-compounds. These contexts call for widening concepts for which co-compounds are a favorable means of expression. The function of concept-widening is associated with the tendency for co-compounds to express superordinate concepts (Section 1.3.2.i). In all these contexts, co-compounds can, however, also add emphasis and/or emotional intensity.

(i) *Negation* Non-referentiality under the scope of negation is a favorable context for co-compounds. In negative contexts the distinction between additive and alternative co-compounds is blurred because, pragmatically, disjunction is stronger in negation (Section 3.3.6). Co-compounds typically have the function of emphasis ('not even') in negative examples such as

'There is no cow in the stable, not (even) sheep-pig' (D 159). Both parts of the compound are on the same minimal pole of the set of items that is denied ('less valuable livestock').[18] In the following extreme example from Mordvin, there are as many as three (perhaps even four) co-compounds. The purpose of the example is to evoke compassion for a tramp.

(39) Erźa Mordvin (D 229)
...a sod.i, kov lotka.ms-čiŕeme.ms... Sonze,
not know.PRS3SG whither stop.INF-lean.INF he:GEN,
Narvatkin.eń,— a śemija.zo-raśke.ze, a
Narvatkin.GEN not family.his-relative.his not
kudo.či.nze-paro.nzo.
house.homestead.PL:his-good.PL:his.
'[Like a cart or the wind he strolls and strolls on the world] and doesn't know where to stay or lean. [The wind is luckier, it drives mills and grinds flour.] He, Narvatkin, neither has a family or relatives nor a house or property.'

In Doronin's novel, from which this example is quoted and which has an emotive style, approximately 5 per cent of all co-compounds are non-referential expressions under the scope of negation. In other, less emotional texts in Mordvin the frequency is considerably lower and then largely restricted to more conventionalized (phraseologized) examples, such as *(son) tarka-eźem a muji* 's/he does not find his/her place (in life) (literally: place-bench)'. These more conventionalized examples are further evidence that negation is a favorable context for the use of co-compounds: *tarka-eźem* 'place-bench' is not conventionalized in Erźa Mordvin in any other context.

Negation is also a favorable context for echo-words (see also Emeneau 1938a/1967: 41):

(40) Lezgian (Haspelmath 1993: 453)
...fadlaj ne.da.j zat'-mat' žaǧu.n t.awu.nwa.j
long eat.FUT.PTC thing-ECHO find.PER NEG.do.PF.PL
rexi žanawur...
gray wolf
'...a gray wolf who had not found anything to eat for a long time...'

(41) Toda (Emeneau 1984: 405)
Püsy xisy kor fit̲.fid̲.ṣk.
tiger ECHO calf carry_off.COMPL.VOL:NEG3SG
'May no tiger or anything carry off the calves!'

The non-referential character of echo-words may be illustrated by a frequent motif in Dravidian folktales where some demon or a tiger takes the echo-word mistakenly for referential (see Emeneau 1938b/1967: 358f; a variant of the my name-is-nobody-motif well-known from Ulysses and the Cyclops), as in the following Toda version from which we have already quoted the sentence (41) with the echo-word:

A Toḍa one evening finished milking all the buffaloes and put the calves in the calfshed. When he had finished putting all the calves in the calfshed, he said, 'My friend! May no tiger (püsy) or anything (kisy) carry off the calves!' ... A tiger, listening to what this man said, was sitting in the ground within the wall behind the calfshed. That tiger thought, and thinking 'If I am a tiger (püsy), what is this other thing, that is the kisy?', it entered the calfshed to seize a calf. At that time a rat (isy) was sitting on the back of a calf there. The rat immediately jumped on the tiger's back. This tiger thought in terror, 'Oh! This is what he calls the kisy. It may do something to me', and at once without at all seizing a calf, it ran away in fright ... (Emeneau 1984: 405).[19]

(ii) *Question* Different types of questions support the use of co-compounds for different reasons. In Section 5.2.9, alternative-approximate and scalar co-compounds in questions were discussed. Another favorable context for co-compounds are TENTATIVE PRESUPPOSITIONS, where the questioner is not sure whether the basis on which the question is grounded is actually true. The following example from Archi is especially illustrative, as the presupposition is rejected in the answer: *jášajémmet dùí-dàbá éťixmur, anx éťixmur, han árši íkir?* (Kibrik et al. 1977: 114) 'If it happened **quarrel and arguing** at yours, if it happened a **fight**, what did you do?' The answer is given: 'Much quarrel and arguing did not happen, much fight did not happen in our village'. Another strategy to mark a presupposition as tentative is to repeat the question in a paraphrase, as is also the case in the Archi example.

(iii) *Irrealis, potentialis, conditional, and future* There are considerably fewer co-compounds in irreal, potential, future, and similar contexts for non-referentiality than in negation in Mordvin written fiction; (42) is an example of a conditional context:

(42) Erźa Mordvin (D 284)
      ...učo.k,   žardo   ružija.t-pejeľ.t'   sťavt.i.t'
      wait.IMP2SG   when   gun.PL-knife.PL   put.PRS.3PL
      karšo.zo.t.
      against.ILL.POSS2SG
      '[(What can you do) if you (as a forest ranger) go against poachers] wait when they direct guns and knives against you.'

The specific type of weapon a forest ranger would be confronted with when meeting poachers cannot be known concretely; it is therefore presented as an alternative (or additive) co-compound (for distributivity see Section 5.5.6).

Prayers are a particularly favorable context for co-compounds, since they tend to accumulate contextual factors that are appropriate for co-compounds (future, negation, emphasis, emotivity, and contrast; see also Section 7.5) and represent persuasive discourse. In Mordvin, traditional prayers undoubtedly have the highest frequency of co-compounds. (Other characteristic features of this register are looser sequences of coordination, unsystematic parallelism, and semantically empty epithetic adjectives. Note also the co-compounds for deities that are reminiscent of the Vedic *Götterdvandvas*; see Section 7.2.1). In the example below co-compounds are given in boldface.

(43) Erźa Mordvin (Paasonen 1941: 4f)[20]

staka-pas ńiške-pas,	God of the heaviness, Great-creator god,
staka-pas veŕe-pas,	God of the heaviness, God of the above,
ontot bontot, mastor langoń stakań **kiŕdit' kandit'**!	**Onto-Bonto** (gods occurring only as a pair), **holder and bearer** of heaviness on the world!
vana, kandińek t'enk kšińek salonok...	look, we bring you our bread and our salt...
paŕak ul'it' vel'ese śadso t'ejićat kadićat, altićat joftićat, muńićat kaśt'ićat,	Perhaps are there in the village-hundred **doers-abandoners** (sorcerers), **cursers-tellers** (sorcerers), **sorcerers-soilers** (sorcerers),
l'iśed'e karčozost **oftoks śardoks**,	go out against them **as bears and elks**,
maksodo **šoždińe parińe** kıld'imańe, ped'amo skalne, čel'ke pona ŕeveńe, il'ado urgat'e mastor lankso **nalkińe čarińe, śt'ińe prińe**!	give **light things and good things** to the cattle and milking cows, to the dust colored sheep, do not attack the **players-rompers** on the earth **those that stand up and fall**!
maksodo šači śuro, sovi eŕme...	give growing corn, coming in income...

noldink **vel'eńe śadońe mirne**
čaxarńe šoždińenk pańińenk!

Let to the **village-hundred**, to the
world-world your light things
and your good things!

5.5.6 Distributivity

According to Gil (1991), distributive expressions contain a <u>distributive key</u> element (the range of things over which something is distributed) and a **distributive share** element (the thing distributed over items, space, or times). In (44) the distributive key is indicated by a quantifier 'each' (underlined) and the distributive share by a distributive numeral 'hundred (years) each' (boldface).

(44) Erźa Mordvin (D 278)
Sire.t'   piče.tńe —   <u>eŕva.nt'eń</u>   **śad.oń-śad.oń**
old.PL   pine.PL:DEF <u>every.DAT:DEF</u> **hundred.GEN-hundred.GEN**
ije.
year
'Old are the pines. Each of them is a hundred years old.'

In distributive contexts, co-compounds can express variation in the distributive share. Just as distributive numerals occur in distributivity without variation, additive or approximate co-compounds of numerals occur in distributivity with variation as in (45), where the number of five or six oxen is distributed alternatively over times ('every winter').

(45) Erźa Mordvin (D 205)
<u>Eŕva</u>   tel'ńa   **vet'e-koto**   buk.ińe   tŕ.i.
<u>every</u> in_winter   **five-six**   ox.DIM   feed.PRS3SG
'He fattens five or six oxen every winter.'

In distributive contexts, the distinction between alternative and additive co-compounds is neutralized as both disjunction and conjunction happen at the same time. Consider (46) with distribution over times. Altogether it is 'mushrooms' and 'berries' that are collected, but for each time it is either 'mushrooms' or 'berries'. The distributive key in (46) is the temporal adverb 'often' together with the frequentative aktionsart of the verb.

(46) Erźa Mordvin (D 277, 321)
...Roza   <u>śejet'ste</u>   jak.<u>ś</u>.eś   marto.nzo
Roza   <u>often:ADV</u>   go.FREQ.pst3SG   with.him
pang.s-jagoda.s...
mushroom.ILL-berry.ILL
'[As a child] Rosa often went with him to pluck mushrooms and berries...'

The neutralization of disjunction and conjunction has to do with the fact that distributivity with co-compounds is usually asymmetric or weakly symmetric in Gil's (1991) terms, as strong symmetric distributivity excludes variation. Strong symmetric distributivity occurs only in specific cases, most of which involve synonymic co-compounds. One possibility is a kind of pseudo-distribution for expressive purposes as in (47):

(47) Erźa Mordvin (D 321)
 Di eŕva.nt' eś.enze t'us.ozo-maziči.ze.
 And each.GEN:DEF self.GEN:POSS3SG color.its-beauty.its
 '[And what (beautiful) trees grow there!] And each has its own color and beauty.'

Co-compounds in distributive contexts range from textually unmarked examples with alternative co-compounds to textually marked expressive examples with synonymic co-compounds.

5.5.7 *Pictorial contexts*

In pictorial contexts, sensation is emphasized, be it outer (sound, cry, gleam, beat, or rapid movement) or inner sensation (fear, joy, sadness). In most cases, it is impossible to distinguish strictly between outer and inner sensation, as a salient outer sensation often evokes a strong feeling while it is generally the function of pictorial expressions to evoke inner sensation. Pictorial contexts are a typical domain for ideophones, so it is not astonishing to find ideophone compounds in pictorial contexts (48b). Especially frequent are synonymic verbal co-compounds and figurative co-compounds, but other types may also occur. Consider (48) from Doronin (1993):

(48) Erźa Mordvin (D 54, 373)
 a ... l'ej.eś t'eke čapaks kepet'et.ś-čovoŕav.ś —
  river.DEF like dough rise.PST3SG-mix.PST3SG
  urn.i-lakord.i ...
  roar.PRS3SG-creak.PRS3SG
  '[When they came to the Dnieper across the forest path] the river rose and mixed like dough, roars and creaks ... '.

 b Uuv-avv, oov-uvv! — kuvśe.ś-lajše.ś   pert'
  Uh-ah, oh-uh!   sigh.PST3SG-lament.PST3SG through
  pel'ks.eś ...
  fear.DEF ...
  '[In a violent blizzard] Uhh-ohh sighed and lamented the fear, [frightened all beings.]'

Abuse of pictorial co-compounds leads to a loss of their expressivity. In fact, there are some conventionalized pictorial co-compounds in Mordvin (all figurative; Section 5.2.7) which now have little expressive power and which testify to earlier abuse: *pij.i-pal.i* 'boils-burns > is excited, suffers pain' and *kišt'.i-mor.i* 'dances-sings > is happy'.

Expressive co-compounds can be toned down not only in a language, but also in a single text. In Doronin's novel, expressions for 'laugh' and 'smile' are typically co-compounds, *pejd'ems-raksems* 'laugh-laugh(loudly):FREQ'. This is, however, not generally the case in Erźa Mordvin texts. As such synonymic co-compounds are used more and more often, the pictorial and emotive connotation fades from them.

In more advanced co-compounding languages such as Vietnamese, pictorial domains have a much higher propensity for co-compounds than in Mordvin. Consider (49) from the Vietnamese translation of the Gospel according to Mark, with three pictorial co-compounds (in boldface):

(49) Vietnamese (Mark 9:3)
Áo-xống   Ngài   trở   nên   **sáng-rực**   và
shirt-skirt   he(deity) return   develop   **bright-bright** and
trắng-tinh   **chói-lòa**...
white-pure   **dazzle-dazzle**
'And his raiment became shining, exceeding white as snow...'

There are no co-compounds in the corresponding Mordvin translation.

5.5.8 Conclusions

Contextual motivation of co-compounds contributes to an expansion of the non-basic types of co-compounds. However, the contextual factors also diminish the contrast between different semantic types of co-compounds and connect co-compounds to other types of compounds. The distinction between additive and alternative co-compounds can be neutralized in distributivity, negation, and irrealis. Ideophone compounds and comparative compounds are closely connected with co-compounds in pictorial contexts. Echo-words have functions very similar to co-compounds in non-referential contexts. Generally, we may say that contextual factors lead to a tightening of the connections between the different types of co-compounds, and between co-compounds and some related types of compounds. This means that the contextual factors strengthen the class component in the lexical class of co-compounds and weaken its lexicalization component. This is in line with a high number of unique occurrences of specific contextually motivated co-compounds. On the other hand, contextual motivation is also a driving force for the conventionalization of certain redundant co-compounds.

Regarding the functions of co-compounds in contextual motivation, the two most recurring tendencies are emphasis and deconceptualization (fuzzy, vague, and general expressions in non-referential contexts). These two general tendencies lead to a high degree of SUBJECTIVITY in contextually motivated co-compounds, because the use of co-compounds is optional in contextual motivation (where co-compounds have not yet been conventionalized).

A further characteristic of conceptually motivated co-compounds is their tendency to lose internal lexico-semantic contrast between the parts as the contrast comes to be located in the context, that is, TEXTUALIZATION of co-compounds occurs (Traugott and König 1991: 208, textualization as a tendency in grammaticalization). In Section 3.3.4 we saw that co-compounds are characterized in general by a low degree of contrast between the parts. This holds even more markedly for contextually motivated co-compounds. Associated with the loss of internal contrast is the overall drift toward non-basic types of co-compounds in contextually motivated co-compounds, facilitating the conventionalization of redundant co-compounds.

5.6 Conclusions

This chapter presented a semantic classification of co-compounds based on the semantic relationship between the parts and the whole (Section 5.2). The semantic types were roughly arranged into two groups: basic (additive, generalizing, collective, alternative-approximate) and non-basic types (synonymic, ornamental, imitative, figurative, and scalar).

The different semantic types of co-compounds are connected in synchronically and diachronically different ways. In addition to this, the process of pair sharpening, which is responsible for determining the meaning of the parts of co-compounds, is strong evidence for a cover meaning of natural coordination for co-compounds (Section 5.3). This cover meaning is, however, not a *Gesamtbedeutung*, because it applies to different semantic groups to varying extents and does not serve as a clear criterion for distinguishing co-compounds from closely related types of compounds.

In Section 5.5 the use of contextually motivated co-compounds was examined. In weakly and moderately co-compounding languages in particular, many co-compounds, notably those that do not belong to non-basic semantic types, must be motivated by the context (emphasis, generalization,

184   A Semantic Classification of Co-compounds

contrast, non-referentiality under the scope of negation, and pictoriality). Contextually motivated co-compounds, depending on style and register to a greater extent than lexicalized co-compounds, were found to lead to an overall drift toward strengthening the role of non-basic co-compounds, to subjectification and textualization of co-compounds, and to strengthening the class component of co-compounds. However, contextual motivation is also the major driving force for the lexicalization of non-basic co-compounds.

Notes

[1] Both additive and collective co-compounds most typically denote collection complexes (Section 1.1.2). The expression of true collectives seems to be secondary and is prominent only in some languages (for example, in Chuvash, but not in Mordvin). Hyperonyms generally seem to be marginal.

[2] There may also be a close phonological relationship between the parts of co-compounds which can be both additive and collective, like Mordvin *alks(t)- pŕalks(t)* 'mattress-pillow > bedding, bedclothes'. In Mordvin only few collective co-compounds with unanalyzable components exist, such as *at'a.t-serd'a.t* 'old_man.PL-?.PL > (late) ancestors'; *serd'a.t* probably derives from *sire at'a.t* 'old old_man.PL'.

[3] Perhaps villages originally had about a hundred inhabitants.

[4] Note that the co-compound is not used to express a hyperonym. It takes the place of a basic level term *ntoo* 'tree'.

[5] Such compounds occur even in West European languages: English *helter-skelter, topsy-turvy, pell-mell* (cf. also Bauer 2001*b*: 12).

[6] In Khasi this might have to do diachronically with the predilection for discontinuous CACB co-compounds.

[7] An additive co-compound.

[8] Cf. however examples, such as in Shakespeare's *Macbeth*: *When the hurlyburly's done,/When the battle's* **lost and won**.

[9] Antonymy is in fact a very complex concept; see Croft and Cruse (2004: ch. 7).

[10] Cruse now conceives of sense relations such as homonymy and meronymy as relations between contextually construed meanings (without treating synonymy explicitly). Meaning is accounted for by contextualized interpretation, purport (consisting partly of pre-meanings and default construals), constraints, and construal (Croft and Cruse 2004: 98). This model of a dynamic construal of meaning is essentially compatible with the approach presented here.

[11] The difference between 'structural' synonymy and contextual synonymy also accounts for the paradox that different languages are considered to have functional equivalents in expression (cross-linguistic synonymy) while there is hardly any

absolute synonymy within languages. In the former case we have to do with contextual synonymy; in the latter with abstract structural synonymy.

[12] Partial reduplication is often thought of as reduplication par excellence, because it is of more interest to morphologists (Marantz 1994: 3486).

[13] Echo-words also occur in Indian English: *'That one, baba, always making joke shoke', 'That club-shub stuff is only for you rich boys!'* (Rushdie 1981/1995: 386, 228).

[14] There is, however, at least one co-compound in (Eastern) Yiddish: *tate-mame* 'father-mother > parents' (Wolf 1991). According to Gold (1991–93: 111) Hebrew *aba-ima* id. is a translation of the Eastern Yiddish co-compound (with a reversed variant *aba-ima*, a Modern Hebrew innovation).

[15] For Vietnamese, Emeneau (1951: 159–200) lists a great number of rules for forming echo-words, most of which seem to be very restricted in productivity and therefore should instead be considered to be imitative co-compounds. This situation is typical of South East Asian languages.

[16] 'The multitude of synonyms has not been invented to satisfy the need of designation, but rather in order to embellish speech or for another similar accidental reason, for, what is expressed by all synonyms can be expressed sufficiently by one of them, and therefore there is no multitude of concepts that would correspond to such a multitude of synonyms.'

[17] Mokša Mordvin has conventionalized the present participle *eŕaj-ašči* 'inhabitant; rich'.

[18] For the general tendency of minimal quantity expressions ('step, word, drop, point') to occur in emphatic negation which can then grammaticalize to a general negation marker, see Jespersen (1917) and Dahl (1979).

[19] Interestingly, the tiger in the story applies pair sharpening to the echo-word.

[20] Co-compounds are not hyphenated in the source but written as two words. The segmentation into lines (mine) is only for the purpose of improving readability.

6

The Areal Distribution of Co-compounds in the Languages of Eurasia

6.1 Patterns of areal coherence

Typological research (Dryer 1989a, Nichols 1992) has shown that many typological features have specific macro-areal patterns of distribution (of subcontinental, continental, or even hemispherical scope). In those macro-areal patterns THE PROPORTION OF LANGUAGES WITH A CERTAIN FEATURE IN A SPECIFIC AREA was the determining characteristic. Thus, in Nichols' sample (1992: 134) only 22 per cent of the languages in the Old World had an inclusive/exclusive opposition in the first person plural ('we'), while the figure was 57 per cent in the Pacific (New Guinea, Australia, and Oceania) and 54 per cent in the New World. Similarly, Dryer found that possessive suffixes were more common in the Old World, whereas languages in the New World tended to have possessive prefixes.

Another kind of areal pattern is the CONTINUOUS AREA WITH A CERTAIN FEATURE, such as dominant OV word order in central Eurasia (including South Asia and the Caucasus, but excluding South East Asia, the Middle East, and West Europe—with a single outlier, Basque, which has OV; Masica 1971, Dryer 1998). Such isoglosses are even stronger evidence for areal relatedness, but are typically of smaller size than the patterns observed by Nichols (1992). Both kinds of macro-areal patterns discussed above apply to discrete typological variables.

In this chapter I will discuss a third kind of areal patterning: CONTINUOUS INCREASE AND DECREASE OF A CONTINUOUS VARIABLE OVER A LARGE AREA. It is the aim of this chapter to show that the text frequency of co-compounds, with some minor exceptions, is distributed continuously over the Eurasian continent. For this purpose, the consideration of co-compounds in other continents is not necessary. However, co-compounds in other continents will be treated in an appendix to this chapter (6.A).

Using frequency of co-compounds as an indicator for areal relationships is not completely new. Tkačenko (1979) investigated the frequency of a single co-compound, 'live-be' (Russian *žili-byli* 'lived-were'), in opening sequences of fairytales in dialects of Eastern Slavic languages and compared it to that of Finno-Ugric languages spoken in the same regions as Russian dialects. In his data co-compounds occur in 56 per cent of opening sequences of Russian fairytales, but only in 8 per cent of Belarusan and in 0.5 per cent of Ukrainian. He further observed that the proportion of 'lived-were' is very similar in Russian dialects and their corresponding Finno-Ugric substrate languages. According to Tkačenko, this is evidence that co-compounds in Eastern Slavic developed because of a Finno-Ugric substrate.

In this chapter I will not investigate whether some languages have acquired or lost co-compounds because of language contact, but will rather concentrate on the synchronic situation. However, languages from all parts of Eurasia will be considered as well as the general frequency of co-compounds as a whole, not just of a single type. For practical reasons, this is best done using parallel texts. Then, in Section 6.3 consideration is given to whether the results from parallel texts can be corroborated by further evidence.

6.2 Consideration of parallel texts

In this section we shall look at the text frequency of co-compounds in a number of Eurasian languages in two parallel texts, the Universal Declaration of Human Rights (UDHR) and the Gospel according to Mark (Mark). Before we come to the discussion of the results, some remarks should be made about the nature of the texts, the quality of the translations, and the procedure for counting co-compounds in the translations.

The Universal Declaration of Human Rights is currently available on the Internet in more than 320 languages and dialects.[1] The text happens to be extremely rich in all kinds of very elaborate coordination, collective, and abstract concepts, and abounds in generalizations which make it a text well-suited to the occurrence of co-compounds.[2] We must, however, take into account that it is a formal, highly organized, written text using language which often deviates considerably from spontaneous spoken language. This formal character has to be taken into account especially for those languages where there are considerable differences between written and spoken language and/or between standard language and dialects. As concerns the quality of the translations, it differs considerably, mainly between languages with official function and others. This has meant that the quality of some translations into some non-official languages is particularly poor. For many non-official languages it is clear that the translation was not from English, but from the official language of a particular country. This is the case for languages of Indonesia (Minangkabau, Aceh, and Sundanese from Bahasa Indonesia) and Hmong (from Mandarin). In those translations what is most interesting are the differences from the texts of the (second) source languages. The publication on the Internet has had the consequence that there are many mistakes in the texts, such as misspellings, wrong characters, omissions of single characters, repeated words, and punctuation. Because most of these mistakes are systematic, most of them could easily be corrected by a bit of Internet philology.[3]

As regards the quality of the translations, the Gospel according to Mark is generally much better than the UDHR. For languages with a limited written tradition we have, however, the opposite problem with respect to expressions for which there is no ready equivalent. While the translations of the UDHR tend to abound in loanwords, foreign sources are in principle avoided in Bible translations. This has the unavoidable consequence that there is some proportion of unusual words in many Bible translations or, put differently, there is a considerable proportion of words in the text belonging to a temporary lexicon and which have been formed in accordance with the general principles for the formation of temporary words in that language. This may effect co-compounds in that their frequency may be slightly higher than expected if co-compounds are a common strategy for forming temporary lexemes in that language. Consider, as an example, the case of the explicative co-compound *undo.st-koron.ost* 'root.their-root.their > root(s)' in the Erźa-Mordvin text discussed in Section 5.2.4.[4]

The shortcomings in quality of the translations call for some discretion when considering whether co-compounds found in parallel texts can be taken as directly representative of the average text frequency of co-compounds in the original texts of these languages. It is clear that, in order to measure the exact extent of text frequency of co-compounds, one would have to consider some representative corpus of original texts including all major text types and it would be necessary to account for the considerable language internal variation. Unfortunately, such sources are not available, so we will have to make the best of not fully reliable data from parallel texts for the present. On the other hand, the robustness of languages, enabling them to retain their characteristic features even in bad translations, should not be underestimated.

The languages whose translations will be examined are listed in Table 6.1, from which it becomes clear that the selection is highly biased. The sample focuses on Eurasian languages with co-compounds, and the languages

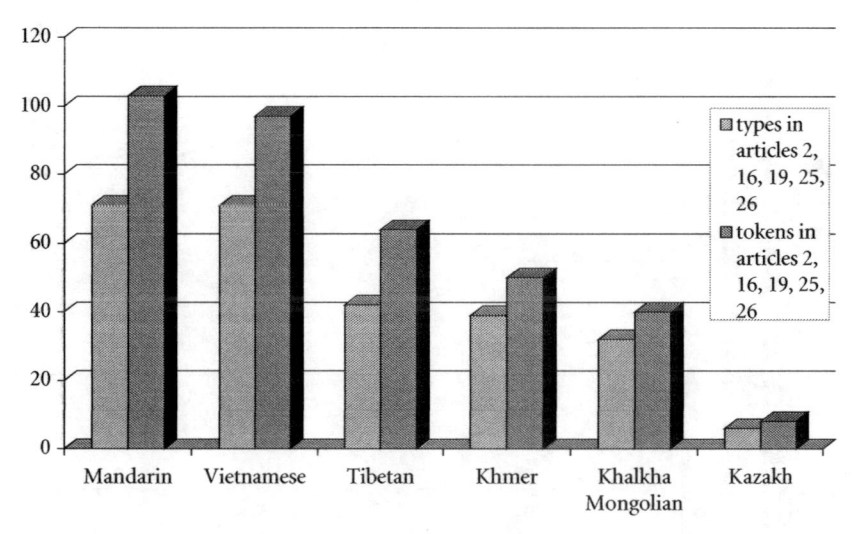

Areal Distribution in the Languages of Eurasia 189

FIG. 6.1. Frequency of co-compounds in the UDHR

represented are only those for which parallel texts were available and where I managed to analyze the text at least as far as to identify co-compounds.

Figures 6.1 and 6.2 show the results for UDHR for the following languages, given here in order of the type frequency of co-compounds: Mandarin (Sino-Tibetan), Vietnamese (Austroasiatic), Tibetan (Sino-Tibetan), Khmer (Austroasiatic), Khalkha Mongolian (Mongolian), Kazakh (Turkic), Uzbek (Turkic), Kirghiz (Turkic), Kannada (Dravidian), Turkmen (Turkic), Abkhaz (North-West Caucasian), Basque (isolate), Malay (Austronesian), Tatar (Turkic), Georgian (Kartvelian), Minangkabau (Austronesian), Bengali (Indo-European), Bahasa Indonesia (Austronesian), Hindi (Indo-European), Finnish (Uralic), Saami (Uralic), Estonian (Uralic), Hungarian (Uralic), and Turkish (Turkic). For the languages with the highest number of co-compounds, co-compounds have been counted in only a part of the entire text (articles 2, 16, 19, 25, 26) amounting to approximately one-fifth of the whole (Figure 6.1). Figure 6.2 shows the number of co-compounds in the whole UDHR text for the other languages listed above.

In East and South East Asia, not all texts that contain co-compounds are represented in Figures 6.1 and 6.2. For practical reasons I refrained from counting the co-compounds in Burmese (Sino-Tibetan) and Laotian (Thai), which contain many co-compounds (probably in the range of Tibetan and Khmer). Neither were counts made in Korean or in the three Hmong varieties because these languages have a high number of co-compounds from

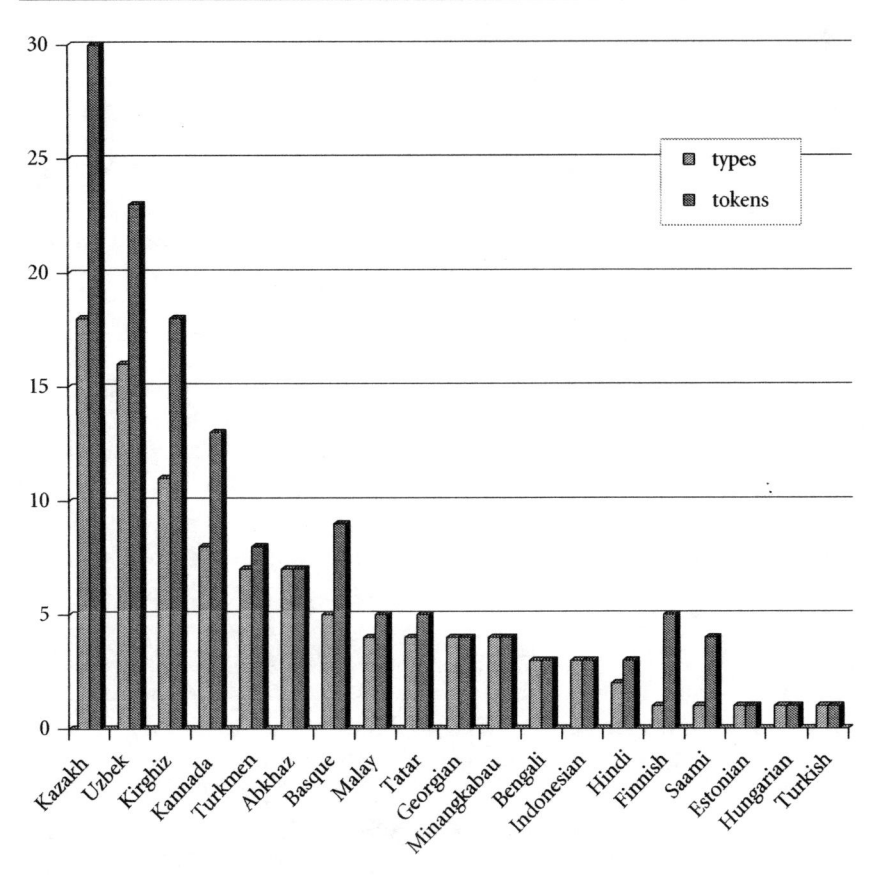

FIG. 6.2. Frequency of co-compounds in the UDHR

Chinese loanwords. It is not clear to me to what extent co-compounds consisting of Chinese morphemes in those languages can be analyzed synchronically as co-compounds. While the Nepali translation is not complete, it can be concluded from that part of the text which is present that the level of co-compounding is about the same as for other Indo-Aryan languages. It has to be noted, however, that the text is written in formal not colloquial Nepali. The level of co-compounding seems to be higher in colloquial Nepali. The proportion of co-compounds in Malayalam (Dravidian) is about the same as in Kannada, but the exact number has not been counted for practical reasons. Not listed are languages in whose translations no co-compounds could be identified (Table 6.1). Outside Eurasia I could find co-compounds in Tok Pisin, in some varieties of Quechua, and in Malagasy, if the *N aman-N* construction (see Section 2.2.1 above) is counted as a co-compound pattern. No usable translations of the UDHR were available for most minority languages in Russia, except for Tatar, which was included.[5]

The most striking result of this quantitative analysis is the huge difference between highly co-compounding languages in East and South East Asia and weakly co-compounding languages in Europe. Even more interesting, however, is that the distribution of frequency of co-compounds across the translations is continuous, coming close to an exponential graph. A further interesting result is that type frequency (the number of different lexical representatives of co-compounds) and token frequency (the number of all instances of co-compounds in the text) behave very much the same in all texts. Put differently, the ratio of type to token frequency does not change greatly as the token frequency increases (the ratio is about 2:3 or above for moderately and highly co-compounding languages). Exceptions to this general tendency in translations with low frequencies seem to be due either to unreliable results with small numbers, or to lexicalizations. Whether there are five, four, three, two, one, or no co-compounds in a text and which they are is very much a matter of coincidence. This becomes especially clear if we compare the Finnish, the Saami, and the Estonian translations. In all of them there is a single (highly lexicalized) generalizing co-compound for 'world' (Finnish *maa.ilma* 'land.air > world'). In the Finnish text this expression happens to occur five times, and in the Saami four times, while it occurs in the Estonian text only once. Similarly, the higher token frequency of Basque is a mere coincidence because a single type ('man-woman > everybody'; see Section 3.3.4 above) happens to have a high token frequency in the text under consideration. However, because of the identity of meaning in the translations (their character as parallel texts), the number of types has some validity even for very small differences in numbers. We may thus conclude that type frequency is the better measure for the frequency of co-compounds in languages with a low level of co-compounding. However, for languages with moderate and high levels of co-compounding, type and token frequencies of co-compounds behave alike and it is therefore sufficient to measure either type or token frequency.

The translations of the UDHR have two major shortcomings for our purposes: First, many central Eurasian languages, while important in the distribution of co-compounds in Eurasia, could not be included here, and second, the UDHR, being a legal formulation, contains language that may deviate considerably from colloquial or written narrative style. Let us, therefore, consider a predominantly narrative text for which translations are available in many central Eurasian languages: the Gospel according to Mark. The complete sample of the languages examined is given in Table 6.1. Figure 6.3

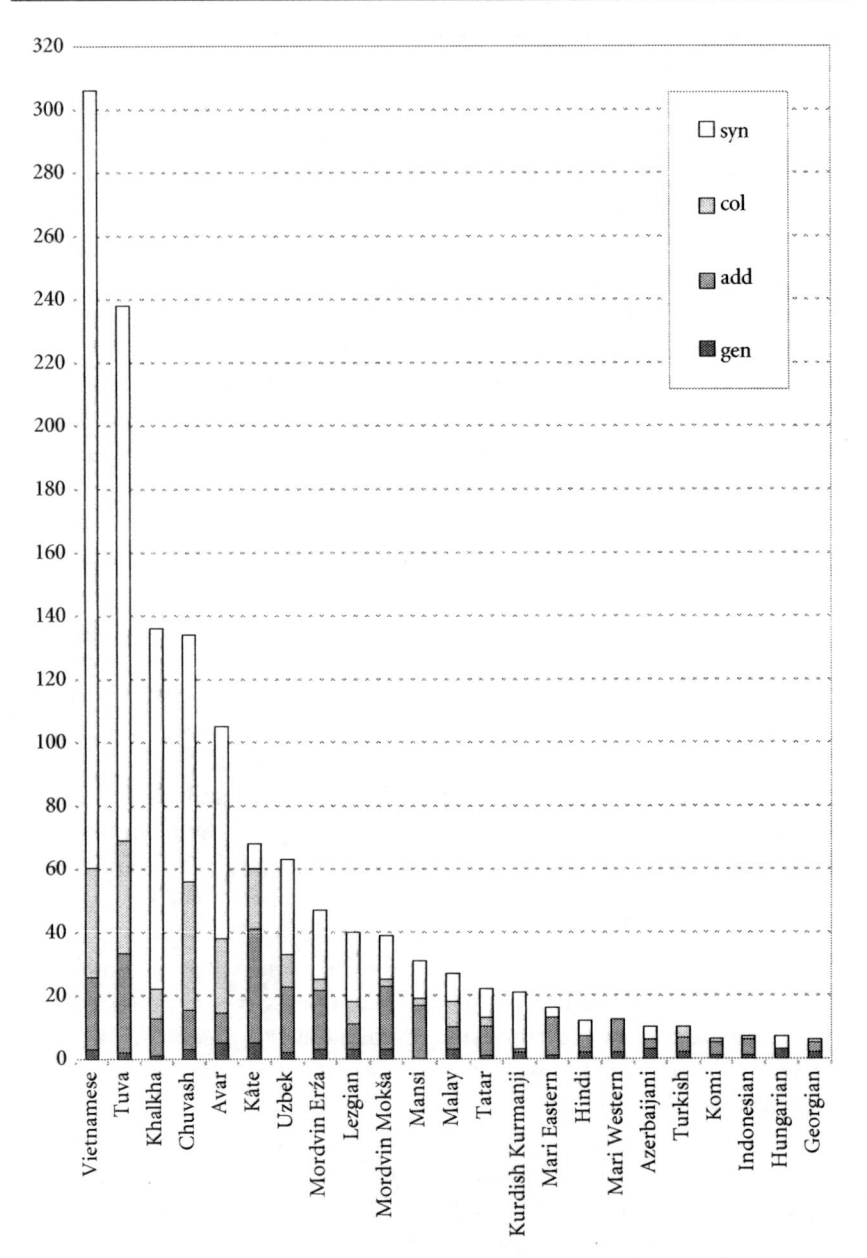

FIG. 6.3. Token frequency of co-compounds in different translations of Mark

shows the token frequency of co-compounds in translations of this text into Eurasian languages (in the order of frequency of co-compounds): Vietnamese (Austroasiatic), Tuva (Turkic), Khalkha (Mongolian), Chuvash (Turkic), Avar (North East Caucasian), Uzbek (Turkic), Erźa Mordvin (Uralic), Lezgian (North East Caucasian), Mokša Mordvin (Uralic), Mansi (Uralic), Malay (Austronesian), Tatar (Turkic), Kurmanji Kurdish (Indo-European), Eastern and Western Mari (Uralic), Hindi (Indo-European), Azerbaijani (Turkic), Turkish (Turkic), Komi (Uralic), Bahasa Indonesia (Austronesian), Hungarian (Uralic), and Georgian (Kartvelian). Languages with only very few generalizing or alternative co-compounds or without co-compounds (see Table 6.1) are not represented in Figure 6.3. One co-compounding language from another continent, Kâte (Trans-New Guinea), has been included. Several other translations have been included, but the exact number of co-compounds was not counted for practical reasons. In the Thai (Thai), Burmese, Lahu, Tibetan (all Sino-Tibetan), and Khmer (Austroasiatic) versions there is a high number of co-compounds, probably somewhere close to that of Tuva. Udmurt (Uralic) is lower than Erźa Mordvin, but higher than Mari. Mokša is lower than Erźa Mordvin, because it lacks a lexicalized co-compound for 'child'. Yakut and Khakas (both Turkic) are in the range of Uzbek and intermediate between Tuva and Turkish. Uyghur is lower than Uzbek, but higher than Tatar. Interestingly, Khalkha is lower than Tuva. The Khalkha translation, however, misses many opportunities to use additive or collective co-compounds such as they occur in other Khalkha texts. In Kalmyk I have counted only the nominal co-compounds and there are fewer (gen 2, add 20, coll 11, syn 30, total 63) than in Khalkha (gen 1, add 10, coll 10, syn 82, total 103). Lak and Tabasaran (North East Caucasian) are close to Lezgian, but certainly lower than Avar. One interesting aspect is the lack of co-compounds in the Classical Georgian text. Needless to say, there are no co-compounds in the translations of West European languages, if we disregard occasional dubious instances, such as 'deaf and dumb' and *Syrophenician*, which were not counted as co-compounds (rather as appositional and fusional compounds). Also noteworthy is the complete lack of co-compounds in Car-Nicobarese (Austroasiatic), given the fact that some Austroasiatic languages, such as Vietnamese and Khmer, have a very high frequency of co-compounds, and that even the Austronesian languages in South Asia (Munda languages and Khasi) have a moderate level of co-compounding.

The type frequency of co-compounds in the translations of Mark has not been counted for practical reasons and because it would convey only a small amount of relevant new information. The only area for which the distinction between type and token frequencies is relevant is New Guinea. In the Tok

Pisin text, which has not been included in Figures 6.3 and 6.4, there are only three types, but a token frequency of 160 (*man.meri* 'man.woman > human beings' 152, *papa.mama* 'father.mother > parents' 5, and *i go i kam* 'go come > go and come' 3; whether *yumi* 'you me > we (incl.)' with 48 should also be counted as a co-compound is unclear; in the UDHR, *manmeri/man meri* occurs 43 times).[6] In the Kâte text, the type frequency is higher than in Tok Pisin but much lower than in texts with a similar token frequency from the languages of Eurasia. In the Kube text (Kube is closely related to Kâte, even if the lexicon is quite different), for which I have not been able to identify all the co-compounds present, the following eight co-compounds together have a token frequency of 106 (only translations are given): 'man woman > - human beings' 59, 'mother father > parents' 9, 'son daughter > children' 8, 'elder_sibling younger_sibling' 7, 'hand leg' 7, 'house fire > home' 4, 'night day' 3, 'go come' 9.[7]

Instead of counting type frequencies I concentrated on the token frequencies of the most important semantic types (Chapter 5), notably the generalizing, additive, collective, and synonymic co-compounds. Alternative co-compounds, which happen to be very rare, were counted together with generalizing co-compounds, because they behave in a highly similar way to generalizing co-compounds cross-linguistically. Ornamental, imitative, and other non-basic types of co-compounds were counted as instances of synonymic co-compounds. Co-compounds in the domain of the concept of 'property' were counted arbitrarily as collective co-compounds in all translations. The frequency of the four semantic types, generalizing (including alternative), additive, collective, and synonymic (including ornamental and imitative), is shown in Figure 6.3 and more clearly in Figure 6.4.

Figure 6.4 shows the proportions of tokens of the four semantic groups irrespective of the overall token frequency of co-compounds; put differently, it shows the proportions of the different semantic types. The most striking facts are that the proportion of synonymic co-compounds (with some minor exceptions) increases directly with the increase in the overall frequency of co-compounds, while the proportion of generalizing (and alternative co-compounds) decreases in inverse correlation with the increase of the overall frequency (in absolute terms, the frequency of generalizing co-compounds remains more or less constant in all languages with co-compounds; see Figure 6.3). Additive co-compounds are the dominant proportion at moderate levels of co-compounding.

The proportions of semantic types shown in Figure 6.4 suggest that co-compounds have characteristic SEMANTIC PROFILES which correlate with the overall text frequency of co-compounds, more or less irrespective of affiliation

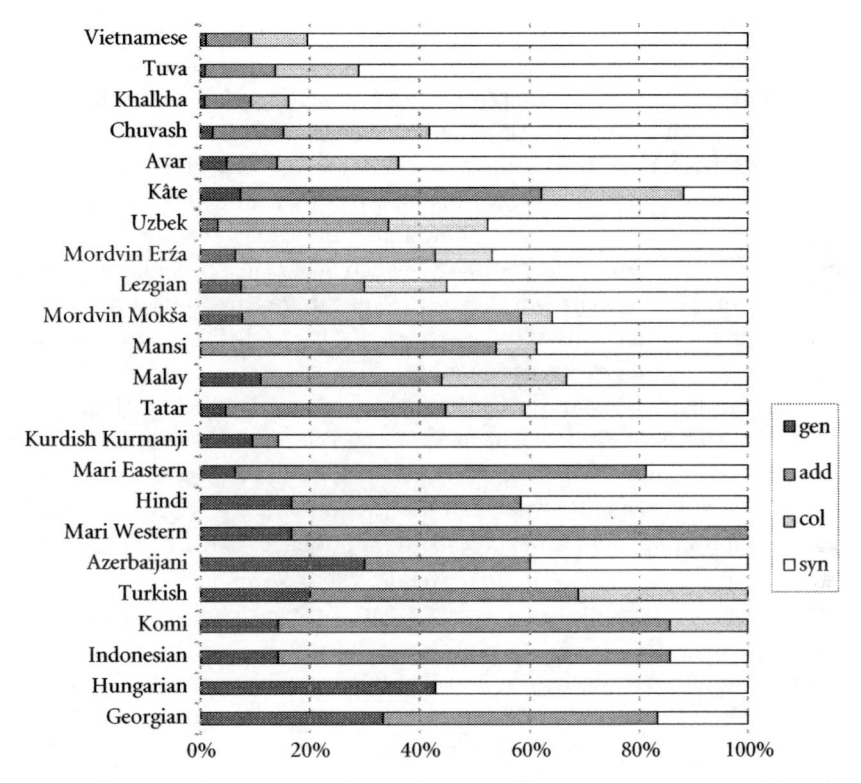

Fig. 6.4. Semantic profiles of co-compounds in different translations of Mark

to linguistic stocks. Further evidence for this claim will be given in Section 6.4 below. The most important properties of the semantic profile of co-compounds which correlate with overall text frequency are the following:

- the proportion of generalizing and alternative co-compounds decreases as overall frequency increases;
- the proportion of synonymic co-compounds increases as overall frequency increases;
- the proportion of additive co-compounds is highest at low-to-moderate levels of co-compounding; it is low at both low and high levels of co-compounding;
- the proportion of collective co-compounding is high at moderate-to-high levels of co-compounding;
- the higher the overall level of co-compounding, the better the profile corresponds to the expected profile. If the overall frequency is low, the profiles may be highly diverse (for instance, Hungarian and Komi).

It is, therefore, possible to rank texts quite accurately according to their overall frequency of co-compounds by considering the semantic profiles of co-compounds alone (especially if the overall frequency is high). Kâte and Kurmanji Kurdish are the exceptions that confirm the rule. For Kâte see above; it would conform more closely if type frequency instead of token frequency were being considered. For Kurmanji Kurdish there is reason to believe that the level of co-compounding in the text is considerably above average. The type *raw-rizim* 'tradition', which occurs five times in the text, is not given in the dictionary but is explained in the glossary to the text. Several synonymic co-compounds of the text are given in the dictionary only in their variant form with an overt coordinator.

It is true that many more texts (both parallel texts and original texts) would have to be considered in order to corroborate the assumption of a general correlation of overall text frequency of co-compounds with proportions of different semantic types. But the data presented in Figure 6.4 should suffice to show that in many texts co-compounds have characteristic semantic profiles which correlate with the overall text frequency in specific ways. Section 6.4 will present further evidence using original texts from an individual language.

Table 6.1 summarizes the levels of text frequency of co-compounds in the two parallel texts, UDHR and Mark. It is clear that the ranking in Table 6.1 and in Figures 6.1, 6.2, and 6.3 does not necessarily correspond directly to the sequence of frequencies of co-compounds in Eurasian languages since the texts are only representative of the languages they are written in to a certain extent, given that they are translations. Nevertheless, it is a valid starting point for the comparison of text frequencies of co-compounds across Eurasian languages.

It becomes clear from the data considered in this section that the frequency of co-compounds is distributed in a highly characteristic areal pattern across Eurasia. Co-compounds are most frequent in continental East and South East Asia, their frequency diminishing as one moves westward. It holds for most pairs of geographically contiguous languages that they have the same or similar levels of co-compounding. There are only a few exceptions to this general tendency, notably Basque, which, with its moderate level of co-compounding, does not fit its location in West Europe. Other exceptions are Modern Tamil and Modern Uyghur, which have too few co-compounds for their geographical location. The material discussed in this section leads us to formulate the following hypothesis about the distribution of co-compounds in Eurasia:

TABLE 6.1. Languages considered in the two parallel texts ranked according to their frequency of co-compounds

UDHR		Mark	
counted	*not counted*	*counted*	*not counted*
Mandarin			
Vietnamese	Hmong (White)	Vietnamese	
Tibetan	Burmese, Laotian		Burmese, Thai,
Khmer	Korean	Tuva	Khmer, Lahu,
Khalkha			Tibetan, Tok Pisin
Kazakh		Khalkha, Chuvash,	Kube
Uzbek		Avar, Kâte	Kalmyk
Kirghiz		Uzbek, Mordvin,	Yakut, Khakas,
Kannada	Malayalam	Lezgian	Toaripi, Melpa,
Turkmen			Uyghur
Abkhaz,		Mansi, Malay, Tatar,	Udmurt, Khanty, Lak,
Basque,		Kurmanji Kurdish,	Tabasaran, Adyghe
Malay, Tatar,	Nepali, Aceh,	Mari (Eastern), Hindi,	
Georgian,	Sundanese,	Mari (Western),	
Minangkabau,	Balinese, Quechua	Azerbaijani,	
Bengali, B.	(Ayacucho)	Turkish, Komi, B.	
Indonesia, Hindi,		Indonesia,	
Finnish, Saami,		Hungarian,	
Estonian,		Georgian	
Hungarian,			
Turkish,			
(Malagasy)			
		only very few generalizing co-compounds:	
		Armenian (Classical), Cebuano, Estonian, Finnish, Modern Greek, Haitian Creole, Tagalog, Yabem	
no co-compounds found:		*no co-compounds found:*	
Azerbaijani, English (and other West European languages), Ewe, Modern Greek, Kurdish, Latvian, Lithuanian, Maltese, Maori, Romani (two varieties), Russian, Samoan, Tagalog		English (and other West European languages), Latvian, Lithuanian, Nicobarese (Car), Russian	

198 Areal Distribution in the Languages of Eurasia

The phenomenon of co-compounding shows continuous diminishment across languages in all directions from the area of highest frequency in continental East and South East Asia and particularly as one moves westward.

In the next section we will look at some of the major linguistic stocks of Eurasia and consider whether the hypothesis about the continuous areal diminishment of co-compounds from east to west can be supported for each particular linguistic stock. We shall also attempt to determine whether the frequency of co-compounds tends to be constant in areas with high genetic diversity and whether language isolates in Eurasia behave in accordance with the hypothesis.

6.3 More evidence for a continuous diminishment of co-compounds from east to west throughout Eurasia

6.3.1 *Turkic, Mongolian, and Tungus*

Turkic is a language family that has dispersed throughout a spread zone (Nichols 1992: 13–24). Turkic languages are extended over a vast area in northern Eurasia from East and North East Asia (Uyghur, Yakut) to North and South Europe (Karaim in Lithuania, Turkish). Furthermore, Turkic languages are much more closely related to each other, both genetically and typologically, than languages of other extended stocks in Eurasia, such as Indo-European, Uralic, Sino-Tibetan, and Austroasiatic. Because of these characteristics, the Turkic languages provide a good illustration of the importance of geography for the distribution of co-compounds in Eurasia. If we look at the Turkic languages considered in the two parallel texts in Section 6.2, we get the picture in Figure 6.5 for the frequency of co-compounds.

It is clear that we should not overinterpret the small differences between texts with frequencies in a similar range. It is, however, obvious from the material that central Asian Turkic languages tend to have a higher frequency of co-compounds than Turkish and Azerbaijani in the Near East, and that by far the highest frequency in the Turkic languages that have been considered is in Tuva, spoken in Mongolia and neighboring parts of Russia, a language that has had very intensive language contact with Mongolian, which is highly co-compounding. To put it differently, the relative frequency of co-compounds in Turkic languages is to a large extent predictable from their present-day geographic position (but less so from their genetic subclassification). This might lead to the assumption that co-compounds in Turkic are of recent origin. However, the oldest attested Turkic sources, Old Turkic (most closely related to Uyghur and attested from various parts of North West China,

```
              low < ----------------------frequency of co-compounds----------------------> high
UDHR:         Azerbaijani < Turkish < Tatar < Turkmen < Kirghiz < Uzbek < Kazakh
Mark:         Turkish < Azerbaijani < Tatar < Uyghur < Uzbek, Yakut, Khakas < Chuvash < Tuva
```

FIG. 6.5. Frequency of co-compounds in Turkic languages

Northern Mongolia, and Siberia about 750–1300 AD), have a high frequency of co-compounds (for instance, see the text in von Gabain 1950: 270). From the high frequency of co-compounds in Old Turkic, we may suppose that the low level of co-compounding found in Modern Turkish should not be reconstructed for Proto-Turkic. Rather, it seems that Turkish languages in the West (probably under the influence of western languages such as Arabic and Russian, Turkish *ve* 'and' < Arabic) reduced their frequency of co-compounds. Eastern Turkic languages, on the other hand, increased their frequency of co-compounds (probably under the influence of Mongolian, Chinese, and other eastern languages), except Modern Uyghur which behaves unexpectedly. Co-compounds containing Mongolian loanwords, frequent in Tuva (but also in Kirghiz, as in the second element in *üj-bülö* 'house/yurta-family/family_member > family' found in the text of the UDHR [Khalkha *ger bül* 'house/yurta-family/family_member > family']), seem to point in this direction. On the other hand, in central Asian Turkic languages there are many co-compounds that contain Arabic loanwords, such as Uzbek *qadr-qimmat* 'worth-preciousness > dignity', evidence that borrowing loanwords does not necessarily entail that a language will assume a degree of co-compounding similar to that of the donor language.

The east to west distribution of co-compounds in Turkic languages is not without exception. Chuvash, the only surviving language of a former Western Turkic branch, has a degree of co-compounding which is considerably higher than that of Tatar, although both languages are spoken in the area of the Volga basin. The higher-than-expected level of co-compounding (from the geographical viewpoint) in Chuvash is evidence that co-compounds in Turkic cannot be a recent innovation from the east. There is no language in the neighborhood of Chuvash from which Chuvash could have got its co-compounds. It can therefore be assumed that co-compounding in Chuvash goes back to Proto-Turkic origins, provided that it did not develop independently, which seems unlikely (see also Ramstedt 1952: 253).

The Turkic languages share many typological features with the Mongolian and Tungus languages, and the three families were formerly believed to form a single genetic stock, Altaic, a theory which is now considered highly controversial.

Mongolian languages have a high level of co-compounds. From the Turkic languages that I have considered there is only one, Tuva, which has an equally high level of co-compounding as Khalkha. The lower frequency in Kalmyk in Mark is at least an indication that this Mongolian language in Europe has a lower frequency than Khalkha.

From the little information I could collect about Tungus languages it seems that they generally have a lower level of co-compounds than Mongolian and Turkic languages. The exception is Manchu, which was exposed to intensive contact with Chinese and Mongolian. Judging from the examples in Gorelova's (2002) Manchu grammar, it seems that co-compounding is quite common in Manchu, even if it is covert (Section 4.4.3), because coordination is often expressed by simple juxtaposition. Clear examples of co-compounds are the following: *ahūn deo* 'elder_brother younger_brother > brothers' (ibid.: 194 and passim) and *(yuan wai) eigen sargan* '(Yuanway) husband wife > Yuanway and his wife' (ibid.: 268). The examples of Manchu synonymic co-compounds given in Gorelova (2002) are all contextually motivated, notably by generalization and emphasis. Consider (1) with emphatic context:

(1) Manchu (Gorelova 2002: 382)
 Emu amba **yafan kūaran** sabu.mbi
 one big **garden courtyard** see.IMPV
 '(He) has seen a big and beautiful garden.'

If this example is typical, it suggests that conventionalization of synonymic co-compounds is quite restricted in Manchu. According to Gorelova (ibid.: 383) co-compounds (pair words, in her terminology) are not characteristic of other Tungus languages, although co-compounds can occasionally be found. In Nanai, they seem to be restricted more or less to some few generalizing co-compounds. In Even, there are co-compounds at least in the western variety described by Sotavalta (1978), which is strongly influenced by Yakut (*buwtüör.u* 'land/world-land.ACC > land' in an example that has been translated from Yakut, where the co-compound *sir-doidu* 'land-place/area > land' appears in the Yakut original; ibid.: 24).

To summarize, evidence from the Turkic languages supports the hypothesis that co-compounding is areally distributed in Eurasia westward from East Asia. The only exception, Chuvash, suggests that co-compounding, in spite of its being continually adjusted in Turkic languages to the level of its neighbors, is not a recent innovation imported from the East. However, more research is needed for Tungus languages.

The high diversity in the level of co-compounding across Turkic languages is important for the typology of co-compounds. Turkic languages are very closely related, which means that they are typologically similar. If they vary greatly in their level of co-compounding, this is strong evidence that the level of co-compounding in a language is not determined by any other features of its structure.

6.3.2 The languages of the Caucasus

The Caucasus is the prototype of a residual zone (in Nichols 1992: 13–15) and bears the following characteristics: high structural and genetic diversity, deviant cast of the sound systems and grammars in comparison to the neighborhood languages, the various languages remain localized over a very long period, while new languages move in from neighboring spread zones (Indo-European: Armenian, Ossete and more recently Russian; Azerbaijani and other Turkic varieties).

In spite of the high genetic and typological diversity of Caucasian languages, co-compounding is very similar throughout the languages of the Caucasus. Consider (2) and (3) with the co-compound 'hand-face' from Abkhaz and Lezgian (for a parallel example from Georgian see Section 1.1.2 example (4)):

(2) Abkhaz (Hewitt 1979: 218)
yə.ç'ə́-yə.nap'ə́   (ø.)j°j°a.nə́
his.face-his.hand   it.wash.CONV
'[The man will enter the house, take off his coat,] wash his hands and face, [sit down at the table and begin to eat.]'

(3) Lezgian (Haspelmath 1993: 108)
Hürmeta   murk   xiz   qaji   ce.l   čin-ǧil
Hürmet:ERG   ice   like   cold   water.SRESS   face-hand
cüxwe.na
wash.AOR
'Hürmet washed his face and hands with icy-cold water.'

Even if the affixation patterns differ considerably (double possessive prefix in Abkhaz, single case suffix in Georgian, no affix in Lezgian), the co-compound 'hand-face' (always associated with 'wash') is the same lexically. As a whole, co-compounding has about the same level and extension in Abkhaz, Georgian,[8] and Lezgian.

A specific parallel between North West Caucasian and Kartvelian are generalizing verbal co-compounds with identical stems and opposite prefixes, such as Adyghe *qe.k°e-me.k°e.žə* 'hither.go-3SG.go.back = he goes here and there' and Georgian *mi.v.di-mo.v.di.var* 'thither.1SG.go-hither.1SG.go.1SG: be:PRS = I go here and there' (see also Section 2.4.3). Nevertheless, this type has characteristics of its own in Adyghe, where the class of locational prefixes is closely associated (and partly identical formally) with incorporated body parts. Consider (4) with the incorporated nouns 'e- 'hand' and ɬe- 'foot'.

(4) Adyghe (Rogava and Keraševa 1966: 293)
    Psə.m   əthele.re   qele.c'əq°ə.r
    water.ERG   suffocate.CONV   child.small.ABS:DEF
    'e.tx̌°e.ɬe.tx̌°e.žə.štəǧ.ep.
    hand.thrash.foot.thrash.again.IMPF.NEG
    'The boy who drowned in the water did not thrash about any more (i.e. with hands and feet).'

There are even ornamental examples, where one of the body parts does not make sense. In the following example 'e- 'hand' cannot be understood in its proper meaning (one does not run with hands): me.'e.će.ɬa.će '3SG.hand.run.foot.run = he runs here and there' (ibid.). The examples show that verbal co-compounding in Adyghe and Georgian can be both very similar and very different at the same time.

Lezgian has no co-compounds of finite verbs, but these are, however, quite common in other Dagestanian languages, such as Hunzib (van den Berg 1995: 114) and Avar. In the translations of the Gospel according to Mark (Section 6.2) Avar has a considerably higher degree of co-compounding than Lezgian, Tabasaran, or Lak. In Avar, synonymic co-compounds, both nominal and verbal, are quite frequent, as shown in (5):

(5) Avar (Mark 1:45)
    ...ġadan-či   heč'.eb   bak'.alda   w.axča-ḣwan
    person-man   NEG:EX.PTC   place.SRESS   M.hide-disappear:CONV:PST
    č'e.ze   kka.na.
    stay.INF   be.PST
    '...but was without in desert places.'

It seems, however, that most synonymic co-compounds in Avar are contextually motivated (Section 5.5). In example (5), ġadan-či 'person-person/man > man' is motivated by negation (it is not used in referential contexts in the same text for 'person, man'), while w.axča-ḣwan 'M.hide-disappear/hide:CONV:PST > hidden' is motivated by the distributive context.

As a rule, languages from stocks that are not autochthonous to the Caucasus (Armenian, Ossete, Russian, Azerbaijani) do have a lower level of co-compounding than the autochthonous Caucasian languages,[9] which suggests that co-compounding is not a recent phenomenon in that region.

The autochthonous languages of the Caucasus, however, which are highly diverse typologically, have a relatively homogeneous level of co-compounding. They are much less diverse in this respect than the Turkic languages which are closely related genetically. Within the Caucasus, the highest diversity in co-compounding seems to be found not between the different linguistic stocks, but within a single one: North East Caucasian (finite verbal co-compounds in Avar and Hunzib, but not in Lezgian).

6.3.3 Indo-European

In the Indo-European languages, co-compounding is characteristic of eastern languages which are not necessarily closely related to each other, notably Tokharian, Indo-Aryan (see Section 7.2.1), some varieties of Russian, and Modern Greek. Some few co-compounds can, however, also be found in the west. In Latin co-compounds are rare, consisting of juxtaposed word forms (Bader 1962: 337–40): *ioc.a sēri.a* 'pleasant.N:PL serious.N:PL > the pleasant and the serious'. Co-compounds in Modern Greek have an affinity with bahuvrihi-compounds (see 1.1.1 and 7.2.1), and are quite different in form from co-compounds in other Eurasian languages.

Tokharian has a high level of co-compounding similar to other languages of Ancient East Asia (see especially Aalto 1964: 70). Let us consider here just a single example to illustrate that it is hardly possible to reconstruct individual co-compounds in Indo-European by means of the comparative method. Tokharian A *ñom-klyu* and B *ñem-kälywe* 'name-glory' has parallels in Old Turkic (Old Uyghur) *at kü* 'name fame/glory > renown', and Mongolian *nere aldar* id., as well as in languages from further away, such as Hungarian *hírnév* 'news name > fame'. Aalto advocates an areal explanation for co-compounds in Tokharian (ibid.: 76). On the other hand, the components Tokharian A *ñom*, B *ñem* 'name' and A *klyu*, B *kälywe* 'fame, glory' represent two well-established Indo-European etyma that also occur in parallel settings in other Indo-European languages. As Campanile (1990: 89) shows, in epic Classical Greek *ónoma* 'name' often appears in similar contexts as *kléos* 'glory' and both collocate with *áphthiton* 'imperishable'. The Vedic-Greek correspondence *śravo akṣitam*, *kléos áphthiton* 'imperishable glory' has been claimed in Indo-European linguistics to go back to a common poetic language. Tokharian A *ñom-klyu*, B *ñem-kälywe* as a word pair (in the sense of words closely associated with each other; Section 1.1.5) might, therefore, very well be inherited from Proto-Indo-European, in which case there is no need for an areal explanation. The two etyma making up the Tokharian compound do not occur, however, as a compound in Classical Greek, and the compounding of the word pair could be claimed to be an innovation of Tokharian based on East Asian influences. This example suggests that it is almost impossible to reconstruct individual co-compounds on the basis of etymological considerations.

For the development of co-compounds in Indo-Aryan from Vedic to Sanskrit, see Section 7.2.1. Modern Indian languages, such as Hindi and Bengali, have low-to-moderate levels of co-compounds (slightly lower than in most Dravidian languages, but higher than in Modern Tamil). Additive co-compounds of pairs of relatives are very common. This is not the case, however, for Romani, an Indo-Aryan language that has moved westward to Europe. There are only some very marginal co-compounds in some varieties of Romani.[10] Usually none are found in parallel texts in Romani, whereas Hindi and other Indo-Aryan languages do have co-compounds. Consider in this context the co-compounds in Indian English (Section 1.1).

It is also interesting to consider the terms for siblings in some Indo-Iranian languages with contacts to Sino-Tibetan or Turkic languages. Indo-European languages usually have single terms for 'brother' and 'sister' and do not make the distinction between elder and younger siblings unlike most Turkic, Dravidian, and Sino-Tibetan languages. Exceptions are colloquial Nepali, which, unlike Hindi, has terms for elder and younger brothers and sisters and forms co-compounds with them, and Tadzhik, which, unlike the closely related Persian, has borrowed the Turkic expressions for elder and younger siblings from a Central Turkic language. There the Turkic expressions continue to exist alongside the inherited Iranian words and may be combined as co-compounds.

In Russian, the degree of co-compounding differs greatly across dialects and varieties. Co-compounds are almost absent from Standard Russian. In Russian folklore, however, co-compounds are used in ways that are very similar to Mordvin (although there are also clear differences, especially formal ones, between co-compounding in Russian and in Mordvin). Russian co-compounds are especially frequent in the 'Byliny' (traditional epic poems; see also Section 7.5), where co-compounds consisting of three parts occur, such as in (6) (I don't know of any parallels from Mordvin):

(6) Russian, Byliny (Putilov 1989–90, 2: 68)
Ne vaše ja p'ju-em-kušaju / I ne vas
Not your I drink:1SG-eat: 1SG-eat:1SG and not you:ACC
xoču i slušati.
want:1SG also hear:INF
'I do not eat and drink yours / And not you I want to serve.'

Because of its association with the folkloristic style, co-compounds in Standard Russian evoke associations with the sphere of folklore. This effect is exploited in (7) from Venedikt Erofeev's *Moskva-Petuški* (written 1969/70; co-compounds and their translation in boldface):

(7) Russian (Erofeev 1990: 7)
I v dorogu bez ogljadki—ajda, rebjata, **uznavat'-vyjaznjat'**, komu na Rusi žit' xorošo, a vot nam-to čto-to počemu-to ploxovato. **Syščem-otyščem**, komu xorošo, vytjanem ego za uško...
'And let's go ahead without looking backward, go on, guys, to **know and find out**, who has a good life in Russia, while we have it somehow rather bad, who knows why. Let us **seek and search** who has a good life, and drag him out by his ear...'

Erofeev uses the co-compounds in this passage to make an allusion to a well-known work in the Russian literature that draws on the folkloristic style where co-compounds are frequent, Nikolaj Nekrasov's (1953) *Komu na Rusi žit' xorošo* (*Who can be happy and free in Russia*, written 1863–77).

According to Keller (1922) co-compounds ('asyndeta') are an archaic trait in Slavic languages. But again, as in Tokharian, it is not possible here to reconstruct individual co-compounds. There is no doubt that there is a parallel between the Russian words in the co-compound *rod-plemja* 'kin-kin' used in the Russian *kakovo ty rody-plemeni?* 'from which kin-kin are you?' and the two words used side by side in Serbian in *ti ne imaš roda ni plemena* 'you have neither kin nor clan' (Dickenmann 1934: 73). It is also undoubtedly the case that in the Mordvin co-compound *rod-pl'ema* as in *T'e lomaneś minek rod-pl'eman* 'This man is of our kin-kin' (Buzakova 1993: 555), both components are borrowed from Russian. Nevertheless, it is Russian and Mordvin, and not Serbian, that use co-compounds.

Among the Baltic languages, co-compounding in Latvian and Lithuanian is considerably less common than in folkloristic Russian and clearly less common than in Estonian (on co-compounds in the Baltic and Finnic languages, see also Uotila 1980). Especially common in modern Latvian are generalizing co-compounds that are mostly written as two words (with two separate word stresses): *krustām šķērsām* 'criss-cross', *šis tas* 'this or that' (but *daudz.maz* 'many.little > about' written as one word with one word stress). A fully univerbated example is *dien.nakts* 'day.night > 24 hours'. As a whole, co-compounding in the Baltic languages does not exceed co-compounding in West European languages very much.

To summarize, co-compounding in Indo-European is marginal, with some few exceptions, notably Tokharian, some varieties of Russian, and of Indo-Aryan languages (see also Kurmanji Kurdish in Section 6.2). Wherever co-compounding occurs above a minimal level in Indo-European languages (with the exception of Modern Greek), it clearly has areal implications. This does not mean, however, that co-compounding in Indo-European languages is exactly identical with co-compounding in the contact languages. Even if the areal factor cannot be denied, Indo-European languages have co-compounds of their own, rather than just borrowed Turkic, Uralic, Caucasian, or Dravidian co-compounds.

6.3.4 *Uralic*

In Uralic linguistics, co-compounds are usually treated in connection with double dual marking (Section 2.3.2), parallelism, and asyndetic coordination[11] (see, in particular, the important monograph by Lewy (1911) on Hungarian, Khanty, and Udmurt). There is little research that focuses exclusively on co-compounds, and especially on their text frequency, among Uralic languages. I deal exclusively here with Finno-Ugric languages since the available evidence from Samoyedic languages is too sparse. From the texts I have considered, it seems to me that Mordvin, which has been treated extensively in Chapter 5, clearly has a higher text frequency than Mari, with Udmurt somewhere between Mordvin and Mari. Khanty and Mansi, in spite of their higher degree of asyndetic coordination and stronger tendency toward parallelism, appear to have a lower text frequency of co-compounds than Mordvin.

The clearest areal differences found are between the westernmost languages in Northern and Central Europe (Finnic, including Finnish and Estonian, Saami, and Hungarian) and the eastern Finno-Ugric languages on both sides of the Ural mountains. Thus, in Estonian, such co-compounds as *isa-ema* 'father-mother' occasionally occur, but *van.em.ad* 'older.CMPR.PL' is the normal word for 'parents'. Such collective co-compounds as *suu-silmad* 'mouth-eye.PL' and *luu.d-liikme.d* 'bone.PL-limb.PL' occur occasionally, especially in expressive contexts as in (8), but these are not the normal words for 'face' and 'body'.

(8) Estonian (Tammsaare 1963: 346 and 241)
    a ...se.l   ol.i.d   suu-silm.ad   tul.d   ja   suitsu
       that.ADESS be.PST.3PL mouth-eye.PL fire.PART and smoke:PART
       täis.
       full
       '[...Pearu shot with his pistol, so that] he (Matu) had the mouth and eyes full of fire and smoke.'
    b ...et luu.d-liikme.d   p.ole.ks.ki   nagu   tema
       thatbone.PL-limb.PL NEG.be.COND.also like   her
       luu.d-liikme.d.
       bone.PL-limb.PL
       '[In the evening Mari sometimes feels] like her bones and limbs were not like her bones and limbs.'

Across Finnic and Hungarian there are some isolated lexicalizations of co-compounds (Estonian *maailm*, Finnish *maailma* 'world' < *maa+ilma* 'land-+*sky', *ilma* now means 'air', Hungarian *arc* 'face' < *orr* 'nose' + *száj* 'eye', see Lewy 1911: 7, and *hír.név* 'news.name > glory') that suggest that co-compounding was more common at earlier stages of Finnic and Hungarian.

To summarize, the geographically western Finno-Ugric languages (Finnic, Saami, and Hungarian) have lower levels of co-compounding than the geographically eastern ones.

6.3.5 *Dravidian*

Co-compounding is not common in all Dravidian languages to the same extent. There is, however, no correlation of the frequency of co-compounds with the genetic subclassification of Dravidian languages. Thus, within South Dravidian, Modern Tamil has almost no co-compounds (Asher 1989 lists only a few examples that are not actually in general use),[12] whereas in Ālu-Kurumba, a small tribal language in the Nilgiri mountains, which according to Kapp (1982: XXIX) is archaic Tamiloid with some features of Kannada, texts abound with co-compounds. In Ālu-Kurumba it is even common to have co-compounds with three parts, such as *mara-cĕḍi-koḍi* 'trees, plants, and climbers', *male-bĕṭṭu-kallu* 'high mountains, mountains and stones' (Kapp 1982: 237, from a creation myth; such co-compounds with three members seem to be predominantly collective co-compounds) and there are also conventionalized synonymic (*uru-bari* 'body-body > [human] body), ornamental (*ka:yi-kaja* 'vegetable-weed > vegetables'), and imitative co-compounds (*go:ḷu-goṭṭe* 'ghost-IMI > ghosts') which seem to have a mainly collective function (ibid.: 199). The highest frequency of co-compounds in Dravidian is found in traditional religious texts (prayers, myths) in small tribal languages, such as Toda (see Emeneau 1984: 215, No. 62). For South and South Central Dravidian, the low level of co-compounds in Tamil[13] seems to be the exception, since co-compounds are common in Kannada and Konda (consider the texts in Krishnamurti 1969 and Steever 1988: 70).

At least some Dravidian languages have co-compounds composed of finite verbs, sometimes difficult to distinguish from temporal sequencing (converbs and serial verbs). While the dominant strategy for temporal sequencing in Dravidian languages is deranking non-final verbs with the same subject to converbs, some languages also have serial verbs (here, this means sequences of two fully inflected verbs). In Konda, non-final verbs in verb sequencing are truncated (example (9), the marker for person and number is reduced to only a single vowel), but not in co-compounds (10).

(9) Konda (Steever 1988: 72)
   vā.t.a   sur.t.an
   come.PST.TPE   see.PST.3SG:M
   'he came and saw'

(10) Konda (Steever 1988: 70; Krishnamurti 1969: text 7.15)
   ...vizu   aya   kulur   poṭi   ti.n.ad   u.ṇ.ad.
   all   that   crane   bird   eat.NPST.3SG:N drink.NPST.3SG:N
   '...that crane consumes everything.'

Generally, co-compounding in most Dravidian languages (at least in South and South Central Dravidian and except Modern Tamil) is slightly more common than in Indo-Aryan languages such as Hindi, although co-compounds will often consist of Indo-Aryan loanwords.

6.3.6 Sino-Tibetan

Co-compounds seem to exist throughout Sino-Tibetan with moderate or high frequency. There is also some diachronic evidence that they are no recent innovation.

Most languages of the Yi branch of Tibeto-Burman have family group classifiers originating from co-compounds (Bradley 2001; what Bradley calls Yi corresponds roughly to Loloish in the Ethnologue). In Yi languages, number + classifier either follow a head noun or serve as a full noun phrase without a head noun, the latter usually being the case with family group classifiers. In some languages, the relationship to a co-compound is still transparent, as in Akha (Southern Yi) sm^{21} da^{33} za^{21} 'three *father children > a father and two sons' (a^{21} da^{33} 'father', za^{21} 'child') where the family group classifier can be said to be synchronically a co-compound. In other languages, such as Lalo (Central Yi) sa^{33} pa^{21} + $\underline{la}^{21}$ 'three father+children > a father and two sons', the co-compound origin of the classifier has become opaque. The elements are not related to a^{55} ti^{33} 'father', za^{21} 'son'. The free form i^{21} 'grandchild', etymologically related to the second part $\underline{la}^{21}$, has lost its initial l, and $\underline{la}^{21}$ / $\underline{li}^{21}$, showing vowel harmony with the first part, occurs now in all four family group classifiers (ma^{33} $\underline{la}^{21}$ 'mother+children, fi^{21} $\underline{li}^{21}$ 'grandparent+children', pi^{21} $\underline{li}^{21}$ id.; free a^{55} ma^{33} is 'mother', fi^{21} 'ancestor', pa^{21} 'male'). Even if family group classifiers are absent from some Yi languages such as Lahu (having nominal co-compounds instead followed by numeral and general human classifier), they can be reconstructed for Proto-Yi, which entails that Proto-Yi had co-compounds.

Compounds have attracted the attention of historical linguists in Tibeto-Burman because their omnipresence in the basic vocabulary makes it difficult to reconstruct the genetic subclassification of Tibeto-Burman into sub-branches. As Matisoff (1978) puts it: 'Each TB language, when faced with the necessity of forming polysyllabic compounds, dips into its inheritance from the proto-treasury in its own unpredictable way' (ibid.: 63), so there is often more diversity between dialects than between languages. Consider the expressions for 'head' in several Tibeto-Burman languages and dialects in Table 6.2.

In none of the languages quoted is the word for 'head' etymologically a simple word; it consists diachronically of a prefix and a root morpheme, of two or three root morphemes, or of a prefix with two root morphemes. This makes it difficult to reconstruct the meaning of the root morphemes, especially as it has to be assumed that many of the prefixes derive diachronically from reduced roots. To this must be added the fact that processes such as clipping (see Section 4.2.3.iii) and synonymic sharpening (Section 5.3) may contribute considerably to the extension and change of meaning of the root morphemes.

Particularly illustrative for co-compounding are the expressions for 'lung' (ibid.: 113–23), where such a complex form as Khaling 'swah-prap is reconstructed as *s-wap-pwar-wap (*FLESH(sya)/LIVER(sin)-LUNG$_1$-LUNG$_3$-LUNG$_1$) and Bantawa som-phu-rok as *s-wap-pwar/pu-wap (*sya/sin-LUNG$_1$-LUNG$_3$/LUNG$_4$-LUNG$_1$). Such examples are evidence for the constant renewal of compounding in Tibeto-Burman.

TABLE 6.2. 'Head' in several Tibeto-Burman languages

'HEAD'	Prefix	*bu (>*wu)	*du(k) 'neck, head'	*s-ko(ŋ) 'hollow object'	*l(y)am/*lum 'round, whole'
Written Tibetan	d-	bu			
Bisu	'aŋ-		tù		
Akha		'ù-	dù		
Written Burmese		'û-		khôŋ	
Lisu		wu^1-	dɯ^3		
Lahu Nâ' (Black Lahu)		ó-		qō	
Lahu Nyi (Red Lahu)	'a-		-tù-	kù	
Lahu Shi (Yellow Lahu)	'a-			kù	
Maru		'áu-			làm
Lashi		'ú-			lèm
Atsi		u-			lum

Source: Matisoff (1978) following Nishida

In Sino-Tibetan linguistics it is common to speak of the cyclicity of compounds (Matisoff 1978: 71 f 'the compounding/prefixation cycle' and Beyer 1992: 95 f 'syllabic cycles'). Associated with this is the idea that languages predominantly comprised of monosyllabic words tend to become disyllabic through compounding (due to homonymy or other reasons) and again predominantly monosyllabic by the fusion of compounds. Trisyllabic examples such as Bantawa *som-phu-rok* show, however, that homonymy and the tendency toward disyllabic structure cannot be the only reason for such extensive compounding of synonyms (see also Section 7.3). What is not disputed, however, is that compounding, including co-compounding, is very well entrenched throughout the Sino-Tibetan stock.

6.3.7 *Austroasiatic*

Austroasiatic is highly diverse typologically. The Munda languages have many similarities to other South Asian languages (the most characteristic being SOV word order). Khasi is a language with both definite articles and gender (a combination which is very unusual for South, South East, and East Asia). Nicobarese has free word order with VOS as a frequent pattern.

Regarding co-compounds, most Austroasiatic languages that I have considered behave similarly to their contact languages. Vietnamese and Khmer, being South East Asian languages, exhibit a high level of co-compounding (Vietnamese being higher than Khmer due at least partly to the large amount of Pali loanwords in Khmer). Santali, Mundari, and Bonda (all Munda languages; for the last, see the texts in Bhattacharya 1968) and Khasi have a moderate level of co-compounding, but rather at the upper range for South Asia (similar to some South Central Dravidian languages spoken in the area of Munda languages) and share with other South Asian languages a predilection for echo-words. Characteristic for Khmer and Khasi, as well as some other Austroasiatic languages, is alliteration in co-compounds (see Section 5.2.6 for Khasi and 6.5 for Khmer). Semelai (Aslian, Malay Peninsula) has at least some co-compounds: *'ma'.bapa* 'mother.father > parents', *(sma') kntək kmpən* '(person) husband wife > married couple' (Kruspe 2004: 228, 217). The material given in Kruspe's grammar suggests that Semelai has a co-compounding level approximately comparable to that of Malay. The outlier is Car-Nicobarese, which has no or almost no co-compounds, at least not in the translation of Mark. Unfortunately, I have no information about the potential contact languages of Nicobarese spoken on the Nicobar and Andamanese islands.

Generally, the Austroasiatic languages support the hypothesis of a continuous diminishment of the frequency of co-compounds as one moves further away from continental East and South East Asia. It is very interesting that there is almost a complete lack of co-compounds in Car-Nicobarese, quite in line with its peripheral status in Eurasia.

6.3.8 Austronesian

Co-compounding in Austronesian languages seems not to be very deep-rooted and is most pronounced in some languages of Indonesia and Malaysia, although a small number of co-compounds may be found in Austronesian languages in the Philippines and Oceania.

Some Indonesian languages have a low-to-moderate level of co-compounds. Aceh has both nominal and verbal co-compounds. Consider (11) with a verbal co-compound (in boldface):

(11) Aceh (Durie 1985: 243)
      hana.meu.jan   ka.sidêk   ka.peurêksa.
      NEG:EX.INTRNS.when   2.consider   2.examine
      'You never consider or examine (anything).'

In Malay there is considerable variation. The literary Malay investigated by Nacaskul (1976) has a much higher level of co-compounding than the translations of the UDHR and of Mark. In Bimanese, an eastern Indonesian language, clear cases of co-compounds without coordinator are rare. However, it is very common to have coordinate syntagms with synonymic parts with the coordinator *ro* 'and', or with a reduced variant of it *ra* or *r* (Jonker 1896: 201). Malagasy, a western Indonesian language outside Indonesia, has a specific construction for natural coordination with a specific coordinator which is used in a similar way as co-compounds (Section 2.2.1).

In the languages of the Philippines, co-compounds are rarer than in Indonesian languages, and seem to be restricted to a few cases of generalizing co-compounds. For Tagalog see Section 5.2.2. A Cebuano example is *nagpang-adto-nganhi* 'coming-going > coming and going' (Mark 6:31). In Yabem, an Austronesian language in New Guinea, co-compounds are almost lacking, but (12) is an example of a repeated generalizing co-compound:

(12) Yabem (Mark 6:31)
      ...gebe   lau   taêsam   sê.ja.sê.mêŋ-sê.ja.sê.mêŋ.
      because people   many   3PL.go.3PL.come-3PL.go.3PL.come
      '...for there were many coming and going...'

Marshallese also has few generalizing verbal co-compounds: *i.to-i.tak* 'go/come.westward-go/come.eastward > travel, go around, journey', *jake.to-jake*.

tak 'give(polite).westward-give(polite).eastward > distribute, pass sth. around'.

In the comparative Austronesian dictionary (Tryon 1995, 2: 154 f), for the word for 'parents' juxtapositions of the words for 'father' and 'mother' are given for the following languages: Sundanese (Java), Balinese (Bali), Da'a (Sulawesi), Ngada, Sika (both Flores), Roti (Roti), Takia, Dami, Motu, and Mekeo (all Papua New Guinea).[14] It does not follow from this that precisely these languages have more co-compounds than other Austronesian languages, and in the UDHR version in Sundanese and in Balinese other expressions for 'parents' are used. It follows, however, that co-compounds do occur at a low level now and again in Austronesian languages in Indonesia and New Guinea, whereas they are not common in the languages of Polynesia and other regions of Oceania. Unfortunately, as regards the Austronesian languages from Taiwan (Formosa) very little material was available to me; this area could be important for the geography of co-compounds in Eurasia, since it seems that co-compounds are not common there. I could not find any, for instance, in Tung's (1964) Tsou texts.

To summarize, co-compounds are lacking or almost lacking in most Austronesian languages, with the exception of some languages of Indonesia and New Guinea, but it seems that the highest levels of co-compounding are nevertheless reached in some elaborate registers of Malay (Nacaskul 1976). Malay, like Russian, is a typical 'transition area' language in which the degree of co-compounding varies across different varieties and registers.

6.3.9 *Language isolates*

Not only stocks but also isolates may supply evidence about the prehistory of typological features, as was pointed out by Nichols (1992).

Basque is an exception to the continuous areal distribution of frequency levels of co-compounds across Eurasia. As a West European language it should not have co-compounds, but it does. This should not, however, be a great surprise for typologists, since Basque also differs in many other respects from its neighboring Romance languages (for instance, its dominant SOV word order, an outlier of the central Eurasian large SOV area).

In Basque (Alan R. King, p.c., Jacobsen 1982), co-compounds consisting of names for the opposite sex are most prominent (*anai-arreb.ak* 'brothers and sisters', *aiton-amon.ak* 'grandparents'). Other co-compounds include *ikasle-irakasle.ak* 'students and teachers', *hortz-agin.ak* 'teeth, (literally:) front teeth and back teeth'. Verbs occur as components of nominalized co-compounds as in *jan.edan.a* 'eat-drink.DEF > food and drink, feasting, banquet', *joan-etorri.a* 'go-come.DEF > going and coming, round trip'. In many domains where, for example, Georgian can use co-compounds such as 'day and night', 'old and young', 'hands and feet', 'gold and silver', co-compounds in Basque, according to Alan R. King, do not sound right. There is also at least one opaque co-compound in Basque: *guraso.a.k* 'parents' is etymologically a co-compound (< *agure-atso 'old man-old woman').[15] Co-compounding in Basque thus seems to be limited to nominal generalizing and additive co-compounds (although parts of co-compounds may be verbal stems, the compounds as wholes will be nouns).

Co-compounding in Basque is not completely isolated areally. Romance languages do not completely lack co-compounds, consider *pankezo, pankero* 'bread-cheese > weasel' in the Romance dialects of the Hautes- and Basses-Pyrénées and of Aragon *paniquesa* id. besides Basque *ogi.gaztai* 'bread-cheese > weasel' (Böhringer 1935: 82, a taboo name), Spanish *vaivén* 'a hither and thither, commuter traffic' (used only as a noun, not as a verbal co-compound as its parts 'go' and 'come' would suggest; this co-compound was already registered by Pott 1862), Italian *fortepiano* (for Italian see also Lindner 2002: 321).

Burushaski, an isolate language in Northern Pakistan, has a low-to-moderate level of co-compounding, which roughly corresponds to the level that would be expected from its geographic position. For the expression of natural coordination there is either single marking for case and indefiniteness with a coordinator, or single marking for case and indefiniteness without coordinator (Lorimer 1935: 105), both of which seem to alternate quite freely. The latter marking type represents co-compounding. Consider (13) with the co-compound in boldface:

(13) Burushaski (Lorimer 1935: 105)
 ja gʊtɛ **hiŋ sʌm** rʌč nɛ hʊru.
 my this **door smoke_hole** guard go stay
 'Stay guarding this door and smoke-hole of mine.'

In the expression for 'parents' the coordinator *kɛ* 'and' may be present or absent. Inalienable nouns in Burushaski always have possessive prefixes and there is always double marking of possessive prefixes (if there are any) in co-compounds: *mu: mu:mi.ɛ ha:lʊm* 'POSS:F:father POSS:F:mother.OBL house: ABL > from her father and mother's house'. The expression for 'children' - *ak -yu* apparently derives from *-ai kɛ -yu* 'daughter and son', with a fossilized reduced form of the coordinator *kɛ* 'and' at the end of the first component.

Co-compounds, at least of the generalizing type, were also used in Sumerian (*an-ki* 'sky-earth', *lú-tur-gal* 'big (and) small people'; Jestin 1951: 65), an isolate language of the Ancient Middle East (about 2500–1600 BC). I have no evidence for other languages of the Ancient Middle East, such as Elamite and Hurrian, which have no cognate languages in modern times.

In Kolyma Yukaghir (Yukaghir is sometimes connected to Uralic, but the evidence is not too convincing, so I will consider it an isolate here), juxtaposition is a common strategy of nominal coordination as well as marking with the comitative (Maslova 2003: 316). Natural coordination can be indicated, however, by single possessive pronouns or single grammatical suffixes (ibid.: 317, 'typical group'). It seems that at least some tight instances of juxtaposition in Yukaghir are co-compounds, such as *amun iŋd'ī* 'bone skinflint' in... *bojs'e amun iŋd'ī.ŋōt gude.delle* 'entirely bone skinflint.TRNSF become.SS:PFV = having become very thin' (ibid.: 317) and *tī-tā* 'here-there > here and there' (ibid.: 9).

For Ainu I cannot register any co-compounds. Ainu has, however, extensive parallelism in legends (see Batchelor 1926/1996: 124).

In isolate languages in Eurasia, the level of co-compounding corresponds approximately to the level expected from their geographical position or is even higher, as in the case of Basque. The presence of co-compounds in Eurasian isolates suggests that co-compounding, at least at a low level, is not a recent phenomenon in Eurasia. Further research is needed here. For example, Ket might be an interesting language to analyse. But, generally, it seems that co-compounding is not common in the 'Paleo-Siberian' languages.

6.3.10 Synthesis

We may conclude that the hypothesis formulated in Section 6.2 on the basis of the investigation of parallel texts has a certain validity. It states that the level of frequency of co-compounds in an Eurasian language is higher the closer that language is located to continental East and South East Asia, a conclusion supported with some minor exceptions by the comparison of languages within stocks and within areas. The findings presented in this and the preceding sections are summarized in Table 6.3 and Map 6.1, where the frequency of co-compounds in a number of languages of Eurasia is represented on a seven-level scale (the levels estimated according to the evidence available). Further research is needed to confirm whether all the languages included have been classified correctly. Extinct languages (Old Turkic, Tokharian, Vedic, and Sumerian) are not represented on Map 6.1.

Four languages could not be assigned to a specific level because different dialects or varieties of them behave differently. Russian ranges between zero and three (standard vs. certain dialects), Kurdish probably between zero and two, Malay between three and four (standard vs. literary Malay), and Nepali between three and four (standard vs. colloquial Nepali). I have abstained

TABLE 6.3. The levels of co-compounding represented on Map 6.1

(6)	upper high level	Mandarin, Vietnamese, Hmong (White)
(5)	high level	Tuva, Khalkha, Tibetan, Lahu, Burmese, Thai, Khmer
(4)	upper moderate level	Manchu, Korean, Japanese, Yakut, Khakas, Kazakh, Kirghiz, Uzbek, Turkmen, Chuvash, Kalmyk, Mordvin, Avar, Khasi, Santali, Bonda, Konda, Kannada, Toda; Kâte, Melpa, Sentani
(3)	moderate level	Khanty, Mansi, Komi, Udmurt, Mari, Tatar, Modern Uyghur, Abkhaz, Adyghe, Georgian, Lezgian, Basque, Burushaski, Hindi, Aceh, B. Indonesia, Sundanese; Toaripi
(2)	upper low level	Finnish, Estonian, Hungarian, Modern Greek, Persian (?), Tadzhik (?), Turkish, Azerbaijani, (Malagasy)
(1)	low level	Modern Tamil, Tagalog, Yabem, Nanai, Even, Latvian, Lithuanian, Ossete, Armenian
(0)	almost none	English (and other West European languages), Maltese, Arabic, Somali, Nicobarese, Tsou, Hua

from putting some languages on the map because I have too little evidence that they really lack co-compounds. Estimating the levels of Paleo-Siberian languages is especially difficult, because in most of them coordinators may be lacking in ordinary coordination.

Another relatively reliable indicator for the presence or lack of co-compounds is the lexical domain 'parents'. Map 6.2 shows in which languages a co-compound (or in the case of Basque, an expression which etymologically derives from a co-compound) is the most lexicalized expression for 'parents' (sources: UDHR, Mark, dictionaries, and grammars). This is the case for almost all languages at level three and above. In some languages at levels two to four, there is another expression in addition to the co-compound which is slightly more lexicalized (light-gray symbols on the map). In Japanese and Korean the co-compounds consist of Chinese morphemes. Burushaski vacillates between a co-compound and an expression with overt coordination. In some languages, there is a coordinate sequence for 'parents', rather than a co-compound, as is the case in Kurdish[16] and Nanai. In Persian and Tadzhik, conjunction with -*u* is intermediate between tight phrase-like coordination and co-compounds (Section 4.4.3). Interestingly, there is no co-compound for 'parents' in many of the peripheral Eurasian languages for which I do not have enough evidence to be sure that they lack co-compounds; notably Ket, Koryak, Evenki, and Paiwan. It may be seen from Map 6.2 that the sequence of

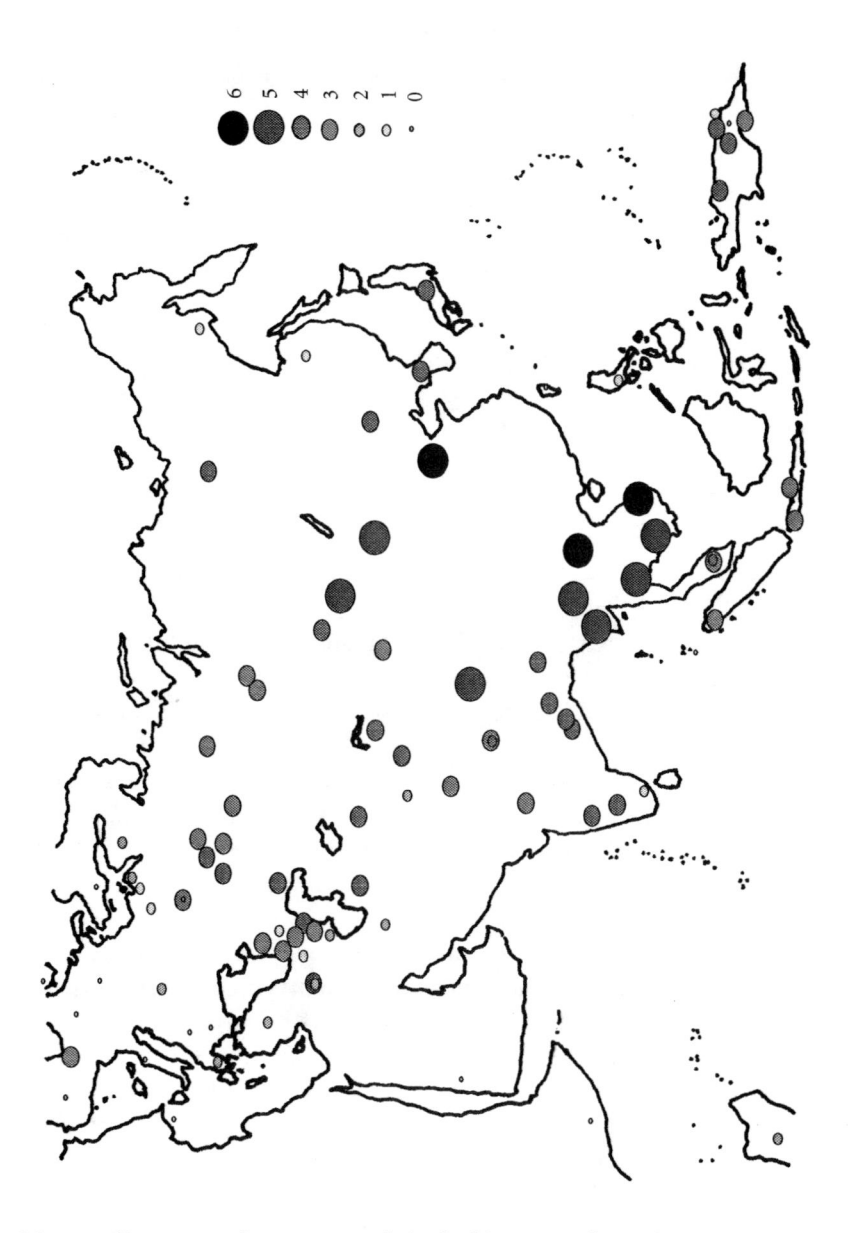

216 *Areal Distribution in the Languages of Eurasia*

MAP 6.1. Frequency of co-compounds in the languages of Eurasia

Areal Distribution in the Languages of Eurasia 217

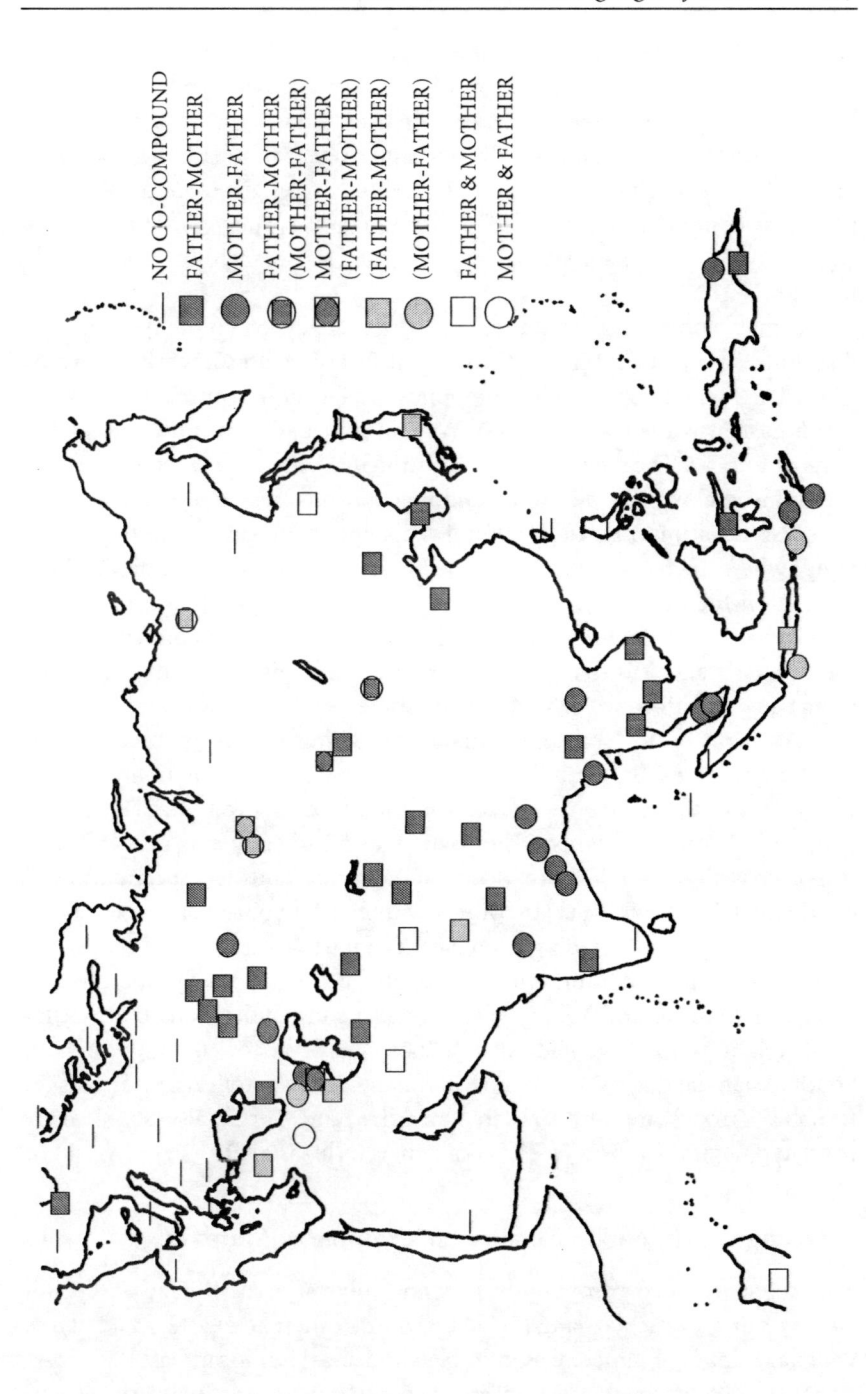

MAP 6.2. Co-compounds in the most lexicalized expression for 'parents'

the parts 'father' and 'mother' varies highly in areally quite unpredictable ways (round symbol: sequence 'mother-father', square symbol: sequence 'father-mother'). In some languages (such as Yakut) the sequence is not even irreversible (circle and square, the inner one symbolizes the dominant order). For the languages of Indonesia, the only ones given are those which have a co-compound for 'parents' in Tryon (1995: 154 f; 6.3.8). This wrongly suggests on Map 6.2 that the languages of Indonesia are highly co-compounding.

We may conclude that the levels of frequency of co-compounds are distributed along a continuum throughout Eurasia with some minor exceptions. The highest levels of co-compounds are found in continental East and South East Asia, the lowest levels in West Europe and some other peripheral parts of Eurasia. The continuous diminishment from east to west is especially pronounced along the Silk Route and neighboring areas to the north which have also been important for cultural exchanges from east to west. Interestingly, where there are exceptions to the general east to west diminishing pattern on the Eurasian continent, the frequency is typically too high. This is true for Basque, the autochthonous Caucasian languages, in the Volga basin for Chuvash and Mordvin, and for Hungarian. This means that co-compounding is slightly more frequent in some residual zones (and in some residues from minor spreading) than in neighboring major spread zones, evidence that co-compounding is not a recent phenomenon in Eurasia. Interestingly, the frequency of co-compounds may drop dramatically in peripheral (insular) regions of Eurasia, as in Nicobarese and probably also in Formosa (Taiwan). The frequency of co-compounds is also low in non-continental South East Asia (Indonesia and the Philippines). There is a rapid falling off in co-compounding from East Asia northward although there is no interruption of the continuum because of the geographically intermediate languages Manchu and Yakut. There are also some indications that north–south relationships have had an influence. The levels of co-compounds in South Asian languages (notably Dravidian) and central Asian languages (notably Turkic) are very similar. Dravidian and Turkic also share many other typological features (see Masica's 1971 'Indo-Altaic').

6.4 Language internal diversity: the example of Mordvin

The frequency of co-compounds does not only vary cross-linguistically, but also within a particular language throughout different registers and styles. Language internal differences can be almost as significant as the cross-linguistic differences that we observed in Section 6.2. In this section let us quantitatively analyze three texts from Erźa Mordvin, two novels and an epic poem, from which many examples have already been considered qualitatively in Chapter 5. The two texts, *Kočkodikeś—Pakśa narmuń* (*The quail is a field bird*) by Aleksandr Doronin (1993) and *Erźan ćora* (*Erzyan fellow*; second part) by Kuźma Abramov (1973), are novels, both telling about the hardship of life in Mordovia (the former in the present, the latter in the past), but they differ considerably in style. Abramov just narrates what happened to a Mordvin sculptor in his youth and does not comment on his experiences. The style is direct and realistic. Doronin's style is more elaborate and there is much introspection into the minds and hearts of the people of the village he describes. The feelings and sorrows of the villagers and even of a mother wolf living in the neighborhood are exposed at length. The third text, *Mastorava* (Šaronov 1994: 9–284), is the Erźa Mordvin national epos which has recently been compiled from traditional folk ballads and epic poems and whose language is that of traditional Erźa Mordvin folk poetry. The three texts will henceforth be called Abramov, Doronin, and Mastorava. Doronin and Abramov each have about 100,000 words, Mastorava about 50,000.[17] Frequencies in the first two texts can thus be compared directly, whereas the numbers in the third have to be doubled for a comparison. I have examined the following data from the three texts:

- The number of all co-compounds that are hyphenated. In Erźa Mordvin orthography all co-compounds, except for the highly lexicalized *ejkakś*,[18] which is the usual word for 'child', are hyphenated. Of course, hyphenated strings which are not co-compounds were not counted. Compounds whose status as co-compounds is dubious (pronominal echo-words, comparative compounds; appositive compounds, and affirmative–negative compounds; Section 5.4) were not counted.
- The word class of the co-compounds in the texts (finite [Vfin] and infinite [Vinfin] verb forms are distinguished, and proper names [Nprop] are counted separately).
- The semantic types of the co-compounds as they have been described in Chapter 5 (alt = alternative-approximate, gen = generalizing, add = additive, col = collective, syn = synonymic, orn = ornamental, and others). Of course, it was not always obvious to which type a co-compound belongs and a number of arbitrary decisions had to be made. Intermediate cases between additive and collective co-compounds were counted as additive. Intermediate cases between alternative and additive co-compounds (especially in distributive and negative contexts) were counted as additive co-compounds. The lexicalized co-compound

220   *Areal Distribution in the Languages of Eurasia*

ul'i-paro 'exists-good > possession', which cannot easily be classified either with respect to word class or with respect to the semantic type, was counted as a nominal collective co-compound.
• Among additive co-compounds, the semantic fields kinship terms [KinT], body parts [BodyP] (including verbs of body care), food (including verbs of ingestion), and clothes (including verbs of clothing) were counted.

Figure 6.6 shows the number of co-compounds in the three texts per 100,000 words and the proportions of the semantic types. In Figure 6.7 the frequency of the different semantic types in the three texts are directly compared to each other. Figure 6.8 shows the proportions of the different semantic types in the three texts (the SEMANTIC PROFILE OF CO-COMPOUNDS). Figure 6.9 shows the proportions of word classes in the three texts (the WORD CLASS PROFILE OF CO-COMPOUNDS). Finally, Figure 6.10 shows the proportions of kinship terms

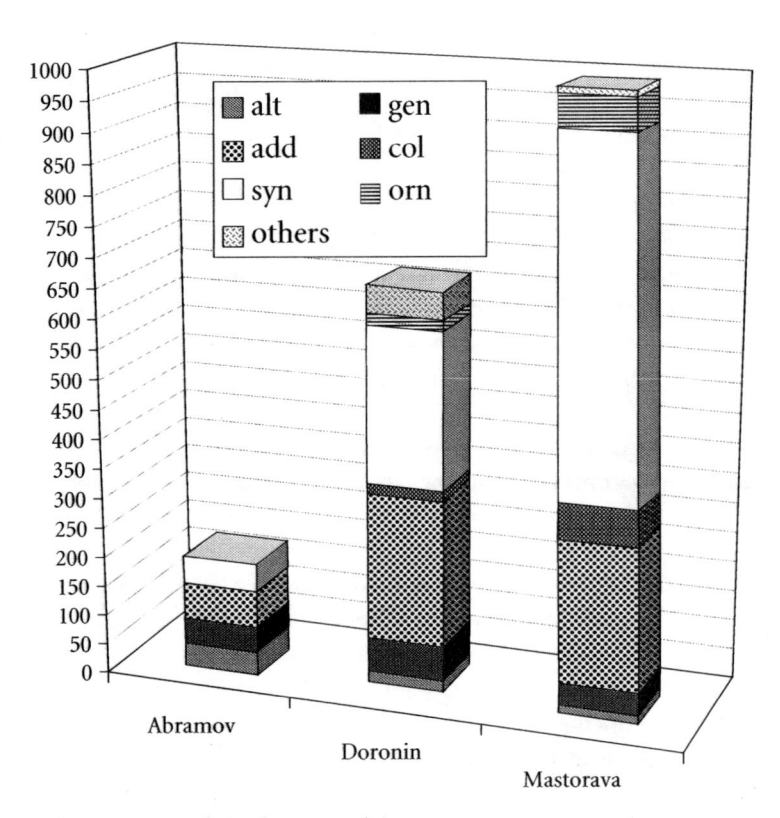

FIG. 6.6. Co-compounds in three Mordvin texts

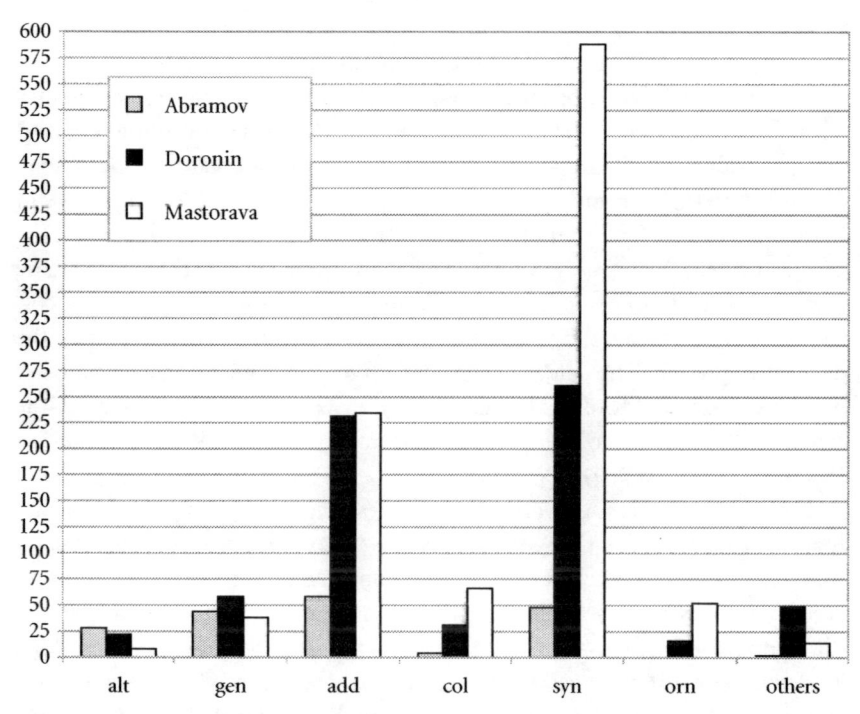

FIG. 6.7. The semantic types of co-compounds in three Mordvin texts

and terms for body parts, food, and clothing in the semantic type of additive co-compounds (the SEMANTIC PROFILE OF ADDITIVE CO-COMPOUNDS). Only token frequencies have been counted.

The most striking result is the huge differences in the overall frequency of co-compounds between the three texts (see Figure 6.6; Abramov and Mastorava differ by a factor of more than five). Interestingly, the differences are bigger between the two texts of the same register than between Doronin and Mastorava. As far as semantic types are concerned (Figure 6.7), alternative and generalizing co-compounds are roughly equally frequent in all three texts (alternative co-compounds happen to be somewhat rarer in Mastorava). Doronin and Mastorava have about the same frequency of additive co-compounds. The number of additive co-compounds differs, however, greatly (by a factor four) between the two fiction texts. The most impressive difference is found in synonymic co-compounds where the proportions are approximately Abramov 1 : Doronin 5 : Mastorava 12. Obviously, synonymic co-compounds are the semantic group with by far the greatest potential for variation in Erźa Mordvin. The frequency of collective and ornamental co-compounds differs in a fashion similar to that of synonymic co-compounds across the three texts, but is generally much lower than for synonymic co-compounds.

The semantic profile of co-compounds (Figure 6.8) varies in accordance with the overall frequency of co-compounds. The proportion of alternative and generalizing co-compounds decreases with an increase in the overall frequency (which means that in absolute figures it is more or less constant in the three texts). The proportion of additive co-compounds is highest at the medium level (Doronin) and is clearly lowest in Mastorava, the text with the highest overall frequency. The proportion of synonymic (and similarly collective and ornamental) co-compounds increases in correlation with the overall frequency. The semantic profiles of co-compounds across the three different texts in Mordvin therefore vary in exactly the same way as the semantic profiles of co-compounds in parallel texts in different languages (Section 6.2, Figure 6.4).

The differences in the word class profiles (Figure 6.9) are much smaller than the differences in the semantic profiles of co-compounds. Generally, we may say that the word class profile of co-compounds is much more constant across registers and styles in Erźa Mordvin than the semantic profile. The differences are largely conditioned by the differences in the semantic profiles. The proportion of numerals (which are strongly represented in alternative co-compounds) and adverbs (which are strongly represented in generalizing co-compounds) decreases with the increase in overall frequency. The proportion of nouns and verbs (which are only weakly represented in alternative and generalizing co-compounds), however, increases in correlation with the overall frequency of co-compounds. The increase in the proportion of verbs (both finite and non-finite) from Abramov to Doronin and Mastorava is

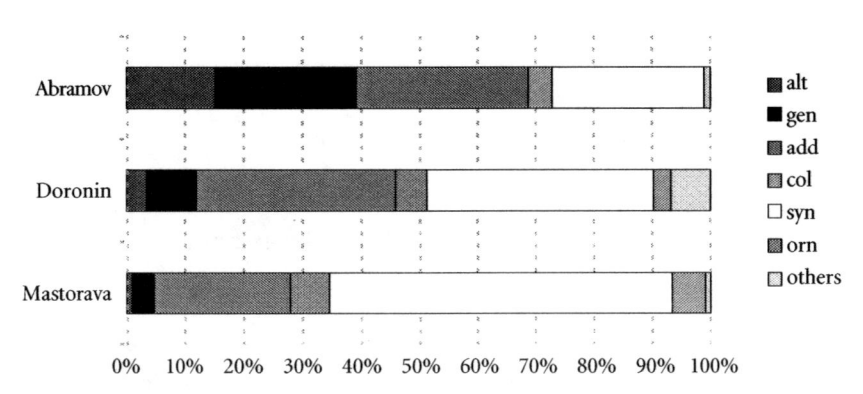

FIG. 6.8. The semantic profiles of co-compounds in three Mordvin texts

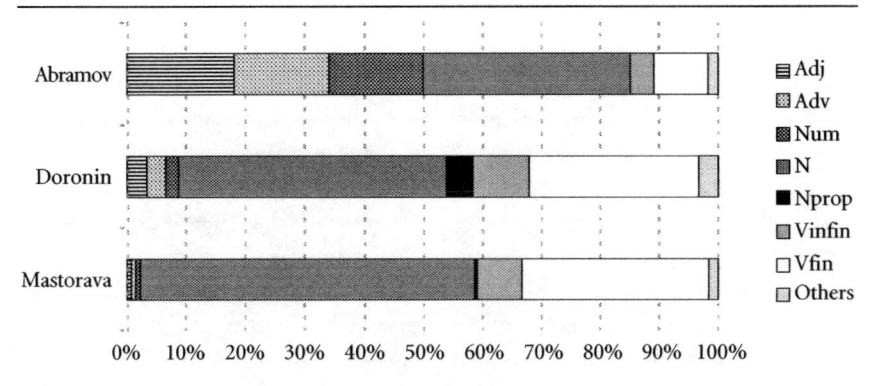

FIG. 6.9. The word class profiles of co-compounds in three Mordvin texts

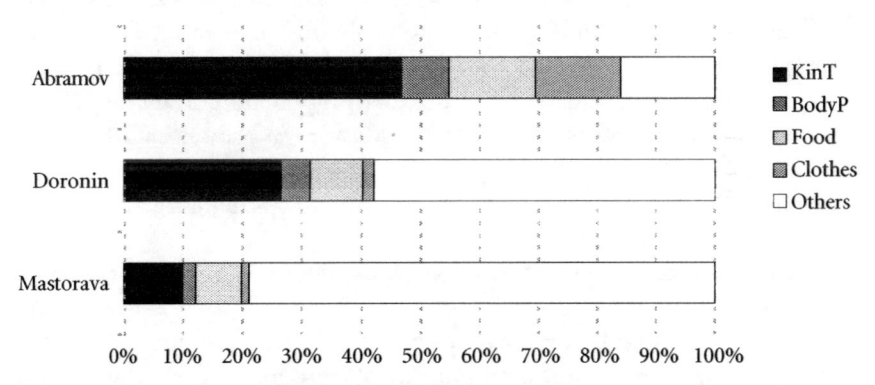

FIG. 6.10. The profile of additive co-compounds in three Mordvin texts

particularly marked. Verbs have their highest potential for development in synonymic co-compounds (they are absent or almost absent from collective co-compounds, but collective co-compounds are marginal in Mordvin anyway).

The semantic profiles of additive co-compounds in the three texts are also very interesting (Figure 6.10). The proportions of terms for kinship, body parts, food, and clothing decrease together with the increase in overall frequency. The Abramov text illustrates how important these groups (and especially the group of kinship terms) may be at a lower overall frequency of co-compounds.

Of course, these are just three texts and many more would have to be analyzed quantitatively to corroborate these preliminary results. However, the three texts were not chosen at random. They behave in their frequencies and profiles of co-compounding as Erźa Mordvin texts typically do and are representative of a low, medium, and high level of co-compounding in Mordvin. It has to be emphasized, however, that the low and high level texts do not represent the lowest and highest possible levels. An example of a text with a maximally high level of co-compounding was given in Section 5.5.5.iii. This traditional prayer has a proportion of co-compounds which comes close to 20 percent (counting a co-compound as one word). Mastorava, in comparison, has a proportion of co-compounds of approximately 1 percent. Lower frequencies of co-compounds than in Abramov may be found, especially in texts of registers and styles which are strongly influenced by Russian and in spontaneous spoken language (which is also often strongly influenced by Russian).

Of course, the differences in the overall frequency across texts of various styles and registers in Mordvin are due to qualitative differences. This is clear from the fact that texts with different overall frequencies differ in their semantic profiles in characteristic ways. Co-compounding in the register of traditional folk poetry, as represented in Mastorava, has several properties that are not typical of the language of modern fiction or colloquial speech. The following are some characteristic properties of epic language in contrast to the language of fiction:

- The same co-compound is often repeated several times in the same passage.
- If a co-compound is repeated, there may be variation in the order of the parts and/or in a lexical slot: *paro-vadŕa* 'good-good > good', (and in the next line) *vadŕa-paro* 'good-good > good' (Mastorava 290), *pra.ś-kulo.ś* 'fall.PST3SG-die.PST3SG > died', (and in the next line) *pra.ś-joma.ś* 'fall.PST3SG-perish.PST3SG > died' (ibid.: 65).
- There are conventionalized (one might say, lexicalized) synonymic and ornamental co-compounds which may come close in text frequency to the corresponding simplex words: *ki.t'-jan.t* 'way.PL-path.PL > way', *ńi-pola* 'wife-spouse > wife', *moda-mastor* 'land-land > land', *vel'e-śado* 'village-hundred > village', *jakams-pakams* 'walk-walk > walk', etc. These are not conventionalized in Mordvin in general, only in some registers of folk poetry.
- Occasionally, one part of a co-compound may consist of more than one word: *valske.ń ška.va-zoŕa.va* 'morning.GEN time.PROL-dawn.PROL > in the morning' (ibid.: 241).
- There are many extreme cases of synonymic sharpening: *tu.jan-mol'.an* 'go_away.PRS1SG-go.PRS1SG > I go away' (ibid.: 62).
- In a few cases, the ornamental part of an ornamental co-compound is extended to another concept by analogy: *oš.ov-śad.ov* 'town.LAT-

hundred.LAT > into town' (ibid.: 336) in analogy to *vel'e-śado* 'village-hundred > village'.
- There are some cases of contextual additive co-compounds (Section 5.5.1).

All these properties of co-compounds in the epic style are characteristics of a higher degree of co-compounding than in the register of fiction and in colloquial Mordvin.

In the same way the difference in quantity between the two fiction texts consists of qualitative differences. There are many fewer synonymic co-compounds in Abramov. Additive co-compounds in Abramov are almost completely restricted to kinship terms and terms for body parts, food, and clothing, while additive co-compounds of these groups are in a minority in Doronin (see Figure 6.10). There are almost no additive co-compounds with partly overlapping coordination in Abramov, while in Doronin overlapping additive co-compounds are frequent.

A similar diversity of co-compounds across texts and registers can be found in many other central Eurasian languages. In Chuvash there is a similar extremely high text frequency of co-compounds in traditional prayers (see Paasonen 1949: 7, 9). An extremely high frequency of co-compounds in prayers is also found in Toda (Emeneau 1984; Section 6.3.5). In Mundari and Khasi there is a high frequency of co-compounds in mythological texts. In Santali texts (Section 2.1) the frequency of co-compounds rises in legally effective speech. For the use of co-compounds in Mewahang ritual language see Section 5.2.6 and Gaenszle (1998).

Generally, it can be assumed that a high language-internal diversity of co-compounding across different registers and different styles is the rule rather than the exception in central Eurasian languages, and that the situation in Erźa Mordvin described in this section is typical for central Eurasian languages in general. But further research is needed to corroborate these preliminary findings.

6.5 Diversity in co-compounding in Eurasia

In Sections 6.2 and 6.3 we concentrated on one aspect of co-compounds, its general text frequency, which behaves consistently across the languages of Eurasia. There is, however, not only similarity in co-compounds in the languages of a particular area, but also diversity. Let us list some aspects of co-compounding which do not give equally neat macro-areal patterns of distribution as the overall frequency of co-compounds:

- The order of the parts in irreversible co-compounds (if they are irreversible at all). Consider the order of the parts 'father' and 'mother' in the co-compounds for 'parents' on Map 6.2.
- The presence and frequency of finite verbal co-compounds. In some languages co-compounds of finite verbs are common (Mordvin, Hunzib), whereas they are lacking or almost lacking in others (Chuvash, Lezgian).
- The frequency and kinds of collective co-compounds (see Section 5.2.3 for a discussion of the differences between Chuvash and Mordvin).
- The marking patterns of co-compounds.

If we compare the six highly co-compounding languages Mandarin, Vietnamese, Khmer, Hmong, Tibetan, and Khalkha, we can identify the following major differences.

In Mandarin and Vietnamese, co-compounds are generally TWO-SYLLABLE UNITS, while this is not the case in Khmer and Khalkha. Another frequent type of two-syllable units formally associated with co-compounds in Mandarin and Vietnamese are sub-compounds. Khalkha, however, has no sub-compounds. Consider (14) from Vietnamese (co-compounds in boldface, other two-syllable units underlined):

(14)   Vietnamese (UDHR 19)

Mọi   ngư'ờ'i   đều   có   quyền   tư do   ngôn luận   và
all   human   all   EX   right   self due_to   speech discuss and
bầy tỏ   quan điểm;   kể cả   tư' do   bảo
display express view point   tell all self due_to say
lư'u   ý kiến   không   phụ thuộc
keep   thought opinion   not   dependent secondary
vào   bất cứ   sự'   can thiệp   nào,
enter not every   CL   concern be_involved what/every

cũng như'   tư' do   tìm kiếm,   thu nhân,
also like   self due_to   seek seek   collect get
truyền bá   thông tin   và
teach/transmit sow/spread communicate inform   and
ý kiến   bằng   bất cứ   phu'o'ng tiện
thought opinion   equal   not every   direction convenient

thông tin	đại chúng	nào	và	không
communicate inform	big people	what/every	and	not

giới' hạn	về	biên giới'i.
limit limit	concerning	border limit

'Everyone has the right to freedom of opinion and expression; this right includes freedom to hold opinions without inference and to seek, receive and impart information and ideas through any media and regardless of frontiers.'

Written Tibetan also has predominantly two-syllable co-compounds and CLIPPING (Section 4.2.3.iii) is very common (*rgyal khab* 'king court > country', UDHR 2, the first part is a clipping from *rgyal po* 'king'). There are, however, also longer co-compounds (*'gro ba mi* 'go NOML man > human being', UDHR 1, *'gro ba* 'goer > human being'; *śes yon slob sbyoŋ* 'know gift teach study > education', UDHR 26). In Written Tibetan, co-compounds of verbs are usually NOMINAL (*dbye 'gog med pa.r* 'separate obstruct NEG:EX NOML.TRNSL > without regard' (UDHR 19), *śes rtogs* 'know understand:IMP > knowledge') while this does not hold for the other five languages.

In Khmer, but not in the other languages, a considerable number of co-compounds display ALLITERATION (*tha:e-tɔam* 'guard-IMI > care', *sɑnte-sok* 'peace-luck > security', *cah-œərẹ:ə* 'old old/old_age > old', *khvah-kha:t* 'lack-lose > to lack', all UDHR 25; 1). See Ourn and Haiman (2000) and Haiman (forthcoming) for discussion.

In Khalkha verbal co-compounds, the first part is a CONVERB, while the other languages do not have converbs. Consider (15) from the UDHR (co-compounds in boldface):

(15) Khalkha (UDHR 19)

üün.d	... alivaa	üzel sanaa,	medeell.ijg
this.LOC	... any	opinion thought	information.ACC

uls.yn	xil.ijn	zaag.aar	ül	xjazgaarla.n
State.GEN	border.GEN	border.INST	not	restrict.CONV

bolomžtoj	**arga zam.aar**	**er.ž survalžl.ax,**
possible	method way.INST	seek.CONV interview.INF

ol.ž ašigl.ax,	**tügee.n delgerüül.ex**
find.CONV use.INF	distribute.CONV distribute.INF

erx	bagtana.
right	be_included:PRS

'... this right includes freedom ... to seek, receive and impart information and ideas ... regardless of frontiers.'

In Hmong, but not in the other four languages, co-compounds are often discontinuous:

(16) White Hmong (Sichuan-Guizhou-Yunnan version of the UDHR)[19]
    a   <Ch> **mual** khed **muas** khed
        <Th> **muas** qhev **muag** qhev
             buy   slave   sell   slave
        'slave trade' (UDHR 4)

    b <Ch> uat   **chongb** uat   **gol**
        <Th> ua   **tshoob** ua   **kos**
             make **marriage** make **marriage**
        'marry' (UDHR 16; 2)

In (17) it can be seen how strongly the White Hmong text is influenced by Mandarin. All the forms with the sign — on the line <Th> are Chinese loanwords that cannot be transliterated to the <Th> orthography because they contain phonological structures that do not occur in White Hmong in Thailand. Even the genitive construction with *nit/ni* is not genuine Hmong (it is not described in Mottin 1978, 1980). Almost the only specific Hmong feature retained in the translation from Mandarin are discontinuous co-compounds, such as *sob said sob trot* 'before choose before?' (I could not identify the meaning of *trot/rhu*, but it most probably means 'choose'; co-compounds are given in boldface):

(17) White Hmong with Mandarin (M.) equivalent (UDHR 26;3)
    <Ch> Naf   zid   duef   dob   ncaik   yinf   gaib
    <Th> Niam   txiv   —   tub   ntxhais   —   —(M. gāi)
           mother father answer son daughter should should
    <Ch> sheuf   zhangd khuab khat dus,   muax   sob
    <Th> —   tshav   qhuab qhia twg,   muaj   xub
           receive manner punish teach which   EX   before
    <Ch> said   sob   trot   nit   ndas dos.
    <Th> xaiv   xub   rhu   ni   ntiag tug.
           choose before ?   GEN property

M.	fú	mǔ	duì	qí	zǐ	nǔ		suǒ	yīng
	father	mother	as_to	their	son	daughter		which	should
M.	shòu	de	jiào	yù	de	zhǒng	kì		yǒu
	receive	GEN	feed	raise	GEN	kind	category		EX

yōu	xiān	xuǎn	zé	de	quán	lì.
excellent	first	choose	choose	GEN	right	power

'Parents have a prior right to choose the kind of education that shall be given to their children.'

From the omnipresence in the Hmong translation of discontinuous co-compounds it can be concluded they are a genuine specific trait of Hmong that is not suppressed even under very strong pressure by language contact.

This is evidence that co-compounding in Eurasia is both highly areally determined and at the same time highly language-specific. Even if the overall relative text frequency of co-compounds in a language is largely predictable from its geographic location in Eurasia, all the other specific properties of co-compounds—and notably their formal properties—are not. This leaves us with a notorious areal-typological paradox: in macro-perspective, the areal influence is undeniable; in micro-perspective, however, it is very hard to prove (except in the cases where loanwords are involved). However, as Inspecteur Maigret says: 'On *imite*, on ne *réinvente* pas' (Simenon 2001).

6.6 The independence of co-compounds from other typological features

In this section some potential predicting factors for co-compounds are discussed. It will transpire that co-compounds are quite independent from other typological features.

6.6.1 *Head and dependent marking*

In Nichols' (1992: 160) areal-typological investigation head and dependent marking turned out to be a very strong predicting factor in typology. We should therefore check whether head and dependent marking might also be a relevant factor for co-compounds. Many co-compounding languages have dependent marking and morphological case, especially in Central Eurasia. On the other hand, many central Eurasian languages also have head marking in nouns (possessive suffixes in Finno-Ugric and Turkic, possessive prefixes in

North-West Caucasian and Burushaski) and some have a high degree of head marking in verbs (notably Basque, Abkhaz, Adyghe, and Georgian). On the other hand, South East Asian languages are well-known for their lack of both head and dependent marking. All this suggests that neither head nor dependent marking is likely to be a predicting factor for co-compounds. Especially impressive is the example of the Caucasian languages, Abkhaz, Georgian, and Lezgian (Section 6.3.2), all of which have roughly the same level of co-compounding, at least for nouns. While Abkhaz is extremely head marking, Lezgian is extremely dependent marking and Georgian has dependent marking in nouns and both head and dependent marking in the clause. The fact that co-compounds may occur with double or single marking for case and/or possessive affixes, or without any marking at all, suggests that the head and dependent marking typology is irrelevant for co-compounding. If it appears that there are few highly head marking languages with co-compounds, this is most probably a mere historical coincidence, as co-compounding is a characteristic feature of Eurasian languages and extreme head marking happens to be rare in Eurasia.

6.6.2 *Isolating morphological type and monosyllabic words*

South East Asian languages are well-known for their isolating morphology. They almost completely lack grammatical affixes. Moreover, at least some East and South East Asian languages (Vietnamese, Classical Chinese) have a strong tendency toward monosyllabic words that consist of only one morpheme. One might thus be tempted to believe that the isolating morphology and the shortness of the words are the relevant factor in explaining why there are co-compounds, and especially synonymic co-compounds, in South East Asian languages, since in languages of the isolating and monosyllabic morphological type, there is a need for longer words, which is why co-compounds are developed.

This cannot be true, for several reasons. First, there are many languages with co-compounds that certainly do not belong to the isolating type. In many of those, co-compounds usually have more than two syllables and occasionally may have many more than two syllables. Consider the following example from Avar, a language with complex morphology, where synonymic co-compounds are frequent in some texts. The following co-compound has seven syllables and consists at least of six morphemes: *aẍd.ole.w-čʼičʼid.ule.w* 'cry.PTC.M-cry.PTC.M = [And always, night and day, he was in the mountains, and in the tombs,] crying' (Mark 5:5).

Second, even in South East Asian languages with predominantly monosyllabic morphemes, co-compounds often have more than two syllables. This is the case in the discontinuous co-compounds frequently found in Hmong, Khasi, Karen, and other languages of the region. Consider the Karen co-compound *tə'.khɔ́.thí tə'.khɔ́.kɔ̀* 'one.side.water one.side.land > travel abroad, far and wide', where the co-compound *thí.kɔ* 'water.land > area, country' occurs discontinuously (Jones 1961: 26).

Nor is there reason to believe that synonymic co-compounds can only be formed with short monomorphemic parts. It is, of course, possible that the especially high frequency of co-compounds in some East and South East Asian languages has to do with the morphological typology of those languages (this issue will be further considered in Section 7.3). But even if this were true, it will be just one among different relevant factors. Typologically there is just no simple correlation between the morphological type of a language and the presence or lack of co-compounds.

6.6.3 *Sub-compounds*

In some languages, such as Mandarin, Vietnamese, and Classical Sanskrit, where co-compounds are formally identical or almost identical to sub-compounds, there is certainly a close relationship between co-compounds and sub-compounds. However, the relevant question here is whether a typologically universal relationship exists between co-compounds and sub-compounds. It is difficult to show that the presence of sub-compounds in a language would have no effect on the incidence of co-compounds, since both sub-compounding and co-compounding are continuous rather than discrete typological variables. Most languages have at least some sub-compounds, but languages that have as many as Mandarin, Mari, German, and Ewe are certainly in the minority. As a whole, I do not see any overall typological correlation in the frequency of co-compounds and sub-compounds. If languages are arranged with respect to their frequency of co-compounds and sub-compounds, almost any combination is possible (Table 6.4).

6.6.4 *The type of ordinary coordination*

It would appear that the typology of coordination is of some relevance for the existence or lack of co-compounds, especially as co-compounds, at least in many cases, diachronically derive from coordination (see Section 7.2 for a discussion). There is, however, little evidence in favor of such an assumption. For example, it is irrelevant for co-compounds whether coordination in a language derives from a comitative construction ('with'-coordination, the coordinator is etymologically a comitative marker 'with', 'accompany', etc.) or from an additive focus particle construction ('also'-coordination, etymo-

TABLE 6.4. Sub-compounds and co-compounds

	No or very few co-compounds	Low-to-moderate level of co-compounding	High level of co-compounding
No or very few sub-compounds	Greenlandic, Arabic	Lezgian, Burushaski	Khalkha
Low-to-moderate level of sub-compounding	English	Turkish, Mordvin	
High level of sub-compounding	Ewe, German	Mari	Mandarin

logically an additive focus particle). It suffices to look at a small number of languages to establish this conclusion (Table 6.5).

Moreover, it is also irrelevant whether the coordinator is bipartite, simple, or zero (Table 6.6).

Neither does there seem to be any correlation between the type of verbal coordination (deranked, that is, with converbs or chaining vs. non-deranked) and the existence of co-compounds (Table 6.7).

Another factor which might be relevant for the emergence of co-compounds is the text frequency of coordination. There is some evidence that languages differ in their token frequency of coordination in noun phrases. Some languages in lowland South America (for instance, Siriono[20] and Huitoto; Preuss 1921) have a considerably lower frequency of coordinated noun phrases in original texts than the average Eurasian language. It might be the case that Eurasian languages have co-compounds because they tend to coordinate much more often in discourse than languages of other continents. Extensive corpus linguistic research in original texts of languages from different continents would be necessary to test this hypothesis. However, at present there is no evidence that any feature of coordination would correlate in any way with the presence or absence of co-compounds in a language.

6.6.5 *Dyad constructions and family group classifiers*

Dyad constructions (Evans 2003, forthcoming) form terms, from kin and other relational expressions K, denoting pairs of the type 'uncle and nephew(s)', 'mother and child(ren)' (two or more people such that one/ several call(s) the other K). Dyads can consist of morphological derivation or of unanalyzable lexical roots. Dyad constructions partly overlap in function with reciprocals, duals, associative duals/plurals, natural comitatives (Section

Areal Distribution in the Languages of Eurasia 233

TABLE 6.5. 'Also'/'with'-coordinators and co-compounds

	No or very few co-compounds	Low-to-moderate level of co-compounding	High level of co-compounding
'Also'-coordination	English	Kannada, Mordvin, Georgian	
'With'-coordination	Ewe, Aymara	Khasi	Mandarin, Tibetan

TABLE 6.6. Relational marking type in ordinary nominal coordination and co-compounds

	No or very few co-compounds	Low-to-moderate level of co-compounding	High level of co-compounding
Zero coordinator	Evenki, Ket	Manchu	Khalkha
Single coordinator	English, Tagalog	Basque, Georgian, Kâte	Mandarin, Vietnamese
Bipartite coordinator	Aymara, Kanuri, Tamil	Kannada, Adyghe, Lezgian	

TABLE 6.7. Deranked vs. non-deranked verbal coordination and co-compounds

	No or very few co-compounds	Low-to-moderate level of co-compounding	High level of co-compounding
Dominant deranked coordination (chaining or converbs)	Tamil	Kannada, Abkhaz, Uzbek	Khalkha
Dominant non-deranked coordination (including serial verbs)	English, Ewe	Mordvin, Georgian, Khasi	Mandarin, Vietnamese

3.3.1), and additive co-compounds. In our context, the question arises as to whether the existence of dyads correlates positively or negatively with the existence of co-compounds. The latter might be the case, because dyads occupy part of a characteristic domain of co-compounds; the former because at least in some languages, dyad constructions develop from co-compounds. However, according to Evans (2003) dyad constructions in Australian languages, where they are especially frequent, derive mainly from possessor morphemes, comitatives and proprietives, complement parals, and source and causal morphemes, but only infrequently from co-compounds.

There are at least two Australian languages which show some relationship between dyads and co-compounds. Kuku Yalanji (Pama Nyungan) has a number of co-compounds in the domain of kinship, such as *yaba yabuju* 'elder_brother-younger_brother > brothers', *babarr jinkurr* 'elder_sister-younger_sister > sisters' (Mark 10:29). Some of the terms are lexicalized dyads with *manda* (on its own 'younger brother's child (of a woman), younger sister's grandchild (of a man)') as a second component: *nganjan-manda* 'father and son together', *ngamu-manda* 'mother and daughter together' (Oates 1993, Evans 2003: 68 f). Wik-Mungkan (Pama Nyungan) forms dyads by combining *ma'* 'hand' with a co-compound: *ma' wanch pam* 'hand man woman > husband and wife', *ma' kaath puk* 'hand mother child > - mother and child', *ma' wanch thum* 'hand woman fire > husband and wife' (seems to contain a clipping from *pam thum* 'husband'; Kilham 1974: 47). Consider also the family group classifiers in Yi languages (Section 6.3.6), which are closely related to dyads (Evans forthcoming). In some languages, co-compounds with dyad function exhibit syntactic behavior which is different from ordinary co-compounds. Thus, in Cantonese, dyadic co-compounds, such as *mou^5-leoi^2* 'mother-daughter', are specific in that they lack numeral classifiers, do not allow possessive attributes, and occur in reciprocal constructions (Stephen Matthews p.c. to Nick Evans).

Generally, however, there does not seem to be any strong overall correlation between co-compounds and dyads. There are languages with both dyads and co-compounds in the kinship domain, such as Oksapmin (Papua New Guinea; Lawrence 1993): *taman* 'father and child' (dyad), *näp gapinir* 'elder_brother younger_sibling > brothers' (co-compound), and there are languages that have dyads but no kin co-compounds, such as Icelandic (*mæðgur* PL.F 'mother and daughter'). The different but partly overlapping areal-typological distribution of dyads and co-compounds also speaks against a strong positive or negative correlation between dyads and co-compounds, dyads being common especially in Australia, New Guinea, and Austronesian languages and co-compounds being common mainly in eastern Eurasia and New Guinea.

6.6.6 Loanwords

Many co-compounds and binomials in many languages contain loanwords or consist entirely of loanwords (see Section 6.3.1 for Arabic and Mongolian loanwords in Turkic co-compounds and Section 6.5 for Sinitic loanwords in Hmong). Thus, one might be tempted to think that extensive borrowing may promote co-compounds and binomials (see also Boeder 1991). Well-known examples are the Romance plus Germanic synonymic pairs in legal English, such as *goods and chattels, fit and proper, keep and maintain, deem and consider, new and novel* (Hiltunen 1990: 54f). However, finding loanwords in co-compounds and binomials is no proof that extensive borrowing would correlate with rising frequencies of co-compounds and binomials. As far as English is concerned, binomials were plentiful in legal Old English (especially with alliteration): *word and weorc* 'word and deed', *sib and socn* 'peace and agreement', *manslagan and manswaran* 'murder and perjury' (ibid.: 25). See also Singh (1982: 351) who argues that Hindi synonymic co-compounds ('redundant compounds') consisting of a native and a non-native component would never have developed without the structural resources Hindi has at its disposal. Generally, it seems there is no direct strong relationship between frequency of loanwords and frequency of co-compounds or binomials, the best example for this being Mandarin Chinese with its very high frequency of co-compounds and rather few borrowings.

6.6.7 Conclusions

Of course, it is not possible to prove that there are no predicting factors for the presence or absence of co-compounds. Many other possible factors could also be taken into account. (The unlikeliness of general typological correlations with properties, such as serial verbs (Section 4.4.2), reduplication (5.4.5), ideophones (5.4.4), group inflection (2.4.1), and parallelism (1.1.5) were discussed in earlier chapters.) But I think it has been well illustrated here that there is no obvious predicting factor for co-compounds, except for geography.

One important fact is that there are no broad correlations with the form of ordinary coordination (Section 6.6.4), with the head and dependent marking type (6.6.1), or with the morphological type (6.6.2). This is strong evidence that the lexical class type of co-compounds is typologically autonomous to a high degree and also suggests that co-compounds, like grammatical classes, do not develop in the first place to fulfill a particular need of a language. Put differently, there is reason to believe that co-

compounds may emerge more or less everywhere, even if high areal restrictions to Eurasia, New Guinea, and a few other places suggests that it is extremely rare for areally unconditioned evolution to give rise to a fully-fledged lexical class of co-compounds.

The purpose of this section has been to show that the existence and level of co-compounding is a highly autonomous typological property, although it will be largely areally determined. It cannot be concluded, however, that there are absolutely no structural factors that correlate with the emergence of co-compounds. On this subject, further research is needed, especially to examine possible lexical and pragmatic correlations.

6.7 Conclusions

In continental Eurasia, co-compounding is distributed in a highly predictable way based on area. As a rule, eastern languages have more co-compounds than western languages, more or less irrespective of their genetic affiliation. In eastern Asia, co-compounding also decreases rapidly in non-continental South Asia and toward North East Asia. There are relatively few discontinuities in this rather monotonous areal pattern, notably Basque, which has too many, and Modern Tamil and Modern Uyghur which have too few co-compounds. Nevertheless, co-compounding is a strong indicator that Eurasia is a relatively homogeneous linguistic area, not in the sense of a *Sprachbund*, but as a CONTACT SUPERPOSITION ZONE (see Koptjevskaja-Tamm and Wälchli 2001: 728). After all, I cannot point to any other typological feature that shows the areal coherence of the languages of Eurasia in a better way than co-compounds. This may be because until now areal typology concentrated on discrete variables and did not consider that continuous variables may give far better results for measuring areal homogeneity in linguistic areas. There is actually some evidence that word order from Central Eurasia to West Europe changes along a continuum from dominant OV to dominant VO (Dryer 1998, Koptjevskaja-Tamm and Wälchli 2001: 704–12).[21] Anyway, the main reason why in linguistics we tend to speak of the languages of Africa, the Americas, New Guinea, and Australia, but rarely of the languages of Eurasia, is doubtless ethnocentrism. Eurasia is the largest continent and has arguably the largest number of languages of all the continents. Typologically, however, Eurasian languages show as much similarity to each other as the languages of other continents, and there is even some reason to believe that Eurasian languages are less diverse typologically and more coherent areally than the languages of other continents.

6.A Appendix: Beyond Eurasia

The kind of areal patterning of co-compounds found in Eurasia does not depend on the areal-typological situation outside Eurasia. However, a comprehensive typology of co-compounds would have to consider the rest of the world more thoroughly than I am able to do here. After surveying the material available to me, I can only make some suggestions about where beyond Eurasia co-compounds might be studied in more detail.

There is much evidence that following Eastern Eurasia, NEW GUINEA is the next largest co-compound area. In New Guinea co-compounds are found, for instance, in Amele (Roberts 1987: 330), Awtuw (Feldman 1986; rare), Baruya (Lloyd 1969: 31, 33; Lloyd 1992, *jilik.yaawarya* 'dog-pig > domesticated animals'), Fore (Scott 1980: 189, 1978: 73), Hatam (Reesink 1999), Kâte (Pilhofer 1933: 94 ff), Kaugel (Blowers and Blowers 1970), West Kewa (Franklin 1971: 52, Franklin and Franklin 1978, *ona-aa/onaa* 'woman-man > people', *ini-agaa* 'eyes-mouth/language > face', *mena-irikai* 'pig-dog > animals', *mena-yapa-yana-yaenu* 'pig-marsupial-dog-things > animals'), Kobon (Davies 1981: 241, *yaur wal* 'bird possum > animal'), Oksapmin (Lawrence 1993, *rum.kin(ä)* 'nose.eye > face'), Sentani (Cowan 1965; see Section 1.1.1 above), Siroi (Wells 1979, *ngaro.su* 'skin-bone(*isu*) > body'), Toaripi (Brown 1968), and Usarufa (Bee 1965, *ara.waa* 'woman.man > people'). The following translations of the Gospel according to Mark into various languages of Papua New Guinea where there are moderate or low-to-moderate levels of co-compounding are available to me: Kâte, Kube (closely related to Kâte), Melpa (closely related to Kaugel), and Toaripi. For Kâte and Kube see also Section 6.2 above. Co-compounds are also found in Tok Pisin, the Creole language of Papua New Guinea (see Section 6.2 above).

There also seem to be languages in New Guinea for which co-compounds are not characteristic, such as Hua (John Haiman, p.c.) and Siane (closely related to Hua; probably no co-compounds in the translation of Mark).

Little information is available about the use of co-compounds in Papuan languages in different styles and registers. Brown's (1988) collection of Toaripi myths is very instructive in this respect. Toaripi has both continuous (*atute. mori* 'son.daughter > children', *pau.marehari* 'elder_brother(*paua*)-younger. brother > friends, kinsfolk') and, in mythological texts, discontinuous co-compounds (*oti haria mea haria karu* 'place different land different people > strangers', *sariva-ére pasi-ére* 'journey-belly stranger-belly > hunger of the journey', Brown 1988: 7, 130). Brown's (1988: x) 'associate names' (*sosoka futai* 'feast feast > feast', *sau-maea tosi-maea* 'ill-body sick-body') correspond to our synonymic, ornamental, and imitative co-compounds, which in Toaripi are characteristic of the language of the myths and serve to add emphasis in ordinary speech (*sosoka futai* 'feast' is used, for instance, in the performative act of opening a feast, ibid.: x). In 'associate names', the second term is rarely used in isolation, but instead is only found together with the common term. Sometimes the second part is a common term in another dialect or language (*futai* is the ordinary word for 'feast' in the Uaripi dialect).

However, co-compounds—and this is remarkable—also play a major role in the Toaripi clan and totem terminology ('parallel names', Brown 1988: ix). Each clan has its specific co-compounds to address persons of different sex and age and to refer to body parts, canoes, houses, axes, water, sago, etc. Thus, in the Melaripi subclan of Iokea, senior males are addressed as *Oa-Melare*, junior males as *Melare-Tivae Isou-Mao* (the latter two are bird names). The traditional term for a canoe when lying beached is *Lala-oroti Sea-oroti* (*Lala-sea* being a tree totem of the clan, *oroti* 'canoe'); for a canoe when afloat, however, *Lalaupota Kiriripota* (derived from fish names, *pota/posa* 'platform'). For body parts, *Meiri... Taura* is added (*Meiri-mai Taura-mai* 'hand', *mai* 'hand'). Note that parallel names can refer—and often do refer—to singular persons or items. The use of discontinuous co-compounds in myths is a feature of eloquence and occurs with high frequency in dramatic passages of the story (ibid.: 67, 104, n. 110). Of course, it would be interesting to know whether there are such parallel names in other parts of New Guinea as well.

Co-compounds seem not to be characteristic of the languages of AUSTRALIA. One example is Gooniyandi (McGregor 1990: 247; *yoowooloo-goornboo* 'man-woman > people'). Kayardild *karndiya dunda* 'wife husband' with fixed order (Evans 1995: 191, 250) might be a co-compound, but this is difficult to determine since conjunction usually lacks coordinators. One language with a moderate level of co-compounding is Wik-Mungkan (Kilham 1974, Kilham et al. 1986); *pam wanch* 'man woman > people' is used very frequently in Mark (reminding me of Tok Pisin *man.meri*; cf. Section 6.2), other examples being *pal-puuy* 'here there > everywhere', *palam-puyam* 'this way and that, everywhere', *(yuk) way min* '(things/wood) bad good > things', *mal thak* 'right left > awkward', *kaa'.wal* 'nose jaw/cheek > face'. For co-compounds in Kuku Yalanji, see Section 6.6.5 above. The otherwise excellent grammar of Kuku Yalanji by Patz (2002) does not mention co-compounds. Thus, the absence of descriptions of co-compounds even in good grammars is not always reliable for the absence of co-compounds in a language. However, the rarity of co-compounds in the domain of dyads (Evans 2003 mentions only Kuku Yalanji) does substantiate that co-compounds are actually rare in Australian languages.

In the AMERICAS, relevant languages for the study of co-compounds are Quechua (Ayacucho Quechua *tayta-mama* 'father-mother > parents', UDHR 16; 3) and some MESO-AMERICAN languages, where I found most evidence for co-compounds in Chinantec and Mixe. For Sochiapan Chinantec see Section 4.2.3.vi. As in Chinantec, co-compounds in Mixe can be discontinuous: *huiiñ.jijp* 'eye-tip/edge > nose' (*jijpput* 'nose'), *huiin.gix jijp.cix* 'eye.LOC face. LOC > face to face', *xuumy.döcy* 'net-mat > things (of the house)', *mij.'ap mij.teedy* 'big.ancestor big.father > ancestors', *y.'ap y.'oc* '3.ancestor 3.clan > offspring'. In Mixe there are also verbal co-compounds ('pares de verbos', express simple concepts according to Hoogshagen and Hoogshagen 1993: 405). Some verbs occur only in pairs and the word order is always fixed. Many verbal co-compounds have identical stems with varying prefixes or identical prefixes with varying stems: *ni.'ix co.'ix* 'surface.look head.look > choose', *ni.'ix pät.'ix* 'down.look up.look > look up and down'. It appears that verbal co-compounds can add emphasis, as far as this can be judged from isolated examples:

(18) Mixe: verbal co-compound (Hoogshagen and Hoogshagen 1993: 158)
 Janch mij je mixy ti nii.yöy ti tü.yöy,
 really big DEF boy already water.go already way.go
 ti y.jäty ya.
 already 3.arrive:PF here
 'The boy traveled a long way to arrive here.'

Co-compounds also occur in at least some Mayan languages. For Tzeltal *čan.balam* 'snake/bug.jaguar > animals' and *te'.ak* 'tree.vine > plants', see Hunn (1977: 134) and Berlin (1992: 195). Examples from Tzotzil are *mól-meʔ.el* 'old/old:man-old:woman > old people' (Cowan 1969: 94), *vinik ants* 'man woman > people' (V. Gast, p.c.), *s.tot s.me'* '3SG.father 3SG.mother > parents'. A number of conversations given in Laughlin (1980) are instructive for the use of co-compounds in Tzotzil and contain instances of persuasive discourse, such as one where a man is arguing with his mother-in-law, trying to persuade her to let him talk to his wife who ran off after he hit her while drunk. This text contains a number of bipartite expressions, some of which are continuously repeated in continuous or discontinuous form, notably *x.laj s.sikub* '3SG.finish 3SG.grow_cold' (the husband: 'maybe [my guilt] will die, will grow cold'; ibid.: 189). (19) is uttered by the mother-in-law:

(19) Tzotzil: co-compound in persuasive discourse (Laughlin 1980: 190)

...7ak'.o	s.tam	tal	s.tzek	s.k'u7	ja7
give/let.IMP2SG	3SG.take	come	3SG.skirt	3SG. blouse	s/he

nox.
only

'Let her bring her skirt and her blouse. That's all.'

For Classical Nahuatl, see Section 5.2.7.

In AFRICA, co-compounds seem to be rare (judging by their absence from many grammars, dictionaries, and texts). What one sometimes finds are a few generalizing co-compounds, such as Kanuri *bonəmwané* 'you lie down (CONJ2SG)—spend the night! (IMP2SG) > day of 24 hours', *lenəmaré* 'you go (CONJ2SG)—come! (IMP2SG) > way to and fro' (Lukas 1937: 15). These are not remarkable for their meaning, but for the form of their parts. Both consist of two verbal elements; the first verb is in a non-final sequential form, called conjunctive, the second is an imperative form.

Sometimes the term compound in African languages is used for tight coordination patterns with a overt marker for coordination, as in the case of as 'verb-verb compounds' in Songhai (Koyra Chiini, Heath 1999: 139f), such as *sar ka julli* 'jump and ? > do somersaults' (*julli* is not attested outside of this expression), where the order of elements is usually fixed and the expression as a whole can be nominalized or can form other verbal derivatives (*ka* 'infinitive' is used for clausal coordination, non-initial clauses being deranked). I do not consider those co-compounds because of the overt marker for coordination.

Co-compounds seem not to be characteristic of CREOLE languages (except Tok Pisin, see above). In French-based Creoles, such as Haitian Creole and Seychelles Creoles, there are some generalizing verbal co-compounds (see Section 4.4.2).

It is not possible to make valid generalizations for global properties of co-compounds from these few remarks. It should be noted, however, that co-compounds are often discontinuous in languages, whatever the continent of their origins (thus enforcing the conclusion of Chapter 4 that co-compounds are not simply words). Furthermore, there is some evidence that the use of co-compounds is sensitive to register and style beyond Eurasia, possible relevant factors being mythological context, persuasive discourse, and emphasis. It is also remarkable that there seems to be no language in Eurasia with a high text frequency of a co-compound 'man-woman > people' which does occur, however, outside Eurasia (Tok Pisin, Wik-Mungkan).

Notes

[1] Cf. Glendon (2001) on the origin of this text, a book that is also very interesting from a philological point of view. Various languages were involved in the development of the original text, especially English and French. The protagonists involved in drafting the UDHR include the Canadian John P. Humphrey, the Frenchman René Cassin, the Lebanese Charles Malik, the Chinese Peng-chun Chang, and the American Eleanor Roosevelt.

[2] For the predilection of binomials in legal English see Hiltunen (1990: 54f, 25).

[3] To mention a few examples, in the Khalkha version *č* is constantly written *jo*. In the Kirghiz version all instances of *r*, *e*, and *ja* are missing and article 26; 3 appears as 17; 3. In the Burmese version some characters are wrong. In the Nepali version the last articles are missing.

[4] It is well-known in philology that glossing synonyms occur frequently in young literatures, especially in translations; see Segre (1963: 62f) for Italian and Liver (1999: 111) for Rhaeto-Romance: *üna libra frya chiaussa* 'a free free thing' for German *ein frey ding*. (Note that *libra frya* is not a co-compound, but just a sequence of two adjectives.) The phenomenon under discussion may, however, cause a translation in a young literature with co-compounds to eventually have more co-compounds than average. This is certainly the case for some translations of Mark in our sample, notably Kurmanji Kurdish and probably Tuva.

[5] There are translations into Even (Tungus) and Yukaghir (isolate) which are, however, summary translations (they much shorter than the other ones). These two texts do not seem to contain any co-compounds.

[6] According to Mühlhäusler (1979: 377) there are more co-compounds (called 'CP Program 1') in Rural Pidgin, such as *banara.supia* 'bow_and_arrow.spear > bow and arrow', *brata.susa* 'brother.sister > brothers and sisters', *han.lek* 'hand.leg > limbs' (also *lek.han*), *su.soks* or *su.soken* 'shoe.socks > footwear', *ritrait* 'reading.writing > s-kills learnt at school'.

[7] I am grateful to Yong-Seop Lee for having sent me his translation of Mark into Kube with a back translation in English.

[8] For other Kartvelian languages see Boeder (1991).

[9] According to Abaev (1958; see also Lewy 1934) the Ossete co-compound *cæskom* 'eye-mouth > face', which has parallels in autochthonous Caucasian languages (Avar 'eye-mouth', Kabardian 'eye-nose', etc.) is one of the clearest examples of a semantic parallel between Ossete and autochthonous Caucasian languages. For 'face' see also Mihatsch and Dvořák (forthcoming).

[10] According to Yaron Matras (p.c.) co-compounds are rare in Romani. He mentions the following examples quoting a paper by Irene Sehidou, 'Neologisms in Romani dialects' presented at the 7th Postgraduate Conference in Linguistics, Manchester, 1999: *phrala phena* 'siblings', *svetos vilagos* 'wide world' (a synonymic co-compound consisting of a Slavic and a Hungarian loanword), *koro mato* 'drunk as a lord', *sasto vesto* 'safe and sound', *dena-lena* 'they do business'.

[11] In many Uralic languages, coordinators are loanwords (Finnish, Estonian *ja* 'and' < Germanic, Mordvin *di*, Mari *da* 'and' < Russian) or recent formations (Estonian *ning* 'and' < *niin kui* 'so how', Mari *den* < *dene* 'with'). It is, therefore, usually assumed that Proto-Finno-Ugric had no grammaticalized overt coordinators.

[12] Verbal co-compounds are present in Old Tamil (see Steever 1988: 41, example 51a).

[13] A Tamil informant from Sri Lanka, when asked to translate 'elder brother and younger brother', asked me whether she could just say 'two brothers'.

[14] Malay, where 'parents' clearly is a co-compound, *ibu bapa* 'mother father', in contrast to Bahasa Indonesia, where *orang tua* 'man old' is more common than *bapak ibu* 'father mother', is not included in Tryon (1995).

[15] Some varieties of Basque have *aita-ama.ak* (father-mother.DEF:PL) instead, while others have the variant *aitatamak*, contracted from *aita-eta-ama.ak* (father-and-mother.DEF:PL) (Alan R. King, p.c.).

[16] In some dictionaries a co-compound is given as a possible variant.

[17] Co-compounds were counted as single words.

[18] This co-compound has, however, been counted in Section 6.2 for Mark. Erźa *ejkakś* consists etymologically of *ejd'e* 'child' and *kakś* 'child'. Instances of co-compounds of the unreduced forms or coordination of the two forms can be found in fairytales and epic texts, especially in negative contexts (such as 'They had no children'). Also attested are instances of *ejkakś.t-kakś.t*. It must be assumed that the co-compound of *ejd'e* and *kakś* was originally used for plural reference and in negative (non-referential) contexts. Because of the local unmarkedness of these uses it could also extend to uses with singular reference.

[19] The Hmong examples are given in two different orthographies, <Ch> is a China orthography for White Hmong (as used in the UDHR) and <Th> is a Thailand orthography for the same language (as used in Bertrais 1978 and Mottin 1978, 1980). In both orthographies final consonant letters mark tones, not consonants, although in a different way; see also Section 4.2.3.vi.

[20] Ö. Dahl, personal communication.

[21] For the comitative and instrumental as a continuous variable in Europe, see Stolz and Gugeler (2000) and Stolz et al. (2003). For word-iteration in the Mediterranean area see Stolz (2003).

7

Some Considerations about the Diachronic Evolution of Co-compounds

A thorough cross-linguistic diachronic description of co-compounds, which ideally should account for everything in the evolution of co-compounds in general and in individual languages (and individual registers and styles within languages), would be a very complex and—given the little evidence available—a speculative undertaking. Therefore, in this short chapter I shall confine myself to a few of the central issues. In Section 7.1 two fundamentally different perspectives on how co-compounds evolve diachronically are introduced, namely their evolution as formal patterns (Section 7.2) and their evolution as lexical classes (Section 7.3). In Section 7.4 the role of textual markedness is considered in the context of the evolution of co-compounds in registers and styles of one language, in particular languages, and in linguistic areas. Finally, in Section 7.5, the question of why co-compounds are especially frequent in the folk poetry of some languages is addressed.

7.1 The evolution of markers, patterns, and constructions vs. the evolution of classes

The framework of grammaticalization (Lehmann 1985, Heine et al. 1991, Hopper and Traugott 2003, Bybee et al. 1994, Haspelmath 1998, 1999, and Dahl 2001) considers along which paths grammatical morphemes and constructions evolve diachronically. Thus, it has been found that markers for tense and aspect will typically evolve from verbs with general meanings, such as 'go', 'come', 'be (at)', 'have', 'take', 'finish', etc., whereas the reverse process, tense and aspect markers developing into lexical verbs, does not occur. The evolution of co-compounds may be considered in a similar way. We can observe that co-compounds often develop from coordination (and notably from phrase-like tight coordination patterns) but that the reverse—

coordination developing from co-compounds—does not occur. The question is raised in Section 7.2 whether coordination is the only, or at least the major diachronic source for formal patterns of co-compounds and what are the difficulties of testing this. The question whether it is reasonable to talk in this context of grammaticalization is not addressed. This depends on how broad or narrow the term grammaticalization is understood. In any case, the result of the process is not the formation of a grammatical class.

The question of how co-compounds evolve as a formal pattern is a rather uninteresting part of the story about how co-compounds evolve diachronically. One reason is that the most typical formal pattern for co-compounding, unmarked juxtaposition of words, may occur spontaneously (as *pappa mamma* in child language), so there is not necessarily a long path of diachronic evolution leading to the emergence of co-compounds.

In my view, the more important diachronic question is how co-compounds evolve as a class, that is, which domains are first occupied by co-compounds, how the semantic profile of co-compounds evolves diachronically, whether a high level of co-compounding evolves gradually or suddenly (does it emerge through many succeeding steps of low and moderate levels of co-compounding), and whether the regression of a class of co-compounds (the movement from a high or moderate level to a low level) proceeds along the same or different stages as the extension of co-compounds.

At the outset of research into grammaticalization, it was not as clear as now that the evolution of morphemes and/or constructions should be the focus of interest. For Kuryłowicz (1965/1976: 70) the evolution of grammatical categories (what he meant by categories corresponds largely to classes in my terminology), rather than the evolution of morphemes or constructions, was the central issue. This led him to view grammaticalization as a reversible process (any grammatical or lexical class can disappear from a language) in contrast to most modern contributions to grammaticalization research (see, for example, Haspelmath 1999).

This does not mean that the irreversibility hypothesis in grammaticalization would be wrong. Rather the question whether there is irreversibility arises only from a certain perspective in grammaticalization. It makes sense only if paths of grammaticalization are considered in which morphemes and/or constructions completely change their nature. If, however, only a single class, or cross-linguistically, a class type, is considered, be it grammatical or lexical irrespective of the diachronic sources of that class type, and if consideration is given to how classes belonging to this class type evolve diachronically, that is, the ways in which they acquire or lose domains of use (measured in terms of both tokens and types), this gives us a completely different perspective. Here, not a grammaticalization path as a whole is considered, but rather a single node in a path or in a bundle of pathways. Again, it is no use discussing whether this process should be called grammaticalization, especially if it is not a grammatical, but a lexical class that is under discussion. In Sections 7.3–7.5, I will consider how co-compounds evolve as lexical classes.

7.2 The diachronic relationship between co-compounds and coordination

In Sections 4.3 and 4.4 we assumed that co-compounds and coordination are synchronically related in the way that coordination is the 'heavy form' corresponding to the 'light form' of co-compounds. In this section I will consider the extent to which co-compounds derive diachronically from coordination. Aside from singular cases of one-form cognate systems, cases where co-compounds and ordinary coordination are formally identical (Section 4.4.3)—which may be considered as evidence for the coordination origin of co-compounds—there are basically two possibilities for co-compounds to be derived from coordination diachronically: co-compounds may represent condensed coordinate constructions (Section 7.2.1) or co-compounds may derive from an old construction for coordination when a new, looser construction is introduced (the introduction of a new 'heavy form'; Section 7.2.2). These two developments, the condensation of co-compounds from a coordinating construction, and the introduction of a new loose construction for coordination, can, however, also occur together and, in practice, it is often difficult to distinguish between the two processes.

7.2.1 *The condensation hypothesis*

Condensation (Frei 1929: 175f, Dahl 2001) is the diachronic process by which a looser construction is transformed into a tighter one (two clauses into one clause, a clause into a phrase, two phrases into one phrase, a phrase into a word). According to Frei, tight constructions always go back to loose constructions: 'Rien n'est dans les syntagmes étroits qui ne soit d'abord dans la phrase, rien n'est dans la morphologie qui ne soit d'abord dans la syntaxe' (Frei 1929: 175f). Condensation is often referred to by the words Givón (1971: 413) ascribed to an anonymous old master: 'today's morphology is yesterday's syntax'.

I call here the CONDENSATION HYPOTHESIS what is generally assumed for the diachronic origin of compounds. Brugmann (1900/1981: 137) puts it like this (my translation): 'One thing is sure right from the beginning and everybody who has written about compounding agrees on it. All compounding derives from a certain tighter connection of two or more words which form a syntactic structure.' As already pointed out by Brugmann, syntactic origin can, of course, not be postulated for each individual instance of a compound, but rather has to apply to patterns of compounds. The condensation hypothesis can thus be restated as follows:

Condensation hypothesis about the origin of compounds:
Patterns of compounds always derive diachronically from semantically corresponding syntactic constructions. Thus, sub-compounds diachronically derive from phrases consisting of a head and a dependent noun, N-Adj compounds derive from phrases consisting of a head noun and an attributive adjective, co-compounds derive from coordinate phrases, object incorporation derives from phrases consisting of a verb and an object, etc.

Strong evidence for the condensation hypothesis comes from compounds that still contain some traces of morpho-syntactic marking, that is, strictly speaking, from incomplete compounding. Thus sub-compounds may contain genitive case morphology as a trace of originally dependent marking constructions, such as German *Kind.s.mutter* 'child mother' (die *Mutter des Kind.es* 'the mother of the child'), or possessive affixes originally from head marking constructions, such as in Turkish *göz.yaş.ı* 'eye.wet.its > tear' (*otel.in oda.lar.ı* 'hotel.GEN room.PL.its > the rooms of the hotel'). Internal inflection marking, even if it is not relational, such as plural markers, as the German *Kind.er.wagen* 'child.PL.carriage > baby carriage', may also be considered as evidence for condensation as it testifies to earlier syntactic constructions. On the whole, traces of morpho-syntactic marking in compounds are strong evidence that some compounds derive from syntactic constructions, but not that all do.

Further, somewhat weaker, evidence for the condensation hypothesis comes from word order. The order of head and dependent in phrases and in compounds is usually the same. In Guaraní, the attributive adjective (or stative verb) follows the noun, whereas the dependent noun precedes the head noun: *kuña r.oga* 'woman house > house of the woman), *oga guasu* 'house big > the/a big house'. The same order is found in compounds: *tesa.y* 'eye-water ('water of the eye') > tear', *kuân.guasu* 'finger-big > thumb' (also *kuân-gusu* id.). In languages where the order is different in phrases and in corresponding compounds, it can usually be shown that the word order in phrases has changed recently, as in German DH in sub-compounds but predominantly HD in noun phrases, the earlier word order in noun phrases having been DH (H is head, D is dependent).

The condensation hypothesis is so widely accepted that a difference in word order between phrases and compounds is usually considered to be a strong argument for a diachronic change of word order in syntax. Consider Rodrigues (1999: 190, 198) for Kipeá (Macro-Ge) with HD order in noun phrases (most Ge languages have DH) and DH in sub-compounds, and Baker (1996: 32, 38) for Sora (Munda, Austroasiatic) with object–verb order in the sentence and verb–noun order in noun incorporation (most Austroasiatic languages, except Munda languages, have verb–object order in the sentence).

Unfortunately, word order may not serve as evidence for the development of co-compounds from coordinate phrases, there being no heads and dependents in coordinate constructions. There is, however, evidence of the first type for co-compounds: traces of morphology of originally coordinating constructions.

Examples of 'incomplete' compounding with traces of coordinators are Classical Greek *kalo.k.agaθ.ía* 'beautiful.'n'.good.ABST' ideal of ethical perfection (Plato), originally the aristocratic ideal of morality' (*kaí* 'and'), Burushaski POSS.*uk* POSS.*yu* 'children' (< POSS.*ui* kɛ POSS.*yu* 'daughter and sons', Lorimer 1935; 6.2.9), and Danish *saft.e.vand* 'juice.'n'.water > diluted cordial', *smør.e.brød* 'butter.'n'.bread > sandwich' (Bauer 2001a: 699). (The latter are, however, fusional compounds, rather than co-compounds.)

The double plural marker in Mordvin co-compounds of the type *t'et'a.t-ava.t* 'father.PL-mother.PL' is strong evidence for condensation, given the fact that other Uralic languages have double dual marking (the dual is lost in Mordvin) in both co-compounds and in phrase-like tight coordination (see examples 11–13 in Chapter 2).

The best-studied example of condensation of co-compounds deriving from coordination is the evolution of dvandva-compounds from Early Vedic to Sanskrit (Justi 1861, Wackernagel 1905: 149–73), where there is direct evidence for different stages. Wackernagel (1905) distinguishes the following steps. Coordination in early Indo-Iranian languages can be syndetic or asyndetic. Examples of the former are *mitráś ca váruṇaś ca* 'Mitra and Varuna' with double coordinator and *mitró váruṇaś ca* id. with single coordinator, an example for the latter is *mitró váruṇaḥ* id. In these three examples all coordinands are in the (nominative) singular. Vedic also has double dual marking in natural coordination, similar to Khanty, Mansi, and Nenets (see Section 2.3.2), *dyáva-pr̥thivī́* (NOM.DU-NOM.DU) 'heaven and earth'. If the case marking is oblique, either both parts may take the same case, such as in *mitráyor-váruṇayoḥ* (GEN.DU-GEN.DU) 'of Mitra and Varuna', or the first part may remain in the nominative, as in *índrā-váruṇayoḥ* (NOM.DU-GEN.DU) 'of Indra and Varuna'. The ending -*ā* of the first part, which is originally a variant of the dual marker of masculine a-stems, may then be extended to forms of other declension classes, such as masculine i-stems in *ágnā-viṣṇū* (dvandva stem-VOC.DU) 'Agni and Vishnu'. In a next step, stress (consistently marked in Vedic orthography) on the first part is lost, as in *indrā-pūṣṇóḥ* (dvandva stem-NOM.DU) 'Indra and Pushna'. Finally, the initial part acquires the general stem form that occurs in other types of compounds (notably sub-compounds), as in *indra-vāyū́* 'Indra and the Wind'.

These stages suggest the diachronic development given in Table 7.1.

Some chronological evidence suggests that there was actually a development from stage 3 to stage 7 from Early Vedic to Sanskrit, while stages 1 to 3 are very likely to have coexisted previously in Proto-Indo-Iranian. While stage 3 is attested in the related Iranian language Avesta, stage 4 is not. The replacement of -*ī* by -*ā* in the first member (5) is an occasional phenomenon. The very use of -*ā*, however, instead of the normal dual ending -*au* of the a-stems is a specialization of the ending of the first part which can be interpreted as the development of a special stem form for first parts of dvandvas. Stress reduction occurred first in dvandvas in which the second member was stressed on the final syllable. This suggests that stress reduction was due to an analogy with the so-called collective compounds (abstract bahuvrihi compounds, such as *tri-yugá-*'period of three life times') that are stressed on the final syllable.[1] There are only two examples of stage 7 in the first nine (older) books of the Vedas, while stage 7 is, however, the common form for new compounds in later texts. Dvandvas of the stages 3 to 6 are very restricted in their choice of declension types, mainly masculine nouns. At stage 7 they acquire full productivity for all declensions. For details, see Wackernagel (1905: 149–73). As can be seen from the examples, dvandvas of names of gods are very important in Vedic, which has to do with the specific ritual register of Vedic hymns (see Section 5.5.5.iii for the use of co-compounds in a ritual register in Mordvin).

TABLE 7.1. The evolution of dvandva compounds from Vedic to Sanskrit

1	syndetic coordination	*mitró váruṇaś ca*
2	asyndetic coordination	*mitró váruṇaḥ*
3	double marking (dual)	*mitráyor-váruṇayoḥ*
4	loss of case inflection in the first part	*índrā-váruṇayoḥ*
5	uniform ending of the first part (dvandva stem)	*ágnā-viṣṇū*
6	stress reduction	*indrā-pūṣṇóḥ*
7	first part has the form of a compound stem	*indra-vāyū́*

In some languages there are also fossilized comitative markers, additive focus particles, and verbal sequence markers, suggesting that co-compounds developed from syntactic constructions that are closely related to coordination, if not from coordination proper.

In Tatar (Turkic) there are co-compounds of kinship terms with both parts marked by -li/-ly, which is an adjectivizing or proprietive suffix (*urman.ly* 'wood.PROP > wooded'), *ata.ly-ul.ly* 'father.PROP-son.PROP > father and son'. This element is of comitative origin and is found in tight coordination elsewhere in Turkic, as in Old Uyghur:[2]

(1) Old Uyghur (Thomsen 1922: 235)
adïy.lï toŋuz.lï art üzä soquš.miš är.miš
bear.PROP wild_boar.PROP pass on meet.VN be.VN
'A bear and a wild boar had been fighting in a mountain pass.'

The Mordvin element *-ńek* that is found on both parts of generalizing co-compounds, in *či.ńek-ve.ńek* 'day.NEK-night.NEK > night and day' (see Section 5.2.2 above), was originally a comitative marker.

Some co-compounds (especially of kinship terms) in Mari have double marking with -*ak*, an additive focus particle. Consider (2), the beginning of a fairytale, where -*ak* cannot be interpreted as an additive focus particle. Double -*ak* is not in use for phrasal coordination and occurs only in a few co-compounds.

(2) Mari (Evseev 1994: 22)
Il.en ul.yt ulm.aš
live.CONV be.PRS3SG be.INF
kum iz.ak-šol'.ak-šamyč.
three elder_brother.also-younger_brother.also-PL
'Once upon a time there were three brothers (it is said).'

In Kanuri (Nilo-Saharan) generalizing co-compounds (*bonəmwané* 'you lie down (CONJ2SG)—spend the night! (IMP2SG) > day of 24 hours'; see Appendix to Chapter 6) the first verb is in a sequential form, termed conjunctive. A similar case is the Kazakh (Turkic) co-compound *žür.ip-tur.ū* 'go.CONV-stand.VN > movement and residence' (UDHR 13; 1) in which the first member is a converb.

While this evidence removes any doubt that co-compounds *can* develop from coordination (and related constructions, such as comitative constructions), it does not prove that co-compounds *always* develop from coordination. Actually, there is some evidence that co-compounds do not derive from coordinating constructions in every case.

Nominal co-compounds in Modern Greek (see Section 1.1.1) might be the result of co-compounds developing from another type of compound, as in *tó anðr.ɔ́.jin.ɔ* 'the:N man.LINK.woman.N > married couple'. In this compound, the parts occur in a stem form and the compound has neuter gender, while the words corresponding to the parts are masculine and feminine, respectively. In Classical Greek *andrógunos* is an adjective 'hermaphroditic' with a nominalized masculine form *andrógunos* 'coward, hermaphrodite'. According to Debrunner (1917) there is only one attested case in Classical Greek where, in an epigram, the adjective can be interpreted as a co-compound, *andróguna* (PL:N) *loutrá* 'baths for men and women', and there it is an adjective. It may therefore be assumed that Modern Greek *anðr.ɔ́.jin.ɔ* derives from a bahuvrihi compound. However, it is difficult to imagine how verbal co-compounds such as *anɛvɔ.katɛvázɔ* 'ascend-descend > go up and down' might have developed from sub-compounds.[3]

Moreover, co-compound-like compounds may occur in child language, even in languages that do not typically have co-compounds in adult speech. Hohenberger (1996)[4] gives such examples as *Messergabel* (2;1) 'knifefork', *Gabellöffel* (2;3) 'forkspoon' for German. This suggests that co-compounds may be formed spontaneously without a complex syntactic diachrony, or that they may be produced after the model of sub-compounds (that begin to occur from 1;10 in Hohenberger's study).

To summarize: Because of their typical lack of overt marking, it is often impossible to prove that co-compounds derive diachronically from co-compounds. There is, however, evidence from co-compounds with fossilized relational marking (that is, strictly speaking, from incomplete co-compounding) that co-compounds in some cases derive diachronically from coordination. In spite of the difficulty of reconstruction, due to the lack of markers (a characteristic property of compounds), there is reason to believe that the condensation hypothesis is true for most cases of co-compounds, bearing in mind that there are no plausible alternatives and that nobody seriously challenges it. We may, therefore, conclude that coordination is a major and even most probably the dominant cross-linguistic source in the evolution of co-compounds.

7.2.2 *The introduction of new 'heavy forms'*

If compounds like German *Kindesmutter* 'child's mother' are now distinct from phrases such as *die Mutter des Kindes* or colloquial *die Mutter von dem Kind*, this is only partly due to condensation in the 'light form'. Diachronically, it is actually the 'heavy form' that has changed. In comparison to

Proto-Germanic, there is a new head-dependent word order in the ordinary attributive possession and articles have been introduced and become obligatory in ordinary attributive possession (*die Mutter des Kindes*).

Such newly introduced 'heavy forms' are very widespread for all kinds of compound-like lexical classes and are well-known as instances of renewal in grammaticalization (von der Gabelentz 1901: 256, Lehmann 1985). In a renewal of a syntactic construction, collocations and lexicalized phrases are less inclined than phrases to participate. This is how lexicalized phrases may split off from syntactic constructions to become compounds. Whenever a new construction takes over in syntax or if a syntactic construction is enlarged by a new formant, this may cause a formal split between the productive syntactic construction and a residue of lexicalized phrases (which may then become a pattern of their own). This is how an alienability split in attributive possession may develop (Koptjevskaja-Tamm 1997 for Maltese). A clear formal differentiation of co-compounds and syntactic coordination may be caused diachronically by the obligatorification of an overt coordinator in syntactic coordination, as has occurred in various Finno-Ugric languages (Mordvin and Mari in contrast to Khanty, Mansi, and Nenets). Often it is impossible to keep condensation neatly distinct from the introduction of a new 'heavy form'. So it is not clear to what extent the lack of articles in German bare binomials and other cases of noun stripping are due to the condensation of binomials (where the article is removed by condensation) or to the introduction of a new 'heavy form' (as with a new construction with articles).

7.2.3 Conclusions

In this section we have seen that, at least in some languages, co-compounds have developed from coordination by condensation, by the introduction of a new construction for coordination, or by a combination of the two. It can be assumed that in most cases co-compounds derive from coordination, but this hypothesis cannot be proved. There is also reason to believe that there are other minor sources for co-compounds (bahuvrihi compounds in Modern Greek, ad hoc juxtaposition), so it has to be assumed that co-compounds, at least in some languages, will have a hybrid origin. Clear examples for co-compounds with a non-coordinate origin are Mordvin *a t'eči-vandi* 'not today-tomorrow > today or tomorrow, soon' and Russian *ne segodnja-zavtra* id. (Section 5.2.8). These clearly derive from sentences with unmarked conditional clauses ('(If) not today (then) tomorrow'). The hybrid origin of a lexical class is, however, not astonishing, given that many grammatical classes have hybrid diachronic origins (e.g. weak and strong past in Germanic languages).

7.3 Co-compounds as a lexical class evolve gradually

In Chapter 6 we found that there is a high degree of correlation between the relative frequency of co-compounds in a text and the related semantic profile of co-compounds. It was found that the proportion of synonymic co-compounds gradually increases as the overall frequency of co-compounds increases. The diachronic interpretation of these synchronic facts must be that synonymic co-compounds, as with any other type of co-compound, do not evolve all of a sudden, but through a long gradual process, step by step, and that a high level of synonymic co-compounds develops only if the basic types of co-compounds, notably additive co-compounds, are well established. More evidence for the hypothesis of a gradual evolution of synonymic co-compounds comes from the conclusion in Chapter 5 that in texts of moderately co-compounding languages, with few conventionalized synonymic co-compounds, non-conventionalized synonymic co-compounds tend to occur in certain specific contexts, such as emphasis, generalization, and negation. This leads me to propose the hypothesis that co-compounds as a lexical class evolve gradually. Thus, a language such as Mandarin, with a high level of co-compounding, would have gone through a long, gradual diachronic evolution from the point where it first developed a low degree of co-compounding (with a dominance of generalizing co-compounds and some additive co-compounds), then gradually rising to a moderate level of co-compounding (with a dominance of additive and possibly collective co-compounds and with contextually motivated synonymic co-compounds), until finally it evolved into a highly co-compounding language with a dominance of synonymic and other non-basic types of co-compounds and with many lexicalized synonymic co-compounds.

Unfortunately, the usual explanations for the evolution of co-compounds in Mandarin (notably the HOMONYMY EXPLANATION and the MINIMAL WORD LENGTH EXPLANATION) are not compatible with the above hypothesis of gradual evolution. A closer look at the more orthodox explanations is therefore in order here.

The traditional view in Sinology that synonymic co-compounds arose through the avoidance of homonymy is expressed in the following passage from Karlgren (1962: 22). 'But, in proportion as the number of homophones increased, [the speaker] had to make elucidative additions to the simple words and thus radically reshape the materials of his language... The additions were of various kinds, the commonest and by far the most important of which was the formation of what may be called synonym-compounds.'[5]

A variant of what may be called the minimal word length explanation is advocated by Feng (1998: 222). According to Feng, disyllabic units (his examples are mostly co-compounds, especially of the synonymic and the ornamental subtype) were created to satisfy the need for two-syllable prosodic units. Throughout Chinese history, syllable length (or syllable weight, as Feng calls it in the framework of prosodic phonology) has continuously declined. Feng holds that the dramatic increase in disyllabicity during the Han dynasty (206 BC–220 AD) was due to the previous loss of final consonants and consonant clusters.[6] Table 7.2 (ibid.: 224) illustrates the reconstructed dramatic change in syllable structure from Old to Middle Chinese.

Even if the two explanations seem to be very different at first glance (the homonymy explanation is a functional explanation, while the overshort words explanation, in the version of Feng (1998), is a hidden-structure explanation), they have some aspects in common, notably they both implicitly assume that redundancy, such as it occurs in synonymic co-compounds, is anomalous and comes into being only if it cannot be avoided.[7] This is a diachronic variant of what Croft (2001: ch. 3) calls the third hidden assumption in semantic relativity (linguistic analysis should minimize redundancy; see Section 1.3.2.iv), a highly problematic position since redundancy is omnipresent in languages of all types. In my view, redundancy should be defined without reference to norm and obligatority. In English *Yesterday she arrived*, the past is expressed twice by the tense marker and by the adverb and this is redundant as I understand the term, even if this is the usual and the shortest possible grammatical way to express that meaning in English.

Let us reconsider the two explanations in terms of Lüdtke's (1980) theory of language change. Lüdtke holds that there are two kinds of language change, qualitative and QUANTITATIVE LANGUAGE CHANGE (*quantitativer Sprachwandel*). Quantitative language change is endogenous (due to language-internal mechanisms), continuous, unconscious, and irreversible. It is due to redundancy management (*Redundanzsteuerung*) in communication. If the linguistic message in speech contains too little information, the hearer

TABLE 7.2. Syllable structure in Old and Middle Chinese

Chronology	Maximal	Minimal
Old Chinese (c. 1000 BC)	CCCMVCCC	CVC
Middle Chinese (c. 800 AD)	{C,S}V{C,S}	CV

C = consonant, V = vowel, M = medial, S = semivowel
Source: Feng (1998)

cannot understand it. In order to be understood, the speaker will tend to make his statement clearer than necessary (implying redundancy) for the audience at which it is directed. Redundancy is also needed because there is noise (in the technical sense of the word) in the transmission of the speech signal. There are basically two dimensions of redundancy: clearer than absolutely necessary phonetic pronunciation, and more morphemes and words ('semantactic units') than absolutely necessary. The two dimensions differ in that the phonetic one is restricted by a maximum (the ideal phonetic realization) and the semantactic one by a minimum (syntactic rules that require a certain basic phrase structure). The phonetic maximum and the semantactic minimum constitute the ideal form of utterance (*Grenznorm*) which is, however, rarely ever realized in spoken communication. The standard is to use more semantactic units than necessary and to pronounce expressions less distinctively than maximally possible. If the standard drifts too far from the phonetic maximum and from the semantactic minimum, the ideal form changes: the phonological structure is reduced and the morphological or syntactic structure is extended. These changes are irreversible. This is why quantitative language change always implies a loss of distinctions in the phonological structure and an accumulation of morphemes in the morpho-syntactic structure. Finally, if morphemes become continuously shorter through reduction of the phonological structure, and if there is a continuous growth in the morphemes required to convey a certain meaning, there will necessarily be a merger of morphemes into new larger morphemes in order to keep the number of morphemes required for a message more or less constant. These three processes, PHONOLOGICAL REDUCTION, MORPHOLOGICAL ACCUMULATION, and MORPHOLOGICAL MERGER, are invariably present in all language change and, since they affect word length and number of morphemes per word (or per any other semantactic unit) in opposite directions, they lead to an equilibrium in word length and morphemes per word. We may call this phenomenon LÜDTKE'S EQUILIBRIUM in language change.

An illustrative example, given below, is the development of adnominal and nominal demonstrative pronouns from Latin to French. As can be seen from the forms in this development, any phonological change is a reduction in the number of phonemes; any morphological change is the addition of a morpheme; and any change in the number of morpheme boundaries is a reduction in the number of morpheme boundaries (optional elements are in parentheses). In spite of massive phonological and morphological changes, the length of the expressions and the number of morphemes contained in them tends to remain constant:

(3) From Latin to French (Lüdtke 1980: 212)
(ecce)ista N > (c)este N > cette N > cette N (-ci)
(ecce)hoc > (ç)o > ço > ce > ce(la) > cela > ça

In the long run, any expression can become too short phonologically in any language (not only in Chinese) and will either be extended by additional morphemes or replaced by a longer expression.[8] This holds for both grammatical forms and lexemes. An example of the extension of a grammatical form is the evolution of personal deixis from Latin to French: *(ego) venio* > *(moi) je viens*. The extension (the personal pronoun) starts by being optional and finally becomes obligatory, after which a new optional extension can be added. An example for accumulation in a lexeme is the evolution from Latin *hodie* > French *hui* which is extended to *au jour d'hui* 'today'. Some French nouns are etymologically Latin diminutives: *auris* / dim. *auricula* > *oreille* 'ear', *genu* / dim. *genuculum* > *genou* 'knee', *agnus* / *agnellus* > *agneau* 'lamb', *sol* / **soliculus* > *soleil* 'sun' (ibid.: 208). In this context, Lüdtke also mentions Chinese synonymic compounds as an example of accumulation (ibid.: 210). Thus, in Lüdtke's model, the homonymy explanation and the overshort words explanation are just two facets of a single process, quantitative language change, which is not restricted to a particular language or language family, but is universal.

The universal process of quantitative language change is very general. It predicts that if several forms compete for the expression of a concept, short forms are replaced in the long run by longer ones (not necessarily during a certain period of time). But, from the point of view of the evolution of individual classes, it is important to note that the model of quantitative language change does not predict which kind of longer, polymorphemic forms (diminutives, sub-compounds, co-compounds, reduplication, etc.) will replace the shorter forms. Thus, while Lüdtke's model and similar approaches can explain why longer forms tend to replace shorter forms, and that this will happen more rapidly in cases of massive phonological reduction, such as from Latin to French and from Proto-Chinese to Mandarin, it cannot explain why Mandarin abounds with synonymic co-compounds while there are none in French. It does not explain why it is diminutives that gave rise to the French expressions for 'ear', 'knee', 'lamb', and 'sun' and not sub-compounds or reduplication. And it does not explain why the French words can no longer be analyzed as diminutives (the Latin lexical class of diminutives has completely disappeared in French), while in Mandarin synonymic co-compounds did not fully merge to one-morpheme units.

We may conclude that the evolution of lexical classes, such as co-compounds and diminutives, cannot be fully accounted for by the mechanism of quantitative language change. Quantitative language change, which, among other things, accounts for the avoidance of too-short words and of homonyms, can help explain why certain representatives of lexical classes (notably those more or less synonymic with their corresponding shorter forms) are used more frequently and may become the norm, and why certain representatives of lexical classes fuse their morphemes (are demotivated from lexical classes; see Section 4.3.4). However, quantitative language change cannot create a new pattern of word formation (or, in our terminology, a new lexical class). That in French *oreille, genou, agneau,* and *soleil* won out was possible only because Latin had diminutives, and because in the temporary lexica of Latin, diminutives could be produced easily. There were no or almost no co-compounds in the temporary lexica of Latin texts, which is why there are no French words which are etymologically synonymic co-compounds. We may, therefore, conclude that co-compounds in Chinese were not created only after the phonological structure of words had already been heavily reduced. Co-compounds, including synonymic co-compounds, must have already existed in Proto-Chinese before the phonological reduction took place, not necessarily as lexemes of the permanent lexicon, but at least as a lexical class in the temporary lexica. If certain compounds are not attested in earlier Chinese texts, this is not proof that they did not yet exist, at least in certain specific styles or registers at that time in the spoken language.

The homomymy and the overshort words explanations are certainly wrong, as follows, in their strong form: 'Synonymic co-compounds were created in Chinese because of the phonotactic simplifications.' But they are likely to be true in a weaker form, as partial explanations: 'Synonymic co-compounds, which already existed, came to be used more frequently and became lexicalized more often because of the phonotactic simplifications.'[9] Evidence against the strong form comes from typology. (The most severe shortcoming of explanations of synonymic co-compounds in Sinology is their lack of any typological perspective.) On the one hand, there are many languages with synonymic co-compounds which, however, do not have a phonotactic structure similar to Mandarin, and notably, no monosyllabic morphemes (such Khmer, Khalkha, and Avar). On the other hand, there are languages which, similar to Mandarin, have either monosyllabic morphemes with a very limited set of phoneme combinations (such as Ewe), or a massive homonymy problem (such as Samoan), and which do not have any co-compounds. It follows that synonymic co-compounds need not necessarily develop under the same phonological and phonotactic conditions as in Mandarin, and that synonymic co-compounds can also develop if there are neither overshort words nor homonymy problems. Add to this that most (possibly all) Sino-Tibetan languages have at least a moderate level of co-compounding. It is thus most likely that Proto-Chinese already had a moderate level of co-compounding where synonymic co-compounds were at least as common as in languages such as Mordvin and Chuvash. Homonymy and overshort words cannot explain why co-compounds developed, and may be only partial explanations why co-compounds, which already existed as a lexical class, came to be used more and more frequently as Classical Chinese evolved toward Mandarin.

The evolution of co-compounds in Chinese thus does not contradict the general assumption of a gradual development of lexical classes of co-compounds.

A well-established class of co-compounds, such as occurs in East and South East Asian languages, exhibits a considerable degree of complexity. But this does not mean that individual co-compounds represent an especially complex structure. Bishop and Tennenbaum (1995/2002) adduce a Mandarin scalar co-compound *dà.xiǎo* 'big.small > size' as the first and only example to illustrate that Chinese has a simple grammar and that its word formation follows logical patterns. However, recall from Section 5.2.9 that scalar co-compounds are extremely marked typologically; they seem to be restricted to some East and South East Asian languages with a high level of co-compounding. Thus, there is reason to believe that a seemingly simple structure like 'big-small > size' develops only if there already is a very complex cluster of similar forms in the lexicon (a lexical class of co-compounds). Put differently, co-compounds, as lexical classes, exhibit a high degree of EVOLUTIONARY COMPLEXITY or MATURITY (Dahl 2004: ch. 6). This stands in contrast to their usually simple formal pattern of mere juxtaposition, a pattern which can be formed spontaneously and does not exhibit evolutionary complexity. This contrast of universally available structure in form with mature structure as a lexical class contributes to the specific areal behavior of co-compounds. As a simple formal pattern, co-compounds can easily emerge in languages of any type; as a complex entrenched phenomenon in the lexicon, they need much time to evolve.

7.4 The role of textual markedness for the acceptability of co-compounds

In this section I will address three crucial questions from a diachronic point of view:
- Why do co-compounds have characteristic recurrent semantic profiles that correlate with their overall text frequency?

- Why do co-compounds cluster into classes?
- And why do co-compounds form macro-areal patterns?

While it is clear that these questions cannot be treated exhaustively here, I would like to suggest that the three are related and require the study of textual markedness (see also Section 2.1).

In Sections 6.2 and 6.4, we saw that basic types of co-compounds, such as generalizing, alternative, and additive, make up a higher proportion of co-compounds where the overall level of co-compounding is low, whereas non-basic types, notably synonymic co-compounds, make up a higher proportion where the overall level of co-compounding in the text is high. Put succinctly, the higher the level of co-compounding, the more non-basic co-compounds there are. In order to understand this general correlation, we may reason as follows. Each potential co-compound has a certain degree of acceptability in each potential context of use. A low degree of acceptability may not necessarily completely block the use of an expression, but it will prevent it from being used frequently. Thus, only those co-compounds which are acceptable in various contexts of use will occur with a higher frequency. We may, therefore, assume that the co-compounds which will have the widest cross-linguistic distribution are the most acceptable and the most easily interpreted even if there is no established class of co-compounds in a language. Acceptability is closely connected to textual markedness. Expressions which are not acceptable are usually more easily accepted in textually marked passages where unusual expressions have the function of attracting the attention of the audience. Generally, however, it is the case that backgrounding expressions (lowering the textual markedness of a passage) are more in demand because many more textually unmarked passages are needed in a text than textually marked ones. Alternative co-compounds, such as 'one-two' or 'once-twice', often have a backgrounding function. Consider (4) from Mordvin:

(4) Erźa Mordvin (D 15)
Ćiľim.eś, keľa, ojmavt.i, nockovt.at vesť-kavkst'
pipe.DEF news calm.PRS3SG draw.PRS2SG once-twice
meľavks.oś suťam.i.
sorrow.DEF drop_off.PRS3SG
'The pipe, they say, calms down, you draw once or twice and the sorrow disappears.'

In this context the precise number is irrelevant. A precise number 'once' or 'twice' would call for the question, 'Why does the author insist on this number?' The alternative co-compound has a backgrounding function in this example (see also example (1b) in Section 2.1 for a tight coordination pattern in the same function). Synonymic and ornamental co-compounds, on the other hand, generally have a high average textual marking potential if they are not conventionalized. Synonymic co-compounds are a kind of repetition, and repetition is insistence which therefore evokes the question: 'Why does the speaker/author insist on this?' This may explain why non-basic co-compounds occur very rarely in texts with a low level of co-compounding and why, in texts with a moderate level of co-compounding, they tend to occur in particular contexts where their effect on textual markedness is mitigated (Section 5.5). Now, it might be argued that it is unfair to compare well-established alternative co-compounds in Mordvin with non-conventionalized synonymic co-compounds. The point is, however, that alternative co-compounds may occur even in languages that have very few co-compounds, such as German *ein-zweimal* 'once-twice' (there are various graphemic variants: *ein-/zweimal*; *ein zweimal*; *ein, zweimal*) and English *once-twice*, as in *Do most patients visit the chiropractor once/twice a week?* (from the Internet).

Speakers use textually marked or—in Haspelmath's (1999) terms—extravagant expressions when endeavoring to catch the attention of the audience. If an extravagant expression is repeated often this may lead to inflation or devaluation (Dahl 2001). For co-compounds this suggests that the higher their frequency in a language (or in a text), the lower their average degree of textual markedness in general. In a next step, co-compounds occurring frequently in certain domains can conventionalize. The collective behavior of co-compounds in respect of devaluation is one of the most crucial aspects of their class character. Co-compounds are a class, not because they would be represented in the language competence in a uniform way (such as a single rule for language production or as a compact list in the lexicon), but because they—however they are represented mentally—influence each other's degree of acceptability. As to the question whether a certain co-compound will lexicalize in a certain language, one of the most important factors is whether other co-compounds already exist in that language and how many. If a co-compound is 'supported' by the existence of other co-compounds, it has a significant advantage over its non-co-compound rivals in the competition for lexicalization in a certain lexical domain. What is not conventionalized sounds odd. In order to become conventional, any means which make an unusual expression sound less obtrusive can be important in support of its further propagation.

It follows from what has been said above that extension of the use of co-compounds occurs in textually marked passages. Here language contact comes into play as a source of inspiration. If a deviation from the norm is required, why not take over an already known expression from a contact language? The kind of language contact which we are concerned with here does not necessarily require much pressure on the side of the donor language, since transfer comes into play only in those contexts where there is already a need for an unusual or different way of expression. Because this kind of language contact is very subtle, it can be observed in operation only under very specific conditions. Such conditions hold for the following example in a German translation of a Hungarian text.[10] A situation of language contact with Hungarian influences on German is undeniable in the context of this translation from Hungarian to German. The inspiring language, Hungarian, has a higher level of co-compounding than German, even if Hungarian, being a central European language, has only few co-compounds, and notably fewer than the more eastern Finno-Ugric languages such as Mordvin. Hungarian has, however, verbal co-compounds in particular. In the Hungarian novel, *A birodalom ezredese* (*The Colonel of the Empire*) by Péter Dobai (Dobai 1985), in most places where there are co-compounds, no co-compounds appear in the German translation by Dorothea Koriath (Dobai 1990). There is one, however, in the following passage:

(5) Hungarian and its German translation
    a Hungarian (Dobai 1985: 432)
        Meglepődött volna Redl, ha tudja, még inkább, ha láthatja is ezt a térdeplő nőt, aki őérte **fohászkodik-fogadkozik** [pray:PRS3SG-commit:PRS3SG], küld imát a Mindenhatóhoz...
    b German (Dobai 1990: 415)
        Redl wäre überrascht gewesen, hätte er das gewusst, ja diese Kniende sehen können, die für ihn **betete-bat**, ihr Gebet zum Allmächtigen sandte...
        'Redl would have been astonished if he knew, if he could have seen this woman on her knees, who **prayed-begged** for him and sent her prayer to the Almighty...'

What is most peculiar about example (5b) in German is that the co-compound *betete-bat*, which is very odd in German out of context, does not sound strange in the context it is found in here. The reason is that the example is from a dramatic central passage of the novel where the heroine Katalin, who is not religious or sentimental in any way, finally, in a desperate situation, does not see any other way to help the male hero, Redl, than to pray for him, a very unexpected action on her part. It is, of course, not a coincidence either that here we have a prayer. We have seen elsewhere (Section 5.5.5.iii) that prayers can be a very favorable context for co-compounds (see also example (39) in Section 5.5.2). Now, I have to admit that the collocation *betete-bat* was probably not used for the first time ever in German in the current context. It is already suggested by the Bernese German co-compound *biti.bäti (mache)* 'beg?-IMI (do) implore' (*bite* 'beg', *bäte* 'pray'; *biti* might derive from *bite di* '(I) beg you', *bäti* is a kind of imitative component). A quick search on the Internet reveals that the two verb forms have occurred with each other in texts and that there are some cases of direct juxtaposition, which tend to be written differently: *betete, bat* in the absence of a characteristic orthographic pattern for co-compounds in German. The clearest indication for inspiration by the contact language is the hyphen in (5b). It must also be taken into account that the specific formal similarity between the verbs lowers the textual marking potential of the form, which would not be paralleled in English *prayed-begged*. Add to this that the former is a strong past, and the latter a weak past, and that it is not unusual in Germanic languages to have coordination of a strong and a weak form of the same verb, as in Swedish *och musiken den gnällde och gnall* 'and the music it moaned and "moant" ' (Gustaf Fröding, *Det var dans bort i vägen*). But all this is only further evidence for the assumption that there are two bundles of factors which make the translation of a co-compound by a co-compound acceptable in this passage: inspiration by the contact language, and factors lowering the oddness of the specific form, among which the most important is to move the passage into the foreground. In the passage given in (6), a Hungarian co-compound has not been translated by a co-compound in German:

(6) Hungarian and its German translation
    a Hungarian (Dobai 1985: 41)
       Katalin nem szívelte Korzelinszkit, és ezt a kapitány **érezte-tudta** [feel:PST:OBJ:3SG-know:PST:OBJ:3SG], nem tolakodott, csak diszkréten hódolt Katalinnak, és Katalin ennyit megengedett, pontosabban, ennyit Katalin észre sem vett...
    b German (Dobai 1990: 39)
       Katalin mochte Korzelinszki nicht, und das **spürte und wusste** der Kapitän, er war nicht zudringlich, er verehrte Katalin nur sehr zurückhaltend, und das gestattete sie ihm, besser gesagt, geruhte sie nicht zu bemerken.
       'Katalin didn't like Korzelinszki, and the captain **felt and knew** this. He didn't make advances, he admired Katalin only hesitantly, and she allowed it, or more precisely, did not deign to notice it.'

In a way, (6) is no less emotional than (5), but captain Korzelinszki happens to be an unimportant figure in the story, so there would be too much highlighting if we had *spürte-wusste* in the German text.

These examples may serve as a point of departure for a hypothesis explaining why co-compounds are distributed in an areally characteristic way in the languages of Eurasia, as is described in Chapter 6. We can take for granted that in texts of every language there will be highlighted passages which call for textually marked expressions. We can further take for granted that contact languages may serve as a source of inspiration in cases where new or unusual expressions are needed. If we now have a language with a low level of co-compounding surrounded by languages with a higher level of co-compounding, this will tend to introduce co-compounds in some contexts where these co-compounds do not feel too odd. In response, the overall frequency of co-compounds in that language will rise slightly, which makes for co-compounds generally having a slightly lower potential for textual markedness in all potential contexts of use than before. This, again, makes it easier for further co-compounds to be introduced through language contact. Given enough time, this process would continue until the recipient language approaches the level of co-compounding of its contact languages. If, however, a language with a higher level of co-compounding is surrounded by languages at a lower level, these other languages will influence it to use various other means of expression in contexts where co-compounds could be used. This can lead to a slight decrease in the overall frequency of co-compounding, which generally makes co-compounds in all contexts acquire a slightly higher potential for textual marking. The consequence of this is that co-compounds are used increasingly less often until the language approximates the low level of its surrounding languages.

This hypothesis for the emergence of the characteristic macro-areal distribution pattern of co-compounding in Eurasia (for which hypothesis there is actually little direct evidence) tries to account for the paradox that, on the one hand, we have a macro-areal pattern which is likely to have developed through language contact and, on the other hand, many language-specific, idiosyncratic properties of classes of co-compounds which cannot be accounted for by language contact. This leads us to the assumption that co-compounds evolve individually in each language, even in the case of strong areal pressure (as in the case of White Hmong; Section 6.5), and that influences through language contact, whether weak or strong, have only an indirect influence on the evolution of the class of co-compounds as a whole.

If we now look at language contact between different registers or between different styles within a single language, the mechanism involved is basically the same as that at work in language contact between different languages, with the reservation that here we are concerned with borrowing rather than loan translation. Of course, it is very difficult to prove borrowing from register to register within a language, but it is very likely that the co-compounds which are textually unmarked in a specific register, having a higher level of co-compounding, may be adopted into passages that call for textual markedness in other registers of the same language, where they are less common. Example (7a) from Mordvin might represent a case in point. Here (7a) is from a novel and (7b) from an epic text. The same synonymic co-compound *prams-jomams* 'fall-perish > perish, die' is used in both examples. While this co-compound is typical of the epic register, where it is not especially marked textually (this can be seen from the fact that it occurs in a sequence with another co-compound *prams-kuloms* 'fall-die > perish, die' which has exactly the same meaning), it is a hapax legomenon (occurring only once) in Doronin's novel. In this novel, *prams-kuloms* is contextually motivated (backgrounded by indefiniteness/lack of evidence and foregrounded by emotivity). There is therefore reason to believe that the co-compound *prams-jomams* 'fall-perish > perish' in the register of written literary fiction was borrowed from the epic register or another register with a higher level of co-compounding:

(7) Mordvin
    a Written literary fiction (D 135)
       Vana   ist'a   eŕamo.ś.kak   kov-but'i
       look   thus   life.DEF.also   where:LAT-INDEF
       pr.i-jom.i.
       fall.PRS3SG-perish.PRS3SG
       'This is how the very life perishes somewhere (P. thought)'.
    b Epic poem (Šaronov 1994: 65)
       Pra.ś-joma.ś   od   Damaj.eń   ava.zo.
       fall.PST3SG-perish.PST3SG   young   Damaj.GEN   mother.his
       '[Died (*Pra.ś-kulo.ś* fall.PST3SG-die.PST3SG) the father of young Damay,] Perished the mother of young Damay.'

Registers in which co-compounding is more frequent may thus occasionally provide co-compounds, from their register-specific lexicons, for registers in which co-compounding is less frequent. This is how highly co-compounding registers may influence the use of others in which co-compounding is less common.

If we now reconsider the question of how homonymy and overshort words may influence the increase of frequency of co-compounds, these can be considered as just two additional factors which may lower the degree of textual markedness of individual co-compounds. If co-compounds are in competition with words that either have homonymy problems or do not have a length suitable for lexical elements, this may lower the degree of textual markedness for those co-compounds. This would have the effect that those co-compounds are more easily lexicalized (or can be more easily borrowed from registers with a higher degree of co-compounding) and that co-compounds thus generally become less marked textually.

To summarize, there is some reason to believe that textual markedness is very important in order to understand why co-compounds develop the way they do in individual languages, in different styles and registers in a particular language, and within linguistic areas. Textual markedness plays an important role for the characteristic development of the semantic profiles of co-compounds, for indirect influence in language contact situations which in the long run may result in macro-areal patterns, and for the high degree of reversibility in the evolution of co-compounds as lexical classes.

7.5 Co-compounds in folk poetry and desemantization

We have repeatedly observed that co-compounds are not equally distributed across registers and styles in central Eurasian languages. Co-compounds are especially frequent in some registers of folk poetry. In the Mordvin epic poem Mastorava (Šaronov 1994), concepts like 'village', 'way', and 'wife' are frequently expressed by co-compounds, whereas this is not the case in fiction or colloquial speech (Section 6.4). Co-compounds can thus have highly different degrees of lexicalization in different registers of the same language and it is an interesting question how this can come about. In Section 5.5.5.iii, I suggested that the extremely high frequency of co-compounds in traditional prayers in Mordvin is due to the fact that this register is especially rich in contexts which favor the use of co-compounds (future, optative, negation, generalization, emphasis). Let us now consider more systematically what might be the main reasons for certain registers of folk poetry to acquire a higher level of co-compounding. It would seem that the following three factors are relevant: (a) accumulation of favorable contexts for co-compounds entailing a higher frequency of co-compounds, which in turn has the consequence that co-compounds in certain domains can be conventionalized, and that the average textual markedness of co-compounds is lowered generally; (b) desemantization in texts with a low information rate—information rate is the amount of new information per time—which favors especially 'redundant' co-compounds of non-basic types; (c) a shift in Lüdtke's equilibrium toward longer words with more morphemes, due to emphatic speech made possible by a low information rate. Factors (b) and (c) are dependent on the low information rate of folk poetry. A passage from Russian Byliny (a kind of epic poem about Russian heroes in the time of the Mongolian-Tatar assault which have been collected especially from Russian dialects in Karelia at the end of the nineteenth century) will serve as illustration. Co-compounds are marked in boldface:

(8) Russian, Byliny (Bogomilov 1950: 96 f)[11]

Tut staryj kazak da Il'ja Muromec,	There Old Cossack and Il'ja Muromec
On poexal po razdol'icu čistu polju,	he PFV:ride:PST along valley: DIM:ACC clean:ACC field:ACC
Ne mog **konca-kraju** siluški naexati.	not can:PST end: GEN-border:GEN force: DIM:GEN on:ride:INF
On povyskočil na goru na vysokuju,	He PFV:out:jump:PST on mountain:ACC on high:ACC
Posmotrel na vse na **tri-četyre** storony,	PFV:look:PST on all on **three-four** side:GEN
Posmotrel na silušku tatarskuju –	PFV:look:PST on force:DIM tatarian:ACC –
Konca-kraju sily nasmotret' ne mog.	end:GEN-border:GEN force: GEN on:see:INF not can:PST
I povyskočil on na goru na druguju,	And PFV:out.jump:PST he on mountain:ACC on other:ACC
Posmotrel na vse na **tri-četyre** storony –	PFV:look:PST on all on **three-four** side:GEN –
Konca-kraju sily nasmotret' ne mog...	end:GEN-border:GEN force:GEN on:see:INF not can:PST

'There the Old Cossack Ilja Muromec, He rode along the valley clean field, Could not reach the end-border of the force. He jumped on a mountain on a high one, Looked at all at three-four directions. Looked at the force the Tatarian—Could not reach with his eyes the end-border of the force. And jumped he on a hill on another one, Looked at all at three-four sides—Could not reach with his eyes the end-border of the force.'

What is characteristic about this passage is that it conveys very little information. The passage quoted is actually only part of a much longer passage which is concerned only with Ilja Muromec seeing the immensity of the Tatarian force. The function of all those words is therefore not to convey new information (most of the audience knows the story anyway), but suspense and emphasis (another factor is the element of play, emphasized by Haiman forthcoming). The consequence for the words used in the passage is that they are devalued in their informative substance. They do not convey as much information as they usually would in other registers; put differently, there is DESEMANTIZATION. A very clear case of desemantization is the co-compound *tri-četyre* 'three-four', which is originally an alternative co-compound '> three or four'. In this passage, however, it is a synonymic co-compound. 'Three-four' means actually 'four = all'. From a communicative point of view, the co-compound is completely superfluous as the idea of 'all' is already expressed by the word *vse* 'all'.

In the language of the Byliny, there is generally a strong tendency toward redundant expression. Synonymic co-compounds are just one facet of this predilection. Other features that raise the element of redundancy in (7) are the following:

- Semantically empty epithetic adjectives, such as *čisto* 'clean' in *čisto pole* 'clean field' for *pole* 'field' (*čisto pole* is sometimes the locally unmarked expression for 'field' in the Byliny).
- Diminutives, such as *sil.uška* 'force.DIM'.
- Multiple verbal prefixes, such as in *po.vy.skočil* 'PREV.PREV.jump:PST'
- The repetition of prepositions before several words or every word in a prepositional phrase, such as *na goru na vysokuju* 'on mountain:ACC on high:ACC'
- Superfluous coordinators, such as *da* 'and', in the first line.

However, these features do not appear exclusively in the language of the Byliny. Diminutives are generally frequent in Russian dialects and multiple prepositions are a specific feature of northern Russian dialects. As far as epithetic adjectives and co-compounds are concerned, it is, however, clear that these features are much more frequent in the Byliny than in colloquial language, even if compared with the colloquial language of northern Russian dialects.

Interestingly, the synonymic co-compounds, even if they are fully redundant in (8), are contextually motivated by generalization (all directions), negation (non-referentiality), and emphasis (see Section 5.5 above; factor (a), accumulation of favorable contexts for co-compounds). This suggests that synonymic co-compounds in the Byliny are not used in a fundamentally different way than in more 'informative' registers.

Neither is desemantization specific for 'less informative' registers. In grammaticalization it is better known under the name of semantic bleaching. In 'informative' registers, semantic bleaching usually occurs together with strengthening of informativeness (see especially Traugott and König 1991), also known as inference or the conventionalization of conversational implicatures (Dahl 1985: 11; Bybee et al. 1994: 285–9). By inference, meaning associated with a specific frequent use of an expression is transferred to that means of expression. The communicative function of language is thus responsible for all kinds of expressions constantly acquiring new meanings, or put more generally, the process of inference guarantees that language is provided constantly with new meanings, whereas old meanings continue to be lost through semantic bleaching. In texts with a high information rate, the two processes, inference and semantic bleaching, can only be considered in their interaction. However, in texts with a low information rate, semantic bleaching without a concomitant semantic strengthening by inference can be expected. It is this general desemantization that we observe in the folk poetry of languages of all continents.

It has been claimed that formulaicity and repetition are found in epic texts because this facilitates the speaker's improvization (Parry 1971; see also Wray 2002: 75ff). If this were their only reason, formulaicity, repetition, and redundancy would just be necessary and unavoidable evils in the production of epic texts. But formulaicity, repetition, redundancy, and parallelism are obviously intrinsic properties of these texts, and are well in line with their semantic structure.

As folk poetry generally seems to favor lexical class types with redundant functions, it can be instructive to look at some languages where co-compounds do not occur, or where they are at least much less common than in Mordvin and the Russian dialects of the Byliny. Interestingly, as far as I know, co-compounds do not occur in folk poetry registers of languages where they are not common in colloquial speech, which suggests that co-compounds are not created in the registers of folk poetry. They only become more frequent and conventionalized to a greater extent in folk poetry if they already exist in the language. Let us look at two examples where the language of folk poetry differs greatly from the language of colloquial speech: Kuna (Chibchan, Panama) and Aranda (Pama-Nyungan). Neither of these two languages has co-compounds. But both languages do have sub-compounds, and sub-compounds are very prominent in the formal registers of the two languages.

Kuna is a language with a number of formally highly divergent spoken registers, whose ethnography of speaking has been described by Sherzer (1983: 25). He writes: 'The varieties are so different from one another that each requires separate learning, and for the most part a variety is not comprehensible without such learning'. There is, however, a general characteristic that holds for all registers: words are longer in the formal or higher registers both phonetically and morphologically, that is, Lüdtke's equilibrium is shifted toward longer words with more morphemes and less phonetic reduction. In colloquial Kuna, words are more reduced phonetically than in formal registers. Thus, the long form *taysasulimoka* can be reduced to the (morphologically identical) form *tachurmo* 'he did not see either'. Sherzer writes: 'Shorter forms (in which final vowels and, in a few cases, the entire final syllable are deleted) are most characteristic of informal, rapid speech. Longer forms occur in slower, more emphatic, more formal, and more ritual speech' (ibid.: 37).

But this distinction is not only demonstrated phonetically; words are also morphologically longer in formal registers. To a large extent, formal registers in Kuna have a different basic vocabulary than everyday Kuna, which consists basically of compounds or affixed words. Many longer forms contain prefixes such as *olo-, mani-, ina-, ikwa-*, and suffixes such as *-kinya, -appi, -lele, -tilli,* and *-liler* (ibid.: 25), some of which still clearly reveal their origin as parts of compounds, such as *olo-* 'gold'. The omnipresence of ornamental compounds in the epic language is illustrated by (9) from the epic poem *Inatoipippiler*:

(9) Kuna (Holmer 1952: 10)
 nana.saila aite.kenae ipe.alulu napa.li
 mother.chief descend.INFL lord.purple near.CONV
 nana.saila ipe.mimiryo ulu.takka.li
 mother.chief lord.food pot.look.CONV
 'The mother descends (from her hammock) toward the fire
 The mother begins to prepare food.'

Long forms can be 'derived' from short forms by adding a communicatively superfluous epithetic component which is often embellishing (thus short *nana* 'mother', long *nana.saila* 'chief mother' [*saila* 'head, principal, hair'], short *ipa* 'day', long *ipekala* 'day way' [*ikala* 'way, road'], short *mimiryo* 'food', long *ipemimiryo* id. [*ipe* 'lord']). In other cases, long and short forms have nothing in common (*muu.tule* 'sea.animal' for '> fish' or 'lord.purple' for '> fire' above).

Another language where sub-compounds abound in folk poetry is Aranda. Strehlow (1971: 186) writes 'the substitute words and metaphorical terms themselves, like most of the nouns, adjectives, and verbs in the songs, tend to be compounds, often of considerable length.' A typical example is the word for 'sun' in the Ibálintja-song which is *Kíntjilbmárilbmára* consisting of *áka* 'head' and the reduplicated **intjilbmara* 'hot gleaming'. Reduplication is another feature that abounds in Aranda songs: 'In all cases reduplication of either the initial or the final syllables of all kinds of words, compound or simple, poetic or prose, long or short, irrespective of where they occur in the line, is a favorite device of native versification. Even poetic nouns, adjectives and verbs of obscure derivation are affected by such polysyllabic accretions.' (Strehlow 1971: 193). An especially interesting case is the reduplication of the copula. In Aranda, the copula *náma*—except in the negative—is usually omitted. 'In verse, however, the copula is not merely inserted but given prominence by reduplication (*nópanáma*) or by the addition of the derivative termination -*la náma*' (ibid.: 191). This is a very impressive example of the shift of Lüdtke's equilibrium due to the conventionalization of emphatic speech (or rather, song). An expression which is typically zero (no expression at all) in colloquial speech has considerable length in the language of songs and its form is even extended by reduplication.

Diminutives are another lexical class, besides co-compounds, sub-compounds, and reduplication, which may be highly extended in folk poetry. In Lithuanian, where diminutives are frequent in the colloquial language, most of the nouns will often be diminutives in the language of the songs (put differently, diminutives are locally unmarked for nouns in traditional songs), as *Subat.ėl.ės vakar.ėl.į / pin.s ses.ul.ei vainik.ėl.į* 'Saturday.DIM.GEN evening. DIM.ACC / bind.FUT3 sister.DIM.DAT garland.DIM.ACC = On Saturday evening / they will bind a garland for the sister' (Kazlauskienė et al. 1994: 202).

These examples suggest that there are general cross-linguistic tendencies for the language of folk poetry to deviate from the language of colloquial speech.[12] It seems that there generally tends to be a shift in Lüdtke's equilibrium toward less phonological reduction and more morphological accumulation. It also appears that morphological accumulation occurs by the extension of lexical classes with redundant function which already exist in the language. Put differently, certain registers of folk poetry simply appear to insist on certain specific tendencies in their language.[13] This is a topic that deserves to be investigated typologically because it promises to be highly relevant for grammaticalization, especially for a better understanding of the processes of semantic bleaching and the strengthening of informativeness.

An important question remains to be asked at the end of this section. Now that we have found that co-compounding reaches high levels both in registers of folk poetry in moderately co-compounding languages and in East and South East Asian languages in general, do we have to conclude that East and South East Asian languages are generally less informative than other languages of the world? To answer this question we have to return to Croft's (2001) critique of semantic relativity (Section 1.3.2.iv), and especially to the first hidden assumption in semantic relativity approaches, according to which a difference in meaning exists if there is a difference in form, not only language-internally (the principle of contrast), but also cross-linguistically.

As Croft points out, there is not necessarily a difference in meaning wherever there is a difference in form across different languages. Therefore, there is no reason to assume that speech in the East and South East Asian languages is generally less informative than in other languages of the world.

7.6 Conclusions

In this chapter two different aspects of the diachronic development of co-compounds have been discussed: (a) the evolution of specific formal patterns of co-compounds, and (b) the evolution of co-compounds as lexical classes. In Section 7.2 we found reason to believe that formal patterns for co-compounds in most cases evolve from tight coordination patterns. However, given the fact that co-compounds in many languages are characterized simply by juxtaposition, it cannot be excluded that co-compounds may emerge spontaneously. Furthermore, a lexical class of co-compounds in a language can arise simply by extension of use of a tight coordination pattern into typical word-domains, without the evolution of a distinct formal pattern.

While a formal pattern of co-compounds can emerge suddenly, a lexical class of co-compounds cannot. In Section 7.3 I argued that co-compounds as a lexical class evolve gradually, and that a language with a high level of co-compounds must have gone through a long history of gradually acquiring higher levels of co-compounding passing through low and moderate levels. Generally it is easier for a co-compound in a language to lexicalize if there are already other co-compounds or, put differently, the higher the frequency of co-compounds in a language, the greater the propensity for co-compounds to lexicalize, not only in prototypical, but also in less prototypical domains for co-compounds. This fact is one of the most important aspects of the class character of co-compounds. In Section 7.4 I tried to find out what lies behind this coherence of individual lexemes and argued that it comes about because the use of specific co-compounds has a cumulative effect on their average degree of textual markedness. The more frequently co-compounds are used in a language (or in a register, or in a style) the lower will be the degree of textual markedness of co-compounds in all potential domains where co-compounds could be used.

In Section 7.4 I further argued that textual markedness might also have played some role in the evolution of the characteristic frequency distribution of co-compounds in Eurasia (Chapter 6). I suggested that contact languages could serve as a source of inspiration to use or not to use co-compounds, especially in textually marked contexts where deviation from the norm is required in any case, thus exercising a very subtle indirect influence on the general level of co-compounding in a language. This persistent indirect influence could have an important cumulative effect over a long period of time.

Textual markedness can also be adduced to explain language-internal differences in the level of co-compounding across registers and styles. Co-compounds will be more frequent in registers where there are more contexts favoring the use of co-compounds. Each register, each style may therefore have its own level of acceptability of co-compounds. If co-compounds often occur because contexts favorable for their use are frequent, they may conventionalize in a register or style. This can be observed in particular for non-basic or 'redundant' types of co-compounds in folk poetry in languages and dialects with moderate levels of co-compounding. In Section 7.5 I tried to show that there is a general tendency in folk poetry to favor lexical classes which are partly redundant, such as sub-compounds and diminutives. There are different reasons to account for this tendency. One is desemantization in texts with a low information rate; another is that longer words are favored by emphatic speech.

It should be restated here that much of what has been claimed in this chapter remains rather hypothetical due to underspecification by research and the absence of what could be considered conclusive evidence, a general problem pervading historical linguistics.

Notes

[1] Vedic also had neuter dvandvas like *iṣṭā-pūrtám* 'sacrificed:PL:N-donated:SG.N > the sacrificed and the donated' in which the second member had singular form in accordance with abstract bahuvrihi compounds, and in which the neuter plural ending of the first part -*ā* happened to be formally identical with the -*ā* originating from a dual ending in non-neuter dvandvas (Wackernagel 1905: 160). This led to a later development of neuter dvandvas with a singular or stem form in the first part, a type which was finally extended to non-neuter stems, such as *candra-tāraká.m* 'moon-star.SG.N > moon and stars' (ibid.: 161; *tāraká* 'star' is feminine).

[2] The matter is actually more complicated diachronically as the proprietive derives from Turkic *lyγ/ liγ and the suffix in natural coordination from *-ly/-li (Ramstedt 1952, von Gabain 1950). At least in Teleutian, however, the original proprietive suffix is used in natural coordination: *aga.lū ačy.lū* 'elder and younger brother' (Teleutian *-lyγ > lū*).

[3] One possibility is that verbal co-compounds might have developed from verbalized nominal co-compounds in examples such as *klið.ɔ.mandaló.n.ɔ* 'lock.LINK.bolt.1SG > I lock and bolt'. There is, however, no nominal co-compound in Modern Greek from *kliðí* 'the lock' and *mándalɔ(s)* 'the bolt', so this is mere speculation.

⁴ Quoted from a handout by Annemarie Peltzer-Karpf.

⁵ DeFrancis (1984), based on research by George A. Kennedy, has challenged the view of Chinese as a monosyllabic language ('monosyllabic myth'). He argues that in Mandarin there are such words as *húdié* 'butterfly' and *pútao* 'grape' (< Iranian **badag(a)*) that are wrongly analyzed as consisting of two synonymic morphemes in Mandarin dictionaries, as none of the syllables *hú, dié, pú,* or *tao* occurs in isolation meaning 'butterfly' or 'grape' at any stage of Chinese. However, the most striking aspect of monosyllabism in Chinese is not that every syllable is a morpheme, but that even syllables that are not morphemes originally can be used incidentally, as if they were morphemes, to produce compounds by the process of clipping (See also 4.2.3.4). Mandarin dictionaries (Hsiung et al. 1995) list several compounds in which the syllables *pú* and *dié* occur without *tao* and *hú* with the meaning 'grape' and 'butterfly', such as *pú.táng* 'grape.sugar > glucose' (short for *pútao.táng*), *dié.xíng.huā* 'butterfly. shape.flower > papilionaceous flower', *dié.yǒng* 'butterfly.swim > butterfly stroke'. The extreme frequency of syllable-morphemes may lead to a situation in which every syllable may occasionally be analyzed as a morpheme and in which any unanalyzable sequence of two syllables can be considered as consisting of two synonymic components (Chao 1968: 139).

⁶ According to Shi (2002: 69) the tendency to disyllabification is, however, a process which started as early as 2,000 years ago and is still at work in Mandarin. While in present day Mandarin more than 75 percent of the 3,000 most common words are disyllabic (ibid.: 70), disyllabic words are attested in the earliest documents and account for approximately 20 percent of the lexicon before 200 BC (ibid.: 72).

⁷ What is common to both explanations is that it is claimed, as Shi (2002: 71) puts it, that the 'disyllabic form of the lexicon... compensates for the historical simplification of the phonological system.'

⁸ One problem with this theory is, of course, that the long run is not always short enough to be empirically observable.

⁹ In a similar way, Shi (2002: 78) claims that the resultative verb compounds of Mandarin ('VR resultative construction'), which are another kind of disyllabic words, developed because of the tendency to disyllabicity from an already existing separable resultative construction, as is also common elsewhere in South East Asia (Cantonese, Vietnamese). Thus, the resultative verb construction did not emerge because of the tendency to disyllabicity, but was instead modified because of disyllabicity.

¹⁰ This does not mean, however, that co-compounds are generally translated by co-compounds. In Section 6.2 we saw that the frequency of co-compounds in parallel texts may vary greatly.

¹¹ The Bylina is from the *Onežskie byliny* first published by A. F. Gil'ferding in 1873 in St. Petersburg. Unfortunately, the original source is not available to me.

¹² The deviating grammar of the language of traditional oral poetry and prose in myths, epic poems, and songs is a topic that calls for systematic typological research (e.g. the altitudinal case markers in Rai languages, Ebert 1999; the Ainu *yukar* epics with considerable differences in grammar from colloquial Ainu, Shibatani 1990: 4 and passim).

[13] An impressive illustration of this point comes from Greenlandic, a language which is well-known for its high degree of morphological synthesis. Rink (1875: 65f) discusses a kind of traditional Greenlandic song that 'is now nearly extinct in the Danish districts of Greenland'. In these songs 'the words themselves [are] rather trifling, the sentences abrupt, and the author evidently [presumes] the audience to be familiar with the whole subject or gist of the song, and able to guess the greater part of it. Every strophe makes such an abrupt sentence, or consists of single and even abbreviated words, followed by some interjectional words only used for songs and without any particular signification' (ibid.: 65). As a consequence, in this type of Greenlandic song, all lines consist of single words embedded at a specific position in a chain of repeated interjections. Here are two lines from the song given by Rink (the orthography of the original is retained; vowels marked with ^ are long, k and q are not distinguished in the orthography):

...haijâ avalag.kumâr.punga [sail_away.FUT.INDISG] imakaja haijâ imakaja ha haijâ umiar.ssuar.ssuar.mik [ship.big.big.INST] imakaja haijâ imakaja ha...
[The wicked little Kukook imakayah hayah, imakayah hah—hayah used to say,...] I am going to leave the country... in a large ship (Rink 1875: 66).

8

Conclusions

Traditional morphology treats the notion of CO-COMPOUNDS as tertiary insofar as they are defined in terms of the primary notion of word via the secondary notion of compounds. In this study another approach was taken. The notion of compounds is viewed as secondary in relation to co-compounds and other types of compounds. Co-compounds are considered LANGUAGE-SPECIFIC FUNCTIONAL–FORMAL CLASSES which form a CROSS-LINGUISTIC CLASS TYPE with characteristic recurrent semantic and formal properties. Co-compounds are thus viewed as a phenomenon on their own which is not restricted to morphology. This CLASS-ORIENTED APPROACH leads to a greater focus on the semantic component of co-compounds than the traditional morphological approach, since the semantic properties of language-specific classes can more easily be generalized cross-linguistically than their formal properties.

Formally, classes of co-compounds have highly different language-specific properties in different languages. What can be stated generally is that co-compounds are WORD-LIKE rather than phrase-like. This means that even if co-compounds in various languages have some formal properties not typically associated with words, co-compounds in all languages have at least some of the characteristics of words. Co-compounds typically LACK OVERT MARKERS OF COORDINATION but can be formally identical to asyndetic phrase-like coordination. Co-compounds can be formally identical or partly identical to other classes of tight forms with more than one lexical slot, such as sub-compounds, appositional compounds, and serial verbs, which are, however, clearly distinct from co-compounds semantically (even if there are some intermediate cases).

As the semantic focus of the class type of co-compounds, NATURAL CO-ORDINATION has been identified. Natural coordination is not a simple semantic feature, but rather a bundle of semantic properties on three different meronomic levels:

1 PART–PART: coordinate relationship between the parts, close lexico-semantic relationship between the parts, parts belong to the same

taxonomic level, inherent or preestablished coordination between the parts.
2 PARTS–WHOLE: whole is superordinate in relation to parts, close lexico-semantic relationship between parts and whole, pair sharpening (see Section 5.3) determines the meaning of the parts.
3 WHOLE: whole expresses a conceptual unit, which represents a superordinate or plural concept rather than a basic level concept.

Natural coordination is, however, not only the characteristic meaning of co-compounds but also of PHRASE-LIKE TIGHT COORDINATION PATTERNS, such as the BARE BINOMIALS in Germanic languages (*brother and sister, bow and arrows*), which have some rather morphological properties in spite of their seemingly syntactic character and are highly formulaic, as can be seen from their strong tendency to the irreversibility of coordinands. Co-compounds differ from phrase-like tight coordination in several respects, both formally and semantically. Formally, co-compounds are more word-like. They notably lack overt markers for coordination. Semantically, it is characteristic in co-compounds that there is a minimal contrast between the parts, whereas in phrase-like coordination a certain amount of contrast is required (Section 3.3.4). Thus, co-compounds are found in typical word-domains, in contexts where most languages without co-compounds would use words, not phrases. Furthermore, co-compounds cluster into classes, whereas phrase-like tight coordination patterns are rather loose accumulations of syntactically deviant formulas. In spite of these general differences there is a considerable area of overlap between co-compounds and tight phrase-like coordination, so that it is sometimes difficult to distinguish between the two, in a similar way as it is sometimes difficult to keep apart demonstrative pronouns and articles that share a number of functions.

One possible approach, taken in Chapters 2 and 3, is to consider the similarities of co-compounds and phrase-like tight coordination rather than the differences. This requires a view on syntax and morphology without a fundamental level difference between the two. A framework which fits this purpose very well is Haiman's 'Natural Syntax'. From this perspective, a general iconic relationship between form and meaning can be identified such that tight conceptual units in coordination (natural coordination) tend to be expressed by formally tight forms of coordination (TIGHT COORDINATION). In Chapter 3, tight coordination was discussed; it turned out to be a highly complex phenomenon with several dimensions (length of coordinate sequence, marking patterns, and semantic correlates).

Languages may have many different patterns in coordination which are sensitive to tightness. Each grammatical affix and functional word may have its individual behavior due to its scope in coordination. A grammatical affix may even behave differently in various functions due to different degrees of grammaticalization. The study of tight coordination with its great many patterns thus reveals that the development of co-compounds as a class is fundamentally different from the development of tight coordination patterns. What is essential for co-compounds is not that they represent a certain formal pattern which is formally distinct from coordination, but that they have certain characteristic semantic and formal properties, and especially that they occur with a certain frequency in lexical domains that are characteristic for co-compounds and not for coordination.

Co-compounds in a particular language are therefore best considered as a LEXICAL CLASS, and co-compounds cross-linguistically as a LEXICAL CLASS TYPE. In Chapter 4 it was claimed that co-compounds, like the middle voice, the diminutive, and noun incorporation, are a lexical class type in contrast to GRAMMATICAL CLASS TYPES, such as future, plural, and definiteness, and in contrast to word classes, such as nouns and verbs. There is, however, no clear borderline between lexical and grammatical classes. Grammatical classes consist mainly of inflectional forms (be they synthetic or analytic), but can, however, also contain some lexicalized forms (such as pluralia tantum within a plural class). Lexical classes are mainly characterized by lexicalized forms, but can also contain some areas with little lexicalization. The concept of lexical classes requires a differentiated view about lexicalization. It is claimed that lexemes emerge in TEMPORARY LEXICA of single texts or conversations, and may then gradually drift toward the permanent pole of the lexicon of a language. Two aspects of lexicalization must be strictly distinguished: drift toward the permanent pole of the lexicon and demotivation of the whole from its parts. Lexemes belonging to lexical classes may have drifted quite a long way toward the permanent lexicon but not reached complete lexicalization, as they are not demotivated. Lexical classes are thus based on incomplete lexicalization; similarly, grammatical classes are based on incomplete grammaticalization since the last step in grammaticalization is the loss of grammatical morphemes.

In Chapter 5, ten major SEMANTIC TYPES OF CO-COMPOUNDS were identified in a classification based on the parts–whole relationship. All of these types are cross-linguistically recurrent, that is, co-compounds in all the languages considered in this study can be classed into the same types, which does not mean that each of the co-compounds can always be unambiguously assigned to a single type, as many co-compounds are intermediate between different types. The existence of many intermediate cases is evidence for diachronic relationships between different semantic types.

According to the degree to which they meet the criteria of natural coordination, these semantic types have been roughly grouped into BASIC (generalizing, additive, collective, alternative, and approximate) and NON-BASIC (synonymic, ornamental, imitative, figurative, and scalar) TYPES. No strict implicational hierarchy for the emergence of different types of co-compounds could be found, except that scalar co-compounds are restricted to a number of highly co-compounding languages. It was found, however, that in most cases basic co-compounds tend to be the dominant types at low and low-to-moderate levels of co-compounding, while non-basic co-compounds (notably synonymic co-compounds) are dominant at moderate-to-high and high levels of co-compounding. Co-compounds in different texts have highly different SEMANTIC PROFILES, with different proportions of different semantic types. There is a high degree of correlation between the level of co-compounding in a text and its semantic profile of co-compounds, both cross-linguistically and within an individual language (Sections 6.2 and 6.4). Non-basic types of co-compounds rely on basic types. There is no language with a substantial number of synonymic co-compounds which would lack additive co-compounds.

The description of LEXICO-SEMANTIC RELATIONSHIPS between the parts of co-compounds necessitates a context-oriented approach to lexical semantics. Lexico-semantic relationships, such as synonymy, are traditionally viewed as applying paradigmatically on the level of lexemes. In Section 5.3 I argued that the synonymy of complete lexical items (with all their meanings) is of highly marginal relevance in contrast to CONTEXTUAL SYNONYMY, which results from the process of SYNONYMIC SHARPENING. In synonymic co-compounds, words with very different meanings, such as 'think' and 'mourn', can become contextual synonyms (Section 5.3).

The special contribution to typology of this investigation is that it tries to establish a CONTINUOUS VARIABLE with a high degree of LANGUAGE-INTERNAL VARIATION by considering data from PARALLEL TEXTS. Traditionally, the comparanda in typology are viewed as discrete variables whose language-internal variation can be neglected, the major sources of material for typological studies being reference grammars and, to a minor extent, data from questionnaires. It is not profitable to view co-compounds as a discrete variable, because it is frequently almost impossible to decide whether a language has co-compounds or not. The most relevant factor of cross-linguistic diversity in co-compounding is not existence vs. non-existence, but frequency. While reference grammars and questionnaires may serve as sources of data for co-compounds in some languages, they are not reliable sources for knowing how frequently co-compounds appear in a language. Parallel texts have many shortcomings; nevertheless they are the only viable source of data for the large scale cross-linguistic study of continuous variables.

One of the most important results of this study comes from areal typology: co-compounds have a MACRO-AREAL PATTERN of distribution, and are salient classes, especially in the languages of continental Asia, easternmost Europe, and New Guinea, but are almost absent from Africa and only marginally present in the Americas (as in Quechua, Chinantec, and Mixe). Within Eurasia the frequency of co-compounds decreases steadily, with only minor exceptions, from continental East and South East Asia westward. Co-compounds are thus evidence for a high degree of areal coherence among the languages of continental Eurasia. The highly regular pattern of areal distribution of co-compounds confirms that the investigation of continuous typological variables in parallel texts is a promising instrument in typological and areal-typological research, in spite of its many methodological and practical difficulties (Chapter 6).

As regards the diachronic investigation of co-compounds, there are two major questions of interest: what is the origin of patterns of co-compounds, and how do co-compounds evolve as lexical classes? There is strong evidence, at least in some languages, that patterns of co-compounds develop partly from coordination (the CONDENSATION HYPOTHESIS; Section 7.2.1). However, as co-compounds in many languages are characterized by the absence of any morphological marker, it cannot be excluded that a pattern of co-compounds may arise spontaneously.

The high degree of correlation between specific semantic profiles and overall text frequency suggests that less prototypical co-compounds (notably of the non-basic types) tend to evolve only after the more prototypical co-compounds. This should not be understood in the sense of an implicational hierarchy, but rather as a shift of the center of gravity away from the semantic core of the class parallel to (and as a consequence of) the increase of frequency. In Chapter 7 it is claimed that what prevents co-compounds from being used in non-co-compounding languages is their high degree of TEXTUAL MARKEDNESS. Co-compounds may only become frequent in texts if there are many contexts in which they are textually unmarked. Textual unmarkedness can be achieved in different ways. One possibility is lexicalization in lexical domains which are favorable for co-compounds. Another is through specific contexts which reduce the odd effect of co-compounds (contextual motivation for the use of co-compounds; Section 5.5). A third possibility are the certain styles and registers which favor the use of co-compounds because they are especially rich in those contexts which are favorable for them. Here the overall frequency comes into play. A higher token frequency of co-compounds generally lowers the potential of textual markedness for all conceivable co-compounds in all conceivable contexts. Thus, the higher the level of co-compounding, the more non-prototypical co-compounds can show up. The higher the frequency of co-compounds, the better established they will be as a lexical class, which makes some divergence from the semantic and the formal prototype tolerable.

For the description of the diachrony of lexical classes and for the understanding of natural coordination, we need a theory of MARKEDNESS (Section 2.1) which is not monistic (where everything is dedicated to a single kind of markedness, be it structural or typological markedness), but rather pluralistic (many different types of markedness independent of each other and interacting with each other in different ways in different areas). In natural coordination there is a systematic clash between formal markedness and structural markedness (where it is marked distinctively, natural coordination tends to be formally unmarked but is structurally marked). This has to do with the fact that coordination, like possession, but unlike tense, number, definiteness, etc. forms TWO-SLOT PATTERNS and not ONE-SLOT PATTERNS (Section 2.1). Especially important for the diachrony of co-compounds are textual markedness (see above) and LOCAL MARKEDNESS. Different behavior with respect to local markedness is one of the major differences between lexical and grammatical classes. Lexical classes become lexical because they become locally unmarked in some lexical domains at a very early stage of development. Grammatical classes become grammatical because they combine with a large number of lexemes before they become locally unmarked and lexicalized in any of them (Section 4.3.5).

Tight coordination patterns and co-compounds (as far as they are not fully univerbated) are an important issue for syntactic theory. In particular, tight coordination is a challenge for syntax. Many tight coordination patterns are evidence for PHONOLOGICAL-SYNTACTIC NON-ISOMORPHISM, where it is possible to attach affixes to syntactic sequences only if affixes can have sufficiently wide scope. Co-compounds, like many other lexical and grammatical classes which have only some properties of words, suggest that there are more things between syntax and morphology than are dreamt of in our linguistics. There is growing evidence in the investigation of formulaic language that collocations, idioms, formulas, and compounds are not just exceptions that break syntactic, morphological, semantic, lexical, and phonological rules, but are at the very center of language processing (Wray 2002: 261). Lexical classes, such as co-compounds, are phenomena that can be located systematically between syntax and morphology. They cannot be accounted for by a listeme model of the lexicon; a procedural or emergent model of the lexicon (Bybee 1998) is needed.

At the end of this study I have to admit that it remains an incomplete treatment of co-compounds and natural coordination. Many important issues have not been given adequate consideration. For instance, co-compounds in spoken language and their phonetic realization remain greatly underexposed. Also, co-compounds in signed languages received inadequate attention. The question of how co-compounds are produced in spontaneous spoken languages was not treated. Another important question not dealt with here is how co-compounds interact with other domains for pairs of lexico-semantically closely related words, such as parallelism in folk poetry and word association (Section 1.1.5). However, this study will have served its purpose if it stimulates other linguists to undertake further and more detailed empirical investigations about the cross-linguistic and language-internal variation of co-compounds and similar phenomena and to develop better theoretical models which can account for the phenomena discussed in this monograph.

Appendix A: Languages and their Linguistic Affiliation

The numbers and capital letters refer to the approximate location of the languages on the map in Appendix B. The same number on the map may refer to several languages if several languages are spoken in a small area. If a language is spoken in several areas or in a large area, only one location is represented. Dialects and other varieties of languages mentioned in the text are given in italics after the language name and are not represented on the map. The major source for genetic classification is Ethnologue (2000).

Abbreviations: I-E Indo-European, S-T Sino-Tibetan, T-B Tibeto-Burman, F-U Finno-Ugric, Aun. Austronesian, M-P Malayo-Polynesian, TNG Trans-New Guinea, S South(ern), N North(ern), E East(ern), W West(ern), C Central

Language stock, family

6	**Abkhaz** NW Caucasian
100	**Aceh** Aun., W M-P, Sundic
5	**Adyghe** NW Caucasian
94	**Ainu** isolate
74	**Akha** S-T, T-B, S Loloish
56	**Ālu-Kuṟumba** Dravidian, S
E	**Amele** TNG, Madang-Adelbert Range
	American Sign Language (ASL) Sign Language
61	**Arabic** Afroasiatic, C Semitic
116	**Aranda (Arrarnta)** Pama-Nyungan, Arandic
3	**Archi** NE Caucasian, Lezgian
8	**Armenian,** *Classical, Eastern* I-E, Armenian
75	**Atsi (Zaiwa)** S-T, T-B, N Burmish
1	**Avar** NE Caucasian, Avar
	Avesta † I-E, Indo-Iranian, Iranian
L	**Awtuw** Sepik-Ramu
159	**Aymara** Aymaran
9	**Azerbaijani** Turkic, S
129	**Babungo (Vengo)** Niger-Congo, Bantoid
103	**Bahasa Indonesia** Aun., W M-P, Sundic
105	**Balinese** Aun., W M-P, Sundic
51	**Bantawa** S-T, T-B, E Kiranti
G	**Baruya** TNG, Main C&W, Angan
16	**Bashkir** Turkic, W
45	**Basque** isolate

24	**Belarusan** I-E, E Slavic
52	**Bengali** I-E, Indo-Iranian, Indo-Aryan
106	**Bimanese (Bima)** Aun., C M-P, Bima-Sumba
74	**Bisu** S-T, T-B, S Loloish
135	**Blackfoot** Algic, Plains-Algonquian
57	**Bonda (Bondo)** Austroasiatic, S Munda
33	**Bulgarian** I-E, S Slavic
73	**Burmese,** *Written* S-T, T-B, S Burmish
69	**Burushaski** isolate
137	**Caddo** Caddoan, S
76	**Cantonese** cf. Chinese
111	**Cebuano** Aun., W M-P, C Philippine
112	**Chamorro** Aun., W M-P, Chamorro
146	**Chinantec(o),** *Sochiapan* Oto-Manguean, Chinantecan
70	**Chinese,** *Classical †, Old †, Middle †, Cantonese, Mandarin* S-T, Chinese
92	**Chukchee (Chukot)** Chukotko-Kamchatkan, N
12	**Chuvash** Turkic, Bolgar
141	**Comanche** Uto-Aztecan, N, C Numic
30	**Czech** I-E, W Slavic
108	**Da'a (Kaili)** Aun., W M-P, C Sulawesi
E	**Dami (Marik)** Aun., E M-P, W Oceanic
40	**Danish** I-E, N Germanic
124	**Dinka** Nilo-Saharan, Nilotic
117	**Diyari** Pama-Nyungan, Karnic
38	**Dutch** I-E, W Germanic
43	**English,** *Modern, Old, Indian* I-E, W Germanic
21	**Estonian** Uralic, F-U, Finnic
86	**Even** Tungus, N
87	**Evenki** Tungus, N
127	**Ewe** Niger-Congo, Kwa
20	**Finnish** Uralic, F-U, Finnic
G	**Fore** TNG, Main C&W
44	**French** I-E, Italic
39	**Frisian** I-E, W Germanic
7	**Georgian,** *Modern, Classical* Kartvelian
37	**German,** *Standard, Swiss [Bernese]* I-E, W Germanic
Q	**Gooniyandi** Bunaban
34	**Greek,** *Classical †, Modern* I-E, Greek
131	**Greenlandic** Eskimo-Aleut, Eskimo, Inuit
156	**Guaraní** Tupi-Gurarani, Guarani
148	**Haitian Creole** Creole, French-based
N	**Hatam** West-Papuan, Hatam
121	**Hausa** Afroasiatic, W Chadic
49	**Hebrew,** *Modern* **(Ivrit)** Afroasiatic, C S Semitic
50	**Hindi** I-E, Indo-Iranian, Indo-Aryan
152	**Hixkaryána** Carib, S
98	**Hmong,** *White* Hmong-Mien, Hmongic
140	**Hopi** Uto-Aztecan, N
G	**Hua (Yagaria)** TNG, Main C&W, East New Guinea Highlands, E-C
154	**Huitoto** Witotoan
29	**Hungarian** Uralic, F-U, Ugric
3	**Hunzib** NE Caucasian, Dido

Appendix A: Languages and their Linguistic Affiliation 283

42	**Icelandic** I-E, N Germanic
125	**Ijo** Niger-Congo, Ijoid
47	**Italian** I-E, Italic
91	**Japanese** Japanese
5	**Kabardian** NW Caucasian
28	**Kalmyk** Mongolian, E
55	**Kannada** Dravidian, S
123	**Kanuri** Nilo-Saharan, W Saharan
23	**Karaim** Turkic, W
71	**Karen** S-T, T-B, Karen
A	**Kâte** TNG, E Huon
J	**Kaugel (Umbu-Ungu)** TNG, Main C&W, Hagen
R	**Kayardild (Gayardilt)** Tangic
66	**Kazakh** Turkic, W
85	**Ket** Yenisey, now isolate
F	**Kewa, West** TNG, Main C&W
82	**Khakas** Turkic, N
51	**Khaling** S-T, T-B, W Kiranti
80	**Khalkha** Mongolian, E
19	**Khanty** Uralic, F-U, Ugric
59	**Khasi** Austro-Asiatic, Khasian
95	**Khmer** Austro-Asiatic, Khmer
153	**Kipeá (Kariri-Xocó)** † Macro-Ge or unclassified
65	**Kirghiz** Turkic, W
138	**Koasati** Muskogean, E
H	**Kobon** TNG, Main C&W, Kalam
15	**Komi** Uralic, F-U, Permic
57	**Konda** Dravidian, S C
90	**Korean** Korean
93	**Koryak** Chukotko-Kamchatkan, N
A	**Kube** TNG, E Huon
57	**Kui** Dravidian, S C
T	**Kuku Yalanji (Kuku-Yalanji)** Pama-Nyungan, Yalandyic
150	**Kuna** Chibchan
36	**Kurdish,** *Bahdinani, Kurmanji* I-E, Indo-Iranian, Iranian
74	**Lahu,** *Nâ', Nyi, Shi* S-T, T-B, S Loloish
1	**Lak** NE Caucasian, Lak-Dargwa
74	**Lalo (Central Yi)** S-T, T-B, N Loloish
97	**Laotian (Lao)** Thai, SW
75	**Lashi** S-T, T-B, N Burmish
47	**Latin** † I-E, Italic
22	**Latvian** I-E, Baltic
2	**Lezgian (Lezgi)** NE Caucasian, Lezgian
74	**Lisu** S-T, T-B, N Lolo
23	**Lithuanian** I-E, Baltic
113	**Malagasy** Aun., W M-P, Borneo
102	**Malay,** *Standard, Literary* Aun., W M-P, Sundic
54	**Malayalam** Dravidian, S
48	**Maltese** Afroasiatic, C Semitic
89	**Manchu** Tungus, S
70	**Mandarin** cf. Chinese
18	**Mansi** Uralic, F-U, Ugric

115	**Maori** Aun., E M-P, C E Oceanic
13	**Mari,** *Eastern (Meadow),* *Western* Uralic, F-U
107	**Marshallese** Aun., E M-P, C E Oceanic
75	**Maru** S-T, T-B, N Burmish
145	**Mayan, Yucatec** Mayan, Yucatecan
77	**Meithei (Meitei)** S-T, T-B, Meitei
C	**Mekeo** Aun., E M-P, W Oceanic
	Melanesian Pidgin cf. Tok Pisin
J	**Melpa** TNG, Main C&W, Hagen
51	**Mewahang (Meohang)** S-T, T-B, E Kiranti
101	**Minangkabau** Aun., W M-P, Sundic
146	**Mixe,** *Coatlán* Mixe-Zoque, E Mixe
136	**Mohawk** Iroquoian, N
10	**Mordvin,** *Erźa, Mokša* Uralic, F-U
B	**Motu** Aun., E M-P, W Oceanic
58	**Mundari** Austroasiatic, N Munda
144	**Nahuatl,** *Classical* †, *Huahtla* Uto-Aztecan, S, Aztecan
88	**Nanai** Tungus, S
142	**Navajo** Na-Dene, Athapaskan
17	**Nenets** Uralic, N Samoyedic
51	**Nepali,** *Standard, Colloquial* I-E, Indo-Iranian, Indo-Aryan
106	**Ngada (Ngad'a)** Aun., C M-P, Bima-Sumba
119	**Ngiyambaa** Pama-Nyungan, Wiradhuric
79	**Nicobarese, Car** Austroasiatic, Nicobar
133	**Nisgha (Niushga'a)** Penutian, Tsimshian
134	**Ojibwa,** *Eastern* Algic, C Algonquian
M	**Oksapmin** TNG Oksapmin
4	**Ossete** I-E, Indo-Iranian, Iranian
109	**Paiwan** Aun., Formosan
	Pali † I-E, Indo-Iranian, Indo-Aryan
57	**Parengi-Gorum (Parenga)** Austroasiatic, S Munda
60	**Persian (Farsi)** I-E, Indo-Iranian, Iranian
158	**Quechua,** *Ayacucho, Huallaga* Quechuan
31	**Rhaeto-Romance** I-E, Italic
45	**Romance,** *Hautes/Basses-Pyrénées, Aragon* I-E, Italic
	Romani I-E, Indo-Iranian, Indo-Aryan
O	**Roti (Rote)** Aun., C M-P, Timor
26	**Russian** I-E, E Slavic
27	**Saami** Uralic, F-U
114	**Samoan** Aun., E M-P, C E Oceanic
	Sanskrit (†) I-E, Indo-Iranian, Indo-Aryan
58	**Santali** Austroasiatic, N Munda
78	**Semelai** Austroasiatic, Mon-Khmer, S Aslian
K	**Sentani** TNG, Main C&W
32	**Serbian** I-E, S Slavic
130	**Seychelles Creole (Seselwa Creole)** Creole, French-based
G	**Siane** TNG, Main C&W, East New Guinea Highlands, E-C
P	**Sika** Aun., C M-P, Timor
157	**Siriono** Tupi-Guarani, Guarayu-Siriono-Jora
E	**Siroi** TNG Madang-Adelbert Range
120	**Somali** Afroasiatic, E Cushitic
122	**Songhai (Songhay)** Nilo-Saharan, Songhai

Appendix A: Languages and their Linguistic Affiliation   285

57	**Sora** Austroasiatic, S Munda
46	**Spanish** I-E, Italic
151	**Sranan** Creole, English based
68	**Sumerian** † isolate
104	**Sundanese (Sunda)** Aun., W M-P, Sundic
41	**Swedish,** *Standard, Northern* I-E, N Germanic
41	**Swedish Sign Language** Sign language
2	**Tabasaran** NE Caucasian, Lezgian
62	**Tadzhik** I-E, Indo-Iranian, Iranian
110	**Tagalog** Aun., W M-P, C Philippine
132	**Takelma** Penutian
D	**Takia** Aun., E M-P, W Oceanic
53	**Tamil,** *Modern, Old* Dravidian, S
11	**Tatar** Turkic, W
I	**Tauya** TNG, Madang-Adelbert Range
83	**Teleutian (Altai, Northern)** Turkic, N
147	**Tepehuan, Southeastern** Uto-Aztecan, S, Tepiman
96	**Thai** Thai SW
72	**Tibetan,** *Classical* †, *Colloquial, Written* S-T, T-B, Tibetic
142	**Tiwa, Southern** Kiowa Tanoan, Tiwa
C	**Toaripi** TNG, Eleman
56	**Toda** Dravidian, S
B	**Tok Pisin** Creole, English based
67	**Tokharian** †, *A, B* I-E, Tokharian
128	**Toura** Niger-Congo, Mande
109	**Tsou** Aun. Formosan
155	**Tupinambá (Old Tupí)** Tupi-Guarani, Tupi
67	**Turkic,** *Old* † cf. Uyghur, Old
35	**Turkish** Turkic, S
63	**Turkmen** Turkic, S
81	**Tuva (Tuvin)** Turkic, N
143	**Tzeltal** Mayan, Tzeltalan
143	**Tzotzil,** *Zinacantán* Mayan, Tzeltalan
88	**Udihe** Tungus, S
14	**Udmurt** Uralic, F-U, Permic
25	**Ukrainian** I-E, E Slavic
G	**Usarufa** TNG, Main C&W, Gadsup-Auyana-Awa
67	**Uyghur,** *Modern, Old* † Turkic, E
64	**Uzbek** Turkic, E
	Vedic † I-E, Indo-Iranian, Indo-Aryan
94	**Vietnamese** Austroasiatic, Viet-Muong
S	**Wik-Mungkan** Pama-Nyungan, M Pama
A	**Yabem** Aun., E M-P, W Oceanic
84	**Yakut** Turkic, N
	Yiddish (Eastern) I-E, W Germanic
126	**Yoruba** Niger-Congo
99	**Yukaghir** isolate
146	**Zoque** Mixe-Zoque

Appendix B: Map of Languages

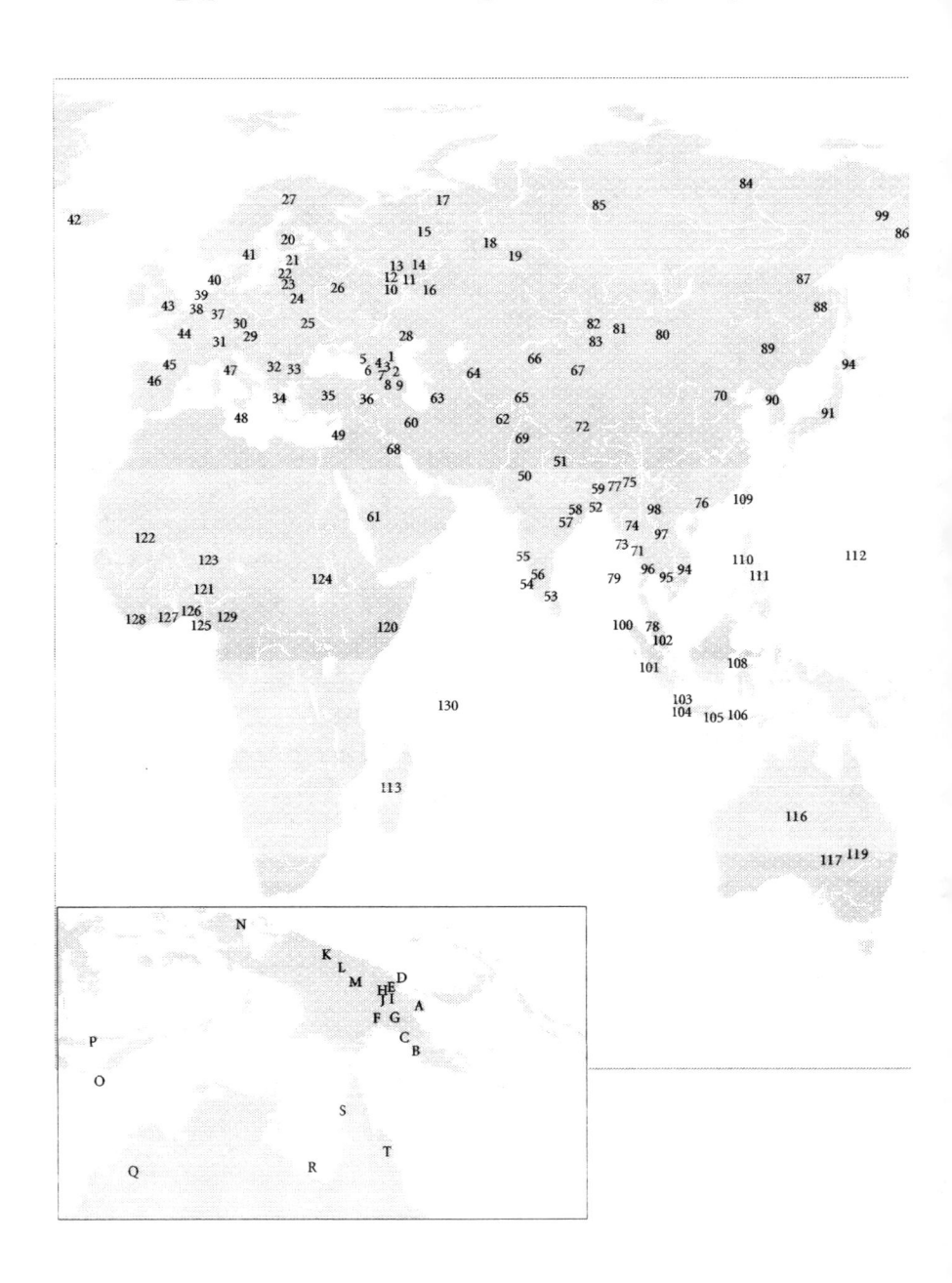

Appendix B: Map of Languages 287

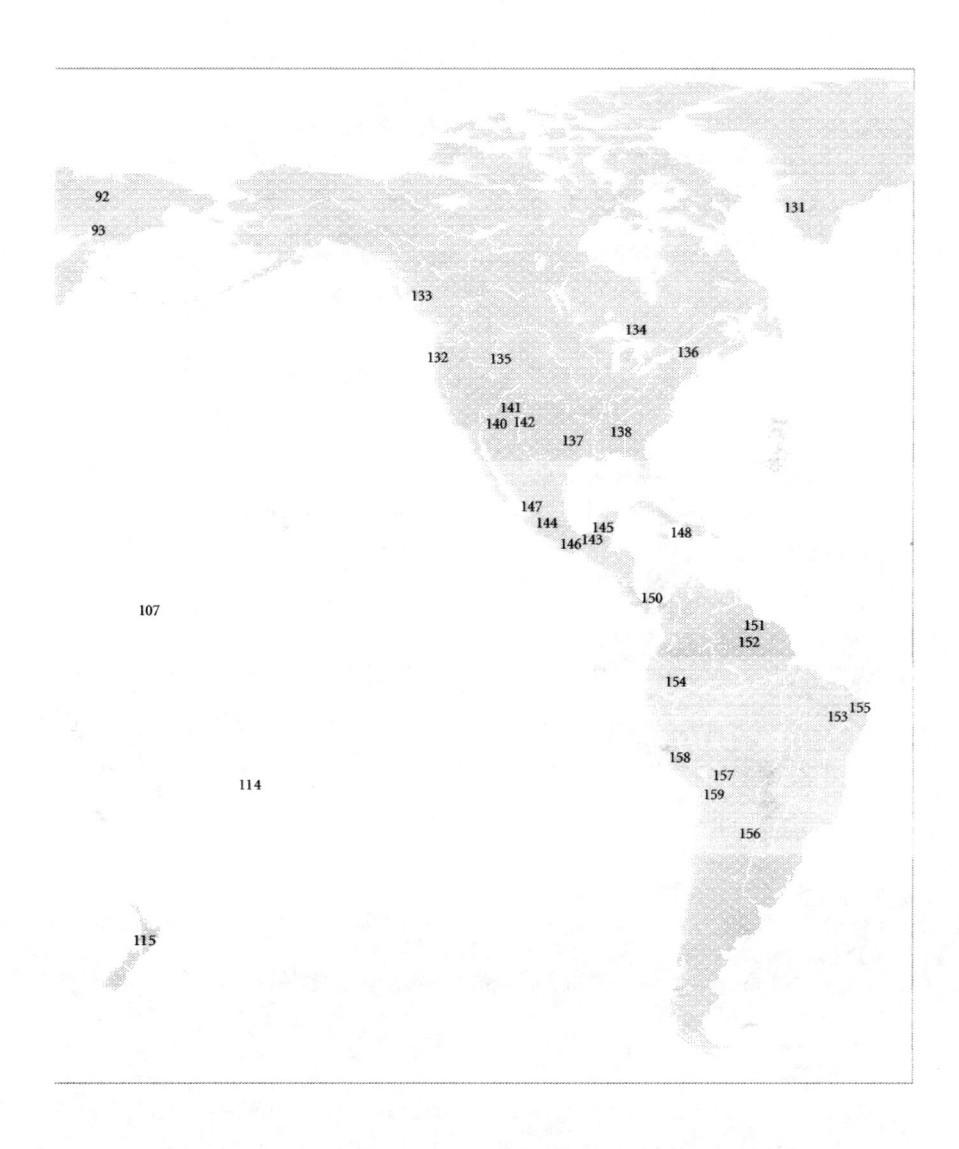

References

A = Abramov 1973.
AALTO, P. (1964). 'Word-pairs in Tokharian and other languages', *Linguistics* 5: 69–78.
ABAEV, V. I. (1958–). *Istoriko-ètimologičeskij slovar' osetinskogo jazyka*. I-. Moskva: Izdatel'stvo Akademii Nauk SSSR.
ABRAMOV, K. (1973). *Erźań ćora. Roman. Omboće kńiga. Pongoso moda*. Saransk: Mordovskoj kńižnoj izdat'el'stvaś.
AIKHENVALD, A. Y. (1999). 'Serial constructions and verb compounding. Evidence from Tariana (North Arawak)', *Studies in Language* 23,3: 469–98.
ALPHER, B. (1994). 'Yir-Yiront ideophones', in L. Hinton, J. Nichols, and J. J. Ohala (eds.), *Sound Symbolism*. Cambridge: Cambridge University Press, pp. 161–77.
ALSINA, A., J. BRESNAN, and P. SELLS (eds.) (1997). *Complex Predicates*. (CSLI Lecture Notes 64). Stanford: Center for the Study of Language and Information.
AMBRAZAS, V. (ed.) (1997). *Lithuanian Grammar*. Vilnius: baltos lankos.
ANDERSEN, H. (1989). 'Markedness theory—the first 150 years', in O. M. Tomić (ed.), *Markedness in Synchrony and Diachrony*. Mouton de Gruyter: Berlin, pp. 11–46.
ANDERSON, S. R. (1985). 'Typological distinctions in word formation', in T. Shopen (ed.) *Language Typology and Syntactic Description*. Cambridge: Cambridge University Press, Vol. 3, pp. 3–56.
—— (1992). *A-morphous Morphology*. (Cambridge Studies in Linguistics 62) Cambridge: Cambridge University Press.
—— (1996). 'How to put your clitics in their place, or why the best account of second-position phenomena may be something like the optimal one', *Linguistic Review* 13,3/4: 165–91.
ANWARD, J. and P. LINELL (1975/76). 'Om lexikaliserade fraser i svenskan', *Nusvenska studier* 55–56: 77–119.
ASHER, R. E. (1989). *Tamil*. London: Routledge.
—— (ed.) (1994). *The Encyclopedia of Language and Linguistics*. 10 vol. Oxford: Pergamon.
AUSTEN, J. (1811/1994). *Sense and Sensibility*. Penguin: London.
AUSTIN, P. (1981). *A Grammar of Diyari, South Australia*. Cambridge: Cambridge University Press Press.
AZE, R. and T. AZE (1973). 'Parengi-Texts', in R. Trail (ed.), *Patterns in Clause, Sentence, and Discourse in Selected Languages of India and Nepal* III: *Texts*. Kathmandu: University Press/Norman: Summer Institute of Linguistics, pp. 213–362.
BADER, F. (1962). *La formation des composés nominaux du latin*. (Annales littéraires de l'université de Besançon 46) Paris.

BAKER, M. C. (1996). *The Polysynthesis Parameter.* New York: Oxford University Press.
BALANDIN, A. N. (1960). *Samoučitel' mansijskogo jazyka.* Leningrad: Učpedgiz.
BATCHELOR, J. (1926/1996). 'An Ainu–English–Japanese dictionary', originally published Tokyo: Kyobunkan, in K. Refsing (ed.), *Early European Writings on the Ainu Language* 4. Richmond: Curzon.
BAUER, L. (1978). *The Grammar of Nominal Compounding. With special reference to Danish, English and French.* Odense: Odense University.
—— (2001a). 'Compounding', in M. Haspelmath, E. König, W. Oesterreicher, and W. Raible (eds.), *Language Typology and Language Universals. An international Handbook* Berlin: de Gruyter, pp. 695–707.
—— (2001b). *Morphological productivity.* Cambridge: Cambridge University Press.
BAUMAN, R. and J. SHERZER (eds.) (1974). *Explorations in the Ethnography of Speaking.* Cambridge: Cambridge University Press.
BEARTH, T. (1971). *L'Énoncé toura (Côte d'Ivoire).* (Summer Institute of Linguistics of the University of Oklahoma 30.) Norman.
BEE, D. L. (1965). Usarufa: a descriptive grammar. Ph.D., Indiana University.
BENDZ, G. (1965). *Ordpar.* Stockholm: Nordstedts.
BERLIN, B. (1992). *Ethnobiological Classification: Principles of categorization of plants and animals in traditional society.* Princeton: Princeton University Press.
BERTRAIS, R. P. (1978). *Dictionnaire Hmong–Français.* Bangkok: Sangwan Surasarang.
BEYER, S. V. (1992). *The Classical Tibetan Language.* Albany: State University of New York Press.
BHATIA, T. K. (1993). *Punjabi.* London: Routledge.
BHATTACHARYA, S. (1968). *A Bonda Dictionary.* Poona: Deccan College.
BIBER, D. (1985). 'A typology of English texts', *Linguistics* 27: 3–43.
—— (1988). *Variation across Speech and Writing.* Cambridge: Cambridge University Press.
—— (1995). *Dimensions of Register Variation. A cross-linguistic comparison.* Cambridge: Cambridge University Press.
—— S. CONRAD, and R. REPPEN (1998). *Corpus Linguistics. Investigating language structure and use.* Cambridge: Cambridge University Press.
BICKEL, B. and J. NICHOLS (forthcoming). 'Inflectional morphology', in T. Shopen (ed.), *Language Typology and Linguistic Description* (2nd edn.). Cambridge: Cambridge University Press.
BIERHORST, J. (1985). *Cantares Mexicanos.* Stanford: Stanford University Press.
BISANG, W. (1986). 'Die Verb-Serialisierung im Jabêm', *Lingua* 70: 131–62.
—— (1988). *Hmong Texte. Eine Auswahl mit Interlinearübersetzung aus Jean Mottin, Contes et légendes hmong blanc.* (Arbeiten des Seminars für Allgemeine Sprachwissenschaft der Universität Zürich 8.) Zürich.
—— (1992). *Das Verb im Chinesischen, Hmong, Vietnamesischen, Thai und Khmer. Vergleichende Grammatik im Rahmen der Verbserialisierung, der Grammatikalisierung und der Attraktorpositionen.* Tübingen: Narr.

BISANG, W. (1995). 'Verb serialization and converbs—differences and similarities', in M. Haspelmath and E. König (eds.), *Converbs in Cross-linguistic Perspective. Structure and meaning of adverbial verb forms—adverbial participles, gerunds.* Berlin: Mouton de Gruyter, pp. 137–88.

BISHOP, T. and P. TENNENBAUM (1995/2002). *Wenlin. Software for Learning Chinese 3.0. Users's Guide.* Wenlin Institute.

BLOCH, J. (1934). *L'indo-aryen du veda aux temps modernes.* Paris: Adrien.

BLOOMFIELD, L. (1917). *Tagalog Texts with Grammatical Analysis.* (University of Illinois Studies in Language and Literature 3,2–4) Urbana: University of Illinois.

—— (1933). *Language.* New York: Holt.

—— (1956). *Eastern Ojibwa. Grammatical sketch, texts and word list.* Leiden: Brill.

BLOWERS, B. L. and R. BLOWERS (1970). 'Kaugel verb morphology', in C. L. Voorhoeve et al. (eds.), *Papers in New Guinea Linguistics* 12: 37–60. (Pacific Linguistics A 25.) Canberra: Australian National University.

BODDING, P. O. (1925–29). *Santal Folk Tales* 1–3. Oslo: Instituttet for sammenlignende kulturforskning.

BOEDER, W. (1991). 'A note on synonymic parallelism and bilingualism', *Studia linguistica* 41,1/2: 91–126.

BOGOMILOV, B. (1950). *Byliny.* Leningrad: Sovetskij pisatel'.

BÖHRINGER, P. H. (1935). *Das Wiesel. Seine italischen und rätischen Namen und seine Bedeutung im Volksglauben.* Inaugural-Dissertation. Zürich.

BÖHTLINGK, O. (1851/1964). *Über die Sprache der Jakuten. Grammatik, Text und Wörterbuch.* The Hague: Mouton.

BÖRJARS, K. (1998). 'Clitics, affixes and parallel correspondence', in M. Butt and T. Holloway King (eds.) *Proceedings of the LFG98 Conference.* Brisbane: University of Queensland.

BOUDA, K. (1933). 'Der Dual des Obugrischen', *Journal de la société finno-ougrienne* 47,2.

BRADLEY, D. (2001). 'Counting the family: family group classifiers in Yi (Tibeto-Burman) languages', *Anthropological Linguistics* 43,1: 1–17.

BRETTSCHNEIDER, G. (1978). *Koordination und syntaktische Komplexität. Zur Explikation eines linguistischen Begriffes.* (Structura 12) München: Fink.

BRICKER, V. R. (1974). 'The ethnographic context of some traditional Mayan speech genres', in R. Bauman and J. Sherzer (eds.). Cambridge: Cambridge University Press, pp. 368–88.

BRODY, J. (1986). 'Repetition as a rhetorical and conversational device in Tojolabal (Mayan)', *International Journal of American Linguistics* 52,3: 255–74.

BROWN, H. A. (1968). *A Dictionary of Toaripi with English–Toaripi index.* 2 parts. Oceania Linguistic Monographs 11. Sydney: University of Sydney.

—— (1988). *Three Elema myths. Recorded in Toaripi, translated and annotated.* (Pacific Linguistics B 98) Canberra: Australian National University.

BRUGMANN, K. (1900/1981). 'Über das Wesen der sogenannten Wortzusammensetzung. Eine sprachpsychologische Studie', *Berichte über die Verhandlungen der* königlich sächsischen Gesellschaft der Wissenschaften zu Leipzig, Philologisch-historische Classe 52: 359–401. Reprinted in L. Lipka and H. Günther (eds.), Wordbildung. Darmstadt: Wissenschaftliche Buchgesellschaft, 135–78.

BÜHLER, K. (1934). Sprachtheorie. Die Darstellungsfunktion der Sprache. Jena: Fischer.

BUZAKOVA, R. N. et al. (1993). Erzań-ruzoń valks. Érzjansko-russkij slovar'. Moskva: Russkij Jazyk.

BYBEE, J. (1985). Morphology. Amsterdam: Benjamins.

—— (1998). 'The emergent lexicon', Chicago Linguistic Society 34, 2: 421–35.

—— and Ö. DAHL (1989). 'The creation of tense and aspect systems in the languages of the world', Studies in Language 13,1: 51–103.

—— R. D. PERKINS and W. PAGLIUCA (1994). The Evolution of Grammar. Tense, aspect, and modality in the languages of the world. Chicago: University of Chicago Press.

—— and S. THOMPSON (2000). 'Three frequency effects in syntax', Berkeley Linguistics Society 23: 378–88.

CAMPANILE, E. (1990). La ricostruzione della cultura indoeuropea. (Testi linguistici 16) Pisa: Giardini.

CARROLL, L. (1865/1994). Alice's Adventures in Wonderland. London: Penguin.

CHAO, Y. R. (1968). A Grammar of Spoken Chinese. Berkeley: University of California Press.

CHARACHIDZÉ, G. (1981). Grammaire de la langue avar (langue du Caucase Nord-Est). Saint-Sulpice de Favières: Favard.

CHELLIAH, S. L. (1997). A Grammar of Meithei. Mouton: Berlin.

CHOMSKY, N. (1970a). 'Remarks on nominalization', in R. A. Jacobs and P. S. Rosenbaum (eds.), Readings in English Transformational Grammar. Waltham: Ginn, pp. 184–221.

—— (1970b/1972). 'Deep structure, surface structure and semantic interpretation', in R. Jakobson and S. Kawamoto (eds.), Studies in General and Oriental Linguistics Presented to Shiro Hattori. Tokio: TEC. Reprinted in N. Chomsky, Studies on Semantics in Generative Grammar. The Hague: Mouton, pp. 62–119.

CHRISTIE, A. (1972/1993). Elephants can Remember. London: Collins.

CLARK, H. H. (1970). 'Word associations and linguistic theory', in J. Lyons (ed.), New Horizons in Linguistics. Hammondsworth: Penguin Books, pp. 271–86.

—— (1992). Arenas of Language Use. Chicago: University of Chicago Press.

—— (1996). Using Language. Cambridge: Cambridge University Press.

COMRIE, B. (1981). Language Universals and Linguistic Typology. Oxford: Blackwell.

—— (1986). 'Markedness, grammar, people, and the world', in F. R. Eckman and E. A. Moravcsik (eds.), Markedness. New York: Plenum, pp. 85–106.

COOPER, W. E. and J. R. Ross (1975). 'World order', Papers from the Parasession on Functionalism. Chicago: CLS, pp. 63–111.

COOREMAN, A. M. (1982). 'Topicality, ergativity and transitivity in narrative discourse: evdience from Chamorro', Studies in Language 6,3: 343–74.

—— (1987). Transitivity and Discourse Continuity in Chamorro Narratives. Berlin: Mouton de Gruyter.

CORBETT, G. G. (1991). *Gender*. Cambridge: Cambridge University Press.
—— (2000). *Number*. Cambridge: Cambridge University Press.
CORDIER, G. (1914). *Littérature annamite*. Hanoï: Impr. d'Extrême-Orient.
COWAN, H. K. J. (1965). *Grammar of the Sentani Language. With specimen texts and vocabulary*. (Verhandlingen van het koniglijk instituut voor taal-, land- en volkenkunde 47). 'S-Gravenhage: Nijhoff.
COWAN, M. M. (1969). *Tzotzil Grammar*. Norman: Summer Institute of Linguistics.
CROCE, B. (1922). *Estetica come scienza dell'espressione e linguistica generale. Filosofia dello spirito* 5th edn. I. Bari: Laterza.
CROFT, W. (2001). *Radical Construction Grammar*. Oxford: Oxford University Press.
—— (2003). *Typology and Universals*. (2nd edn.). Cambridge: Cambridge University Press.
—— and D. A. CRUSE (2004). *Cognitive Linguistics*. Cambridge: Cambridge University Press.
CRUSE, D. A. (1986). *Lexical Semantics*. Cambridge: Cambridge University Press.
CYSOUW, M. (2003). *The Paradigmatic Structure of Person Marking*. (Oxford studies in typology and linguistic theory) Oxford: Oxford University Press.
D = Doronin 1993.
DAHL, Ö. (1979). 'Typology of sentence negation', *Linguistics* 17,1: 79–106.
—— (1985). *Tense and Aspect Systems*. Oxford: Blackwell.
—— (2001). 'Grammaticalization and the life cycles of constructions', *RASK-Internationalt tidsskrift for sprog og kommunikation* 14: 91–134.
—— (2004). *The Growth and Maintenance of Linguistic Complexity*. Amsterdam: Benjamins.
DALRYMPLE, M., I. HAYRAPETIAN, and T. H. KING (1998). 'The semantics of the Russian comitative construction', *Natural Language and Linguistic Theory* 16: 597–631.
DAVIES, J. (1981). *Kobon*. (Lingua Descriptive Studies 3) Amsterdam: North-Holland.
DEBRUNNER, A. (1917). *Griechische Wortbildungslehre*. Heidelberg: Winter.
DEFRANCIS, J. (1984). *The Chinese Language. Fact and fantasy*. Honolulu: University of Hawaii Press.
DERBYSHIRE, D. C. (1977). 'Discourse redundancy in Hixkaryana', *International Journal of American Linguistics* 43,3: 176–88.
DESMEEDT, K. and G. KEMPEN (1987). 'Incremental sentence production, self-correction and coordination', in G. Kempen (ed.), *Natural Language Generation. New results in artificial intelligence, psychology and linguistics*. Dordrecht: Nijhoff, pp. 365–76.
DEZ, J. (1980). *La syntaxe malgache* I/II. Thèse 1977 Paris. Paris: Honore Champion.
DICKENMANN, E. (1934). *Untersuchungen über die Nominalkomposition im Russischen*. I: *Einleitung und Material*. (Veröffentlichungen des Slavischen Instituts an der Friedrich-Wilhelms-Universität Berlin.) Leipzig: Harrassowitz.
DISCIULLO, A.-M. and E. WILLIAMS (1987). *On the Definition of Word*. Cambridge, MA: MIT Press.

DIXON, R. M. W. and A. Y. AIKHENWALD (eds.) (2002). *Word. A cross-linguistic typology.* Cambridge: Cambridge University Press.
DOBAI, P. (1985). *A birodalom ezredese.* Budapest: Magvetö.
—— (1990). *Oberst Redl. Roman über die Donaumonarchie.* Deutsch von D. Koriath. Budapest: Corvina.
DONALDSON, T. (1980). *Ngiyambaa. The language of the Wangaaybuwan.* Cambridge: Cambridge University Press.
DORONIN, V. (1993). *Kočkodikeś—Pakśa narmuń.* Saransk: Mordovskoj kńižnoj izdat'el'stvaś.
DRESSLER, W. U. and L. MERLINI BARBARESI (1994). *Morphopragmatics. Diminutives and intensifiers in Italian, German and other languages.* (Trends in Linguistics. Studies and Monographs 76) Mouton: Berlin.
DRYER, M. P. (1989a). 'Large linguistic areas and language sampling', *Studies in Language* 13: 257–92.
—— (1989b). 'Plural words', *Linguistics* 27,5: 865–95.
—— (1995). 'Frequency and pragmatically unmarked word order', in P. Downing and M. Noonan (eds.), *Word Order in Discourse.* Amsterdam: Benjamins, pp. 105–35.
—— (1998). 'Aspects of word order in the languages of Europe', in A. Siewierska (ed.), *Constituent Order in the Languages of Europe.* (Eurotyp 20–1) Berlin: Mouton de Gruyter, pp. 283–319.
DURIE, M. (1985). *A Grammar of Acehnese on the Basis of a Dialect of North Aceh.* Dordrecht: Foris.
—— (1997). 'Grammatical structures in verb serialization', in A. Alsina et al. (eds.), *Complex Predicates.* Stanford: Center for the Study of Language and Information, pp. 289–354.
EBBING, J. E. (1965). *Gramática y diccionario Aimara.* La Paz: Don Bosco.
EBERT, K. (1999). 'The UP–DOWN dimension in Rai grammar and mythology', in B. Bickel and M. Gaenszle (eds.), *Himalayan Space. Cultural horizons and practices.* Zürich: Völkerkundemuseum Zürich, pp. 105–31.
ECKMAN, F. R. and E. A. MORAVCSIK (eds.) (1986). *Markedness.* New York: Plenum.
EDMONSON, M. S. (1971). *The Book of Counsel: The Popol Vuh of the Quiche Maya of Guatemala.* (Middle American Research Institute Publication 35) New Orleans: Middle American Research Institute.
—— (1973). 'Semantic universals and particulars in Quiche', in M. S. Edmonson (ed.), *Meaning in Mayan Languages.* The Hague: Mouton, pp. 205–33.
EMENEAU, M. B. (1938a/1967). 'Echo-words in Toda', *New Indian Antiquary* 1: 109–17; Reprinted in Emeneau 1967: 37–45.
—— (1938b/1967). 'An echo-word motif in Dravidian folk-tales', *Journal of the American Oriental Society* 58: 553–70. Reprinted in Emeneau 1967: 357–70.
—— (1951). *Studies in Vietnamese (Annamese) grammar.* Berkeley: University of California Press.
—— (1967). *Dravidian Linguistics, Ethnology and Folktales.* Collected papers. Annamalainagar: Annamalai University.

EMENEAU, M. B. (1969). 'Onomatopoetics in the Indian linguistic area', *Language* 45: 274–99.

—— (1980) *Language and Linguistic area.* Stanford: Stanford University Press.

—— (1984). *Toda Grammar and Texts.* (American Philosophical Society, Memoirs Series 155) Philadelphia: American Philosophical Society.

EROFEEV, V. (1990). *Moskva-Petuški.* Moskva: Prometej.

ETHNOLOGUE. (2000). = B. F. GRIMES (ed.) *Ethnologue.* 1: *Languages of the world*, 2. *Maps and indexes* (14th edn.). Dallas: Summer Institute of Linguistics.

EVANS, N. D. (1995). *A Grammar of Kayardild: With historical-comparative notes on Tangkic.* Berlin: Mouton de Gruyter.

—— (2003). *An Interesting Couple: The semantic development of dyad morphemes.* (Arbeitspapier 47, Neue Folge.) Institut für Sprachwissenschaft, Universität zu Köln.

—— (forthcoming). 'Dyad constructions', to appear in *Encyclopedia of Language and Linguistics* (2nd edn.).

EVSEEV, T. E. (1994). *Kalyk ojporo.* Joškar-Ola: Marij Kńiga Savyktyš.

FANSELOW, G. (1985). 'What is a possible complex word', in J. Toman (ed.), *Studies in German Grammar.* Dordrecht: Foris, pp. 289–318.

FELDMAN, H. (1986). *A Grammar of Awtuw.* (Pacific Linguistics B 94) Canberra: Australian National University.

FENG, S. (1998). 'Prosodic structure and compound words in Classical Chinese', in J. L. Packard (ed.), *New Approaches to Chinese Word Formation.* Berlin: Marton de Gruyter, pp. 197–260.

FORIS, D. P. (2000). *A Grammar of Sochiapan Chinantec.* (Studies in Chinantec Languages 6) Dallas: Summer Institute of Linguistics.

FOX, J. J. (1988). *To Speak in Pairs: Essays on the ritual languages of eastern Indonesia.* Cambridge: Cambridge University Press.

FRANKLIN, K. J. (1971). *A Grammar of Kewa, New Guinea.* (Pacific Linguistics C 16) Canberra: Australian National University.

FRANKLIN, K. J. and J. FRANKLIN (1978). *A Kewa Dictionary. With supplementary grammatical and anthropological materials.* (Pacific Linguistics C 53) Canberra: Australian National University.

FRANTZ, D. G. (1990). 'Null heads and noun incorporation in Southern Tiwa', *Berkeley Linguistics Society* 16S: 32–8.

FREI, H. (1929). *La grammaire des fautes.* Paris: Geuthner.

GABAIN, A. VON (1950). *Alttürkische Grammatik. Mit Bibliographie, Lesestücken und Wörterverzeichnis.* (2. verbesserte Auflage.) Leipzig: Harrassowitz.

GABELENTZ, G. VON DER (1901). *Die Sprachwissenschaft, ihre Aufgaben, Methoden und bisherigen Ergebnisse* (2nd edn.) Leipzig: Tauchnitz.

GAENSZLE, M. (1998). *Ancestral voices: oral ritual texts and their social contexts among the Mewahang Rai of East Nepal.* Habilitationsschrift. Heidelberg.

GARIBAY, K. Á. M. (1953). *Historia de literatura nahuatl.* México: Porrua.

—— (1961). *Llave del nahuatl. Collection de trozos clasicos, con gramatica y vocabulario para utilidad de los principantes* (Segunda edicion revisada y augmendada). México: Porrua.

GAUDES, R. (1985). *Wörterbuch Khmer–Deutsch*. 2 Bde. Leipzig: Enzyklopädie.
GENIUŠIENE, E. (1987). *The Typology of Reflexives*. Berlin: Mouton de Gruyter.
GIL, D. (1991). Nouns, verbs, and quantification. *Eurotyp Working Papers* 10, 1. The European Science Foundation, Eurotyp Programme, Berlin.
GIVÓN, T. (1971). 'Historical syntax and synchronic morphology: an archeologist's field trip', *Chicago Linguistic Society* 7: 391–415.
—— (1995). *Functionalism and Grammar*. Amsterdam: Benjamins.
GLENDON, M. A. (2001). *A World made New. Eleanor Roosevelt and the Universal Declaration of Human Rights*. New York: Random House.
GLONTI, A. (ed.) (1975). *K'art'uli zyap'rebi* [Georgian folk-tales]. (1975). T'bilisi: ganat'leba.
GOLD, D. L. (1991–3). 'Reversible binomials in Afrikaans, English, Esperanto, French, German, Hebrew, Italian, Judezmo, Latin, Lithuanian, Polish, Portuguese, Rumanian, Spanish, and Yiddish', *Orbis* 36: 104–18.
GORELOVA, L. M. (2002). *Manchu Grammar*. Leiden: Brill.
GOSSEN, G. H. (1974a). *Chamulas in the World of the Sun: Time and space in a Maya oral tradition*. Cambridge, MA: Harvard University Press.
—— (1974b). 'To speak with a heated heart: Chamula canons of style and good performance', in R. Bauman and J. Sherzer (eds.). Cambridge: Cambridge University Press, pp. 389–413.
GREENBERG, J. H. (1960). 'A quantitative approach to the morphological typology of languages', *International Journal of American Linguistics* 26: 178–94.
—— (1966). *Language Universals*. The Hague: Mouton.
—— and C. O'Sullivan (1974). 'Frequency, marking and discourse styles with special reference to substantival categories in the Romance languages', *Working Papers on Language Universals* 16: 47–72.
GRICE, H. P. (1975). 'Logic and conversation', in P. Cole and J. Morgan (eds.), *Syntax and Semantics 3. Speech acts*. New York: Academic Press, pp. 41–58. Reprinted in H. P. Grice 1989: 22–40.
—— (1981). 'Presupposition and conversational implicature', in P. Cole (ed.), *Radical Pragmatics*. New York: Academic Press, pp. 183–98.
—— (1989). *Studies in the Way of Words*. Cambridge, MA: Harvard University Press.
GROVER, C. (1994). 'Coordination', in R. E. Asher (ed.), *The Encyclopedia of Language and Linguistics*. Oxford: Pergamon, vol. 2: 762–8.
HAIMAN, J. (1985). *Natural Syntax*. Cambridge: Cambridge University Press.
—— (1988). 'Incorporation, parallelism, and focus', in M. Hammond, E. Moravcsik, and J. Wirth (eds.), *Studies in Syntactic Typology*. Amsterdam: Benjamins, pp. 303–20.
—— (1994). 'Ritualization and the development of language', in W. Pagliuca (ed.), *Perspectives on Grammaticalization*. Amsterdam: Benjamins, pp. 3–28.
—— (forthcoming) *Playful Reproduction*.
HALL, T. A. (1999). 'The phonological word: a review', in T. A. Hall and U. Kleinhenz (eds.), *Studies on the Phonological Word*. Amsterdam: Benjamins, pp. 1–22.

HAMPE, B. (2002). *Superlative Verbs. A corpus-based study of semantic redundancy in English verb–particle constructions.* Tübingen: Narr.

HARRIES-DELISLE, H. (1978). 'Coordination reduction', in J. H. Greenberg (ed.), *Universals of Human Language 4 Syntax.* Stanford: Stanford University Press, pp. 515–83.

HARRIS, A. C. (2002). 'The word in Georgian', in R. M. W. Dixon and A. Y. Aikhenvald (eds.), *Word. A cross-linguistic typology.* Cambridge: Cambridge University Press, pp. 227–42.

HASPELMATH, M. (1993). *A Grammar of Lezgian.* Berlin: Mouton de Gruyter.

—— (1997). *Indefinite Pronouns.* Oxford: Clarendon.

—— (1998). 'Does grammaticalization need reanalysis?', *Studies in Language* 22,2: 315–51.

—— (1999). 'Why is grammaticalization irreversible?', *Linguistics* 37,6: 1040–68.

—— (2002). *Understanding Morphology.* London: Arnold.

—— (2003a). 'The geometry of grammatical meaning: semantic maps and cross-linguistic comparison', in M. Tomasello (ed.), *The New Psychology of Languages* II. Mahwah: Erlbaum, pp. 211–42.

—— (2003b). 'Creating economical morphosyntactic patterns in language change'. Draft of paper presented at the workshop 'Explaining Linguistic Universals: Historical Convergence and Universal Grammar', UC Berkeley, 7–8 March.

—— (2003c). 'Against iconicity and markedness'. Paper presented at Stanford University, 6 March.

—— (2004). 'Coordinating constructions: an overview', in M. Haspelmath (ed.), *Coordinating Constructions.* Amsterdam: Benjamins, pp. 3–39.

—— (forthcoming). 'Coordination', in T. Shopen (ed.), *Language Typology and Linguistic Description* (2nd edn.). Cambridge: Cambridge University Press.

—— E. KÖNIG, W. OESTERREICHER, and W. RAIBLE (eds.) (2001). *Language Typology and Language Universals. An international handbook* (HSK 20). Berlin: Mouton de Gruyter.

HEATH, J. (1999). *A Grammar of Koyra Chiini. The Songhay of Timbuktu.* Berlin: Mouton de Gruyter.

HEINE, B. (1997). *Possession. Cognitive sources, forces, and grammaticalization.* Cambridge: Cambridge University Press.

—— U. CLAUDI, and F. HÜNNEMEYER (1991). *Grammaticalization: A conceptual framework.* Chicago: University of Chicago Press.

HEINE, H. (1826/1997). *Die Harzreise.* Reclam: Stuttgart.

HELFFER, M. (1977). *Les chants dans l'épopée tibétaine de Ge-sar d'après le livre de la course de cheval. Version chantée de Blo-bsaŋ bstan-'jin.* Genève: Droz.

HEWITT, B. G. (1979). *Abkhaz.* (In collaboration with Z. K. Khiba). (Lingua Descriptive Studies 2) Amsterdam: North-Holland.

—— (ed.) (1996). *A Georgian reader (with texts, translations and vocabulary).* London: School of Oriental and African Studies.

HEYNE, M. (1888). *Beowulf. Mit ausführlichem Glossar* (5. Auflage). Paderborn: Schöningh.
HILDEBRANDT, K. A. (forthcoming). Review of R. M. W. Dixon and A. Y. Aikhenvald (eds), 'Word: A cross-linguistic typology'. *Linguistische Berichte.*
HILTUNEN, R. (1990). *Chapters on Legal English. Aspects past and present of the language of the law.* (Suomalaisen Tiedeakatemian Toimituksia B 251.) Helsinki: Suomalainen Tiedeakatemia.
HINTON, L., J. NICHOLS, and J. J. OHALA (eds.) (1994). *Sound Symbolism.* Cambridge: Cambridge University Press.
HOHENBERGER, A. (1996). *Functional Categories and Language Acquisition: Self-organization of a dynamic system.* Frankfurt-am-Main: Frankfurt University.
HOLMER, N. M. (ed.) (1952). *Inatoipippiler or The adventures of three Cuna boys: According to Maninibigdinapi (Belisario Guerrero).* (Ed., translated, and commented by N. M. Holmer). Göteborg: Etnografiska museet.
HONTI, L. (1997). 'Numerusprobleme (Ein Erkundungszug durch den Dschungel der uralischen Numeri)', *Finnisch–Ugrische Forschungen* 54: 1–126.
HOOGSHAGEN NOORDSY, S. and H. HALLORAN DE HOOGSHAGEN (1993). *Diccionario mixe de Coatlán, Oaxaca.* (Vocabularios indígenas 32) México: Instituto Lingüístico de Verano.
HOPPER, P. J. (1979). 'Aspect and foregrounding in discourse', in T. Givón (ed.), *Discourse and Syntax. Syntax and Semantics* 12: 213–41. New York: Academic Press.
—— (1987). 'Emergent grammar', *Berkeley Linguistics Society* 13: 139–57.
—— and E. C. TRAUGOTT (2003). *Grammaticalization* (2nd edn.). Cambridge: Cambridge University Press.
HORN, L. R. (1989). *A Natural History of Negation.* Chicago: University of Chicago Press.
HSIUNG, D. N. et al. (1995). *A Chinese–English Dictionary* (revised edition). Beijing: Foreign Language Teaching and Research.
HUMBOLDT, W. VON. (1836). *Über die Verschiedenheit des menschlichen Sprachbaues und ihren Einfluss auf die geistige Entwickelung des Menschengeschlechts.* Berlin. Reprinted in *Gesammelte Werke* (1848/1988) 6: 1–425. Berlin: Reimer/Berlin: Mouton de Gruyter.
HUNN, E. (1977). *Tzeltal Folk Zoology: The classification of discontinuities in nature.* New York: Academic Press.
HYMAN, L. M. (1975). 'On the change from SOV to SVO: evidence from Niger-Congo', in C. N. Li (ed.), *Word Order and Word Order Change.* Austin: University of Texas Press, pp. 113–47.
JACOBS, Judith (1979/1993). 'Observations on the uses of reduplication as a poetic device in Khmer', in T. L. Thongkum et al. (eds.), *Studies in Tai and Mon-Khmer Phonetics and Phonology in honour of E. J. A. Henderson.* Bangkok: Chulalongkorn University Press, pp. 111–30. Reprinted in Jacobs 1993: 225–42.
—— (1993). *Cambodian Linguistics, Literature and History. Collected articles.* (Ed. by D. Smyth). London: School of Oriental and African Studies.

JACOBS, Joachim (1988). 'Fokus-Hintergrund-Gliederung und Grammatik', in H. Altmann (ed.), *Intonationsforschungen*. Tübingen: Niemeyer, pp. 89–134.

JACOBSEN, W. H. JR. (1982). 'Basque copulative compounds: a problem in irreversible binomials', *Berkeley Linguistics Society* 8: 384–97.

JAKOBSON, R. (1936/1971). 'Beitrag zur allgmeinen Kasuslehre. Gesamtbedeutungen der russischen Kasus', *Travaux du cercle linguistique de Prague 6/Selected Writings* 1. 'S-Gravenhage: Mouton, pp. 23–71.

JESPERSEN, O. (1917). 'Negation in English and other languages', *Kgl. Danske Videnskabernes Selskab, Historisk-Filologiske Meddelelser* 1, no 5.

—— (1942). *A Modern English Grammar on Historical Principles*. 6: *Morphology*. Copenhagen: Munksgaard.

JESTIN, R.-R. (1951). *Abrégé de grammaire sumérienne*. Paris: Geuthner.

JOHANNESSEN, J. B. (1998). *Coordination*. (Oxford studies in comparative syntax) New York: Oxford University Press.

JONES, R. B. (1961). *Karen Linguistic Studies. Description, comparison, and texts.* Berkeley: University of California Press.

JONKER, J. C. G. (1896). *Bimaneesche spraakkunst*. (Verhandelingen van het Bataviaasch Genootschap der Kunsten en Wetenschappen 48:3). Batavia.

JURAFSKI, D. (1996). 'Universal tendencies in the semantics of the diminutive', *Language* 73,3: 533–78.

JUSTI, F. (1861). *Die Zusammensetzung der Nomina in den indogermanischen Sprachen zunächst in Hinsicht ihrer Form*. Inauguraldissertation. Marburg: Pfeil.

KAPLINSKI, J. (2002). 'Jos Heidegger olisi ollut mordvalainen', http://jaan.kaplinski.com/philosophy/ugrimugri.html.

KAPP, D. B. (1982). *Ālu-Kuṟumbaru Nāyaⁿ. Die Sprache der Ālu-Kuṟumbas. Grammatik, Texte, Wörterbuch*. Wiesbaden: Harrassowitz.

KARLGREN, B. (1962). *Sound and Symbol in Chinese* (revised edn.). Hong Kong: University Press.

KATRE, S. M. (1987). *Aṣṭādhyāyī of Pāṇini*. Austin: University of Texas.

KAZLAUSKIENE, B. et al. (1994). *Vestuvinės dainos* 4. (Lietuvių liaudies dainynas 8) Vilnius: Lietuvių literaturos ir tautosakos institutas.

KEENAN, E. L. (1985). 'Passive in the world's languages', in T. Shopen (ed.) *Language Typology and Syntactic Description*. Cambridge: Cambridge University Press, 1: 243–81.

KELLER, G. S. (1922). *Das Asyndeton in den balto-slavischen Sprachen*. Heidelberg: Winter.

KELLER, R. (1994). *Sprachwandel. Von der unsichtbaren Hand in der Sprache* (Zweite, überarbeitete und erweiterte Auflage). Tübingen: Francke.

KEMAJKINA, R. S. (ed.) (1993). *Jovksoń kužo. Erźań jovkst*. Saransk: Mordovskoj kńižnoj izdat'el'stvaś.

KEMMER, S. (1993). *The Middle Voice*. Amsterdam: Benjamins.

KIBRIK, A. E. et al. (1977). *Arčinskij jazyk. Teksty i slovari*. Moskva: Izdatel'stvo Universiteta.

KILBY, D. (1981). 'On case markers'. *Lingua* 54: 101–33.
KILHAM, C. (1974). 'Compound words and close-knit phrases in Wik-Munkan', *Papers in Australian Linguistics* 7: 45–72. (Pacific Linguistics A 37) Canberra: Australian National University.
—— J. ADAMS, J. BELL, and G. NAMPONAN (1986). *Dictionary and Source Book of the Wik-Mungkan language*. Darwin: Summer Institute of Linguistics, Australian Aborigines Branch.
KLAVANS, J. L. (1985). 'The independence of syntax and phonology in cliticization', *Language* 61: 95–120.
KLIMA, E. S., U. BELLUGI et al. (1979). *The Signs of Language*. Cambridge, MA: Harvard University Press.
KOLJADENKOV, M. N. (1959). *Struktura prostogo predloženija v mordovskix jazykov. Predloženie i ego glavnye členy*. Saransk: Mordovskoe knižnoe izdatel'stvo.
KONONOV, A. N. (1960). *Grammatika sovremennogo uzbekskogo literaturnogo jazyka*. Moskva: Akademija Nauk.
KOPČEVSKAJA-TAMM, M. and A. ŠMELEV (1994). 'Alešina s Mašej stat'ja (O nekotoryx svojstvax russkix 'pritjažatel'nyx prilagatel'nyx')', *Scando-Slavica* 40: 209–28.
KOPTJEVSKAJA-TAMM, M. (1993). *Nominalizations*. London: Routledge.
—— (1997). 'Possessive noun phrases in Maltese: alienability, iconicity and grammaticalization', *Rivista di Linguistica* 8,1: 245–74.
—— and B. WÄLCHLI (2001). 'The Circum-Baltic languages. An areal-typological approach', in Ö. Dahl and M. Koptjevskaja-Tamm (eds.), *Circum Baltic Languages 2: Grammar and Typology*. Amsterdam: Benjamins, pp. 615–750.
KRISHNAMURTI, B. (1969). *Koṇḍa or Kūbi. A Dravidian Language (texts, grammar and vocabulary)*. Hyderabad: Tribal Cultural Research & Training Institute.
KROHN, K. (1994). *Hand und Fuss*. Göteborg: Acta Universitatis Gothoburgensis.
KRUSPE, N. (2004). *A Grammar of Semelai*. Cambridge: Cambridge University Press.
KURYŁOWICZ, J. (1965/1976). 'The evolution of grammatical categories', *Diogenes* 51; *Esquisses linguistiques 2*, 38–54. München: Fink.
K'Z = Glonti, A. (ed.) (1975).
LABOV, W. (1972). *Sociolinguistic Patterns*. Philadelphia: University of Pennsylvania Press.
LAMBRECHT, K. (1984). 'Formulaicity, frame semantics and pragmatics in German binomial expressions', *Language* 60,4: 753–96.
LANG, E. (1977). *Semantik der koordinativen Verknüpfung*. (Studia grammatica 14) Berlin: Akademie.
LARSSON, E. and S. SÖDERSTRÖM (1980). *Hössjömålet. Ordbok över en sydvästerbottnisk dialekt. På grundval av E. Larssons samlingar* (2. uppl.). Umeå: Skrifter utgivna av Dialekt-, ortnamns- och folkminnesarkivet i Umeå.
LAUDE-CIRTAUTAS, I. (1980). *Chrestomathy of Modern Literary Uzbek*. Wiesbaden: Harassowitz.

LAUGHLIN, R. M. (ed.) (1980). *Of Shoes and Ships and Sealing Wax: Sundries from Zinacantán*. (Smithsonian contributions to anthropology 25) Washington: Smithsonian Institute.

LAWRENCE, M. (1993). *Oksapmin Dictionary*. Ukarumapa, Papua New Guinea: Summer Institute of Linguistics.

LEGENDRE, G. (2000). 'Positioning Romanian verbal clitics at PF: an optimality-theoretic analysis', in B. Gerlach and J. Grijzenhout (eds.), *Clitics in Phonology, Morphology and Syntax*. Amsterdam: Benjamins, pp. 219–54.

LEHMANN, C. (1985). 'Grammaticalization: synchronic variation and diachronic change', *Lingua e stile* 20: 303–18.

LEHMANN, W. and G. KUTSCHER (1949). *Sterbende Götter und christliche Heilsbotschaft. Wechselreden indianischer Vornehmer und spanischer Glaubensapostel in Mexiko 1524*. (Quellenwerke zur alten Geschichte Amerikas III.) Stuttgart: Kohlhammer.

LEISI, E. (1971). *Der Wortinhalt* (4. durchgesehene und erweiterte Auflage). Heidelberg: Quelle.

LEVELT, W. J. M. (1983). 'Monitoring and self-repair in speech', *Cognition* 14: 41–104.

—— (1989). *Speaking. From intention to articulation*. Cambridge, MA: MIT Press.

LEVINSON, S. C. (2003). *Space in Language and Cognition. Explorations in cognitive diversity*. Cambridge: Cambridge University Press.

LEWIS, G. L. (1967). *Turkish Grammar*. Oxford: Clarendon.

LEWY, E. (1911). *Zur finno-ugrischen Wort- und Satzverbindung*. Göttingen: Vandenhoeck.

—— (1934). 'Sprachgeographische Probleme des mediterranen Gebietes', *Studi etruschi* 8,2: 171–8.

LIDDELL, S. K. and R. E. JOHNSON (1986). 'American sign language compound formation processes, lexicalization, and phonological remnants', *Natural Language and Linguistic Theory* 4: 445–513.

LINDBLOM, B. (1992). 'Phonological units as adaptive emergents of lexical development', in C. A. Ferguson, L. Menn, and C. Stoel-Gammon (eds.), *Phonological Development: Models, research, implications*. Timonium: York, pp. 131–63.

LINDNER, T. (2002). *Lateinische Komposita. Morphologische, historische und lexikalische Studien*. Innsbruck: Innsbrucker Beiträge zur Sprachwissenschaft.

LINELL, P. (1982). *The Written Language Bias in Linguistics*. Linköping: University of Linköping.

LIPKA, L. and H. GÜNTHER (eds.) (1981). *Wortbildung*. Darmstadt: Wissenschaftliche Buchgesellschaft.

LIVER, R. (1999). *Rätoromanisch. Eine Einführung in das Bündnerromanische*. Tübingen: Narr.

LLOYD, J. A. (1992). *A Baruya-Tok Pisin-English Dictionary*. (Pacific Linguistics C 82). Canberra: Australian National University.

LLOYD, R. G. (1969). 'Gender in a New Guinea language. Baruya nouns and noun phrases', *Papers in New Guinea Linguistics* 10: 25–67. (Pacific Linguistics A 22). Canberra: Australian National University.

LONGOBARDI, G. (1994). 'Reference and proper names: a theory of N-movement in syntax and logical form', *Linguistic Inquiry* 25,4: 609–66.
LORD, C. (1993). *Historical Change in Serial Verb Constructions*. Amsterdam: Benjamins.
LORIMER, D. L. R. (1935). *The Burushaski Language* I. *Introduction and grammar*. Oslo: Instituttet for sammenignende kulturforskning.
LÜDTKE, H. (1980). *Kommunikationstheoretische Grundlagen des Sprachwandels*. 'Sprachwandel als universales Phänomen', pp. 1–19; 'Auf dem Weg zu einer Theorie des Sprachwandels', pp. 182–252. Berlin: de Gruyter.
LUKAS, J. (1937). *A Study of the Kanuri Language*. London: Oxford University Press.
LUUTONEN, J. (1997). *The Variation of Morpheme Order in Mari Declension*. (Suomalais-ugrilaisen seuran toimituksia 226.) Helsinki.
LUVSANDENDEV, A. (1957). *Mongol'sko-russkij slovar'*. Moskva: Gosudarstvennoe izdatel'stvo inostrannix i nacionalnyx slovarej.
MCCAWLEY, J. D. (1974). 'Prelexical syntax', in P. A. M. Seuren (ed.), *Semantic Syntax*. London: Oxford University Press, pp. 29–43.
MCGREGOR, W. (1990). *A Functional Grammar of Goonijandi*. Amsterdam: Benjamins.
MAHOOTIAN, S. (1997). *Persian*. London: Routledge.
MAJAKOVSKIJ, V. V. (1969). *Stixotvorenija. Poèmy*. Moskva: Xudožestvennaja literatura.
MALKIEL, Y. (1959). 'Studies in irreversible binomials', *Lingua* 8: 113–60.
MALLINSON, G. and B. J. BLAKE (1981). *Language Typology. Cross-linguistic studies in syntax*. Amsterdam: North-Holland.
MALOTKI, E. (1979). *Hopi-Raum. Eine sprachwissenschaftliche Analyse der Raumvorstellungen in der Hopi-Sprache*. Tübingen: Narr.
MARANTZ, A. (1994). 'Reduplication', in R. E. Asher (ed.), *The Encyclopedia of Language and Linguistics*. Oxford: Pergamon, vol. 3: 3486–7.
MASICA, C. P. (1971). *Defining a Linguistic Area*. Chicago: University of Chicago Press.
MASLOVA, E. (2003). *A Grammar of Kolyma Yukaghir*. Berlin: Mouton de Gruyter.
MATISOFF, J. A. (1978). *Variational Semantics in Tibeto-Burman. The 'organic' approach to linguistic comparison*. (Occasional papers of the Wolfenden society on Tibeto-Burman linguistics 6). Philadelphia: Institute for the Study of Human Issues.
MAUGHAM, W. S. (1919/1965). *The Moon and Sixpence*. Harmondsworth: Penguin.
MIHATSCH, W. (2000). 'La relation partie-tout aux confins de l'hyponymie', *Scolia* 12: 237–60.
—— (2003). Kognitive Grundlagen lexikalischer Hierarchien untersucht am Beispiel des Französischen und Spanischen. Phil. Dissertation. Tübingen.
—— and B. DVOŘÁK (forthcoming). 'The concept FACE: paths of lexical change', in W. Mihatsch and R. Steinberg (eds.), *Lexical Data and Universals of Semantic Change*. Tübingen: Stauffenburg.
MILLER, J. and R. WEINERT (1998). *Spontaneous Spoken Language*. Oxford: Clarendon.
MINASSIAN, M. (1980). *Grammaire d'armenien oriental*. Delmar: Caravan.

MINER, K. (1986). 'Noun stripping and loose incorporation in Zuni', *International Journal of American Linguistics* 52: 242–54.
MIRAMBEL, A. (1959). *La langue grecque moderne. Description et analyse.* Paris: Klincksieck.
MITHUN, M. (1984). 'The evolution of noun incorporation', *Language* 60: 847–95.
—— (1988). 'The grammaticization of coordination', in J. Haiman and S. Thompson (eds.), *Clause Combining in Grammar and Discourse.* Amsterdam: Benjamins, pp. 331–59.
MORAVCSIK, E. A. (1994). 'Associative Plurals'. Handout. Pre-inaugural meeting, ALT, Konstanz, November.
—— and J. WIRTH (1986). 'Markedness—an overview', in F. R. Eckman and E. A. Moravcsik (eds.), *Markedness.* New York: Plenum, pp. 1–11.
MOTTIN, J. (1978). *Eléments de grammaire hmong blanc.* Bangkok: Don Bosco.
—— (1980). *Contes et légéndes hmong blanc.* Bangkok: Don Bosco.
MTK = Modern Türk Klasikler. (1994). *Moderne türkische Klassiker.* Auswahl und Übersetzung von W. Riemann. München: dtv.
MÜHLHÄUSLER, P. (1979). *Growth and Structure of the Lexicon of New Guinea Pidgin.* Camberra: Australian National University.
MUKAŘOVSKÝ, J. (1940/1982). 'O jazyce básnickém', *Slovo a slovesnost* 6: 113–45. Reprinted in J. Mukařovský, *Studie z poetiky.* Praha: Odeon.
—— (1976). *On Poetic Language.* Lisse: Ridder. [Translation of Mukařovský (1940)].
NACASKUL, K. (1976). 'Types of elaboration in some Southeast Asian Languages', in Ph. Jenner, L. Thompson, and S. Starosta (eds.), *Austroasiatic Studies* 2: 873–89. Honolulu: University Press of Hawaii.
NEBEL, P. A. (1948). *Dinka Grammar (Rek – Malual dialect). With texts and vocabulary.* Verona: Istituto Missioni Africane.
NEKRASOV, N. A. (1953). *Sočinenija* III. Moskva: Gosudardstvennoe Izdatel'stvo.
NESPOR, M. and I. VOGEL (1986). *Prosodic Phonology* (Studies in generative grammar 28). Dordrecht: Foris.
NGUYỄN, Đ. H. (1965) 'Parallel constructions in Vietnamese', *Lingua* 15: 125–39.
NGUYEN, D. H. (1995). *NTC's Vietnamese–English Dictionary.* Lincolnwood: NTC.
NGUYỄN, V. H. (1933). *Les chants alternés des garçons et des filles en Annam.* Paris: Geuthner.
NICHOLS, J. (1992). *Linguistic Diversity in Space and Time.* Chicago: University of Chicago Press.
NIETZSCHE, F. (1999). *Der Fall Wagner. Götzen-Dämmerung. Der Antichrist. Ecce homo. Dionysos-Dithyramben. Nietzsche contra Wagner. Kritische Studienausgabe.* München: dtv/de Gruyter.
NIKOLAEVA, I. and M. TOLSKAYA (2001). *A Grammar of Udihe.* Berlin: Mouton de Gruyter.
NÜBLING, D. (1992). *Klitika im Deutschen. Schriftsprache, Umgangssprache, alemannische Dialekte.* Tübingen: Narr.

OATES, L. (1993). *Kuku–Yalanji Dictionary* (2nd printing). Albury: Graeme van Brummelen.
OCKHAM, W. of (1984). *Texte zur Theorie der Erkenntnis und der Wissenschaft*. Stuttgart: Reclam.
OLSEN, S. (2001). 'Copulative compounds: a closer look at the interface between syntax and morphology', in G. Booij and J. van Marle (eds.), *Yearbook of Morphology* 2000: 279–320. Dordrecht: Kluwer.
OURN, N. and J. HAIMAN (2000). 'Symmetrical compounds in Khmer', *Studies in Language* 24,3: 483–514.
PAASONEN, H. (1938). *Mordwinische Volksdichtung* I. Herausgegeben und übersetzt von P. Ravila (Suomalais-ugrilaisen seuran toimituksia 77). Helsinki: Suomalais-ugrilaisen seuran toimituksia.
—— (1941). *Mordwinische Volksdichtung* III. Herausgegeben und übersetzt von P. Ravila (Suomalais-ugrilaisen seuran toimituksia 84). Helsinki.
—— (1949). *Gebräuche und Volksdichtung der Tschuwassen*. Herausgegeben von E. Karahka und M. Räsänen (Suomalais-ugrilaisen seuran toimituksia 94). Helsinki.
PACKARD, J. L. (ed.) (1998). *New Approaches to Chinese Word Formation*. Berlin: Mouton de Gruyter.
PARRY, M. (1971). *The Making of Homeric Verse. The collected papers of M. Parry*. Ed. by A. Parry. Oxford: Clarendon.
PATZ, E. (2002). *A Grammar of the Kuku Yalanji Language of North Queensland* (Pacific Linguistics 526). Canberra: Australian National University.
PAUL, H. (1903/1981). 'Das Wesen der Wortzusammensetzung', *Indogermanische Forschungen* 14: 251–8. Reprinted in L. Lipka and H. Günther (eds.), *Wortbildung*. Darmstadt: Wissenschaftliche Buchgesellschaft, pp. 179–86.
—— (1904). *Prinzipien der Sprachgeschichte* (4. Auflage). Halle: Niemeyer.
PAYNE, J. R. (1985a). 'Negation', in T. Shopen (ed.) 1: 197–242.
—— (1985b). 'Complex phrases and complex sentences', in T. Shopen (ed.), *Language Typology and Syntactic Description*. Cambridge: Cambridge University Press, vol. 2: 3–41.
PILHOFER, G. (1933). *Grammatik der Káte-sprache in Neu Guinea* (Beihefte zur Zeitschrift für Eingeborenen-Sprachen 14). Berlin: Reimer.
POTT, A. F. (1862). *Doppelung (Reduplikation, Gemination) als eines der wichtigsten Bildungsmittel der Sprache, beleuchtet aus Sprachen aller Welttheile*. Lemgo: Meyer.
PREUSS, K. TH. (1921). *Religion und Mythologie der Uitoto. Textaufnahmen und Beobachtungen bei einem Indianerstamm in Kolumbien, Südamerika. I. Einführung und Texte (Erste Hälfte)*. Göttingen: Vandenhoeck.
PULKKINEN, P. (1966). *Asyndeetine rinnastus suomen kielessä* (Suomalaisen kirjallisuuden seuran toimituksia 281). Helsinki.
PUSTET, R. (1992). *Diskursprominenz und Rollensemantik—eine funktionale Typologie von Partizipationssystemen*. Inaugural-Dissertation. Köln.
PUTILOV, B. N. et al. (1989–90). *Pesni sobrannye P. N. Rybnikovym. 1–2: Byliny*. Petrosavodsk: Karelija.

RABEL, L. (1961). *Khasi, a Language of Assam*. Baton Rouge: Louisiana State University.

RAMSTEDT, G. J. (1952). *Einführung in die altaische Sprachwissenschaft* II. *Formenlehre* (Suomalais-ugrilaisen seuran toimituksia 104: 2). Helsinki: Suomalais-ugrilaisen seuran toimituksia.

RAVILA, P. (1941). 'Über die Verwendung der Numeruszeichen in den uralischen Sprachen', *Finnisch-ugrische Forschungen* 27.

REESINK, G. P. (1999). *A Grammar of Hatam: Bird's Head Peninsula, Irian Jaya* (Pacific Linguistics C 146). Canberra: Australian National University.

RINK, H. J. (1875/1975). *Tales and Traditions of the Eskimo: With a sketch of their habits, religion, language and other peculiarities*. Edinburgh: Blackwood; New York: AMS.

ROBERTS, J. R. (1987). *Amele*. London: Croom Helm.

RODRIGUES, A. D. (1999). 'Macro-Jê', in R. M. W. Dixon and A. Y. Aikhenvald (eds.), *The Amazonian Languages*. Cambridge: Cambridge University Press, pp. 165–206.

ROGAVA, G. V. and Z. I. KERAŠEVA (1966). *Grammatika adygejskogo jazyka*. Krasnodar: Krasnodarskoe knižnoe izdatel'stvo.

ROSCH, E. (1975). 'Cognitive representations of semantic categories', *Journal of Experimental Psychology: General* 104: 192–233.

—— C. B. MERVIS, W. GRAY, D. JOHNSON, and P. BOYES-BRAEM (1976). 'Basic objects in natural categories', *Cognitive Psychology* 8: 382–439.

Ross, J. R. (1986). *Infinite Syntax!* Reprinted Ph.D. dissertation. Norwood: Ablex.

RŪĶE-DRAVIŅA, V. (1959). *Diminutive im Lettischen* (Acta Universitatis Stockholmiensis, Études de Philologie Slave 8). Lund.

RUSHDIE, S. (1981/1995). *Midnight's Children*. London: Vintage.

SAIDOV, M. (1967). *Avarsko-russkij slovar'*. Moskva: Sovjetskaja Ènciklopedija.

SALTARELLI, M. (1988). *Basque*. London: Croom Helm.

SAMARIN, W. J. (1967). *Field Linguistics. A guide to linguistic field work*. New York: Holt.

SAPIR, E. (1909). *Takelma Texts* (Anthropological Publications 2.1). Philadelphia: University Museum.

—— (1911/1990). 'The problem of noun incorporation in American languages', *American Anthropologist* 13: 250–82/ *The collected works of Ed. Sapir* V: 27–59. Berlin: Mouton de Gruyter.

—— (1922/1969). 'Takelma', in F. Boas (ed.), *Handbook of American Indian Languages* 2: 1–296. Oosterhout N.B.: Anthropological Publications.

ŠARONOV, A. M. (1994). *Mastorava*. Saransk: Mordovijań kńigań izdat'el'stvaś.

SAUSSURE, F. DE (1916). *Cours de linguistique générale*. Publié par Charles Bally et Albert Sechehaye. Lausanne: Payot.

SCHACHTER, P. and F. T. OTANES (1972). *Tagalog Reference Grammar*. Berkeley: University of California Press.

SCHAUB, W. (1985). *Babungo*. London: Croom Helm.

SCHULTZE-BERNDT, E. (2001). 'Ideophone-like characteristics of uninflecting predicates in Jaminjung (Australia)', in F. K. E. Voeltz and C. Kilian-Hatz (eds.), *Ideophones*. Amsterdam: Benjamins, pp. 355–73.

SCHUSTER, R. (1995). *Synonymität im Text. Eine Untersuchung an russischen Textbeispielen.* Slavistische Beiträge 327. München: Sagner.

SCOTT, G. (1978). *The Fore Language of Papua New Guinea* (Pacific Lingistics B 47). Canberra: Australian National University.

—— (1980). *Fore Dictionary* (Pacific Linguistics C 62). Canberra: Australian National University.

SEBBA, M. (1987). *The Syntax of Serial Verbs* (Creole Language Library 2). Amsterdam: Benjamins.

—— (1994). 'Serial verbs', in R. E. Asher (ed.), *The Encyclopedia of Language and Linguistics.* Oxford: Pergamon, vol. 7: 3858–61.

SEGRE, C. (1963). *Lingua, stile e società. Studi sulla storia della prosa italiana.* Milano: Feltrinelli.

SEILER, H. (1972). *Zum Problem der sprachlichen Possessivität.* Arbeitspapier des Institutes für Sprachwissenschaft der Universität Köln 20.

SHERZER, J. (1983). *Kuna Ways of Speaking.* Austin: University of Texas.

SHI, Y. (2002). *The Establishment of Modern Chinese Grammar: The formation of the resultative construction and its effects.* Amsterdam: Benjamins.

SHIBATANI, M. (1990). *The Languages of Japan.* Cambridge: Cambridge University Press.

SHOPEN, T. (ed.) (1985). *Language Typology and Syntactic Description.* 3 vol. Cambridge: Cambridge University Press.

SIMENON, G. (2001). *Maigret et l'inspecteur Malgracieux* (18. Auflage). München: dtv.

SINGH, R. (1982). 'On some "redundant compounds" in Modern Hindi', *Lingua* 56: 345–51.

ŠKETAN, M. (1991). *Čumyren lukmo ojporo II. Ojlymaš, myskara, novella, očerk, stat'ja, korrespondencij, fel'eton-vlak.* Joškar-Ola. Marij kniga izdatel'stvo.

SKVORCOV, M. I. (ed.) (1982). *Čuvašsko-russkij slovar'.* Moskva: Russkij Jazyk.

SOTAVALTA, A. (1978). *Westlamutische Materialien.* Bearbeitet und herausgegeben von H. Halén (Suomalais-ugrilaisen seuran toimituksia 168). Helsinki: Suomalais-ugrilainen seura.

SPENCER, A. (1991). *Morphological Theory.* Oxford: Blackwell.

—— (2000). 'Verbal clitics in Bulgarian: a paradigm function approach', in B. Gerlach and J. Grijzenhout (eds.), *Clitics in Phonology, Morphology and Syntax.* Amsterdam: Benjamins, pp. 355–86.

—— (2003). 'Does English have productive compounding?', in B. Geert, J. DeCesaris, A. Ralli, and S. Scalise (eds.), *Topics in Morphology. Selected papers from the Third Mediterranean Morphology Meeting (Barcelona, September 20–22, 2001).* Barcelona: Institut Universitari de Lingüística Applicada, Universtitat Pompeu Fabra, pp. 329–41.

SRIDHAR, S. N. (1990). *Kannada.* London: Routledge.

STASSEN, L. (1985). *Comparison and Universal Grammar.* Oxford: Blackwell.

—— (2003). 'Noun phrase conjunction: the coordinative and the comitative strategy', in F. Plank (ed.), *Noun Phrase Structure in the Languages of Europe.* Berlin: Mouton de Gruyter, pp. 761–817.

STEEVER, S. B. (1988). *The Serial Verb Formation in the Dravidian Languages*. Delhi: Motilal Banarsidass.

—— (1993). *Analysis to Synthesis. The development of complex verb morphology in the Dravidian languages*. New York: Oxford University Press.

STEIN, R. A. (1956). *L'épopée tibétaine de Gesar (dans sa version lamaïque de Ling)*. Paris: Presses universitaires de Paris.

STOLZ, T. (2003). 'Mediterraneanism vs. universal process: word iteration in an areal perspective. A pilot-study', *Mediterranean Language Review* 15: 1–47.

—— and T. GUGELER (2000). 'Comitative typology—Nothing about the ape, but something about king-size samples, the European community and the little prince', *Sprachtypologie und Universalienforschung* 53,1: 53–61.

—— C. STROH, and A. URDZE (2003). 'Solidaritäten', *Lingua Posnaniensis* 45: 69–92.

STREHLOW, T. G. H. (1971). *Songs of Central Australia*. Sydney: Angus.

TALIBOV, B. and M. GADŽIEV (1966). *Lezginsko-russkij slovar'*. Moskva: Sovetskaja Ènciklopedija.

TALMY, L. (2000). *Toward a Cognitive Semantics* I–II. Cambridge, MA: MIT Press.

TAMMSAARE, A. H. (1963). *Tõde ja õigus* I. Tallinn: Eesti Riiklik Kirjastus.

TAYLOR, J. R. (1989). *Linguistic Categorization. Prototypes in linguistic theory*. Oxford: Clarendon.

TEREŠČENKO, N. M. (1973). *Sintaksis samodijskix jazykov*. Leningrad: Nauka.

THOMPSON, L. C. (1987). *A Vietnamese Reference Grammar*. Honolulu: University of Hawaii.

THOMSEN, V. (1922). *Samlede Afhandlinger* III. København: Gyldendalske Boghandel.

THUMB, A. and R. HAUSCHILD (1959). *Handbuch des Sanskrit. Mit Texten und Glossar.* II. *Formenlehre* (3. stark überarabeitete Auflage). Heidelberg: Winter.

TIERSMA, P. M. (1982). 'Local and general markedness', *Language* 58,4: 832–49.

TIMUŠEV, D. A. (ed.) (1971). *Obrazcy komi-zyrjanskoj reči*. Syktyvkar: Akademija Nauk SSSR.

TKAČENKO, O. B. (1979). *Sopostavitel'no-istoričeskaja frazeologija slavjanskix i finno-ugorskix jazykov*. Kiev: Naukova dumka.

TL = Xlebnikov 1993.

TRAUGOTT, E. C. and E. KÖNIG (1991). 'The semantics-pragmatics of grammaticalization revisited', in E. C. Traugott and B. Heine (eds.), *Approaches to Grammaticalization* 1: 189–218.

TRIVEDI, G. M. (1990). 'Echo formation', in S. Krishan (ed.), *Linguistic Traits across Language Boundaries*. Calcutta: Anthropological Survey of India, pp. 51–82.

TRUBETZKOY, N. S. (1939). *Grundzüge der Phonologie* (Travaux du Cercle Linguistique de Prague). Prague: Ministère de l'instruction publique de la République Tchéco-Slovaque.

TRYON, D. T. (ed.) (1995). *Comparative Austronesian Dictionary*. 4 vol. Berlin: Mouton de Gruyter.

TSCHENKÉLI, K. (1965–1974). *Georgisch–Deutsches Wörterbuch*. 3 Bde. Zürich: Amirani.

TSCHUDI, J. J. VON (1853). *Die Kechua-Sprache. Sprachlehre, Sprachproben, Wörterbuch.* Wien: K.-K. Hof- und Staatsdruckerei.
TUCKER CHILDS, G. (1994). 'African ideophones', in L. Hinton, J. Nichols, and J. J. Ohala (eds.), *Sound Symbolism.* Cambridge: Cambridge University Press, pp. 178–204.
TUNG, T. (1964). *A Descriptive Study of the Tsou Language, Formosa* (Institute of History and Philology Academia Sinica. Speical Publications 48). Taipei.
UDHR (Universal Declaration of Human Rights) (1999–2002). http://www.unhchr.ch/udhr/navigate/alpha.htm.
UNGERER, F. and H.-J. SCHMID (1996). *An Introduction to Cognitive Linguistics.* London: Longman.
UOTILA, E. (1980). 'Asyndeton in the Baltic and Finnic languages: an archaic construction in its typological periphery', *Journal of Baltic Studies* 11,1: 86–91.
VAN DEN BERG, H. (1995). *A Grammar of Hunzib.* München: Lincom.
VAN OIRSOUW, R. R. (1987). *The Syntax of Coordination.* London: Croom Helm.
VIETZE, H.-P. (1969). *Lehrbuch der mongolischen Sprache.* Leipzig: Enzyklopädie.
VOLLMANN, R. (1989/90). *Die Bildung der Komposita im umgangssprachlichen Tibetisch*—Seminar: Morphologische Analyse. Dressler & Stefanescu.
VYGOTSKIJ, L. S. (1962). *Thought and Language.* Cambridge, MA: MIT Press.
WACKERNAGEL, J. (1905). *Altindische Grammatik II, 1. Einleitung zur Wortlehre. Nominalkomposition.* Göttingen: Vandenhoeck & Ruprecht.
WÄLCHLI, B. (2001a). 'Ist Koordination in syntaktischer Hinsicht symmetrisch oder asymmetrisch?', in B. Wälchli and F. Zúñiga (eds.), *Sprachbeschreibung und Typologie.* Bern: Sprachwissenschaft, pp. 45–64.
—— (forthcoming). 'Typology of heavy and light "again", or, the eternal return of the same', *Studies in Language.*
—— and F. ZÚÑIGA (eds.) (2001). *Sprachbeschreibung und Typologie. Publikation zum Workshop vom 16. Dezember 2000.* (Arbeitspapiere 38) Bern: Insitut für Sprachwissenschaft.
WALLIN, L. (1983). 'Compounds in Swedish sign language in historical perspective', in J. Kyle and B. Woll (eds.), *Language in Sign: An international perspective on Sign Language.* London: Croom Helm.
WEBER, D. J. (1989). *A Grammar of Huallaga (Huánuco) Quechua.* Berkeley: University of California Press.
WELLS, M. A. (1979). *Siroi grammar* (Pacific Linguistics B 51). Canberra: Australian National University.
WERLEN, I. (2002). *Sprachliche Relativität.* Tübingen: Francke.
WESTERMANN, D. (1930). *A Study of the Ewe Language.* Transl. by A.-L. Bickford-Smith. London: Oxford University Press.
WHORF, B. L. (1945/1956). 'Grammatical categories', *Language* 21: 1–11; *Language, thought, and reality.* Selected Writings of B. L. Whorf (ed. by J. Carroll). New York: MIT Press, pp. 87–101.
WIEDEMANN, F. J. (1884). *Grammatik der syrjänischen Sprache mit Berücksichtigung ihrer Dialekte und des Wotjakischen.* St. Petersburg: Eggers.

WIERZBICKA, A. (1985). *Lexicography and Conceptual Analysis*. Ann Arbor: Karoma.
WILLETT, T. L. (1988). *A Reference Grammar of Southeastern Tepehuan*. Ann Arbor: UMI.
WISNIEWSKI, E. J. and G. L. MURPHY (1989). 'Superordinate and basic category names in discourse: a textual analysis', *Discourse Processes* 12: 245–61.
WITKOWSKI, S. R. and C. H. BROWN (1983). 'Marking-reversals and cultural importance', *Language* 59,3: 569–82.
WOLF, S. A. (1991). *Jiddisches Wörterbuch*. (2. Nachdruck der 2. durchgesehenen Auflage). Hamburg: Buske.
WRAY, A. (2002). *The Transition to Language*. Oxford: Oxford University Press.
XLEBNIKOV, G. J. (ed.) (1993). *Tăvan literatura. Učebnik-xrestomati 7 klass valli*. Šupaškar: Čăvaš kĕneke izdateľstvi.
YOUNG, R. W. and W. MORGAN (1980). *The Navajo Language. A grammar and colloquial dictionary*. Albuquerque: University of New Mexico.
ZIPF, G. K. (1935/1965). *The Psycho-biology of Language. An introduction to dynamic philology*. Cambridge, MA: MIT Press.
ZUBIN, D. A. and K.-M. KÖPCKE (1986). 'Gender and folk taxonomy: the indexical relation between grammatical and lexical categorization', in C. Craig (ed.), *Noun Classes and Categorization*. Amsterdam: Benjamins, pp. 139–80.

Translations used of the Gospel According to Mark:

Adyghe NT 1992 Stockholm; **Armenian (Classical)** B. O. Künzle (ed.) 1984 *Das altarmenische Evangelium*. Bern: Lang; **Avar** Mk 1996 Stockholm; **Aymara** Mk 1930 n.p.; **Azerbaijani** NT 1998 Stockholm/Moskva; **Bahasa Indonesia** http://www.bit.net.id/SABDA-Web/Mar/T_Mar1.htm; **Burmese** NT 1989 n.p.; **Cebuano** http://hole-in-one-golftours.com/bibledatabase/online/cebuano/41_001.htm; **Chuvash** NT 2001 Moskva; **English (Early)** http://www.bibleontheweb.com/Bible.asp; **Estonian** NT 1991 n.p.; **Finnish** http://www.funet.fi/pub/doc/religion/christian/Bible/html/finnish/1933,38/Mark.html; **Georgian (Classical)** NT 1963 Tbilisi; **Georgian (Modern)** NT 2001 Stockholm/Moskva; **German (Bernese)** H. und R. Bietenhard (übers.), *Ds Nöie Teschtamänt bärndütsch*. Bern: Haller; **Greek (Modern)** NT 1988 Atena; **Haitian Creole** B 1985 Port-au-Prince; **Hindi** NT n.d. Bangalore; **Hopi** Gsp. 1929 New York; **Hungarian** NT 1996 Budapest; **Kalmyk** NT 2002 Moskva; **Kâte** B 1978/1990 Port Moresby; **Khakas** Mk 1995 Stockholm; **Khalkha** B 2000 n.p.; **Khanti** Mk 2000 Helsinki/Stockholm; **Khmer** B 1999 n.p.; **Komi** Mk 1995 Stockholm/Helsinki; **Kube** Mk unpublished; **Kuku Yalanji** Mk 1967 Darwin; **Kurdish (Kurmanji)** NT 2000 Stockholm/Moskva; **Lahu** Mk NT 1962 Rangoon; **Lak** Mk 1996 Stockholm/Moskva; **Latvian** B 1993 Rīga; **Lezgian** Mk 1996 Stockholm/Moskva; **Lithuanian** NT+ 1984 n.p.; **Malay** Mk 1976 Petaling Jaya; **Maltese** Mk 1934 London; **Mansi** Mk 2000 Helsinki/Stockholm; **Mari (Eastern)** Mk 1995 Stockholm/Helsinki; **Mari (Western)** Mk 1997 Stockholm/Helsinki; **Marshallese** NT 1899 New York; **Melpa** NT 1965 London; **Mordvin (Erźa)** Mk 1995 Stockholm/Helsinki; **Mordvin (Mokša)** Mk 1995 Stockholm/Helsinki; **Nico-**

barese (Car) NT 1950 Rangoon; **Russian** http://www.irrtv.org/Russian/Bible/Mar-1.html; **Seychelles Creole** NT 1999 Victoria (Seychelles); **Siane** NT 1996 South Holland, IL; **Songhai** NT 1936 Paris; **Tabasaran** Mk 1997 Stockholm; **Tadzhik** B 1992 Stockholm; **Tagalog** B 1980 Manila; **Tamil** NT 1981/1989 Colombo; **Tatar** NT 2001 Kazan; **Thai** NT 1977 Colorado Springs; **Tibetan** B 1968 (reprint of) Bangalore; **Toaripi** NT 1938 London; **Tok Pisin** 1987/2000 NT Morsbi; **Turkish** http://www.funet.fi/pub/doc/bible/html/turkish/Mr.1.html; **Tuva** Mk 1996 Stockholm/Moskva; **Udmurt** Mk 1992 Stockholm/Helsinki; **Uyghur** Mk 1982 n.p.; **Uzbek** NT+ 1996 (Stockholm/Moskva); **Vietnamese** B 2000 New York; **Wik-Mungkan** Mk 1969 Darwin; **Yabem** NT 1924 London; **Yakut** Mk 1995 Stockholm; **Zoque** NT 1967 México.

Index of Persons

Aalto, P. 17, 153, 203
Abaev, V. I. 241 n. 9
Abramov, K. 80, 135, 219–25
Aikhenvald, A. Y. 92, 94, 124
Allen, N. J. 148
Alpher, B. 164
Ambrazas, V. 167
Andersen, H. 39
Anderson, S. R. 20–1, 34, 61–2, 66 n. 17, 91, 97–8, 133 n. 11, 136
Anward, J. 21, 95, 98, 101, 133 n. 13
Asher, R. E. 207
Austen, J. 76–7
Austin, P. 130
Aze, R. and T. 57

Bader, F. 203
Baker, M. C. 247
Balandin, A. N 51
Batchelor, J. 214
Bauer, L. 18–9, 97–8, 104, 184, 247
Bearth, T. 88 n. 1
Bee, D. L. 237
Bellugi, U. 19–20, 27, 132 n. 4
Bendz, G. 21
Benveniste, E. 96
Bergman, B 37 n. 10
Berlin, B. 239
Bertrais, R. P. 242 n. 20
Beyer, S. V. 99, 153, 210
Bhatia, T. K. 17
Bhattacharya, S. 210
Biber, D. 37 n. 13, 96
Bickel, B. 132 n. 1
Bierhorst, J. 151
Bisang, W. 22, 102, 124, 134 n. 22, 146
Bishop, T. 257

Blake, B. J. 68
Bloch, J. 167
Bloomfield, L. 18, 101, 110, 139
Blowers, B. L. and R. 111, 168, 237
Bodding, P. O. 45, 85
Boeder, W. 17, 235, 241 n. 8
Bogomilov, B. 265
Böhringer, P. H. 213
Böhtlingk, O. 48
Börjars, K. 66 n. 17
Bouda, K. 52
Bradley, D. 208
Brettschneider, G. 20, 36, 66 n. 16, 67, 89 n. 10, 96
Bricker, V. R. 151
Brody, J. 151
Brown, C. H. 27
Brown, H. A. 79, 81, 237–8
Brugmann, K. 97, 99, 101, 245–6
Bühler, K. 18
Buzakova, R. N. 140, 172, 205
Bybee, J. 23, 33, 95, 105–6, 133 n. 8, n. 11, 243, 267, 280

Campanile, E. 203
Carroll, L. 41, 82
Chao, Y. R. 100, 150, 272
Chelliah, S. L. 143
Chomsky, N. 21, 68
Christie, A. 82
Clark, H. H. 15, 65 n. 5, 115
Comrie, B. 44, 66 n. 18
Cooper, W. E. 21, 104
Cooreman, A. M. 24
Corbett, G. G. 54, 66 n. 13, 156
Cordier, G. 150
Cowan, H. K. J. 4, 8, 168, 237

Cowan, M. M. 239
Croce, B. 55
Croft, W. 29, 31, 39, 40, 65 n. 3, 122–3, 184 n. 9, n. 10, 253, 269–70
Cruse, D. A. 138, 159, 184 n. 9, n. 10
Cysouw, M. 89 n. 7

Dahl, Ö. 23, 29, 33, 105–6, 133 n. 8, 134 n. 19, 185 n. 18, 242 n. 21, 243, 245, 257, 259, 267
Dalrymple, M. 88 n. 4
Davies, J. 237
Debrunner, A. 250
DeFrancis, J. 273 n. 5
Derbyshire, D. C. 164
DeSmeedt, K. 84
Dez, J. 47
Dickenmann, E. 205
DiSciullo, A.-M. 94–5, 132 n. 2
Dixon, R. M. W. 92, 94
Dobai, P. 260–1
Donaldson, T. 53
Dorjgotov, E. 153
Doronin, V. 12, 135, 141, 144–5, 150, 154, 162–4, 167, 169, 172–3, 176–8, 180–2, 219–25, 258, 263
Dressler, W. U. 110
Dryer, M. P. 24–5, 65 n. 1, 105, 186, 236
Durie, M. 22, 124, 211
Dvořák, B. 241 n. 9

Ebbing, J. E. 74
Ebert, K. 272 n. 12
Edmonson, M. S. 151
Emeneau, M. B. 20, 164, 168, 177–8, 185 n. 15, 207, 225
Erofeev, V. 204
Evans, N. D. 21, 89 n. 5, 232, 234, 238
Evseev, T. E. 249

Fanselow, G. 19
Feldman, H. 237
Feng, S. 97, 134 n. 21, 156, 253
Foris, D. P. 102–3, 125
Fox, J. J. 15
Franklin, J. and K. J. 237
Frantz, D. G. 133 n. 12
Frei, H. 245
Fröding, G. 261

Gabain, A. von 53, 199, 271 n. 2
Gabelentz, G. von der 51
Gadžiev, M. 104
Gaenszle, M. 148, 225
Garibay, K. Á. M. 151
Gast, V. 239
Geniušienė, E. 136
Gil, D. 180
Gil'ferding, A. F. 272 n. 11
Givón, T. 24, 245
Glendon, M. A. 241 n. 1
Gluxova, N. 50, 64, 140, 142
Gold, D. L. 185 n. 14
Gorelova, L. M. 128, 200
Gossen, G. H. 151
Greenberg, J. H. 24, 39
Grice, H. P. 81
Grover, C. 86
Gugeler, T. 242 n. 22

Haiman, J. 13, 18, 21–2, 30, 38, 54–5, 80, 98, 101, 147, 150, 227, 237
Hall, T. A. 92
Halloran de Hoogshagen, H. 239
Hampe, B. 120
Harries-Delisle, H. 79, 89 n. 10
Harris, A. C. 3
Haspelmath, M. 9, 23, 27, 28–9, 35 n. 1, 36 n. 5, 48, 52, 65 n. 2, 72–3, 81, 83, 89 n.7, 111, 122, 134 n. 18, 137, 145, 177, 201, 243–4, 259
Hauschild, R. 91
Heath, J. 240
Heine, B. 23, 111
Heine, H. 67–8, 149, 243

Index of Persons

Helffer, M. 153
Helgason, P. 55
Hewitt, B. G. 8, 135, 138, 140–1, 144, 163, 165–6, 174–5, 201
Heyne, M. 149
Hildebrandt, K. A. 94
Hiltunen, R. 36 n. 6, 235, 241 n. 2
Hohenberger, A. 250
Holmer, N. M. 268
Honti, L. 54, 66 n. 12
Hoogshagen Noordsy, S. 239
Hopper, P. J. 26, 65 n. 4
Horn, L. R. 243
Hsiung, D. N. 272 n. 5
Humboldt, W. von 31
Hunn, E. 239
Hyman, L. M. 86

Jacobs, Joachim 80
Jacobs, Judith 147
Jacobsen, W. H. Jr. 212
Jakobson, R. 28
Jespersen, O. 18, 185 n. 18
Jestin, R.-R. 213
Johannessen, J. B. 60
Johnson, R. E. 132 n. 4
Jones, R. B. 231
Jonker, J. C. G. 211
Jurafski, D. 133 n. 10
Justi, F. 17, 247

Kaplinski, J. 37 n. 16
Kapp, D. B. 20, 207
Karlgren, B. 18, 252
Katre, S. M. 37 n. 9, 91
Kazlauskienė, B. 269
Keenan, E. L. 65 n. 4
Keller, G. S. 205
Keller, R. 26
Kemajkina, R. S. 1, 6
Kemmer, S. 23, 30, 106–8, 126, 136
Kempen, G. 84
Kennedy, G. A. 272 n. 5

Keraševa, Z. I. 202
Kibrik, A. E. 178
Kilby, D. 93
Kilham, C. 234, 238
King, A. C. 212–13, 242 n. 15
Klavans, J. L. 21, 60
Klima, E. S. 19–20, 27, 132 n. 4
Koljadenkov, M. n. 2
König, E. 183, 243
Kononov, A. N. 136
Köpcke, K.-M. 36 n. 4
Koptjevskaja-Tamm, M. 23, 88 n. 4, 120, 236, 251
Krishnamurti, B. 207–8
Krohn, K. 13
Kruspe, N. 210
Kuryłowicz, J. 244
Kutscher, G. 151

Labov, W. 37 n. 13
Lambrecht, K. 11, 13–14, 21, 104, 141, 173
Lang, E. 20
Larsson, E. 120
Laude-Cirtautas, I. 175
Laughlin, R. M. 239–40
Lawrence, M. 234, 237
Lee, Y.-S. 241 n. 7
Legendre, G. 66 n. 17
Lehmann, C. 103, 243, 251
Lehmann, W. 151
Leisi, E. 6
Levelt, W. J. M. 84
Levinson, S. C. 32
Lewis, G. L. 111, 147–8, 168
Lewy, E. 17, 31–2, 46, 66 n. 12, 206–7, 241 n. 9
Liddell, S. K. 132 n. 4
Lindblom, B. 26
Lindner, T. 213
Linell, P. 21, 92, 95, 98, 101, 133 n. 13
Liver, R. 241
Lloyd, J. A. 237
Lloyd, R. G. 237

Longobardi, G. 55
Lord, C. 124
Lorimer, D. L. R. 213, 247
Lüdtke, H. 26, 253–5
Lukas, J. 81, 240
Luutonen, J. 50
Luvsandendev, A. 159

McCawley, J. D. 19
McGregor, W. 63, 238
Mahootian, S. 129
Majakovskij, V. V. 163
Malkiel, Y. 21, 104
Mallinson, G. 68
Malotki, E. 130
Marantz, A. 185 n. 12
Masica, C. P. 167, 186, 218
Maslova, E. 214
Matisoff, J. A. 209–10
Matras, Y. 241 n. 10
Matthews, S. 234
Maugham, W. S. 77
Mayakovski see Majakovskij
Merlini Barbaresi, L. 110
Mihatsch, W. 6, 241 n. 9
Miller, J. 37 n. 13
Minassian, M. 49
Miner, K. 95, 113
Mirambel, A. 3
Mithun, M. 20, 23, 45, 52, 112, 157
Moravcsik, E. A. 39, 66 n. 13
Morgan, W. 120
Mottin, J. 146, 152, 228, 242 n. 20
Mühlhäusler, P. 241 n. 6
Mukařovský, J. 65 n. 5
Murphy, G. L. 6, 89 n. 8

Nacaskul, K. 18, 211–12
Nebel, P. A. 38
Nekrasov, N. A. 205
Nespor, M. 5, 66 n. 14, n. 15, 93–4

Nguyen, D-H. 104
Nguyên, Đ-H. 36 n. 8
Nguyên, V. H. 150
Nichols, J. 5, 25, 65 n. 6, 101, 132 n. 1, 186, 198, 201, 212, 229
Nietzsche, F. 84
Nikolaeva, I. 89 n. 5, 165
Nübling, D. 21, 60–1

Oates, L. 234
Ockham, W. of 171
Olsen, S. 7, 22, 37 n. 11
O'Sullivan, C. 24
Otanes, F. T. 133 n. 7
Ourn, N. 18, 147, 227

Paasonen, H. 15, 179, 225
Pāṇini 37 n. 9
Parry, M. 267
Patz, E. 238
Paul, H. 18, 101
Payne, J. R. 23, 48, 75
Peltzer-Karpf, A. 272 n. 4
Pilhofer, G. 126, 237
Pott, A. F. 20, 148, 168, 213
Preuss, K. T. 232
Pulkkinen, P. 52
Pustet, R. 65
Putilov, B. N. 204

Rabel, L. 147
Ramstedt, G. J. 199, 271 n. 2
Ravila, P. 54
Reesink, G. P. 237
Rink, H. J. 273 n. 13
Roberts, J. R. 237
Rodrigues, A. D. 247
Rogava, G. V. 202
Rosch, E. 27, 37 n. 14
Ross, J. R. 21, 86, 104
Rūķe-Draviņa, V. 110
Rushdie, S. 1, 185 n. 13

Index of Persons

Saidov, M. 123
Saltarelli, M. 58
Samarin, W. J. 133 n. 15
Sapir, E. 31, 89 n. 5, 133 n. 15
Šaronov, A. M. 160, 173, 219, 263–4
Saussure, F. de 116
Schachter, P. 133
Schaub, W. 74
Schmid, H.-J. 37
Schultze-Berndt, E. 165
Schuster, R. 159–60
Scott, G. 237
Sebba, M. 86, 124
Segre, C. 241 n. 4
Sehidou, I. 242 n. 10
Seiler, H. 5, 96
Shakespeare, W. 184 n. 8
Sherzer, J. 37, 267–8
Shi, Y. 272 n. 7, n. 9
Shibatani, M. 272 n. 12
Shokri, N. 51
Simenon, G. 229
Singh, R 235
Šketan, M. 140
Skvorcov, M. I. 143, 147, 165
Šmelev, A. 88 n. 4
Söderström, S. 120
Sotavalta, A. 200
Spencer, A. 21–2, 60, 66 n. 17, 91–2, 99, 132 n. 4
Sridhar S. N. 72, 123, 167
Stassen, L. 20, 23, 45, 52
Steever, S. B. 22, 169, 207–8, 242 n. 12
Stein, R. A. 153
Stolz, T. 166, 242 n. 22
Strehlow, T. G. H. 268–9

Talibov, B. 104
Talmy, L. 141
Tammsaare, A. H. 206
Taylor, J. R. 27, 110
Tennenbaum, P. 257

Tereščenko, N. M. 51
Thompson, L. C. 4
Thompson, S. 106
Thomsen, V. 249
Thumb, A. 91
Tiersma, P. M. 39–40
Timušev, D. A. 10
Tkačenko, O. B. 18, 187
Tolskaya, M. 89 n. 5, 165
Traugott, E. C. 183, 243
Trivedi, G. M. 167
Trubetzkoy, N. S. 42
Tryon, D. T. 212, 218, 242 n. 14
Tschudi, J. J. von 76
Tucker Childs, G. 164
Tung, T. 212

Učaev, Z. 64
Ungerer, F. 37 n. 14
Uotila, E. 205

van den Berg, H. 202
van Oirsouw, R. R. 68
Veselinova, L. 11
Vietze, H.-P. 146
Vogel, I. 5, 66 n. 14, n. 15, 93–4
Vollmann, R. 154
Vygotskij, L. S. 6

Wackernagel, J. 17, 91, 170, 247–8, 271 n. 1
Wallin, L. 133 n. 7
Weber, D. J. 76
Weinert, R. 37 n. 13
Wells, M. A. 237
Werlen, I. 31
Westermann, D. 49, 102
Whorf, B. L. 31–2, 36 n. 7, 39, 87, 122
Wiedemann, F. J. 31–2
Wierzbicka, A. 37 n. 14
Willett, T. L. 47
Williams, E. 94–5, 132 n. 2

Wirth, J. 39
Wisniewski, E. J. 6, 89 n. 8
Witkowski, S. R. 27
Wolf, S. A. 185 n. 14
Wray, A. 21, 95–6, 134 n. 17, 267, 279

Xlebnikov, G. J. 135, 150

Young, R. W. 120

Zipf, G. K. 27
Zubin, D. A. 36

Index of Languages

Abkhaz 189 90, 197, 201, 215, 230, 233
Aceh 188, 197, 211
Adyghe 197, 201–2, 215, 230, 233
Ainu 214, 272 n. 12
Akha 208–9
Ālu-Kurumba 20, 207
Amele 237
American Sign Language (ASL) 19–20, 37 n. 10, 132 n. 4
Arabic 129, 199, 215, 232, 235
Aranda 16, 267–9
Archi 178
Armenian 168, 201–2, 215
   Classical 167, 201–2, 215
   Eastern 44, 49
Atsi 209
Avar 39, 123, 125, 142, 192–3, 195, 197, 202–3, 215, 230, 241 n. 9, 256
Avesta 53, 148
Awtuw 237
Aymara 74–5, 233
Azerbaijani 58–9, 61, 192–3, 195, 197, 198–9, 201–2, 215

Babungo 74–5
Bahasa Indonesia 119, 126–8, 188–90, 192–3, 195, 197, 215, 242 n. 14
Balinese 197, 212, 242 n. 17
Bantawa 209–10
Baruya 237
Basque 58–9, 61, 79, 111, 186, 189–91, 196–7, 212–4, 215, 218, 230, 233, 236, 242 n. 15
Belarusan 187
Bengali 189–90, 197, 204
Bimanese 211
Bisu 209

Blackfoot 112
Bonda 210, 215
Bulgarian 11, 34, 43, 55, 62–3
Burmese 18, 189, 193, 197, 209, 215, 241 n. 3
Burushaski 213, 215, 230, 232, 247

Caddo 112
Cantonese 234, 272 n. 9
Cebuano 197, 211
Chamorro 40, 61
Chinantec, Sochiapan 102–3, 125, 239, 278
Chinese 18, 20, 134 n. 21, 190, 199–200, 215, 228, 235, 253, 255–7, 272 n.5, *see also* Mandarin; Cantonese
   Classical 97, 156, 230
   Old 253
   Middle 253
Chukchee 112
Chuvash 112, 126, 135, 138, 141–3, 145–6, 149–51, 164–6, 184 n. 1
Comanche 112
Czech 126–7

Da'a 212
Dami 212
Danish 98, 247
Dinka 38
Diyari 130
Dutch 40, 66 n. 16

English 2, 11–13, 19, 22, 27, 18, 36 n. 6, 14–18, 46, 48–9, 55, 59, 61, 69, 74–7, 79, 81, 85, 88 n. 1, 89 n. 9, 91, 94, 96, 98–100, 105, 107, 109, 111–12, 116, 118–20, 126–7, 132 n. 2, 133 n. 8,

134 n. 20, 141, 157, 161–2, 164, 170, 174–5, 184 n. 5, 197, 215, 232–3, 235, 241 n. 2, 253, 259
Indian 1, 25, 185 n. 13, 204
Old 149, 235
Estonian 83, 88 n. 1, 100, 132 n. 1, 152, 189–91, 197, 205–7, 215, 242 n. 11
Even 200, 215, 241 n. 5
Evenki 215, 233
Ewe 49, 102–3, 110–11, 125, 197, 231, 233, 256

Finnish 52–3, 75, 82–3, 108–9, 189–91, 197, 206–7, 215, 242 n. 11
Fore 237
French 7, 39, 72–3, 80, 105, 108, 127, 161–4, 254–6
Frisian 40

Georgian
  Classical 193
  Modern 3, 8, 11, 46, 61–2, 66 n. 16, 93, 103, 112, 114, 135, 137–8, 140–1, 144, 163, 165, 166, 174–5, 189–90, 192–3, 195, 197, 201–2, 213, 215, 230, 233
German 7, 8, 11–15, 19, 36 n. 4, 43, 55–6, 66 n. 16, 67, 79, 81, 84, 88 n. 1, 96, 99, 101, 103, 107–8, 110–11, 112, 120, 127, 132 n. 5, 141–4, 161, 173, 175, 231–2, 241 n. 4, 246, 250–1, 259–61
  Swiss (Bernese) 7, 12, 61, 79, 115, 169, 261
Gooniyandi 63, 238
Greek
  Classical 54, 162, 175, 203, 247, 250
  Modern 3, 5, 18, 37 n. 11, 94, 96, 114, 123, 163, 197, 203, 205, 215, 250–1, 271 n. 3
Greenlandic 232, 273 n. 13
Guaraní 246

Haitian Creole 125, 197, 240
Hatam 237

Hausa 53
Hebrew, Modern 184 n. 14
Hindi 59, 114, 189–90, 192–3, 195, 197, 204, 208, 215, 235
Hixkaryána 164
Hmong, White 4, 102–3, 123, 135, 138, 142, 146, 150, 152, 156–7, 175, 188–9, 197, 215, 226, 228–9, 231, 235, 242 n. 20, 262
Hopi 130
Huitoto 232
Hua 215, 237
Hungarian 17, 189–90, 192–3, 195, 197, 203, 206–7, 215, 218, 241 n. 10, 260–1
Hunzib 125, 202–3, 226

Icelandic 55, 107, 234
Ijo 125
Italian 13, 55, 110, 213, 241 n. 4

Japanese 19, 81, 215

Kabardian 241 n. 9
Kalmyk 193, 197, 200, 215
Kannada 53, 72, 123, 167, 189–90, 197, 207, 215, 233
Kanuri 53–4, 81, 233, 240, 249
Karaim 198
Karen 102, 231
Kâte 21, 80, 126, 192–7, 215, 233, 237
Kaugel 111, 168, 237
Kazakh 113, 189–90, 197, 199, 215, 249
Kayardild 238
Ket 214–5, 233
Kewa, West 237
Khakas 193, 197, 199, 215
Khaling 209
Khalkha 46, 48, 113–14, 129, 135, 138, 140, 144, 146, 153, 159, 189, 192–3, 195, 197, 199–200, 215, 226–7, 232–3, 241 n. 3, 256
Khanty 17, 46, 51–4, 197, 206, 215, 247, 251

Index of Languages

Khasi 102, 138, 147–9, 184 n. 6, 193, 210, 215, 225, 231, 233
Khmer 18, 22, 124, 147, 149, 189, 193, 197, 210, 215, 226–7, 256
Kipeá 247
Kirghiz 113, 189–90, 197, 199, 215, 241 n. 3
Koasati 81
Kobon 237
Komi 10, 31, 53, 192–3, 195, 197, 215
Konda 48, 207–8, 215
Korean 189, 197, 215
Koryak 215
Kube 194, 197, 237, 241 n. 7
Kui 169
Kuku Yalanji 234, 238
Kuna 16, 267–8
Kurdish
   Bahdinani 34, 50–1
   Kurmanji 192–3, 195–7, 205, 214–15, 241 n. 4

Lahu 112, 193, 197, 208–9, 215
Lak 193, 197, 202
Lalo 208
Laotian 189, 197
Lashi 209
Latin 13, 53–4, 83, 108, 111, 120, 133 n. 9, 170, 203, 254–6
Latvian 82–3, 110, 119, 152, 197, 205, 215
Lezgian 104, 111, 114, 122, 137, 145, 177, 192–3, 195, 197, 201–3, 215, 226, 230, 232–3
Lisu 209
Lithuanian 118–19, 152, 167, 197, 205, 215, 269

Malagasy 47, 190, 197, 211, 215
Malay 18, 189–90, 192–3, 195, 195, 197, 210–12, 214, 242 n. 14
Malayalam 190, 197
Maltese 119, 197, 215, 251
Manchu 128, 200, 215, 251

Mandarin 18, 20, 48, 93, 97, 98, 114, 122, 124, 134 n. 22, 136, 150, 153–4, 171, 188–9, 197, 215, 226, 228, 231–3, 235, 252, 255–7, 272 n.5, n. 6, n. 9
Mansi 51–3, 192–3, 195, 197, 206, 215, 247, 251
Maori 197
Mari 27, 34, 50–1, 53, 60, 63–4, 114, 119, 126–7, 140, 142, 192–3, 195, 197, 206, 215, 231–2, 242 n. 11, 249, 251
Marshallese 211
Maru 209
Mayan, Yucatec 112
Meithei (Meitei) 142–3
Mekeo 212
Melanesian Pidgin *see* Tok Pisin
Melpa 197, 215, 237
Mewahang 148, 225
Minangkabau 188–90, 197
Mixe, Coatlán 239, 278
Mohawk 112
Mordvin
   Erźa 1–3, 6, 11–16, 34, 36 n. 2, n. 3, 52–3, 55, 59, 80, 100, 104, 110, 114, 122–3, 125–6, 128, 135, 137–46, 148–52, 154, 157–8, 160, 162–4, 166–7, 169, 172–82, 148–52, 154, 157–8, 160, 162–4, 166–7, 169, 172–82, 184 n. 1, n. 2, 188, 192–3, 195, 197, 204–6, 215, 218–26, 232–3, 242 n. 11, 247–9, 251, 257–60, 263–4, 267
   Mokša 36 n. 2, 185 n. 17, 192–3, 195
Motu 212
Mundari 210, 225

Nahuatl 112 13, 151
Nanai 139, 200, 215
Navajo 75, 120
Nenets 51, 53, 247, 251
Nepali 190, 197, 204, 214, 241 n. 3
Ngada 212
Ngiyambaa 53–4

Index of Languages

Nicobarese, Car 193, 197, 210–11, 215, 218
Nisgha 112

Ojibwa, Eastern 110
Oksapmin 234
Ossete 201–2, 215, 241 n. 9

Paiwan 215
Pali 210
Parengi-Gorum 57
Persian (Farsi) 111, 129, 204, 215

Quechua 75–6, 190, 197, 239, 278

Rhaeto-Romance 241 n. 4
Romance (Hautes/Basses-Pyrénées, Aragon) 213
Romani 197, 204, 241 n. 10
Roti 212
Russian 13, 18, 39, 46, 82, 88, n. 4, 107–8, 111, 132 n. 4, 146, 162–3, 169, 187, 197, 199, 201–5, 212, 214, 224, 242 n. 11, 251, 165–7

Saami 189–91, 197, 206–7
Samoan 197, 156
Sanskrit 17–19, 37 n. 9, n. 11, 91, 103, 123, 166, 170, 204, 231, 247–8
Santali 44–5, 85, 125, 210, 215, 225
Semelai 210
Sentani 4, 8, 125, 152, 168, 215, 237
Serbian 205
Seychelles Creole 240
Siane 237
Sika 212
Siriono 232
Siroi 237
Somali 215
Songhai 119, 240
Sora 247
Spanish 40, 213
Sranan 86

Sumerian 213
Sundanese 188, 197, 212, 215, 242 n. 17
Swedish 7, 21, 48, 88 n. 1, 95, 98–101, 166, 261
 Northern 120
Swedish Sign Language 37 n. 10, 133 n. 7

Tabasaran 193, 197, 202
Tadzhik 129–30, 204, 215
Tagalog 46, 61, 66 n. 13, 105, 132 n. 7, 139, 166, 197, 211, 215, 233
Takelma 89 n. 5
Takia 212
Tamil
 Modern 53, 119, 196, 204, 207–8, 215, 233, 236, 242 n. 13
 Old 242 n. 12
Tatar 59, 189–93, 195, 197, 199, 215, 249
Tauya 53
Teleutian 271 n. 2
Tepehuan, Southeastern 47–8
Thai 18, 189, 193, 197, 215
Tibetan 48, 59, 99, 153–4, 189, 197, 209, 215, 226–7, 233, 257
Tiwa, Southern 129
Toaripi 79, 81, 197, 215, 237–8
Toda 20, 168, 177–8, 207, 215, 225
Tok Pisin 79–80, 106, 125, 190, 194, 197, 237–8, 240, 241 n. 6
Tokharian 17, 153, 203, 205
Toura 88 n. 1
Tsou 212, 215
Tupinambá 112
Turkic, Old 198–9, 203
Turkish 69–73, 80, 111, 119, 147, 148, 157, 168, 189–90, 192–3, 195, 197, 198–9, 215, 232, 246
Turkmen 189–90, 197, 199, 215
Tuva 170, 192–3, 195, 197, 198–200, 215, 241 n. 4
Tzeltal 239
Tzotzil 151, 239–40

Index of Languages

Udihe 89 n. 5, 165
Udmurt 17, 31, 53, 152, 169, 193, 197, 206, 215
Ukrainian 187
Usarufa 237
Uyghur
  Modern 193, 196–7, 198–9, 215, 236
  Old 138, 153, 198, 249
Uzbek 104, 113–14, 136, 138, 144, 175, 189–90, 192–3, 195, 197, 199, 215, 233

Vedic 17, 37 n. 11, 53–4, 122, 203–4, 247–8, 271 n. 1

Vietnamese 4, 36 n. 8, 43, 48, 103–4, 112, 113, 119, 122, 135, 138–9, 143, 140, 153, 174, 182, 185 n. 15, 189, 192–3, 195, 197, 210, 215, 226, 230–1, 233, 272 n. 9

Wik-Mungkan 234, 238, 240

Yabem 125, 197, 211, 215
Yakut 48, 193, 197, 211, 215
Yiddish, Eastern 168, 185 n. 14
Yoruba 125
Yukaghir 214, 241 n. 5

Zoque 134 n. 23

Index of Subjects

abbreviation 99
ablaut 133 n. 8, 148, 166
abstract (nouns) 144, 150, 152, 187
acceptability 257–61, 271
accidental coordination 5, 11–13, 43, 52, 74, 83
accusative 41
additive co-compounds 137–9, 141–5, 156–9, 192–5, 219–25, 234
  contextual 173, 225
  pairing 138
  non-pairing 139
adjectives 78, 98, 126, 152–4, 161, 174, 246
  denominal 88 n. 4
  epithetic 179, 266
adposition 93, 132 n. 1
adversative coordination 36 n. 1, 78–9
adversative sequences 175–6
affirmative 81–2
affirmative-negative compounds 170
affix 49–50, 60–2
  phrasal 61–2, 66 n. 17, 96
affix order 50, 63–4
Africa 164, 240, 278
afterthought coordination 89 n. 10
agent nominal 106
agglutinative form 119
alienability split 251
alienable possession 5
alliteration 18, 131, 147–8, 210, 227, 235
alternative co-compounds 138, 151–2, 156–7, 258–9, 266
Americas 239, 278
analogy 10, 39, 121, 155, 224–5, 248
analytic form 105, 111, 276
animacy hierarchy 66 n. 13
'and'-coordination, *see* conjunction

'animal' 8, 113, 128–9, 137, 142, 237, 239
antonyms 124, 136, 159
apodosis 21
apposition 43–4, 76
appositional compounds 7, 18, 22, 99, 161–4
approximate co-compounds 138, 151–2, 156–8, 163, 180
arbitrariness 30, 116
areal coherence (patterns of) 186–7, 236, 278
areality 17–18, 25, *see* ch. 6, 262, 278
article 11–12, 47, 55, 61, 69, 251
associative dual 89 n. 5, 232
associative plural 54, 66 n. 13, 76, 81, 169, 232
assonance 147
asymmetry 21, 56, 60
asyndetic coordination 36 n. 1, 128, 205–6, 247, 274
attributive possession 4, 41–4, 49–51, 161, 251
Australia 164, 186, 234, 238–9
auxiliary 21, 57
  directional 112

backgrounding 41, 65 n. 4, 258, 263
bahuvrihi compounds 91, 133 n. 7, 248, 250–1, 271 n. 1
bare binomials 11–15, 21, 54–5, 96, 141, 251, 275
  contextual 14, 17
  irreversible 21, 104
basic level concept 6, 27–8, 37 n. 14
bias, areal 25, 135, 188
binomials 85, 104, 148, 155, 235, 241 n. 2, *see also* bare binomials

bipartite stems 101
bipartite tools 138
bleaching, *see* semantic bleaching
blocking 19, 258
body parts 126–7, 137–8, 149, 201–2, 220–1, 223
book titles 83, 89 n. 9
borrowing, *see* loanwords
bound morpheme 100
bound stems 100
'brothers' 114, 237, 242 n. 13
'but'-coordination, *see* adversative coordination
Byliny 204, 265–7, 272 n. 11

case 55, 58–60, 92–3, 132 n. 1, 229
causative 106
cause 21, 124
'child(ren)' 194, 213, 219, 237, 242 n. 19, 247
child-directed speech 110
child language 244, 250
class 23–4, 87–8, 105, 274–6 *see also* functional-formal class
class-character 15
class, emergence of 258
class type 23
classifier 102, family group 208, 232, 234
clausal coordination 21
cliché phrases 101
clipping 99–100, 132 n. 4, 209, 227, 234, 272 n. 5
clitics 21, 58, 60–4, 66 n. 10, n. 14, n. 17, 92
  second-position 61–2
  phrase-level 63
'clothes' 113, 128
co-compounds *see* 1.1, *see* **chs. 4–8**
  basic 6, 154–6, 171, 252, 258, 277
  connective 156
  disjunctive 156
  form of 2–5, 130–1
  macro-synonymic 156

meaning of 5–8
non-basic 154–6, 171, 183–4, 258, 264, 277
prototypical 155, 278
translational 156, use of 8–10
see also additive; alternative; approximate; collective; discontinuous; figurative; generalizing; imitative; ornamental; scalar; synonymic co-compounds
coexistent formants 109–11, 114
cohesive expression 36 n. 5
cohesiveness, *see* continuity
collection complexes 6, 139, 143, 184 n. 1
  homogeneous 143
  mixed 143
collective 6–7, 75, 81, 118, 141–2, 184 n. 1
collective co-compounds 137–9, 141–3, 145–6, 156–8, 192–5
collective compounds 248
collective concepts 20, 187
collective coordination 88 n. 3
collectivity 81
collocations 96, 149, 251, 279
colloquial speech, deviation from 224, 267–9
colloquial style 168
comitative 47, 52–5, 69–71, 74–6, 139–40, 231–4, 249
comma intonation, *see* intonation break
common ground 115
comparative 54, 102
comparative compounds 163–4, 170
competence 121, 259
competition 117, 255, 263
complexity 257
  evolutionary 257
compositionality 95, 97, 104–6, 109, 111, 117
compound(ing) *see* **ch. 4**, 274
  incomplete 246–7
  ornamental 268
compound pronouns 89 n. 7

compounding cycle 210
compounding forms 99–100
concept-widening 176
concepts 27–8, 32
conceptual unit 2, 5–6, 8, 45, 134 n. 16, 275
condensation 245–7, 250–1
condensation hypothesis 245–6, 278
conditional 178
conditional clause 152, 251
conjunct, *see* coordinand
conjunction 35–6 n. 1, 52, 81–2
conjunctive 249
connective prosody 98
constructions 23–4
contact superposition zone 236
context 8, 14–15, 32–3, 135–7, 171, 277
context sensitivity 116–17
contextual motivation 171–84, 200, 202, 263, 266, 278
contextual sharpening, *see* sharpening
contextually established coordination 14–15
continuity 94, 101–3
continuous variables 44
contrast 78–80, 154–5, 175–6, 183, 275
  principle of 269
contrastive coordination 53–4
conventionalization 171–4, 177, 182–3, 224, 259, 267
conventionalized meaning 94
converb 71, 129, 227, 232, 249
converses 138
coordinand 35 n. 1, 45–52, 59–64, 67–9, 78–81, 83–4
coordinate sequence 36 n. 1, 60, 63–4, 67–8
  length of 67–8, 275
coordinate structure constraint 86
coordinated phrase 36 n. 1
coordination 35 n. 1, *see* chs. 2–3
  coordination counter-to-expectation 48, 75, 78

coordination, nominal 47, 55, 69–70, 129, 130, 214
coordination reduction 68
coordination, verbal 71, 129, 232–3
coordinator 35 n. 1, 45–8
  emphatic 75
  reduction of 46, 211, 213
copula 269
copulative compounds 1, 7, 22, *see also* co-compounds
corpus linguistics 96
couplet 151
cover meaning 28, 32, 136, 155–6, 161
covert marking 36 n. 7, 39, 87, 122
cranberry-compound 100, 126
cranberry-word 100, 147, 155
Creole languages 125, 237, 240
culture 8, 27, 37, 151
cyclic events 157

dative 50, 73
deconceptualization 183
decorative imagery 22
deep structure 68
definita tantum 120
definiteness 38, 55
deletion operations 68
delimitative aktionsart 169
demonstrative pronouns 254–5
demotivation 115–16, 134 n. 17, 276
dependent marking 65 n. 6, 229–30, 246
deponents 108, 136
deranked coordination 232–3
derived words 27
desemantization 264, 266–7, 271
determinative compounds, *see* sub-compounds
devaluation 259
deviation from the norm 41–2
diachronic evolution 118, *see* ch. 7, 278
diachronic identity 30
diachronic relationships 156–7, 183, 277
dictionary-metaphor 114

diminutive 110–11, 120–1, 133 n. 10, 255–6, 266, 269
directional markers 106, 111–12
disambiguation 14
discontinuity 4, 101–3, 131
discontinuous co-compounds 4, 102–3, 146–7, 228–9, 231, 237–40
discontinuous coordination 47–8, 89 n. 10
discourse communities 115
discrete variables 44
disjunction 36 n. 1, 81–4, 151–2, 169–70, 176
  in questions 82
distance, minimal 55–7, 60, 67
distinctive markedness 38–9, 42–3
distributive coordination 74, 88 n. 3, n. 4
distributive key 180
distributive share 180
distributivity 82, 175, 179, 180–1, 202
disyllabicity 210, 226–7, 272 n. 6, 7, 9
diversity 201–2, 210, 225–9
  language-internal 218–25, 277
domains
  communicative 23
  construction 23
  semantic 23
double barreled names 8
double citizenship 60–1
double dual marking 51–3, 206, 247–8
double marking 50–4, 56–7, 122–3, 247–9
drift toward permanent lexicon 115–16, 276
dual 40, 51–4, 66 n. 12, 232, 247–8, 271 n. 1
dummy element in disjunction 82
dvandva 1, 17, 91, 166, 247–8, see also co-compounds
dyad constructions 21–2, 89 n. 5, 232, 234
dynamic construal (of meaning) 184 n. 10

echo-words 20, 167–70, 177–8, 185 n. 13, 210, pronominal 168–9
economy of encoding 9
effect 124
effort 65 n. 5
elliptic plural/dual 54
embellishing 268
emergent lexicon, see model of the lexicon, emergent
emergent structure 10, 26, 122
emotive style 176
emotivity 162, 176, 179, 182, 263
emphasis 144, 146, 172–6, 179, 238–40, 266
emphatic speech 264, 269, 271
enumeration 81, 85
epic poem (register) 153, 172–3, 203–4, 224–5, 263, 264–8
epistemic possibility 81
equipollent opposition 42 n.
ergative 41
establishment 5, 14–15
ethnography of speaking 37 n. 13, 267
Eurasia 17, 135, 186–236, 240, 262, 279
exclusive 'or' 82
exhaustive listing 139
exhaustive listing coordination 81–3
explanations
  emergent-structure 26
  functional 26, 253
  hidden-structure 25–6, 253
  historical 26
explicative disjunction 83, 89 n. 9, 145–6
explicativity 18
explicit marking 44
extravagance 259

'face' 113, 142, 206–7, 237–8, 241 n. 9
fairytale (register) 1–2, 6, 13, 172, 187, 249
'family' 113
fiction (register) 135, 172, 178, 219, 221, 224, 260, 263

figurative co-compounds 138, 149–51, 154, 156–7, 181–2
figurative sense 80–1, 163
fixation 103
fixed order 94, 104, 132 n. 7, see also irreversibility
focus 54, 80, contrastive 84
focus particles (additive) 52–3, 72, 140, 231–2, 249
folk poetry 16, 150, 224, 264–71, 272 n. 12
folkloristic style 204–5
folktales 178
'food' 113, 128–9
'foot' 119
foregrounding 41, 65 n. 4, 261, 263
form-meaning relation 9, 14, 31, 275
form-use relation 9, 14
formal identity 30
formal markedness 38, 42–3, 45, 279
formal register 16, 151, 187, 267–8
formative 132 n. 1
formulaicity 13, 21, 95, 267, 275, 279
free morpheme 100
frequency (text) 9, 24–5, 33–4, see 6.1–4, 257–64, 278–9
  relative 118–20
  token 106, 116, 118, 189–94, 221, 279
  type 106, 116, 121, 189–91, 193–4
frequentative (aktionsart) 180
functional word 49–50
functional-formal class (type) 105, 121, 125, 130–2, 274
fusional compounds 7–8, 99
future 105, 178–9

gapping 89 n. 10
gemination 166
gender (grammatical) 3, 155–6, 210
generalization 80, 82, 146, 172–5, 187
generalizing co-compounds 138–41, 156–9, 191–2, 194–5, 219–22, 240
generative grammar 68

generative perspective 121
generative semantics 19
generic collectives 6
generic use 139, 157
genitive 41, 123, 167, 246, 250–1
Gesamtbedeutung 28, 37 n. 15
Götterdvandvas 179, 247–8
gradual development 252
gram 105, 133 n. 8
grammatical category 106
grammatical class 105–10, 117–21, 131–2, 276, 279
grammatical word 5, 93–5
grammaticalization 72–3, 87–8, 118–20, 243–5, 266–9, 276
  incomplete 134 n. 19, 276
  irreversibility of 243–4
grammaticalization paths 28, 243–5
grammaticalness 120
group collectives 6
group coordination 74–6, 88 n. 3, n. 4
group inflection 58–9
  in coordination 58–60, 62
  in subordination 58–9
Gruppenflexion, see group inflection

hapax legomenon 263
'head' 209
head marking 65 n. 6, 229–30, 246
'heavy form' 108–9, 111, 114, 127–8, 245, 250–1
  introduction of new 245, 250–1
hendiadys 6
'here-there' 52, 139–40, 152
hesitation 84
hidden absoluteness 31
hierarchical level 1
hierarchy of increase 157
homonymy 184 n. 10
  avoidance of 18, 171, 210, 252, 255–7, 263
host 61
hyperonyms 6, 184 n. 1

hyphenation 2, 4, 92, 99, 162, 261
hysteron proteron 126

iconicity 9, 13–14, 30, 55–7, 60, 174, 275
ideal form 254
ideophone compounds 164–6, 170, 181
ideophones 164–6
idioms 13, 94, 96
idiosyncrasy 9, 28, 105–13, 116, 262
imitative co-compounds 137–8, 141–2, 147–9, 156–7, 207 reciprocally 147, 149, 165
imperative 71, 249
imperfective aspect 107, 118
imperfectivity 65 n. 4
implicational hierarchy 112, 157, 277–8
implicatures, conversational 267
important passages 41
improvization 267
inalienable possession 5, 30, 120, 213, 251
inchoative verbs 120, 145
inclusive 'or' 82
inclusive/exclusive pronouns 24, 80, 186, 194
inclusory coordination 89 n. 7
incomplete compounding 246–7
incorporation (object/noun incorporation) 95, 112–13, 133 n. 10, 11, 202, 246
indefinite pronouns 140
inessive 44
inference 267
infinite verb forms 125–6
infix 61
inflation 259, *see also* use, inflationary
inflection harmony 3, 131
inflectional form 105, 117–18, 134 n. 18, 276
informal register 169
information rate 264–71
informativeness 81–2, 267
inherence 5, 98, 275
intensity 103

intermediate-denoting compounds 7, 99, 162–4, 170
interrogatives 154
intersection 76
intersective coordination 76–7, 83–4, 161
intonation break 45
intonation unit 67, 79
irrealis 178
irreversibility 21, 218, 226, 244, 253, 275
isogloss 186
isolates 212–14
isolating morphology 230–1
item-generalization 139
iterative 118, 141
iterativity 103
izafe 50

juxtaposition 4–5, 36 n. 1, 128, 130, 244, 257

kinship terms 137–8, 220–5, 232

lack of evidence 81–2, 151, 157, 263
language contact 259–62
language production 121
language-internal diversity 37 n. 13
legends (register) 214
level of abstraction 27–8
level of co-compounding 9, 157, *see* ch. 6, *see* 7.3–5, 277–9
lexemes 105–7, 114–17 *see also* listemes
  contextual 110
  permanent 116–17, 133 n. 15, 276
  temporary 116–17, 134 n. 16
lexical category, *see* word class
lexical class (type) *see* 4.3, 155–6, 243–5, *see* 7.3, 276, 279
lexical domains 9, 15, 259, 279
lexical plurals, *see* pluralia tantum
lexical slot 106, 130, 167–70, 274
lexicalization 114–21, 139, 264, 276, 278–9
  incomplete 276

lexicalized phrases (lexphrases) 21, 95–6, 98, 251
lexico-semantic relationship 154, 158, 161–2, 274–5, 277
lexicon 94–5, 114–18, 121, 257, 259, 280
  permanent (or long-term) 114–17, 133 n. 15, 276
  temporary (or short-term) 33, 114–17, 133 n. 14, 188, 256, 276
light 'again' 112
'light form' 108, 111, 128, 245, 250
light verb constructions 106, 111
listemes 94, 114
loanwords 199, 208, 210, 235, 262–3
local markedness 40–4, 118–20, 175, 266, 279
locative 44, 73
loose coordination 13, 67–72, 78, 88 n. 1
Lüdtke's equilibrium 254, 264, 268–9
lumping 122–3

m-doublets 168
macro-areal patterns 25, 186, 258, 262, 278
macro-perspective 229
Mark, Gospel according to 187–8, 191–7, 199–200, 202, 210, 215
markedness 38–45, 65 n. 2, 279
markedness clash 40, 43, 45, 279
markedness reversal, *see* markedness clash
marker (formal) 38, 43
marking patterns of coordination 69–73, 275
'marking-reversal' 27
mass nouns 12
maturity 257
meaning 26–33
meronomic levels 5, 28, 122
meronomic structure 130–1
meronymy 184 n. 10
Meso-America 27, 102, 151, 239
metalinguistic disjunction 83

metaphor 149–51, 161
metonymy 149
micro-perspective 229
middle 106–9, 118, 127, 133 n. 9
  logophoric 107, 118, 136
minimal distance, *see* distance
minimal pole 177
minimal quantity expressions 185 n. 18
minimal word length 171, 252–3, 256, 263–4
minimalism 60
model of the lexicon
  emergent (procedural) 95, 280
  listeme 94–5, 114, 280
monistic view about markedness 39
monosyllabism 230–1, 272 n. 5
morpho-syntactic word, *see* grammatical word
morphological accumulation 254, 268–9
morphological typology 230–1
morphology 13, *see* 4.1–2, 245, 274–5, 279
  traditional 90–2, 121
motion verbs 134 n. 23
motivation (relative) 116
mouthing 37 n. 10
myths (register) 147, 207, 225, 237–8

names, *see* proper names
narrative discourse 65 n. 4
narrative style 191
natural comitative 47, 75–6, 89 n. 5, 140, 232
natural coordination 1, 5–6, 11–13, *see* ch. 2, *see* 3.3, 97–8, 154–6, 274–5
natural relationship 44
Natural Syntax 13, 21, 54, 275
negation
  affixal 170
  as context for co-compounds 172, 176–9, 202, 242 n. 19, 265–6
  emphatic 185 n. 18,
negative marker 140
neuter (gender) 36 n. 4, 248, 250, 271 n. 1

Index of Subjects

neutralization 39
New Guinea 21, 168, 186, 193–4, 234, 237–8, 278
New World 186
nominalization marker 142–3
non-compositionality, *see* compositionality
non-contrastive coordination 79
non-distinctiveness 121–30, 132
non-exhaustive listing 141–2
non-exhaustive listing coordination 53, 81–3
non-intersective coordination 76
non-isomorphism 94
  phonological-syntactic 60–4, 279
non-overlapping coordination 77–8
non-referentiality 172, 176–9, 182–3
non-relational marking 41, 43, 48–64, 71
norm 41–2
noun incorporation, *see* incorporation
noun stripping 95, 251
novel, *see* fiction (register)
number 39, 49–50, 55, 63, 72
numerals 152
  complex 8
  distributive 166–7, 180

obligatorification 251, 255
obligatoriness 105
Oceania 186, 211–12
one-form (cognate) systems 108, 114, 126, 245
one-slot pattern 41, 43, 279
onomatopoeia 164
opacity 117
opposite poles 139, 152, 175
'or'-coordination, *see* disjunction
oral poetry, *see* folk poetry
order 19–20, 21, 218
ordinary coordination (as opposed to natural coordination) 43, 47–8, 52, 231–3, 245
original texts 33–4, 188, 196

ornamental co-compounds 6, 138, 142, 146–8, 156–7, 160, 219–24
overlapping coordination 77–9, 84, 144, 160
overshort words, *see* minimal word length
overt coordinator 11, 45–6, 79, 84–5, 240, 274–5
overt marking 36 n. 7, 39

pair 45, 78, 82, 137–8
pair sharpening, *see* sharpening
pair words 1, *see* co-compounds
pairing 137–9, 141
paradigmaticity 118
paradigms 105, 117
parallel focus structure 80
parallel names 238
parallel texts 33–4, 187–98, 277
parallelism 15–16, 17, 36 n. 8, 44, 179, 267
parameter setting 19
'parents' 10, 44–5, 113–14, 120, 136–7, 155, 158, 185 n. 14, 194, 210, 212–13, 215, 217–18, 242 n. 14, 15, 17
part 5–6, 130–1, 136–7, 154–5, 274–6
part of speech, *see* word class
partial cover meaning 28, 74, 126
passive 107, 118, 133 n. 9
past (tense) 120, 161
patterns 24
'people' 237–40
perception 31
perfect tense 28
perfecta tantum 120
perfective aspect 107
perfectivity 65 n. 4
periods of time 152
permanent lexicon, *see* lexicon, permanent
persuasive discourse 176, 239–40
phonetic maximum 254–5
phonological merger 254
phonological reduction 254–5, 268–9

phonological similarity (between parts) 147–9, 167, 184 n. 2, 261
phonological word, *see* prosodic word
phrasal affix, *see* affix
phrasal verbs 111, 120, 132 n. 2
phrase 91–8, 121–2, 126–30, 245–7
phrase-like tight coordination 10–15, 96, 114, 157–8, 243, 275
pictorial context 163, 181–2
play 22, 266
plural 38–41, 50–3, 105, 118–20, 143, 242 n. 19, 246
   etymologically double plural 40
plural action verb 169
plural concept 155, 275
plural word 105, 119
pluralia tantum 53, 105, 107, 118–21, 276
pluralistic view about markedness 39
plurality 143
polysemy 14, 31
possession, *see* attributive; predicative possession
'possession', *see* 'property'
possessiva tantum 120
possessive affixes 41, 49–50, 52–3, 75, 186, 229, 246
possessive pronoun 50, 62, 77
potentialis 178
prayer (register) 179–80, 207, 224–5, 260, 264
predicative possession 66 n. 11
predicting factors 229–36
prefabs 10, 121
prefixes (verbal)
   directional 61–2, 111, 140
   inseparable 66 n. 16
   locational 201–2
   separable 101, 120, 132 n. 5
prelexical transformation 19
preposition 55, 69, 266
presupposition, tentative 178
preverbs, *see* prefixes
privative opposition 42 n.

productivity (morphological) 116
pronominal agreement 41
pronouns 80
   clitic 80
   in figurative sense 80
proper names 12, 14, 63
'property' 44, 80, 113, 123, 128–30, 157, 194, 219
proprietive 52–5, 66 n. 11, 81, 89 n. 5, 249, 271 n. 2
prosodic patterns (in compounds) 98–9
prosodic phonology 66 n. 14, n. 15, 93–4, 253
prosodic word 5, 65 n. 10, 93–4
protasis 21
prototype 27, 37 n. 14, 93, 96–8, 141
   formal 122
   semantic 122, 155
prototypical concepts 27, 37 n. 14
prototypicality 155
proverbs 10
pseudo-coordination 85–6
pseudo-distribution 181
pseudo-dynamic situation 141
pseudo-inflection 99
pseudo-repair 84

qualities 174
   extreme 149
quality scales 153
quantifier 48, 180
quantitative language change 253–6
quantitative typology 24
question 82, 153–4, 178
   indirect 153, 157, 170
questionnaires 34

radical cover meaning 29
reciprocal constructions 234
reciprocity 21
recurrence 30
redundancy 22, 31, 171–2, 253–4, 264–9
redundancy management 253–4

reduplication
    partial 166, 185 n. 12
    word (full) 17, 20, 119, 166–70, 242 n. 22, 268–9
referentiality 96
reflexive 108, *see also* middle
register 9–10, 33–4, 237–40, 218–25, 262–71, 278
reinforcement 174
related meanings 29–30
relational compounds 7, 99
relational marking 41, 43, 45–8, 86
    fossilized 250
relational nouns 137
relative clauses 66 n. 18
relativity, *see* semantic relativity
repair 84
repetition 22, 36 n. 8, 57, 224, 259, 267
repetitive, *see* light 'again'
residual zone 201, 218
restricted 100
result 21
resultative verbs 125, 134 n. 21, 272 n. 9
rhyme 147
ritual language 146, 148, 225, 248, 268
ritualization 150

saliency 10
salient events 164
Sammelbedeutung 37 n. 15
sampling 25
Sapir/Whorf hypothesis, *see* semantic relativity
scalar co-compounds 138, 152–4, 156–7, 170, 178, 277
scope 60, 62, 68, 86–8, 276, 279
    of quantifiers 175
    of negation 176
semantactic minimum 254–5
semantic bleaching 266–7, 269
semantic classification 135–7, 276
semantic core 107, 109, 278
semantic correlates *see* 3.3, 275

semantic maps 28–9, 107, 156
semantic nucleus 155
semantic profile 194–6, 220–4, 244, 252, 264, 277–8
semantic prototype 155
semantic relativity 30, 253, 269
sensation (outer or inner) 181
sentence coordination 46, 68
separate coordination 53, 74–5, 78, 88 n. 3
serial verb construction 57, 86, 102, 124–6, 134 n. 22, n. 23, 207–8
shape, lack of 28, 144
sharpening
    antonymic 159
    contextual (semantic) 14, 32–3, 158–61
    member-class 32
    meronomic (part-whole) 161
    pair 154, 158–9, 185 n. 19, 275
    synonymic 160, 209, 224, 277
'siblings' 113, 139, 194, 204
sign, linguistic 8
signed language 19–20, 37 n. 10, 132 n. 4, 133 n. 7
simple words 27
single marking 49–51, 56–64
singular 38–40, 51, 118
situation types 29
slogans 13
sociolinguistics 37 n. 13
songs (register) 268–9, 273 n. 13
sound symbolism 148
source-goal compounds 141
space-generalization 139
specific use 157
specifier 111, 168
splitting 122–3
spontaneous spoken language 37 n. 13
Sprachbund 236
spread zone 198, 218
stem forms 99
strengthening (of informativeness) 267, 269

stress 93, 96, 98–9
  contrastive stress 98
stress reduction 4, 248
structural markedness 39–40, 42–3, 45, 279
structural oppositions 39
stub-compounds 132 n. 4
style 218–19, 224–5, 262
sub-compounds 2–3, 27–8, 90–2, see 4.2.3, 121–8, 231–2, 246–8, 267–8
subjectivity 183–4
subordinate (level) concept 27–8, 32, 36 n. 4, 126, 161, 170
subordination 124, 126
subordinator 11, 36 n. 1, 43, 65 n. 8
summary conjunction 48, 75
superfluous meaning 160
superordinate (level) concept 27–8, 89 n. 8, 141, 154–5, 176, 275
subordinating compounds, see sub-compounds
suppletion 109
Swadesh list 133 n. 15
symmetrical compounds 22
symmetry 21, 55–7, 62, 64
synchronic connections 156, 183
synchronic semantic relationships 28
syndetic coordination 36 n. 1, 247
synonymic co-compounds 6, 136–8, 141–7, 156–7, 159–60, 171–2, 192–6, 219–24, 252–6, 266
  explicative 145–6, 188
synonymity, see synonymy, contextual
synonyms 17–18, 78, 124, 136, 159, 171
  cognitive 159
synonymy 159–60, 184 n. 11
  contextual 60, 184 n. 11, 277
syntactic paraphrase 91
syntax 13, 90–1, 96, 121, 245, 275, 279
  syntax of coordination 57–64
synthetic form 105, 111, 276

taboo name 213
tags 154
tantum-forms 108–10, 119–21
tatpurusha compounds 91, see also sub-compounds
taxonomic level 5–6, 154, 275
taxonomy 27–8, 32, 161
temporal sequence 85–6, 126, 129, 207
temporary lexicon, see lexicon, temporary
text frequency, see frequency
texts 33–4
textual markedness 40–2, 44–5, 181, 257–64, 270–1, 278–9
textualization 183–4
thinking 31
tight construction 245
tight coordination 13, see ch. 3, 275, 279
tight sequences 105
tightness 35, 62, see ch. 3, 276
time-generalization 139
'to do'-second coordinand construction 169
token 106
tone neutralization 93
tone sandhi 132 n. 6
tone simplification 103
topic 65 n. 4
topicalization 65 n. 4
totem 238
transition area language 212
transitive verb construction 41
translation 31–2, 228, 241 n. 4, 260–1, see also parallel texts
transparency 117
two-form systems
  cognate 108, 111–12
  non-cognate 108, 111–12
two-slot pattern 41, 43–4, 130, 161, 279
two-syllable units, see disyllabicity
type 106
typological correlations (of features) 125, 167, 229–6

typological markedness 40, 42, 65 n. 3, 257
typological variables
  continuous 24–5, 125, 186, 231, 277
  discrete 24, 186, 277
typology 9, 16, 19, 22–6, *see* ch. 6, 256, 277
typology of texts 33, 37 n. 13

unbalanced coordination 60
union 77
unitarity 97–8
Universal Declaration of Human Rights (UDHR) 187–91, 194, 196–7, 199, 215, 241 n. 1
use 8–9
  inflationary 174

vacillation (within concepts) 108–9, 114
valency 108
values of a category 39, 41
variables, *see* typological variables
variation 82
verb serialization, *see* serial verb constructions
versatile 100
vocativic contexts 162
voice 24, 65 n. 4
vowel harmony 66 n. 10

whole 5–6, 130–1, 136–7, 154–5, 275–6
word 90–105, 121, 132 n. 1, 274–5, 279
  classical definition 90, 96
  deconstruction of the notion of 93–6
  prototypical definition of 96
word association 15
word class 91, 106, 121–2
word-domain 10, 15, 128–30, 154–5, 270, 275
word form, *see* inflectional form
word formation 90, 121, 256
word iteration, *see* reduplication, word
word-like 1, 4, 9–10, 96, 105, 274–5
word order 24, 41, 132 n. 7, 186, 236, 246–7
word pair 15, 151, 203
word slots 4, 101
word stress 2–3, 36 n. 3
wordhood 97–104, 128
written-language bias 33, 37 n. 13

yes/no-question 82
young literatures 241 n. 4

zero marking 30, 43, 45, 54–7, 122
zero morphemes 62